Nothingness in the Heart of Empire

Nothingness in the Heart of Empire

*The Moral and Political Philosophy
of the Kyoto School in Imperial Japan*

HARUMI OSAKI

Published by State University of New York Press, Albany

© 2019 State University of New York

All rights reserved

No part of this book may be used or reproduced in any manner whatsoever without written permission. No part of this book may be stored in a retrieval system or transmitted in any form or by any means including electronic, electrostatic, magnetic tape, mechanical, photocopying, recording, or otherwise without the prior permission in writing of the publisher.

For information, contact State University of New York Press, Albany, NY
www.sunypress.edu

Library of Congress Cataloging-in-Publication Data

Names: Osaki, Harumi, author.
Title: Nothingness in the heart of empire : the moral and political philosophy of the Kyoto School in imperial Japan / Harumi Osaki.
Description: Albany : State University of New York, [2019] | "This book was written based on [the author's] doctoral dissertation at McGill University"—Acknowledgements. | Includes bibliographical references and index. Identifiers: LCCN 2018015532 | ISBN 9781438473093 (hardcover) |
ISBN 9781438473116 (ebook) | ISBN 9781438473109 (perf.)
Subjects: LCSH: Philosophy, Japanese—20th century. | Nothing (Philosophy)
Classification: LCC B5241 .O825 2019 | DDC 181/.12—dc23
LC record available at https://lccn.loc.gov/2018015532

10 9 8 7 6 5 4 3 2 1

Contents

Acknowledgments	vii
Abbreviations	ix
Preface	xi
Introduction	1

Part 1
"Overcoming Modernity" and "The Philosophy of World History"

Chapter 1
Nishitani Keiji and the *Bungakukai* Symposium
"Overcoming Modernity" — 23

Chapter 2
The *Chūōkōron* Symposia Concerning the Philosophy
of World History — 41

Chapter 3
The Unity between the Subject and the Substratum of the State:
The First Characteristic of Japanese National Subjectivity — 51

Chapter 4
The Interpenetration between the National and the International:
The Second Characteristic of Japanese National Subjectivity — 67

Chapter 5
The Reciprocal Determination between the Virtual and the Actual:
The Third Characteristic of Japanese National Subjectivity — 85

CHAPTER 6
The Outcomes of the Two Projects at Stake in
Japanese National Subjectivity   101

Part 2
A Political Dimension of Nishida Kitarō's Philosophy of Nothingness

CHAPTER 7
Questions Concerning Nishida and Japanese Subjectivity   117

CHAPTER 8
Nishida's Political Thoughts Concerning Japanese National Subjectivity   127

CHAPTER 9
The Significance and Problems of Nishida's Arguments about *Kokutai*   163

CHAPTER 10
Nishida's Criticism of Hegel with an Eye to Overcoming
Western Modernity   179

CHAPTER 11
Examining Nishida's Philosophical Project of Overcoming
Western Modernity   217

CHAPTER 12
Reconsidering the Issues of *Kokutai* and Overcoming Modernity   243

CONCLUSION   257

NOTES   259

BIBLIOGRAPHY   275

INDEX   283

Acknowledgments

This book was written based on my doctoral dissertation at McGill University. Foremost, I would like to express my sincere gratitude to my supervisor, Thomas Lamarre, for overseeing my PhD studies and research, and for his advice, support, and encouragement throughout the entire dissertation process and the preparation of the manuscript for this book.

Beyond my supervisor, a number of people gave me valuable advice, suggestions, comments, and criticisms. I would like to thank my comprehensive examination committee members, Adrienne Hurley and Brian Massumi; the internal examiner, Gavin Walker; and the external examiner, Naoki Sakai. My sincere thanks also go to the reviewers of my book manuscript selected by the State University of New York Press, Richard F. Calichman and Kimoto Takeshi. Without their thoughtful comments and useful suggestions, this book would not have taken form. While incorporating all of these people's advice and responding to each criticism was beyond the scope of this book and my capacity, I will keep their excellent input in mind as tasks to address in future research.

During the time I was writing the manuscript for this book, I have benefitted from the invaluable support, encouragement, and inspiration from many people. I would like to express my gratitude to Nadine Powell, Elyse Amend, Christine Lamarre, Danielle Barkley, Yumiko Kanao, Timothy Forster, Klaus Hammering, Chang Zhang, dear members of CPNM, and Michel Brousseau.

Portions of chapters 10 and 11 in part 2 of this book were previously published in the *European Journal of Japanese Philosophy*, vol. 2 (Oct. 2017) under the title, "The Dialectic of Hegel and Nishida: How to Deal with Modernity." I thank the journal editors for their generous permission to use the content of the essay in this book. I am also grateful to the editors of SUNY Press, Christopher Ahn, Chelsea Miller, Eileen Nizer, Anne Valentine, and Aimee Harrison for all of their support and help in completing this book.

Lastly, I wish to thank my parents without whom it would have been impossible to continue my scholarly pursuits.

Abbreviations

OM   *Overcoming Modernity: Cultural Identity in Wartime Japan.* Edited and Translated by Richard F. Calichman. Columbia University Press. 2008.

SR   *Sekaishi no riron.* Edited by Mori Tetsurō, *Kyoto tetsugaku sensho* XX. Tōeisha, 2000.

NKC   *Nishitani Keiji chosakushū*, 26 vols. Sōbunsha, 1986–1995.

NKZ   *Nishida Kitarō zenshū*, 19 vols. 1947–1953. Iwanami Shoten, 1978–1980.

SN   "*Sekaishiteki tachiba to nihon*," Kōsaka Masaaki et al., *Chūōkōron* 57 (1) Jan. 1942: 150–92.

TRR   "*Tōa kyōeiken no rinrisei to rekishisei*," Kōsaka Masaaki et al., *Chūōkōron* 57 (4) Apr. 1942: 120–61.

ST   "*Sōryokusen no tetsugaku*," Kōsaka Masaaki et al., *Chūōkōron* 58 (1) Jan. 1943: 54–112.

HW   *Werke*, in 20 Bänden, Georg W. F. Hegel. Edited by Eva Moldenhauer and Karl M. Michel, Suhrkamp, 1969–1971.

Preface

This book is a critical examination of the Kyoto School philosophers' prewar and wartime political discourses, with specific reference to the philosophical and metaphysical theories that worked to reinforce them. Prior critical works on the Kyoto School have tended to focus on the philosophers' alignment with Japan's war effort. However, as such critiques do not address the philosophy in depth, they have tended to leave open the possibility that the problem lies not in the Kyoto School thinkers' philosophical endeavors, but in their historical circumstances. By the same token, even when critiques seem to hit the mark, advocates of the Kyoto School have tended to blame the critics for not understanding the philosophy, and have ignored these assessments peremptorily. With a goal of moving the dialogue beyond this rupture, this book argues that the Kyoto School's moral and political philosophy tends to align itself with nationalist and imperial formations, conceptually and logically. By undertaking a philosophical investigation of the problems found in the Kyoto School thinkers' political discourses, this book shows that there is no strict separation between "lofty" philosophy and "vulgar" politics. Instead, it argues that seemingly genuine philosophy can be a source of political problems.

In this examination, despite the Kyoto School philosophers' frequent emphasis on the uniqueness of Japan, the East, or the Orient, I do not adopt such particularism. Rather, I elucidate how the particularistic assumptions of these philosophers constitute an essential part of the problems their political discourses gave rise to. There is a persistent tendency for Western thinkers to read into the texts of non-Western philosophers something particular to their own cultural tradition. Although I do not completely disagree with such an approach, the arbitrary insertion of idealized images of "Japan," "the East," or "the Orient" often obscures what is written in these texts and covers up the difficulties that exist there. Reading philosophers' texts in this way makes an intellectual dialogue with them almost impossible. For, when people idealize others, they treat them simply as the representatives of cultural stereotypes and refuse to face them as status-equal interlocutors. Moving against such a tendency, I read the Kyoto School philosophers' discourses without reducing their meanings to cultural particularities, and present the problems in these discourses in a way sharable with anybody, in principle, regardless of whether they are of the West or the East. In doing so, I hope to pave the way for future dialogues and exchanges that can traverse such dichotomous divisions.

The founder of the Kyoto School, Nishida Kitarō, once dreamed of a philosophy in which the particularity of the national culture of his own country could contribute to the universality of humanity. However, he seemed to be swayed by the ambition of identifying this particularity with true universality. His followers, even in the present, do not seem to be free from a similar desire to celebrate "Japaneseness" over and above the particularities of other cultures. Still, in his philosophy, there is a line of thought that gestures toward another universality that can enable all such particularities to coexist and interact, without being superior or inferior to one another. Although Nishida conceived place or nothingness to be such a universality, the sense of cultural superiority he retained in the name of the dignity of particularity prevented him from fully developing the potential of this line of thought. Thus, to locate a point from which we can start this pursuit differently than Nishida did—that is, to open a "place" where dialogues and exchanges of particularities actually can occur—is also a key objective of this book.

Introduction

The first aim of this book is to read the philosophy of Japan's Kyoto School *as philosophy*. As I shall explain in greater detail below, such a project is not without precedents. However, those who have read Kyoto School work as philosophy have tended to introduce a divide between philosophy as such and politics, often to avoid being critical of the Kyoto School or to redeem its philosophers. In contrast, in reading Kyoto School philosophy as philosophy, I hope to provide a more detailed account of the political implications of its intellectual project, neither to dismiss nor to redeem it, but to open up questions about the project of modern philosophy more generally. As such, the second aim of this book is to explore the *politics* of Kyoto School philosophy *as philosophy*.

The Kyoto School was a group of Japanese philosophers who were under the tutelage or influence of Nishida Kitarō, the school's founder. Nishida is often regarded as the first Japanese philosopher who tried to express religious insights from Zen Buddhism through the medium of Western philosophy in order to establish a mode of philosophy unique to East Asian cultural traditions. Although some Japanese scholars still identify themselves as members of the Kyoto School, or descendants of Nishida's philosophy, the school was at its zenith before and during the Second World War, when Nishida was still alive. In postwar Japan, the Kyoto School philosophers' involvement with Japan's wartime situation as famous intellectuals aroused much controversy: in the prewar and wartime periods, some of Nishida's disciples frequently made statements supporting wartime policies, and even had meetings with military authorities. While not as active as his followers, Nishida published works in line with the ideology of the wartime regime, and also offered his work to military authorities who asked for his advice.

In contrast, when the Kyoto School's philosophers first became known in Europe and North America, their involvement with Japan's wartime situation was not brought to the public's attention. The ways in which the Kyoto

School's thinking was received went through gradual changes until issues surrounding their wartime involvement started to draw notice. In the preface to *Rude Awakenings*, a 1995 anthology that was intended to "examin[e] the relationship between Japanese nationalism and intellectuals in the Kyoto school" (vii), James W. Heisig and John C. Maraldo give a short overview of these changes. According to these two scholars, the Kyoto School philosophers' ideas began to spread through translated texts in Western countries in the 1980s. At the time, they were warmly welcomed as Zen thought, which, as specific to Oriental culture, had gained some popularity in the West. However, since Heidegger's association with the Nazis had drawn substantial attention within academia in the late 1980s, people also started to scrutinize the Kyoto School's commitment to the wartime politics (*Rude Awakenings* vii–viii).

In 2011, Bret W. Davis, Brian Schroeder, and Jason M. Wirth published *Japanese and Continental Philosophy: Conversations with the Kyoto School*, which addressed intellectual dialogues between the Kyoto School and continental philosophers. In the introduction to this collection, they review the reception of the Kyoto School's philosophies and emphasize the fact that "the members of the Kyoto School thought of themselves first and foremost as *philosophers*, rather than as religious, cultural, or political theorists" (*Japanese and Continental Philosophy* 2). From this standpoint, the three editors intended their volume to be "the first anthology to be fully committed to developing *philosophical exchanges* between the Kyoto School and modern and contemporary Western philosophers in the Continental tradition" (*Japanese and Continental Philosophy* 2). What is expressed here is concern about the Kyoto School thinkers' inquiry into philosophy as such that goes beyond mere introduction to or interpretation of their thought, which formerly tended to be understood in the context of politics or Eastern religions.

Even before this, the increasing interest in philosophical approaches to the Kyoto School had manifested itself in its study. In the introduction to *Re-Politicising the Kyoto School as Philosophy* in 2008, Christopher Goto-Jones describes this anthology as "the search for the politics of the Kyoto School *qua* philosophy" and explains its goal as "shifting scholarly priorities *away* from 'historical evaluation and assessment of socio-political implications' at a specific point in history and *towards* the quest to 'apprehend philosophical architectonic and conceptual coherence' in philosophical texts" (11). While addressing the Kyoto School's political thought by following the general trend of scholarship since 1990s, Goto-Jones emphasizes the importance of philosophical inquiries, rather than socio-politico-historical investigations that have previously been carried out. For example, seven years before the publication of this anthology, Heisig, who wrote the forward of *Re-Politicising the Kyoto School as Philosophy,* published his book, *Philosophers of Nothingness: An Essay* on the Kyoto School. Heisig's 2001 work is an extensive study of three major philosophers of the school, namely Nishida, Tanabe Hajime, and Nishitani Keiji. Other similar examples, such as Goto-Jones's 2005 *Political Philosophy in Japan: Nishida, the Kyoto School, and Co-Prosperity* and Robert Wilkinson's 2009 *Nishida and Western Philosophy* point to a kind of "philosophical turn" that has been going on in Kyoto School scholarship, so to speak.

However, this philosophical turn cannot be celebrated without reserve, since it seems to include some problematic tendencies, depending on how "philosophy" is understood. If one assumes, even if tacitly, that only Western philosophy is philosophy in the exact sense, from this standpoint, the Kyoto School's philosophy, which was created outside the region called "the West," could be judged as not properly philosophical. In *Nishida and Western Philosophy*, Wilkinson seems to take this stance. What matters is not that Nishida's philosophy is compared with Western philosophy, but rather how this comparison is conducted.

For example, annexing the proviso that, "It is a mistake, of course, to regard either East or West as monolithic," Wilkinson insists "there are general tendencies of the kind" between them (158). Then he discusses what he believes to be a main difference between them with regard to rationality, which in his view consists of "working out rigorously the consequences of one's foundational beliefs, the beliefs in turn being dependent on equally foundational experiences":

> Rationality manifests itself in the same way both in the East and in the West. The chief difference (if one may simplify so complex a matter) lies in the centrality given to non-dual or mystical experience in the East by comparison to its relative non-centrality in the West. (Wilkinson 159)

Although Wilkinson may seem to simply present his idea of a general difference between the East and the West here, his further statements on Nishida suggest, although avoiding explicit mention, he reduces this difference to a matter of degree to which thought is worth being called philosophy. For example, Wilkinson states:

> The fact that Nishida's philosophy rests on experiences of the kind described is not in itself a problem. From the *philosophical* point of view there is a greater problem in the fact that he does not try to argue that the insights which he tries to conceptualize are veridical. (159)

To sum up Wilkinson's claim here in his own terms, Nishida intended his account of his Zen experience to be "a philosophy in the western sense, not an account of a mystical world-view beyond the reach of logic," aiming at "giving a coherent and systematic conceptual rendering of experience in the western manner" (102). Yet, Wilkinson concludes Nishida could not accomplish this, and so his thought was assimilated to mysticism as a result (160). In thus judging that Nishida did not provide a sufficiently logical account of his Zen experience and mystified it, Wilkinson describes Nishida's thought as the exemplary of the aforementioned Eastern tendency, in which the centrality is given to mystical experience. When Wilkinson denounces Nishida's allegedly mystical account as a problem viewed "[f]rom the philosophical point of view" (159), he tacitly assumes that Eastern tradition has something which, at its core, prevents thought from becoming philosophy, and that philosophy proper is basically Western philosophy. In the same vein, Wilkinson betrays his belief that rationality proper is the Western style of rationality when he states that Nishida "had to accept that reason could be used in this endeavour or he would not have set out to do western-style philosophizing at all, but this is not to be taken as implying that he was a thoroughgoing rationalist in all respects (which, as has been seen, he was not)" (155).

Furthermore, Wilkinson stretches his conclusion on Nishida and his implied failure in being thoroughly rational and philosophical in the Western sense to a matter of Eastern systems of thought: he asserts the incommensurability of Eastern and Western cultures, namely, "the more general *décalage* . . . between those central oriental systems of thought aiming at nirvana or one of its close analogues and those western philosophies" (161). Through this statement, Wilkinson practically affirms monolithic stereotyping of the East and the West, which he professed to deny. His selective and inconsistent usage of the term "philosophy" for Western thought illustrates his assumption that philosophy proper is Western philosophy and as if, strictly speaking, Oriental or non-Western philosophy did not really exist.

There would be plenty of room to explore whether Nishida really failed to "giv[e] a coherent and systematic conceptual rendering of experience" (Wilkinson 102), or if it is in fact an issue of interpretation. Regardless of the East or the West, depending on respective philosophers, such rendering can take a variety of forms, as does rationality, which may not be confined within the sphere of reason in the narrow sense. Generally speaking, scholars work hard to elucidate and explicate such various forms of rendering and rationality. Strangely enough, however arcane Western philosophies are, it is rare that scholars ascribe the difficulties of the texts to the different cultural backgrounds of the philosophers, or blame them for making their philosophies unintelligible due to their cultural nature. On the other hand, such gestures often go unchallenged in Western scholars' research of non-Western philosophers. What is operative here is again the assumption that only Western philosophy is philosophy proper, and that only Western rationality is rationality proper. This provides a pretext for judging anything that does not meet certain standards of this rationality as non-philosophical, and for abandoning efforts to elucidate or explicate non-Western philosophy as "philosophy" on its own terms. This seems to be nothing but an obstacle to philosophy and its understanding, especially given that the existence of various non-Western forms of philosophy has been claimed for so long.

Considering the perniciousness of Western-centric biases on philosophy, one may expect that taking into account cultural particularities that underlie different non-Western philosophies, with respect for them, would help us to understand them better, and avoid subjecting them to unfair judgments based on Western-centric biases. When this stance is taken, philosophy is understood as an expression of underlying culture, and largely determined by it. Although this approach may promote our understanding to a certain extent, it is also true that excessive emphasis upon such particularities, especially when they are arbitrarily picked up (or even invented), often runs the risk of hindering understanding not only of philosophy, but also of underlying culture. This seems to be the case with Goto-Jones's *Political Philosophy in Japan*.

Taking into account the fact that Buddhist thought constituted significant parts of both the tradition of Japanese political thinking and social discourses in early twentieth century Japan (Goto-Jones, *Political Philosophy in Japan* 26), Goto-Jones insists "it is not possible to substantiate the existence of a clear-cut break between the sites of religion, politics and philosophy in Nishida's work" (*Political Philosophy in Japan* 27). From this viewpoint, Goto-Jones explicates Nishida's political philosophy as elaborated by using concepts from Japanese Buddhist tradition and, as such, able to relativize and challenge Western political philosophy. In light of Nishida's political philosophy thus explicated, Goto-Jones re-examines Nishida's wartime discourses and discerns in them "the 'civil war' against ultra-nationalist and imperialist interpretations of the state-sanctioned terminology using the tools of his wider philosophical system" (*Political Philosophy in Japan* 1).

In this re-examination, Goto-Jones gives a key role to conditionals, which he believes Nishida must have used based on Nichiren, a Japanese Buddhist monk in the Kamakura period (*Political Philosophy in Japan* 33). Goto-Jones draws out and summarizes a conditional phrase that, for him, seems to play a significant role in Nichiren's teachings: "*buppō* [Buddha's law] is primary and *ōbō* [national law] is only legitimate to the extent that it accords with *buppō*" (*Political Philosophy in Japan* 33). His point here is that national law is legitimate only when it accords with Buddha's law; when national law does not accord with Buddha's law, people could judge this disaccord and understand the above statement as an implicit criticism of national law, as an allusion to its illegitimacy.

However, doubt arises as to whether it is possible to read the conditional into the texts in which it does not appear, and to find it functioning in the way as Goto-Jones claims. An example, which he uses to attest to the above usage of conditionals in Japanese Buddhist history, rather seems to disprove this claim. Goto-Jones states that Japanese Buddhist monk "Shaku Sōen famously called on the Imperial Japanese Army to seek 'the subjugation of evils hostile to civilization, peace and enlightenment' during the Russo-Japanese War of 1904–05" (*Political Philosophy in Japan* 35), and adds, in a note, "Sōen also notes that by seeking the destruction of this evil, Japan 'pursues no egoistical purpose'" (*Political Philosophy in Japan* 144). Asserting a tacit assumption of a conditional phrase in these statements, Goto-Jones finds in them the following dual meaning:

> On the one hand there is a simple justification of expansion "in the name of the Buddha." But, on the other hand, the justification of war is importantly conditional: war must not be the result of personal ambition . . . (*Political Philosophy in Japan* 35–36)[1]

Shaku's original statements, as quoted by Goto-Jones, do not include any conditional clause. Most simply understood, they plainly describe that Japan's war efforts accord with the moral ideal of Buddha's law. Nevertheless, once the author's tacit assumption of the conditional is asserted, the distinction between this moral ideal and the state's actual acts is introduced. Based on this distinction, it becomes possible to read into these statements a criticism of the state's acts in the name of the Buddhist moral ideal. It is questionable whether the author intended this complication in such simple statements. As it is uncertain whether Shaku supposed this distinction in them, there is no guarantee that he meant by them such a criticism. Most likely, he genuinely praised the state's war efforts as consonant with Buddha's law, while assuming the enemy's evilness.[2]

It is by drawing upon similar tacit assumptions of the conditional that Goto-Jones reads a criticism of the Japanese empire into Nishida's nuanced claim. Formulating a sentence that he believes Nishida would approve of, "*only enlightened states can form genuine transnational groupings,*" Goto-Jones interprets it as follows:

> . . . *only if/when* (. . . *tara*) states are enlightened will they become able to form legitimate transnational groupings. That is, the Japanese Empire is immoral if Japan (or Korea, or China . . .) is not

an enlightened state. From Nishida's concern about the problems of heteronomous political ethics, we can judge that Imperial Japan (with its state controlled Neo-Shintō-Confucian ideology) was not an enlightened state. Hence, the Japanese Empire was not a genuine or moral particular world. (*Political Philosophy in Japan* 65)

Again, it is uncertain whether a conditional clause is in fact tacitly assumed in Nishida's above sentence. On the contrary, if the accord between ideal and the state's actual acts is taken for granted, especially if it is supposed that it could be achieved exclusively in that very state as Shaku's statements indicate, the sentence at issue would present a different claim than what Goto-Jones presents as "misreading," that is, "Imperial Japan . . . was enlightened *because* it had an empire" (*Political Philosophy in Japan* 65). Here, Japan is enlightened, or at least at an advanced stage of enlightenment compared to other countries. If one were to suppose that, "*only if/when* states are enlightened will they become able to form legitimate transnational groupings," it would follow that only Japan can do so. Based on such assumptions, one might conclude that it is legitimate for Japan to guide other countries that do not have this ability, and to form transnational groupings under its leadership. In other words, the formation of a Japanese empire is not only legitimate here, but also moral. As I will argue later, this seems close to the overall claim expressed in Nishida and his disciples' prewar and wartime discourses, as far as they are read on their own terms, and before thinking about a risk that "such sentences could be *used* by political figures" (Goto-Jones, *Political Philosophy in Japan* 65).

Goto-Jones's above argument provides an illustration of the difficulty we may face in conducting research on philosophy by taking into account its supposed "cultural background." His strategy is to extract such a logic that would be characteristic of a certain Eastern religious tradition and, in light of this logic, change the interpretations of the works of those thinkers who belong to this tradition. Certainly this strategy, considered in itself, can sometimes contribute to discovering new meanings that have formerly gone unnoticed. However, on the pretext that understanding certain thinkers is linked to understanding their culture, when their works are loaded with too much extrapolation of alleged cultural specificities even if there is no inkling of them, the meanings of texts tend to be distorted rather than elucidated. This is similar to the case in which cultural stereotypes for certain people are so strong that interpretations of their works amount to the applications of these stereotypes.

Thus, not only is the position of insisting on the universality of Western philosophy an impediment, but the position of asserting the particularity of Eastern or Japanese philosophy can also be an obstacle to philosophical investigation, especially regarding cultural stereotypes that both these positions produce and promote. Then, a hope may be that, if philosophical dialogues are held between the West and the East or Japan, this may help break such stereotypes and remove obstacles to philosophical investigation and mutual understanding. Although this possibility cannot be denied, it seems to depend on the ways in which such dialogues take place. For example, in the introduction to *Japanese and Continental Philosophy*, the editors describe how they believe dialogues between the two cultures could take place:

> If one of the gifts that Western philosophy has been able to offer the Japanese is its methods of rational inquiry and critical dialogue, one of the gifts that the Japanese tradition has to offer the West is an existential-religious path that proceeds by way of holistic practice as well as conceptual thought. (14)

The editors here seem to repeat the same dichotomous stereotypes as Wilkinson, namely that Western philosophy represents rationality, while Eastern tradition (not "philosophy" proper) draws upon mystical experience and, as such, is essentially religious. When dialogues are held by taking such stereotypes as unchanged presuppositions, they most likely will end up confirming stereotypes held by both those who claim Western philosophy's universality and those who claim Japanese thought or tradition's particularity. If this is the case, doubt arises as to whether these positions are really in dialogue with each other. For, insofar as both apply their stereotypes not only to others, but also to themselves, they just confine themselves within their own fixed ideas rather than actually addressing to each other.

What is more important is that these two positions, Western universalism and Eastern or Japanese particularism, in spite of their seeming opposition, strangely cooperate to endorse and reinforce cultural stereotypes. Relevantly to this matter, in the final chapter of *Re-Politicising the Kyoto School as Philosophy* titled "Resistance to Conclusion: The Kyoto School Philosophy under the Pax Americana," Sakai Naoki draws our attention to "the complicity of universalism and particularism" that persists in studies of Japanese thought:

> What we must be aware of is the on-going presence of a peculiar, reciprocal connivance between the Orientalist exoticization of Japanese thought by Western scholars and the culturalist endorsement by Japanese intellectuals of such exoticism. (186)

Orientalism is famously formulated by Edward Said as "a Western style for dominating, restructuring, and having authority over the Orient" (3). It is a way of thinking discerned in Westerners' discourses on the Orient, intended to shape the Orient into an object to be ruled by the Occident. It authorizes Westerners to impose a specific view upon the Orient for this purpose.[3] In Sakai's words, "the West represents on behalf of the East, thereby establishing hierarchical relationships between the West and the East" ("Resistance to Conclusion" 186). It is through this Orientalist strategy that Western universalism works in the study of non-Western philosophy, excluding non-Western modes of thought from alleged "philosophy proper," or marginalizing the former within the field of the latter. Sakai's claim is that Japanese particularism, adopted to counter Western universalism (although it is not exclusively Japanese intellectuals who take this position) does not necessarily challenge its supposed opponent, but rather provides water for turning the enemy's mill. Ironically, particularizing Japanese thought and making scholars recognize this particularity has the effect of endorsing, or even reinforcing, Orientalists' assertion of the universality of Western thought as essentially different from Japanese thought as particular. Based on this view, Sakai warns that reading Japanese philosophers' works in particularist manners runs the risk of falling into the pitfall of this "mutual endorsement" between Western universalism and Japanese particularism, which he calls "the civilizational transference" ("Resistance to Conclusion" 183).

> . . . the exoticizing projection of Asia, "the Oriental mind," or "the outside of Western metaphysics" onto the texts of Japanese philosophy has made it impossible for students to work through the constraints of civilizational transference" ("Resistance to Conclusion" 190)

Contrary to Western universalists, who undervalue Japanese philosophy, Japanese particularists try to enhance its value, and yet the latter are drawn into mutual endorsement with the former. This is because particularists share with universalists the intention of establishing hierarchical relationships based on the dichotomy of the West and Japan; the fact that the two parties uphold opposite hierarchies does not prevent both from supporting this dichotomy itself, while working to solidify it together. Both Western universalism and Japanese particularism not only reduce interpretation of philosophical texts to an application of cultural stereotypes, but also lend themselves to the dichotomous division of Western philosophy as universal and Japanese philosophy as particular. Considering this, investigations of Japanese philosophy must avoid taking either the Western universalism or Japanese particularism approaches to philosophy in order to do justice to its object while neither idealizing nor belittling it.

What, then, would a philosophy that stands outside of these two positions look like, and how might we reconceive universality, particularity, and their relation differently based on it? These are big questions, and answering them fully is beyond the scope of this book and my ability. What can be said, at least, is that if a philosophy is not satisfied with being confined within the dichotomy of these positions, it should critically examine the assumed ideas of universality and particularity, and their relation to each other, as well as question how and under what conditions these ideas are produced, and what limitations or constraints they consequently involve. If such restrictions were disclosed, it would help exploring how universality, particularity and their relation can be reconceived differently, while also correcting the problems resulting from such restrictions, or caused by disregard for them. After all, particularity and universality are only there as we conceive of them. As such, they are neither as unchangeable nor essential as they seem to be. Rather, they are continually produced, transformed, undermined, and re-produced, while new problems entailed in them are discovered. No universality, no particularity, thus produced, can be the perfect final solution. So, what one can do is to accept the difficulty of this ongoing production and join its process, rather than substantiating universality/particularity as a fixed standard.

From this standpoint, a critical eye should be turned not only to the above two positions in the study of the Kyoto School's philosophy, but also to this philosophy itself. For this very philosophy exemplifies the pitfalls that we should avoid when trying to get out of the dichotomy between Western universalism and Japanese particularism.

At a glance, the fact that the Kyoto School philosophers engaged in the production of universalist philosophical discourses, which seem to have validity beyond particular, local concerns of Japanese intellectual society, may give the appearance that these philosophers already surmounted this dichotomy. This, however, does not only concern their theoretical position. Their engagement in universalist philosophical projects is often invoked as a reason to distinguish their political stance from those of other Japanese intellectuals around the time of the Asia-Pacific War, especially literary figures, who enthusiastically celebrated Japan's war and colonial invasion solely in defense of its national interests. In fact, what is presupposed here is another dichotomy, namely one of emotional particularism associated with nationalism and philosophical universalism associated with cosmopolitanism.

Sakai points out that the Kyoto School philosophers used their universalistic discourses for the particularistic purpose, that is, to legitimize Japan's colonial rule over other Asian countries and establish its hegemony over them:

> Not only Japan's relationship with Korea, Taiwan, China and other peoples in Asia but also the fact that the members of the Kyoto School clearly participated in the production of the legitimacy of

Japanese colonial rule in Asia in universalistic philosophical terms have been persistently overlooked in the study of Kyoto School philosophy. ("Resistance to Conclusion" 194)

Sakai describes those who use universalistic philosophical terms and privilege their own country or people as part of the "particularization of the universal project of transcendental philosophy" ("Resistance to Conclusion" 195). Given that this particularization of the universal project in the Kyoto School's philosophy lent itself to legitimizing Japan's colonial rule, the philosophers' pursuit of universality cannot be enough reason for judging their philosophy as unaccountable for the legitimization of colonialism. For this very pursuit of universality becomes a pretext to disguise and justify this particularist purpose.

Moreover, this particularization of the universal does not necessarily overcome the dichotomy between Western universalism and Japanese particularism. As aforementioned, Western universalism, in asserting the exclusive universality of the West, which is basically one of many particular cultural regions, is not really universal in the exact sense of the word. Rather, insofar as it makes universality serve to privilege particular people or their culture, Western universalism entails particularization of the universal, which is indeed parallel to the Kyoto School's philosophical discourses. The Kyoto School's universalist discourses, legitimating Japan's colonial rule, simply aim to put Japan and Japanese people in the same position that the West and Westerners occupy in Western universalism. They replace it with Japanese universalism, without questioning the problems implied in such a positioning itself. Thus the philosophical pursuit of universality does not necessarily amount to opposing certain people's subjugation of others. Western philosophy already has a lot of precedence to show this.

The same applies to the cases in which allegedly universal "morality" or "ethicality" is pursued. Having a different view from that of Sakai, Heisig, in the forward of *Re-Politicising the Kyoto School as Philosophy*, states, "for these philosophers self-awareness is intended as a moral yardstick that aims to be every bit as 'universal' as the principles on which their wartime opinions have been chastised" (xxv). Heisig then continues that revealing these philosophers' "universal" moral principles would "[turn] the philosophy of the Kyoto School on itself as a way to cleanse it of the stains that the conditions of its birth left upon it" (*Re-Politicising the Kyoto School* xxv). Heisig's claim is that the universal moral principles, upheld by the philosophers, could judge their own wartime engagement determined by a particular historical situation. Therefore, disclosing such universal moral principles would be enough to release them from the accusation of their wartime engagement. It is in the same vein that Heisig claims, in his *Philosophers of Nothingness*, that "anything approaching or supporting the imperialistic ideology of wartime Japan" was "an aberration from their own intellectual goals" (6).[4] Heisig here seems to have trust in the impeccability of the philosophers' universalist and moral project, which he views as fundamental and unspoilable by their involvement in particular situations.

In his 1995 essay, "The Consequences of the 'Philosophy of World History: From Wartime to the Postwar Era'" ["*Sekaishi no tetsugaku*" *no kiketsu: Senchū kara sengo e*], Yonetani Masafumi offers significant insight into this point. He discusses the continuity between the four Kyoto School thinkers' wartime and postwar discourses, and underscores that they shared a specific philosophy of world history and advocated for the war with recourse to the moral ideal backed up by their philosophy. This continuity, Yonetani argues, demonstrates these philosophers' belief that the moral ideal they upheld in wartime was right, even though the war, which was justified based on their very beliefs, was wrong. He thus asks, "even if that ideal criticized what was going on in reality, still, at the same time, wasn't it also this ideal that consequently supported this reality?" Yonetani also points to these philosophers' lack of awareness of this "complementarity between ideal and reality" (229). Here, both the ideal and the reality worked in tandem to allow the war to procced, and have also bolstered recent efforts to resuscitate wartime ideologies in Japan (228). If these philosophers' moral ideal truly criticized the actual war, it would not have lent itself to a revival of ideologies today that promoted this very war in the past. In other words, this resurgence of wartime ideologies confirms that this moral ideal harbors the very factors that allow this to happen. Thus, "the complementarity between ideal and reality" was not simply forced upon this moral philosophy by its historical situation. It does not necessarily seem to be the case that their moral philosophy—despite its profound truthfulness that arguably could constitute a criticism of, or resistance to, the war—was misrepresented and abused by the forces behind the wartime situation.

Of course, the Kyoto School's entire philosophy cannot be reduced to the philosophers' prewar and wartime discourses, and it is undeniable that exploration of their philosophies, conducted independently of political matters, has its own significance. Still, the fact remains that these philosophers engaged in Japan's wartime situation based on their philosophies and argued for particularist stances by using universalistic terms of philosophy. Emphasizing merely "universal" and "moral" aspects in the philosophers' project, as if this were enough to prove their unaccountability, would preclude the questions as to how their concepts of universality and morality worked to advocate particularism, and consequently what effects their philosophy contributed to certain social, historical, and political situations. Then, we run the risk of misrepresenting the philosophers' statements that privilege their own particular country or people as expressions of their genuine universalist aspirations, or worse—allowing for similar abuses of philosophy on the pretense of its profundity, even though inadvertently.

Likewise, we could not assume a clear-cut division between the Kyoto School philosophers' pure philosophy and their political discourses while taking the latter as mere deviation forced to occur by historical conditions. Through legitimating Japan's colonial rule by using universalistic terms in particularist manners, the Kyoto School's philosophy itself straddled the dividing line between philosophy and politics. To this extent, it would be relevant to ask how allegedly "pure" philosophy could become a source of political problems, rather than assuming the clear-cut split between philosophy and politics.

Nevertheless, thematizing the philosophers' involvement in colonialism tends to be avoided in the study of the Kyoto School's philosophy. Although this might be partly because of academia's general tendency to separate pure philosophy and politics, Sakai finds the cause of this avoidance in the aforementioned dichotomous scheme dividing the West and Japan.

> What has been evaded in the study of Kyoto School philosophy because of the binarism of the West and Japan is an inquiry into the essential alliance between colonialism and the transcendental project of universalist philosophy. ("Resistance to Conclusion" 195)

Why does this binarism work to make scholars avoid such an inquiry? If the schema of the binary opposition between the West and Japan as a part of the non-West is taken too punctiliously, and each of the opposing terms to be united within itself as homogeneous, Japan's challenge to Western hegemony is regarded as benefitting the non-West as a whole. The non-West, then, is put in a disadvantageous position in relation to the West. In turn, Japan's position in relation to other members of the non-West is left unquestioned, and criticisms of Japan's colonial rule in Asia are hastily equated with advocacies of Western domination. Similarly, raising questions about the Kyoto School's philosophical legitimation of Japanese colonialism is mistaken as standing on the side of Western colonialism and denigrating Japan and Japanese philosophers' challenge to Western hegemony. Here, non-Westerners' challenge to Western hegemony provides an excuse for Japan's colonial rule and Japanese philosophers' legitimization of it. Sakai warns us that "it is important to keep in mind that a certain denunciation of Eurocentrism, particularly of white supremacy, was used to legitimate Japanese imperialist ventures in Asia before and during the Asia Pacific War" ("Resistance to Conclusion" 186). In other words, when we avoid inquiry into the Kyoto School's legitimation of

Japanese colonialism on the pretense of the philosophers' just cause of challenging Western hegemony, the logic at work here is the same which was used to justify Japan's colonial aggression in Asia under the banner of fighting against Western colonialism. To avoid being trapped by this logic, Sakai suggests turning a critical eye to "the structural complicity between the West and Japan" ("Resistance to Conclusion"186), beyond their binary opposition, with regard to their common, but different, particularist desire for hegemony and their use of universalistic terms to justify this desire.

What complicates things is that the Kyoto School's philosophers themselves often argued for Japanese particularism and privileged Japan and the Japanese in their works. Still, exploring their philosophy does not necessarily require one to share their particularist stance, including its ethnocentric assumptions, unless one willingly adopts such a stance. It is possible to critically analyze their particularist discourses, and elucidate how these philosophers used universalistic terms to particularize their own country and people, and the problems involved in their philosophy thus articulated. This critical analysis of particularist discourses should not be carried out in a particularist manner that reduces these problems to matters distinct to Japan or the Japanese, thus repeating the errors of particularism in question. Rather, it should address these problems as those which could occur to anybody, anywhere, in generalized terms. This would also help cast light upon the aforementioned "structural complicity between the West and Japan" based on their commonality.

In this book, I take the following stance in my exploration of the Kyoto School's philosophy: (1) we must avoid both Western universalism and Japanese particularism. Specifically, we must neither undervalue the Kyoto School's philosophy based on allegedly universal standards of Western philosophy, nor interpret the school's philosophy as an expression of alleged Japanese particularities. (2) Rather than assuming the division between the school's pure philosophy and their political engagement, this book treats the school's philosophy as already straddling this dividing line, and addresses this philosophy as underlying the philosophers' political engagement and endorsing politically problematic power structures. (3) Instead of taking the thinkers' universalist project of philosophy as evidence of political innocence or silent opposition to colonialism, I question how they used universalistic philosophical terms to authenticate Japanese particularism and legitimate the colonization of others. (4) In the same vein, I question how these philosophers used moral terms for the same purpose. For it was their moral project that also contributed to this authentication and legitimation.

In exploring the Kyoto School's philosophy with this stance, I will adopt a textual approach. While this approach has its own limits, my objective is not to divine or represent the true intentions of these philosophers based on records or testimonies, whether their own or those of others. Rather my objective is to clarify what is stated in these philosophers' discourses, explore what thoughts these discourses articulate (and the thoughts thus articulated may be called "intentions" in another sense), and elucidate what problems are involved with these thoughts. It will be argued that, even if these philosophers really wished to resist the wartime regime as a whole, the presentation of various elements in these philosophers' discourses undermines the possibility of such resistance. What matters here is that the presentation and arrangement of these philosophers' texts ultimately captured people's hearts and mobilized them for the war.

An objection to this approach may be that these philosophers did not intentionally present and arrange their discourses in such ways. In fact, a typical defense of the Kyoto School, in terms their public discourse, is that due to censorship and the suppression of free speech, they could not express their true ideas, and instead were forced to publicly state what they did not really mean. This was undeniably the case with much of the Japanese population at that time. However, this defense tends to ignore or exclude the possibility of any commonality or overlap between the ideology of the wartime government and the ideology of the people who underwent censorship. In his contribution to *Re-Politicising the Kyoto School as Philosophy*, Davis responds to this defense by writing, "a political philosophy must be judged not just on its intentions but also on its effects" (32). Certain kinds of beliefs work to justify terrible thoughts and actions carried out on others, including one-sidedly killing them without remorse. Such beliefs are not reducible to a matter of intentions. People sometimes try to put beliefs into practice with well-meaning goals, and then defend their deeds in the name of their good intentions. It bears remembering other historical events where one group of people conquered others who they regarded as "uncivilized" in order to "enlighten" them, or massacred them with the ostensibly good intention of "liberating" them. It seems that similar beliefs to these manifest themselves in the discourses of the philosophers at hand. Therefore, rather than putting too much trust in these philosophers presumed "good intentions," it is necessary to question the thoughts (or "intentions" in another sense, that are inseparable from and defined by the effects they produce) expressed or formed through the arrangements and presentation of various elements in their discourses.

Indeed, the Kyoto School philosophers' prewar and wartime discourses as a whole exemplify the inseparable unity of their political and moral philosophy, ultimately grounded in their metaphysical thought. However, as dealing with all such discourses risks leading to a desultory argument, I focus on two central themes, namely: (1) overcoming modernity, and (2) Japanese national subjectivity. I then examine these philosophers' public discourses in which these themes conspicuously manifest themselves.

"Overcoming Modernity" was the title and theme of a symposium organized soon after the beginning of the Asia-Pacific War. Its goal was to discuss the war's significance, which the symposium's title was supposed to represent. Famous intellectuals, including a few members of the Kyoto School, were invited to contribute essays and exchange their opinions. Before and after this symposium, a series of three other symposia also took place. Only four prominent members of the Kyoto School participated, including the two who attended the "Overcoming Modernity" symposium. Since all four thinkers shared a particular conception of world history, their philosophy was a consistent topic across these symposia. In pursuit of the symposium's goal, these thinkers discussed the importance of a Japanese national subjectivity that could lead to the overcoming of modernity, and also bring world history into perspective. Thus, for these four philosophers, the themes of overcoming modernity and Japanese national subjectivity were inseparably connected, reflecting their thoughts about not only what the Second World War was, but also what it should be. Although their mentor, Nishida, distanced himself from his four disciples' project during these symposia, this does not necessarily mean the former's philosophy was completely removed or resolutely opposed to that of the latter. As I will discuss, the ideas of similar subjectivity and the lines of thought that constituted another attempt to overcome modernity can be discerned in Nishida's philosophy in the same period. Nishida's thinking thus conceptually buttressed the ideas his disciples expressed during these symposia.

The Kyoto School philosophers' pursuit of universality and their concern for overcoming modernity have an inherent connection. Modernity, as we usually understand it today, originated in the West and then spread globally. As such, it appeared as something universal, but only as an effect of historical processes of universalizing. The nation-state, as a polity that is characteristic of modernity, is also the universal in a similar sense. Indeed, it is an amalgam of the universal and the particular, a combination of the state as a universalized form of a political body and the nation as a particular (or particularized) human group. In Japan's case, Japanese people largely equated modernization with Westernization at that time. It, along with the importation of Western philosophy, began almost concomitantly with the establishment of the nation-state in the Meiji period. Following this time of importation and adaptation, "Japanese" modern philosophy developed and culminated in the emergence of the Kyoto School. The Kyoto philosophers' bid for universality only took place under specific conditions, in which the Japanese nation-state had already been established and universalized. More precisely, in the prewar and wartime periods when these philosophers were most active, Japan struggled to expand its power beyond itself as a particular nation-state. Considering this situation, it is not a coincidence that the Kyoto School's bid for universality, in line with Japan's policies and war efforts, sought the universality beyond that of modernity and the West. Reflecting the amalgam of the universal and the particular in the Japanese nation-state, these philosophers' pursuit of this "higher" universality was permeated by their allegiance to the values of the particularity of their nation. Therefore, it is not surprising that these philosophers viewed the task of overcoming modernity and the West as connected to the realization of this "higher" universality to Japanese national subjectivity in particular.

Doubt has been cast on the success of the Kyoto School's attempts to overcome modernity. As the title of his 2002 book, *Overcome by Modernity*, suggests, Harry Harootunian evaluates the philosophers' attempts as failures, claiming the Kyoto School was overcome by the modernity they tried to surmount. This claim might be criticised as a sweeping generalization that does not inquire deeply into the philosophy at issue. Still, his formulation on the general historical context concerning the theme of "overcoming modernity" is helpful to situate the Kyoto School's philosophy within a broader scope, and explore it in line with "the structural complicity between the West and Japan," which Sakai emphasized.

Harootunian's statement may be misunderstood as a Western-centric claim that non-Western countries must follow the same path of modernization as the West, and therefore are fated to be overwhelmed by the West forever. However, this is not what he means. When he qualifies Japanese modernity as "co-eval" in the sense that it "shared the same historical temporality of modernity (as a form of historical totalizing) found elsewhere in Europe and the United States" (Harootunian xvi), he does not propose that European or American modernities are/were at more advanced stages than Japanese modernity in a single, linear course of progress. As history shows, Japan was urged to modernize through its encounters with Western modernity, and it achieved modernization through its confrontation with the West. To this extent, Japanese modernity was born from the same historical process as Western modernity. This coevality does not necessarily imply that the latecomer is doomed to be overwhelmed by the predecessor. The point is that, as the result of this coevality, Japanese modernity, in spite of or precisely because of its rivalry with Western modernity, ran the risk of internalizing its structural oppression against the non-West. This is the same oppression which Japanese modernity is supposed to counter to achieve a non-Western form of modernity for itself. More concretely, Harootunian raises the question of whether it can be said that a Japanese modernity overcame Western modernity when the former appropriated the latter's modes of imperialism and colonialism that have historically tormented the non-West. It is from this perspective that Harootunian claims the Kyoto School was overcome by the modernity they tried to surmount. What he means is not that the West defeated, and will continue to defeat Japan, but that Japanese modernity has been, and will be challenged by its own self-contradiction, just as Western modernity has been, and will continue to be. Another question raised is whether the Kyoto School philosophers, in their discourses on overcoming modernity, could develop ideas that aimed to break such complicity between Japanese and Western modernity.

Along this line of thinking, this book asks: Could the Kyoto School philosophers' thoughts about overcoming modernity offer a valid prospect for the Japanese people to overcome modernity, rather than being overcome by it? Could their ideas about a Japanese national subjectivity, as the agent for this overcoming, offer visions of a mode of existence that differs from Western-centric subjectivities? Attending to these questions by focusing on the two themes of overcoming modernity and Japanese national subjectivity, and by thoroughly examining these philosophers' discourses, are the tasks this book sets out to achieve. The criteria for evaluating these philosophers' attempts will be taken from their own criticisms of Western modernity and the subjectivity that is characteristic of it. Thus, evaluating their attempts entails examining whether their moral and political philosophies were true to the ideals they themselves professed to uphold and, relatedly, elucidating how these philosophers particularized their own country and people by using universalistic philosophical terms against their own ideals. It will be shown that this particularization of the universal, in terms of how it was expressed, will take the shape of the universalization of the particular in terms of the content of expression in the discourses at issue.

In part 1 of this book, I will examine the discourses of four prominent members of the second generation of the Kyoto School: Kōsaka Masaaki, Kōyama Iwao, Suzuki Shigetaka, and Nishitani Keiji. While only Suzuki and Nishitani participated in the "Overcoming Modernity" symposium, all four thinkers participated in the three subsequent symposia, during which they discussed their philosophies of world history. I will explicate these thinkers' philosophy, as expressed in these symposia, on Japanese national subjectivity and the philosophy of world history, based on which they asserted the significance of this subjectivity and the necessity to create it. By looking into its three salient characteristics, I will inquire whether this subjectivity could become the agent for overcoming modernity, as these thinkers envisioned. I will also question whether this subjectivity could become the agent for ethically transforming the Japanese wartime state or its military government, as recently claimed by some scholars.

In part 2, I will turn to these thinkers' mentor, Nishida, and examine his discourses, published almost contemporaneously with these symposia. My analysis will turn an eye to the overlaps and continuity between his lines of thought and that of his disciples. In reference to the above three characteristics of Japanese national subjectivity, I will argue that Nishida not only promoted ideas of a similar subjectivity, but also elaborated a theory of the structure of the Japanese state that could condition the possibility of this subjectivity. By unpacking the visions of the state and the world that Nishida believed this subjectivity would create, I will inquire whether such views could offer alternatives to the forms of the state and world that are characteristic of modernity, thus constituting a successful project to overcome modernity.

Part 1

"Overcoming Modernity" and
"The Philosophy of World History"

Chapter 1

Nishitani Keiji and the *Bungakukai* Symposium "Overcoming Modernity"

In part 1, I will investigate the discourses of several members of the Kyoto School's second generation, as presented in two symposia that took place in the early 1940s. One is the "Overcoming Modernity" roundtable discussion held by the *Bungakukai* (Literary World) journal in 1942 (published in the same year). The other is a series of three roundtable discussions, organized by the *Chūōkōron* (Central Review) journal in 1941 and 1942 (published from 1942 to 1943). In his landmark 1959 essay, "Overcoming Modernity," Takeuchi Yoshimi remarked: "On the level of ideas, the 'Overcoming Modernity' and 'World-Historical Standpoint' symposiums share much in common" (104). Takeuchi's approach was to find a close link between the discussions in both symposia. Recently, however, doubt has been cast on this methodology. For example, Minamoto Ryōen proposes to treat these events separately: "Unlike the *Chūōkōron* debates, which dealt more with the philosophy of history, the "Overcoming Modernity" symposium dealt with the nature of civilizations" (199); "[the participants'] common concern was modern Western civilization and its acceptance on the one hand, and the possibilities for Japanese and Eastern traditions on the other. At least in this symposium, the question of the Greater East Asian War was not central for them" (207). The discussions in the *Chūōkōron* symposia were developed around this war. Minamoto distinguishes these deliberations from those in the *Bungakukai* symposium, and claims their central topic to be the nature of Eastern/Western civilizations and cultures. For him, this is basically independent of the debates about the war.

However, this stance is not without problems. Although Minamoto equates the differences between the two symposia's main topics, and the dissimilarities of the discussions that took place within them, doing so precludes the question concerning the ways in which these topics were discussed. Even though matters pertaining to civilization or culture cannot be reduced to the issue of warfare, the two topics were not broached completely independently of each other. Rather, it seems the war and its historical context cast a shadow upon the discussions and determined the ways it was debated. Besides, as many scholars have already shown, and as I will also demonstrate, the Kyoto philosophers' discussions on the philosophy of world history during the *Chūōkōron* symposia significantly overlap with their arguments about overcoming modernity during the *Bungakukai* symposium. To this extent, Takeuchi's remarks should still be taken seriously.

Negating the commonality between the two symposia and putting excessive emphasis upon the distinctions between the *Bungakukai* and *Chūōkōron* events, during which topics concerning the war predominated, seems to be a tactic to exonerate the Kyoto School from blame of wartime engagement. In fact, reading the discussions on civilization and culture as independent to the war is quite similar to the approach of interpreting the discourses that explicitly supported the war as opposing it. There is also another tactic, which consists of emphasizing the Kyoto philosophers' distinction from those literary figures who attended the "Overcoming Modernity" symposium, and from nationalists in general, even though this differentiation is not so clear-cut in reality. This tactic works to generate an impression these philosophers were immune to nationalism.

In view of refuting such arguments, and by interpreting the Kyoto philosophers' thoughts as expressed through their discourses, in this chapter I will scrutinize the Kyoto School's position articulated in relation to the "Overcoming Modernity" symposium. A special focus will be cast upon Nishitani Keiji, who was a representative figure of the Kyoto School's second generation. First, I will investigate the Kyoto School philosophers' approach by analyzing how they differed from both literary figures at this symposium, and nationalists at that time. I will question whether the distinctions between these groups were really decisive enough to separate and label them as either pacifists or jingoists. Second, by reading Nishitani's essay contribution to the symposium, I will show that his argument about Oriental religiosity and Japanese tradition in contrast to Western modernity implies the assertion of the superiority of Japanese culture, attesting to this argument's affinity with typical nationalist claims of the time. Third, I will examine excerpts of this same essay, in which Nishitani discusses the Greater East Asia Co-Prosperity Sphere, in reference to the morality that concretizes this Japanese tradition. This examination will draw out how his arguments, made in the name of this morality, practically provided justification for Japan's bid to establish its hegemony in Asia and the war it waged for that purpose.

Section 1: The Putative Division between the Kyoto School and Nationalists

The roundtable discussion, titled "Overcoming Modernity," was held in 1942, just after the outbreak of the Asia-Pacific War in 1941, and sought to address the war's impact upon Japanese intellectuals. In the "Concluding Remarks" of this discussion, Kawakami Tetsutarō mentions the "intellectual trembling" caused by the war that led to the coordination of the discussion itself (OM 149). In the Annotation (*kaidai*) of the Japanese text, Matsumoto Ken'ichi explains that, to Japanese intellectuals at the time, this "intellectual trembling" meant that "the Greater East Asia War [*daitōa sensō*], in its ideal, attempted to resist the Western modernity that Japan had imitated and pursued until then" (v).[1] For Japan at that time, which from the Meiji period onward had embarked on modernization by importing Western culture, modernization was equal to Westernization. In short, the model of the modernity to be achieved by Japan was that of the West. Therefore, when it launched the war against Western countries, Japan's urgent task, as perceived by Japanese people, was not only to surpass the West, but also to overcome the modernity equated with the West. Thus, "overcoming modernity," in view of Japan's rivalry with the West, was a timely discussion topic for Japanese intellectuals. Speaking of the dominant tendency in the roundtable discussion, Richard F. Calichman, in his preface to the English translation of "Overcoming Modernity," notes, "the modernity to be overcome was associated with the West itself, such that overcoming modernity and overcoming the West were seen as essentially the same thing" (IX).[2]

Though gathered under the same slogan, the intellectuals selected to participate in this symposium had differing views on the task at hand. Kawakami mentions "the strange sense of chaos and rupture that dominated the symposium" (OM 149), because in many instances, these intellectuals did not engage respectfully with each other's opinions or have actual conversations with each other. Such "chaos and rupture" occurred mainly due to the differences between the groups or factions they belonged to, which was further complicated by their individual differences. The symposium's participants are often classified under three groups: the associates of the journal *Bungakukai*, in which the record of this roundtable discussion would be published; the Japan Romantic School; and the Kyoto School. The differences between the literary figures part of these first two groups and the philosophers of the Kyoto School have been particularly emphasized. It is often said that while the literary figures, especially those from the Japan Romantic School, opposed modernity and exhorted the return to Japanese indigenous tradition from antiquity, the Kyoto School philosophers situated Japan's modernization in the context of world history and explored how Japan, thus modernized, could go beyond modernity.

The difference between these two stances is not only a matter of dividing opinion within this symposium—rather, the split overlaps with that between the positions of the wartime Kyoto School, and of typical nationalists who were intent on celebrating Japan and the uniqueness of its genuine traditions, completely independent of foreign influence. For example, Minamoto emphasizes the Kyoto School's "open-mindedness to the world," and distinguishes these philosophers from "the narrow-minded nationalists" (204). The difference is often interpreted as decisive, and it is invoked to distinguish these philosophers, not only from fanatic nationalists, but from nationalism in general. For example, David Williams characterizes the position of the wartime Kyoto School as "[r]ejecting the reigning assumption of all Japanese ultra-nationalists and most moderate nationalists alike." He further characterizes the philosophers of the Kyoto School as "free of ethnocentric bias" (*Defending Japan's Pacific War* 62), thus differentiating them from the nationalists.

Even though the existence of a number of dissimilarities is undeniable, whether these differences are decisive enough to conclude the Kyoto School's immunity or opposition to nationalism or ethnocentrism is another matter. According to Kevin M. Doak, the very difference that distinguishes the stance of the Kyoto School from one form of nationalism was crucial to the school's contribution to another. In the 1930s and 1940s, Doak observes there were tensions between the modern Japanese state and ethnic nationalists, who attached importance to the ethnic nation and viewed it as to be built upon shared ethnicity and pure indigenous tradition. They opposed the modern state, as they viewed it as contaminated by foreign influence. To prevent ethnic nationalism from constituting an oppositional force, the modern state of Japan must have conciliated it so as to create a seamless national identity that included it (Doak, "Nationalism as Dialectics" 182–92).

It is against this backdrop that the Kyoto School, insofar as it is distinguished from the Japan Romantic School, played an important role. In the late 1930s, Doak explains, Yasuda Yojūrō, a representative figure of the Romantic School, started to insist on "a natural 'blood and soil' as a more authentic expression of the Japanese soul than such historical constructs as the modern nation-state" ("Nationalism as Dialectics" 186), while shifting his position to ethnic nationalism. Inevitably, Yasuda and the Romantic School were prone to ethnic nationalism's ambiguous attitude toward the nation-state. That is, they exhorted the significance of the ethnic nation based on pure indigenous tradition on the one hand, and criticized the corruption of the modern state due to foreign influence on the other. However, Doak continues:

> In contrast to the Romantic School, the Kyoto school was less troubled by the ambiguities of nationalism and argued for a historical perspective that would reappropriate 'moral energy' for the state. By explicitly connecting 'blood and soil' with the Japanese state, the Kyoto school played such a critical role in asserting a clear and unequivocal identification of nationalism with the nation-state. . . . ("Nationalism as Dialectics" 186)

Differently from the Romantic School that emphasized the emotional ties with ethnic tradition, the Kyoto School grasped the world and history through the lens of philosophical rationality. From this standpoint, the Kyoto School could provide theories that compatibly supported the modern state, without having to worry about the ambiguities that troubled ethnic nationalism. Moreover, the Kyoto School's ideas of morality, backed up by rational thought, could offer an alternative to ethnic nationalism's criticisms of state corruption. At the same time, they could channel their forces in the service of the state, rather than in opposition to it. As such, the Kyoto School could even incorporate in their theories the "blood and soil" as essential elements of ethnic nationalism, and relevantly associate them with the modern state, conceived as a nation-state without posing a threat to it. Thus, in Doak's view, the Kyoto School's very difference from ethnic nationalists enabled these philosophers to represent another type of nationalism that was more suitable for the modern state, and also had the capacity to integrate these nationalists into it.

Specifically, Doak insists that the "Overcoming Modernity" symposium was "a good example of the state's attempt to provide 'proper guidance' to moral and nationalist critiques." Furthermore, he states, "the very purpose of the symposium was, arguably, to co-opt much of the force of these nationalist critiques within the state structure." Doak also notes the pivotal role played by Nishitani with regard to this purpose: "No one expressed the bond between moralism and the state better than Nishitani Keiji" ("Nationalism as Dialectics" 193).

Seen in this light, the Kyoto philosophers' difference from literary figures at the symposium, and ethnic nationalists in general, proves neither the Kyoto School's immunity, nor opposition to any nationalism, nor the lack of its point of contact with ethnocentrism. The Kyoto School's theories that appropriated the essential elements of ethnic nationalism, and gave them rationalized forms, could not but undergird its basic tenets, rather than undermine them. Even though these theories tended toward taming the force of ethnic nationalism, this worked to integrate it into another form of nationalism that urged people to serve the modern state. Furthermore, on the consequence of the state's efforts to control ethnic nationalism, Doak comments, "movements that the state attempted to control actually had a good deal of influence over the subsequent character of the nation-state itself" ("Nationalism as Dialectics" 192). Through the Kyoto School's promotion of rational thought, the modern state was assimilated to the nation-state, which ethnic nationalists, at the same time, promoted emotional devotion to. Even though they held different ideals, both groups' positions essentially amounted to the same thing. Thus, the divisions between the Kyoto School and ethnic nationalists, as well as between the philosophers and literary figures at the symposium, are not strictly dichotomous. Rather, the two sides, regardless of their differences, coordinated, and even cooperated, to move in the same direction.

Harootunian remarks that, despite dissident views among the participants from different groups, "the symposium shared with the prevailing discourse on cultural authenticity the fantasy that neither history nor techno-economic development had managed to change what was essentially and eternally Japanese" (*Overcome by Modernity* 40).[3] The convergence of the concerns of different groups upon this essential and eternal Japaneseness at the symposium can be understood against the backdrop of Japan's historical situation, which was just after the outbreak of the Pacific War. Sun Ge also observes the schism in the symposium between the literary figures who "tended to associate the 'anti-modern' with an affirmation of a native 'pure tradition' " and the scholars who "saw the discussion of the superiority of Japan as a constitutive element in the narrative of world history." Sun formulates this schism as tradition versus modernity, insistence on sensibility, or daily experience versus abstract theoretical investigation (59). However, by regarding this difference as an extension of "an opposition (and complex admixtures) between a position that centered on Japan and one that centered on the West" (Sun 60), developed around Japan's drive for modernization in the Meiji Period, Sun does not ignore the moment in which these positions were unified on the occasion of the war:

> The outbreak of the Pacific War tipped the scales toward a unified position that centered on Japan. In sum, at this pivotal moment in the Asia-Pacific War, it became possible to set aside differences regarding the shock produced by Western modernity in Japan, at least temporarily. (60)

The position of negating modernity and returning to native tradition, and that of going beyond modernity in world history, shared the common objective of establishing Japan's cultural superiority to the West, in line with the former's task to surpass the latter. The difference between the two positions resided merely in the ways in which they believed they could achieve this objective. In Sun's view, this was the case not only with these two positions at the "Overcoming Modernity" symposium, but also with Japanese intellectuals in general at that time:

> . . . while there did not exist any real difference of position among Japanese intellectuals of the 1940s, a single problematic held sway: that of *how to narrate* 'Japan' and the 'West' within the putatively larger narrative of modernity. (61)

This problematic created a context in which all symposium participants could agree on the question of how to overcome modernity, in spite of their miscommunication—the slogan "Overcoming Modernity" attracted many of their intellectual contemporaries. In this context, the Kyoto School philosophers on the one hand, and literary figures of the *Literary World* and the Romantic School—or more broadly ethnic nationalists—on the other, sought different solutions to the same problematic, namely how to establish Japan's cultural superiority to the West, as implied in the question of how to "overcome modernity."

With this problematic in mind, in the next two sections, I will look into Nishitani's essay contribution to the "Overcoming Modernity" symposium. In it, he thematizes the uniquely Japanese sensibility that should incarnate Japanese "blood and soil" in his own way. This, Harootunian's words, exemplifies Nishitani's concern for "what was essentially and eternally Japanese." Nishitani discusses this sensibility as permeated by a certain kind of morality. As Doak notes, he believes this morality has been cultivated characteristically of Japan, while "express[ing] the bond between moralism and the state." Examining this essay will reveal not only how Nishitani's thought had affinity with ethnic nationalism, but also how his seemingly innocuous arguments about culture and civilization were permeated by a desire to establish Japan's cultural superiority that could ascertain its hegemonic status.

Section 2: Nishitani on Japanese "Tradition" and "Sensibility"

In his essay "My Views on 'Overcoming Modernity,' " which he contributed to this roundtable discussion, Nishitani finds the potential for overcoming modernity in Oriental religiosity. For him, the reason this overcoming is necessary resides not only in modernization's harmful effects on the non-Western world, but also in a defect of Western modernity itself. He asserts that Western culture had long lost its unity in its place of origin before it was imported into Japan in a fragmented manner that caused the division of specialized spheres alienated from wholeness. This loss of unity was the result of the unbridgeable gap between God and humans unconditionally presupposed in Western religiosity, and more precisely in the religiosity of Christianity. Driven by the disconnection between the transcendent and the immanent, humanity as the immanent was negated in the name of God as the transcendent. Thus, this negation never led to the affirmation of humanity. When people pushed to spread faith in God throughout secular life while retaining this gap, a strong reaction occurred. A large part of culture became secularized and moved away from religion. The split within Western modern culture accompanied the loss of the truly comprehensive unity that can subsume all spheres for the realization of holistic humanity. Nishitani insists, "an absolute negation of humanity must at the same time involve a way to affirm humanity through that negation" (OM 54). This, however, is impossible in Christianity. To overcome this, Nishitani invokes Oriental religiosity, modeled after Zen Buddhism. This religiosity is endowed with fundamental unity and, by virtue of its fundamental unity, negates humanity and reaffirms it through this negation.

Nishitani posits the most important facet of Oriental religiosity is the standpoint of subjective nothingness. In Western modern science, which has developed independently of religiosity, humans are turned into objects and observed merely with regard to their body and consciousness. However, in Nishitani's view, true subjectivity cannot be objectified and therefore must reside outside such a science:

> Even more profoundly than "life," the human's subjectivity can be apprehended only by the fact of one's self-interiority, the fact that this subjectivity operates genuinely through spontaneous freedom. When one penetrates within this subjectivity, which appears in free acts, it can in no sense be determined as being. Rather, it negates the ontic apprehension of the self and, in this sense, presents itself strictly as nothing. (OM 55; translation modified by referring to Kawakami et al. 24)[4]

Just as life can be grasped only through one's inner intuition of living, true subjectivity can be apprehended only by the fact of one's interiority that is spontaneously operating beyond personal will. This true subjectivity, which consists of free acts on its own terms, cannot be reduced to one's body or consciousness as substantialized selfhoods. As such, it can be discovered only as nothingness, through the negation of these superficial selfhoods in the ontic dimension. Here the negation of humanity from the standpoint of its true subjectivity leads to the affirmation of humanity on a more profound level.

Furthermore, this negation does not entail a complete break with the entities in the status of being: "The true mind qua subjective nothingness absolutely negates both body and mind in their status as being, and yet at the same time it gives life to these in its unity with being" (OM 55–56). "When we thus transcend [the conscious] 'self' and become aware of our true self, such awareness comes to us inseparably from both the body and its natural world and the mind and its cultural world" (OM 55). Through the apprehension of nothingness as true subjectivity, we still recognize our body and mind and their worlds, yet they come to appear to us differently, as permeated by the acts of their fundamental ground. Realizing that everything, including our own selves, is interconnected through this ground, we attain a holistic view of the world and humanity. Here there is no separation between the transcendent and the immanent, as humans, once immersed into the nothingness transcending them, return to the selves, which have become aware of the immanence of the transcendent in this world. Due to this intimate connection between the transcendent and the immanent, Nishitani believes Oriental religiosity can provide the means to recover the unity in our worldview, once lost in Western modernity, and to make way for overcoming it. It should be noted that the overcoming of Western modernity by Oriental religiosity thus conceived entails a change in humanity's sensibility to the body, mind, and world, which are given new lives by being negated by subjective nothingness.

Nishitani finds the epitome of this Oriental religiosity in the Japanese spirit, allegedly realized in Japanese people's actual lives and constituting their sense of ethics:

> If, therefore, the religiosity of subjective nothingness can be generally understood as Oriental religiosity, then it was Japan's particular circumstances that allowed this religiosity to discover the way to permeate throughout real life and become unified with the people's sense of ethics [*rinrishin*]. I see here the deepest aspect of Japanese spirit. (OM 59)

Nishitani's association of Oriental religiosity with Japanese spirit is understandable if one considers the moral implication of his idea of nothingness as true subjectivity. He sees the moral virtues of "selflessness" (*muga*) and "no-mindedness" (*mushin*) in the state that is characteristic of this religiosity, in which superficial selfhoods such as ego and mind do not exist (OM 55; translation modified by referring to Kawakami et al. 25).[5] It follows that truly free acts coming from subjective nothingness are altruistic acts, such as self-sacrifice and service to others. He asserts that following Japanese Shintoism's Way of the gods (*kannagara no michi*), as a Japanese indigenous tradition from ancient times and the source of Japanese spirit, has enabled Japanese people to do such acts in their real lives. This Way of the gods, he explains, "lies in actualizing the ethics of service while coming directly in touch with the gods' minds and achieving creative freedom" by "negating one's self-interest and returning to the source of one's mind" (OM 59; translation modified by referring to Kawakami et al. 30).[6] As such, the Way of the gods typically illustrates Oriental religiosity in that it leads people to negate themselves and become aware of their true origin, in contact with which they can attain true freedom and live ethically. In Nishitani's view, it is because Japanese people have followed this way throughout the ages that Oriental religiosity has permeated these people's real lives, and has been unified with their sense of ethics, taking the shape of Japanese spirit. It follows that this sense of ethics involved in Japanese spirit can be regarded as a concretization of the sensibility of mind, body, and the world enabled by Oriental religiosity in Japanese society. This is the sensibility through which people feel everything in their intimate interconnection as the emotional basis for altruism. In his essay, "My Views on 'Overcoming Modernity,'" Nishitani thus promises the success of Japan's project of overcoming Western modernity by reasoning that Oriental religiosity, which can resolve the defect of Western modernity, is effectuated by Japanese tradition and Japanese people's real lives, where this tradition is brought to life in their sense of ethics. Rather than disregarding the tradition and sensibility unique to Japanese people, he bases the success of this project upon them and endorses their importance in establishing Japan's cultural superiority to the West. Aside from the fact that the tradition and sensibility at issue here are those that are theoretically investigated and philosophically explored, his basic stance is in line with that of the literary figures who attended the same symposium and were usually characterized by their appeal to pure Japanese tradition, or uniquely Japanese sensibility.

Nishitani argued that Japanese tradition epitomized Oriental religiosity, which he viewed as more comprehensive than Western modernity, and as in a position to enable its overcoming. This position designates his inclination to establish the cultural superiority of Japanese tradition, and implies the superiority of the people who bear it. This way of argument, which has an obvious ethnic nationalist tone, cannot be reduced to a matter of "the attempt to bring the possibilities latent in traditional culture into encounter with Western culture" (Minamoto 217) in the face of the destruction of Japanese tradition after the reception of modern Western civilization. In the following section, I will explore how, in his essay, Nishitani conceived of the morality that he believed should concretize this Japanese tradition epitomizing Oriental religiosity, and what significance he gave this morality while considering Japan's historical situation at that time. The relevance of his assertion of Japan's cultural superiority to the given situation, and the relevance of his argument about culture and civilization in view of his advocacy for violence against others, reveal themselves in his discussion of the Greater East Asia Co-Prosperity Sphere. We will see that Nishitani's essay exemplifies Calichman's comment on the "Overcoming Modernity" symposium, that the "appeal to cultural nationalism and the country's military expansionism were in fact two sides of the same coin" (OM IX).

Section 3: Colonial Rule and Aggression Based on "Morality"

Depending on the situation, recourse to indigenous tradition can provide an effective countermeasure against the imposition of global hegemony from the outside. Even if unconditional approval of this recourse might be dangerous, the claim to resist such hegemony, if made alone, stands to reason. However, in many cases, such a claim does not stand by itself, but is connected with other claims, or even with practical acts. Therefore, we must question how such recourse works with or in relation to these claims and acts. In fact, Nishitani's insistence on Japanese tradition as the epitome of Oriental religiosity, in view of overcoming Western modernity, is not simply an assertion of Japan's cultural dignity in resisting Western hegemony. It is also connected with the claims to endorse and the acts to consolidate another hegemony Japan was establishing based on assumed cultural superiority.

Nishitani finds a prominent manifestation of the Oriental religiosity of subjective nothingness in Japanese people's self-annihilation and devotion to public service (*messhi hōkō*), which are ordinarily regarded as traditional virtues. He maintains that it is moral energy that incites Japanese people to annihilate themselves and devote themselves to public service, and as such, this energy realizes national ethics among them and makes their state ethical. He then underlines:

> If moral energy worked in only these ways, however, it would be unrelated to that worldwide ethicality I have mentioned and could on occasion become linked to such justices as the colonial exploitation of other races and states. Moral energy could then serve a kind of national self-interest. For our country [*waga kuni*]

at present, however, moral energy as the driving force behind state ethics must at once be the driving force toward world ethics. (OM 60; translation slightly modified by referring to Kawakami et al. 33)[7]

If people are satisfied with realizing the ethics of selflessness or no-mindedness only within their own state, they may end up pursuing its self-interest while neglecting to care about the harm they cause to other states in this pursuit. In order for this not to happen, it is necessary to realize this ethics among multiple states beyond one's own borders:

> From the perspective of past state behavior, therefore, the globality revealed by state life today must signify the negation of that behavior. The state has gone beyond the standpoint of merely emphasizing itself alone and arrived at a self-awareness of the horizon of inter-national communality, as based on the nonduality of self and other. It has opened up a horizon in which self and other put an end to their selves so as to create a communal totality where both can live. In this sense, the state has necessarily revealed the aspect of what may be called "self-negativity" that lies at its root. (OM 61)

Nishitani's assertion that states should give up their self-interests and achieve international communality may sound innocuous. However, his statement immediately after this citation disproves this impression. Referring to Japan, he continues: "Moreover, the state can today claim authority for itself as a leading state precisely because it bears such a spirit of communality" (OM 61). His conclusion of the necessity of realizing Japan's authority as a leading state in this communality is obviously problematic. The "self-negativity," on which this communality should be based, does not have the same meaning for Japan as it does for others. Whereas "self-negation" for Japan means expanding its authority beyond its limits and over other states, the "self-negation" for others means renouncing their sovereignties and subjecting themselves to Japan's authority. Therefore, there is no actual "communality" between Japan and others. Nevertheless, if a pretense of communality is made, it is the effect of the statement that Japan bears the spirit of communality qua the ethics of selflessness and no-mindedness. It is Nishitani's claim that Japan epitomizes in its national spirit the Oriental religiosity of subjective nothingness that lays the groundwork for his problematic argument here.

The "Overcoming Modernity" symposium took place in the aftermath of the outbreak of the Asia-Pacific War or, in other words, just after Japan had launched aggression toward, and had effectively taken control of, some

Asian countries. What Nishitani designates by the term "inter-national communality" is the Greater East Asia Co-Prosperity Sphere, which Japan aimed at constructing through such aggression and control. What he designates by Japan's authority as a leading state in this communality is Japan's status as the ruler of this sphere, gained after its aggression toward these countries.

Minamoto favorably views Nishitani's claim on the "construction of Greater East Asia" and asserts that Japan's "activity in Asia must in no way be taken to mean the acquiring of colonial territories" (219). However, the claim that gaining the sphere through such violent measures is not the same thing as acquiring colonial territories is hardly convincing. Nishitani's recourse to the ethics of selflessness and no-mindedness for the purpose of ensuring Japan's status as the ruler of this sphere does not authenticate his claim that this sphere is not composed of colonial territories.

Bret W. Davis fairly points out "a marked gap between Nishitani's idealistic vision of a non-imperialistic Co-Prosperity Sphere and the brutal reality of Japan's imperialistic actions across Asia" and insists that "this gap itself calls for critical examination" (31) from the standpoint that "a political philosophy must be judged not just on its intentions but also on its effects" (32). And yet Davis trusts Nishitani's good intentions when he asserts, "Nishitani did attempt to offer ethical instruction to the state, albeit in the form of 'cooperative' rather than confrontational resistance," and that, via his ideal of a "nation of non-ego," "he carried out his immanent critique of the political reality of wartime Japan" (35). However, an examination of the actual text of Nishitani's essay, "My Views on Overcoming Modernity," does not reveal such an attempt to moralize the state and its military policies from within.

To anticipate my claim, clarification of how we understand morality or ethicality must be done to evaluate whether Nishitani's essay can be taken as an attempt at moral or ethical transformation. Although Nishitani discusses the morality or ethicality exceptionally inherent in a certain state or certain people, I would question whether the morality or ethicality thus conceived is really moral or ethical, or if those to whom such morality or ethicality is attributed are inclined to improve themselves morally or ethically in any way.

When Nishitani claims Japan's authority in the international communality, backed by his reasoning that Japan bears the spirit of communality qua the ethics of selflessness and no-mindedness, he assumes that this ethics has been realized in Japan and not in other countries. This assumption is expressed in his statement, "it was Japan's particular circumstances that allowed [Oriental] religiosity to discover the way to permeate throughout real life and become unified with the people's sense of ethics" (OM 59). The stance of thus taking the realization of this ethics in Japan as the ground of its authority over other countries would hardly be compatible with the commonly held view that the Kyoto School philosophers offered ethical instruction to Japan and its control over other countries.

Nishitani's statement that "moral energy as the driving force behind state ethics must at once be the driving force toward world ethics" (OM 60; translation slightly modified by referring to Kawakami et al. 33) may seem to encourage Japan's further moral completion beyond the scope of national ethics. However, as we have seen, what he designates as the development of moral energy from Japanese national ethics into world ethics is the creation of the international communality under Japan's authority, indeed, achieved by invading and conquering other countries. If the aggression toward and rule over other countries are thus regarded as the advancement from national ethics to world ethics, it follows that Japan does not need to do anything more for its moral completion. The way in which Nishitani's argument proceeds leaves no room for understanding it as an attempt to moralize Japan's colonial policies. Given this, Minamoto's statement that "Nishitani's aim was a world ethics that went beyond the national level and he warned against colonization" (219–20) does not hold water. For, here, it is colonization that provides the basis for this world ethics. Ironically, when Nishitani states that moral energy, if it finds its realization only within one state, "could on occasion become linked to such injustices as the colonial exploitation of other races and states" (OM 60), he endorses Japan's colonial rule under the pretext of avoiding colonial rule. In doing so, he simply echoes typical wartime ideology that Japan's colonial rule is different from the usual, indeed Western, colonial rule because of the ethicality it accomplishes.

Still, when Nishitani advises readers to "attain the source of their minds and become grounded in subjective nothingness by devotedly practicing self-annihilation and deepening their grasp of the 'clean and bright mind' [*seimeishin* or *kiyoki akaki kokoro*]" (OM 62; translation modified by referring to Kawakami et al. 35),[8] he may seem to exhort the efforts for moral advancement. But here, he simply presses Japanese people to annihilate themselves and devote themselves to public service through their work activities. Whereas he once said that if moral energy works through such behaviors, it runs the risk of serving national self-interest unrelated to worldwide ethicality, now he states:

> In thus saying that the state's moral energy is manifested by means of each individual serving the public and annihilating their selves in their work, this means that, while these individuals acquire clean and bright minds in their efforts at professional mastery and self-annihilation, they can merge with the fountainhead of state life that runs throughout national history as well as come in touch with that world ethics that lies at the bottom of world

history (what the ancients called the "way of heaven"). (OM 61–62; translation modified by referring to Kawakami et al. 35)[9]

In short, Nishitani here states that individuals, by serving the public and annihilating themselves, can not only merge with the fountainhead of national life, but also encounter world ethics. He explains the reason why they can do so in what follows:

> The fact that "professional service" can actually signify this—in other words, that the work activities of each and every person directly involve a path that reaches down to the deepest levels of world religiosity and state ethicality—is due to our nation's traditional spirit, as created out of the secret harmony between Oriental religiosity and our own spiritual path. It is also due to the fact that, as I have remarked, this spirit has in its radical development today become part of world-historical reality. (OM 62)

The "radical development" of "our nation's traditional spirit," which has "become part of world-historical reality," means that the moral energy behind this spirit has become the driving force toward world ethics. As we have seen, through this change in moral energy, Nishitani designated the construction of the Greater East Asia Co-Prosperity Sphere as the international communality based on the ethics of selflessness and no-mindedness.

Then, his statement that "the work activities of each and every person directly involve a path that reaches down to the deepest levels of world religiosity and state ethicality" due to this "radical development" means that Japanese people's self-annihilation and devotion to public service now come in touch with world ethics due to Japan's colonial aggression and rule over other countries. The idea expressed here, that the state's colonial rule and aggression gives the people's work activities a meaning related to world ethics, merely encourages the people to support such policies and work harder for the state. It never offers ethical instruction to the state. Doak's comment on the "Overcoming Modernity" symposium, that it "did succeed in providing a new moral mission to the wartime state and thereby distracts some attention from the contradictions that rested at the heart of its aggression in Asia" ("Nationalism as Dialectics" 194), typically applies to Nishitani's essay contribution to the symposium.

Thus, rather than having ended up producing harmful effects against his good intentions, Nishitani's arguments themselves reveal the causes that actively allowed the production of such effects. Attributing morality or ethicality exclusively to the single state and its military policies, as he does in his arguments, cannot but boost the state's self-confidence, so as to turn it into arrogance and embellish its brutal actions without encouraging its modest reflections on them. Therefore, we cannot conclude, simply from his insistence on morality or ethicality, that he offered "ethical instruction to the state," or carried out "his immanent critique of the political reality of wartime Japan" (Davis 35). Even though Nishitani tried to distinguish himself from nationalists, he shared their basic assumptions by positioning Japan as a privileged state and the Japanese as privileged people. He simply based this ethnocentrism upon the morality or ethicality allegedly inherent in Japan and Japanese people. As such, this ethnocentrism becomes cloaked in the ideal of selflessness and no-mindedness, and is seemingly free of the self-importance attributed to ethnocentrism. My point is not that this ethnocentrism is justifiable based upon such morality or ethicality but, given that its essentialism in Japan and Japanese people is dubious, this ethnocentrism cannot be justified. Even if it takes on the ideal of selflessness and no-mindedness, it is merely as a disguise.

This veiled ethnocentrism hangs on Nishitani's assertion that the ethics of selflessness and no-mindedness has been realized in Japan, has been fostered by its traditions and takes shape in the Japanese people's self-annihilation and devotion to public service. However, concerning this assertion, his argument seems to turn on itself. On the one hand, he describes these virtues as if they were a *fait accompli* in the people's real lives. On the other hand, he claims, "the state requires of its citizens both mastery in one's work and self-sacrifice (or self-annihilation) in one's work activities" (OM 56). He then continues:

> The state requires of each of its citizens efforts of self-sacrifice or self-annihilation, through which they become ethical—and through which, conversely, the state can first become ethical qua this community of citizens. (OM 57; translation slightly modified, referring to Kawakami et al. 28)[10]

Here Nishitani seems to be trapped in a circular logic, equating the outcome of the state's compulsory policy and the current lived circumstances with the people's real lives.

In fact, Kobayashi Hideo—who was a leading figure of *Literary World*, yet who, according to Takeuchi Yoshimi, became closest to the Romantic School at the time of the symposium ("Overcoming Modernity" 113)—moves within a similar circular logic. He insists that, "[s]ince this language is the traditional language of Japan, no matter how sincerely or logically expressed, its flavor must appear in one's style as that which can be achieved only by Japanese people" (OM 196). However, if this is truly the case, it would be impossible that Japanese philosophers' "essays lack the sensuality of Japanese people's language" (OM 196), as Kobayashi lamented during the symposium. When he states, "This [to make the aforementioned flavor appear in one's style] is what writers always aim for in their trade" (OM 196), Kobayashi, similarly to Nishitani, insists on the necessity of realizing what he claims to have already been realized among the people in his own country, thanks to its tradition.

In light of the historical situation in Japan in the 1930s, in which intellectuals "contested the meaning of what constituted the actual (*genjitsu*), usually in an effort to lay claim to defining daily life," Harootunian regards this roundtable discussion as "a culmination of and, perhaps, a closure to the interwar attempt to grasp daily life in its 'actuality' rather than its mere virtuality" (*Overcome by Modernity* 37). Although Harootunian points to the common ground on which Nishitani and Kobayashi stand, it seems that something slightly different from literal actuality is at issue in both men's thinking. Both invoke what is supposed to have been realized and at once should be realized, what is actually there and is to be virtually there. They do not mind throwing themselves into the circle between these two aspects, as if they were one.

It was not only Nishitani and Kobayashi who struggled between two similar aspects. Calichman mentions that Hayashi Fusao, who was a member of the *Literary World*, made "a distinction between Japan in its actual existence and Japan in its essential being" (OM 2). In reference to these two aspects, Calichman notes: "[Hayashi's] entire project consisted in reducing the former to the latter, or rather in allowing the potential contained within the latter to express itself in such a way as to reshape or transform the former" (OM 2). Generally speaking, when people try to assimilate a present state of affairs into an ideal one, equated with the authentic way of being of the thing at issue, they are apt to distinguish the two states and at once equate them. The two become assimilated, and a circular correlation between them is inevitably established.

In fact, speaking specifically of Nishitani and other philosophers of the Kyoto School, they have their own reason for throwing themselves into the circle between what is actually there, or has already been realized, and what is to be virtually there, and therefore should be realized. This point will be further explained in the next chapter through the examination of the subsequent *Chūōkōron* symposia, held by four philosophers of the second generation of the Kyoto School, including Nishitani.

Chapter 2

The *Chūōkōron* Symposia Concerning the Philosophy of World History

Between 1941 and 1942 four prominent figures of the Kyoto School's second generation, referred to as *shitennō* (the gang of four)—Kōsaka Masaaki, Kōyama Iwao, Suzuki Shigetaka and Nishitani Keiji—coordinated three other consecutive roundtable discussions. These were held under the auspices of the Japanese journal *Chūōkōron*, which also published the discussion transcripts between 1942 and 1943. The titles of these symposia were "The World-Historical Position and Japan" (*Sekaishiteki tachiba to nihon*), "The Ethicality and Historicity of the East Asia Co-Prosperity Sphere" (*Tōa kyōeiken no rinrisei to rekishisei*) and "The Philosophy of Total War" (*Sōryokusen no tetsugaku*). As these titles show, the philosophers taking part in these symposia attempted to theorize Japan's position in world history in relation to important world-historical events of the era. In spite of minor differences of opinion, these thinkers shared their particular philosophy of world history, which they believed could buttress their attempt at this theorization.

During these three symposia, held contemporarily with the *Bungakukai* symposium, these young philosophers' beliefs, as revealed through Nishitani's arguments related to the latter symposium, manifested themselves more clearly in rather friendly conversations among comrades. These philosophers' discussions at the three symposia also demonstrate how these philosophers situate the theme of overcoming modernity and the West in a wider perspective of their philosophy of world history. In this way, the discussions in the *Chūōkōron* symposia show overlap and continuity with those in the *Bungakukai* symposium. Therefore, reading these discussions may offer a viewpoint from which to reevaluate Nishitani's arguments addressed in the previous chapter.

In what follows, I will illuminate the *shitennō* thinkers' philosophy of world history as it relates to the theme of "overcoming modernity." My objective here is to critically evaluate their philosophy and the project of "overcoming modernity" they pursued. As the prerequisite for this evaluation, I will formulate a coherent picture of the four thinkers' arguments as articulated in their discourses. In the process of doing so, these thinkers' ideas of Japanese national subjectivity, as the key player in their philosophy of world history, will come to the fore. These ideas will suggest a possibility of reconsidering Nishitani's arguments regarding Japan and the Greater East Asia Co-Prosperity Sphere. Therefore, after explaining the basic framework of the four thinkers' philosophy of world history, I will take on the characteristics and problems of their ideas of this subjectivity.

This chapter will begin with an outline of the philosophy of world history conceived by these four thinkers. Here, I will elucidate their stance toward world history determined by this philosophy, as well as their ideas about Japan's position in the world and its history. Then, I will observe how, from this position, the four thinkers found it necessary to create a Japanese national subjectivity based on their grasp of the world-historical situation. The discussions as to how they conceived this subjectivity, and the problems involved in their views, will be drawn out in subsequent chapters in part 1.

In what follows, I will consult the transcripts of the three roundtable discussions as they were published in the *Chūōkōron* journal.[1] In addition, to elucidate the four thinkers' thoughts and their implications, I will occasionally consult relevant works of these respective thinkers. I will treat the themes or motifs they pursued across the three roundtable discussions, rather than address each separately. I will also focus on exploring the lines of thought traversing the four thinkers' thought, rather than looking deeply into their differences.

Section 1: Japan in the World-Historical Position

At the beginning of the series of the roundtable discussions, Suzuki concisely spoke to modern philosophy in consideration of the course of world history, and stated that it should be "a discipline which clarifies in what position one is in the course of history and suggests in what direction one will proceed." To this, he added that it should be "a discipline which directs historical changes, advancing one step further than that which merely lays the foundations of existing things" (SN 151). Speaking to the tasks he believes a philosophy of world history should fulfill, Suzuki seems to juxtapose two contradictory objectives: discerning the direction of history so that one can follow it and, on the other hand, giving direction to history. However, the four thinkers who participated in the discussion—including Suzuki himself—see no contradiction between these two tasks. Instead, they take for granted that they are one and the same.

In fact, the unity of these two tasks is possible when they are seen from a certain standpoint, which these four thinkers adopt in their philosophy of world history—that is, the standpoint of the practical subject who engages in world history, rather than simply watching it as an independent object. However, when the four thinkers attach importance to such engagement in world history, they do not simply attach it to any form of involvement. As Kōyama says, "it is always moral vitality that moves world history" (SN 183). These philosophers see world history as driven by moral power. Thus, world history imposes morality upon humans, which is equal to the necessity of world history, even though they are not aware of it. This belief is evident in Nishitani's statement that, "ethics is not something which is far away from historical actuality, but that which is found in the midst of it and pushed out of historical necessity, so to speak" (TRR 124). The practical subject should find this ethics in world history and act in accordance with it. In turn, world history does not exist as what it is without such acts by the practical subject. Unless the subject acts in accordance with this ethics, world history does not move according to its necessity. If moral vitality is the driving force of world history, it is only to the extent that the practical subject, by his or her moral acts, exercises this force to drive world history in the right direction. Therefore, Suzuki emphasizes, "after all, necessity does not reside where we hold our arms and wait, but only where we take action as the subject. That is to say, historical necessity is subjective or indeed a practical necessity" (TRR 122). This necessity as world-historical ethics consists of, in Kōsaka's words, "responding to the call from world history and constituting the world itself" (TRR 145). The task for the practical subject who tries to act in compliance with this ethics as necessity, then, is to discern it in the course of history and, by following this ethics, to constitute the world so that its historical course rightly realizes this necessity. In this way, from the standpoint of this subject, to discern the direction of history in order to follow it and to give direction to history are two sides of the same coin; that is, the subject's acts in response to world-historical ethics are a necessity.[2] What theoretically underlies the unity of these two aspects is the equation between world-historical necessity and ethics, and the idea of moral vitality, which drives world history in accordance to this necessity qua ethicality, and which these four thinkers elsewhere call *moralische Energie*, following German historian Leopold von Ranke.[3]

The four thinkers agree that, in their time, Japan in particular has the mission to follow and realize this necessity qua ethicality, and act as the practical subject of world history. In their view, world history now exclusively calls upon Japan to exercise moral power through following and realizing world-historical necessity qua ethicality. Even though these philosophers' assertions sound pretentious, they have their reasons and are based on their view of world history and grasp of the world-historical situation in their time.

For the four thinkers, the world in the exact sense of the word should be a totality including all states or nations neutrally. However, this idea of the world was born as a result of the global expansion of the sphere of domination and influence of Europe in modern times. Thus, the world could not but be represented as the Eurocentric world, ignoring non-European countries or subordinating them to European ones. Such a world is not truly worthy of being called "the world." Thus, Kōyama in his "The Dynamics of World History" (*Sekaishi no dōgaku*) states, "the modern world in which Asia is slavishly subjugated to Europe is not yet the true world" (SR 245). In his "The Ideal of World History" (*Sekaishi no rinen*), Kōyama also declares how we should view world history: "We must recognize *many world histories* and *many historical worlds* in the world of humanity on the earth. Being based on the plurality of historical worlds once is the indispensable condition for the consideration of true world history" ((1) 341).[4]

This change in the view of history is inseparable from the creation of a world that can accept pluralistic worlds and histories, a true world deserving of its name. Suzuki claims, in "The History of the View of World History" (*Sekaishikan no rekishi*), that "our view of world history is exactly built upon the recognition that the true world is not the existing one, but must be created hereafter" (SR 110). After stating that "this constructive and practical standpoint itself exactly entails overcoming so-called historicism" (SR 111), which consists merely in approving the *fait accompli*, he describes this move as "overcoming modernity in historical science" (SR 114). In the eyes of the four thinkers, it seems that this move corresponds to those actually happening in the world. Kōsaka, in his "Types of the View of World History" (*Sekaishikan no ruikei*), relates these moves as follows: "Spatially, centering around the Oriental world, the worlds that have been subjugated to the Western world and ignored so far are coming to the fore, and temporally, so-called modernity has been already overcome and is about to pass into a new present" (SR 60). The rise of non-Western worlds is positioned as parallel to the movement of overcoming modernity, as the time in which the West identified itself with the world. To create the new world that includes all different worlds neutrally is thus to pass into a new present by constructing such a world and making world history. It is only from the standpoint working toward creating the world proper and making world history that we can create a new version of world history and overcome the modern view of it, which equates the world with the West and ignores other worlds.[5]

In the world-historical situation of the time when the four thinkers conceived the philosophy of world history, Japan was viewed as the only state that could achieve modernization and succeed in developing itself so as to rival European states by winning the wars with Russia and China and extending its territory. It is this situation that made the four thinkers believe that Japan's mission was to follow and realize world-historical necessity qua ethicality that consisted of correcting the Western-centered world system and creating the true world. Thus, Kōsaka insists, "The mission of being the subject of world history is assigned to our state, from within and without, by historical necessity, even beyond whether each of us wills to accept this mission or not" (SR 60–61). Nishitani explains the reasoning behind this insistence in "The Philosophy of World History" (*Sekaishi no tetsugaku*): "[The world] did not show itself in its genuine neutrality as the 'world' itself. It came to show itself after Japan, by the enhancement of its national power, had objected to the Eurocentric world and pulled apart Europe and the world [which had formerly been equated]" (SR 18; NKC IV 223). He also claims, "In the 'world' which has truly become a fact, each of the actions of the state in that world also becomes a fact of the world, and being based on the subjectivity of the state leads to directly touching the world as the fact" (SR 51; NKC IV 251–52). Speaking of Japan, if it acted to establish the true world, such actions, while being made from the standpoint of a particular state, contributed to the good of the whole of this new world. In the eyes of the four thinkers, this appeared to be Japan's role around the time of the three roundtable discussions, just after Japan had declared war against Allied Western countries.

Section 2: The Necessity of Creating Japanese National Subjectivity

Being Japanese, the four philosophers themselves cannot be unrelated to the aforementioned task of exercising moral power through following and realizing world-historical necessity qua ethicality. As a prerequisite for the fulfillment of this task, Kōsaka emphasizes "the thought supported by this moral power" must be "established first in Japan with conviction," and that "there is a responsibility of establishing [such a thought] first at home. Here is, I believe, our subjectivity in thought" (ST 70). The four thinkers' philosophy of world history was an attempt at establishing such thought. Creating this philosophy was an act of making moral power manifest itself, and calling upon other Japanese people to do so together through different kinds of acts, as to move world history toward the construction of the new world order. In doing so, the four thinkers were in themselves the practical subjects, following and realizing the necessity qua ethicality of world history. After stating that "ethics is not something which is far away from historical actuality but that which is found in the midst of it and pushed out of historical necessity," Nishitani adds, "in turn, the ethics in this sense is at its basis connected with the philosophy of world history" (TRR 124). Here he does not simply mean that this philosophy consists in elucidating the ethicality qua necessity of world history. Since doing so is inseparable from effectuating this ethicality qua necessity, from the standpoint of the philosophy of world history, he also suggests that this philosophy is in itself a double act of elucidating and effectuating this ethicality qua necessity, first in the field of thought, then possibly affecting reality. Thus, this philosophy is intended to be an ethical and necessary act upon world history to carry it forward—an act whose practical subjects the four thinkers themselves are.

Ironically, in spite of the four thinkers' ambition, Kōsaka's claim that thought supported by moral power must be established in Japan betrays the fact that such a thought has not yet been established, at least enough to permeate through the Japanese population. Kōsaka is not the only member whose statement reveals the reality in Japan. Kōyama insists, "Today, to ensure that the order in the world and that in East Asia are renewed, the order of the society in the state of Japan itself must be suitably renewed. . . . Japanese people also need to become quite new Japanese who are different from those in the past." He adds, "The creation of new humans brings about the creation of a new world" (TRR 156). As is the case with Kōsaka, Kōyama's emphasis on the necessity of creating new Japanese also discloses the reality that that new subjectivity of Japanese people, who will be able to renew the world order by assuming the world-historical necessity qua ethicality, has not yet matured. Immediately after Kōyama, Nishitani explicitly states this reality:

> So far I have said that *moralische Energie* vividly works in Japan as actuality. But, at the same time, in this respect, I also feel like there is a great difficulty in present Japan, I mean, in its depths, so to speak. This difficulty is, I think, that Japanese people nowadays are not given an ideal type or a standard type, a so-called paradigm of humanity. (TRR 156)

Nishitani confesses that it is hard to say that *moralische Energie*—that is, the moral vitality that the four thinkers believe manifests itself in Japan—actually does so once they turn to the current condition of Japanese people. As a cause of this difficulty in Japan in his time, he refers to the absence of an ideal human type for Japanese people to follow. He argues that the traditional Japanese ideal human type disappeared a few decades after the Meiji

Restoration. In new generations, severed from the spiritual culture of the past, some intellectuals found a way to cultivate humanity in Western culture. However, most of the general public could learn nothing fruitful neither from Japanese traditional culture, nor from Western culture. As a result, most people suffered from indirection, as they were unable to find a norm to follow. In Nishitani's view, it is this lack of the ideal human type that prevents Japanese people from acting suitably for their world-historical mission and for moral vitality to manifest itself through their acts. As a result of this lack, Nishitani posits, Japanese people do not know how to establish their own subjectivity strongly enough to complete this mission, or are otherwise unaware of it, precisely at the time when this mission has been assigned to Japan by its world-historical situation. Agreeing on this vision of the current condition of Japanese people, the four thinkers continue to discuss, in Kōsaka's words, the need for "the creation of a new type of Japanese," "the Japanese with a global character, so to speak, who assume the task of world history and are achieving it" (TRR 159).

In line with this act of creating Japanese national subjectivity, the significance of the circular reasoning into which Nishitani fell at the "Overcoming Modernity" symposium becomes understandable. On the one hand, Nishitani insists that Japanese people's self-annihilation and devotion to public service are their traditional virtues, realized in their daily lives. On the other hand, he insists that the state should demand of its members this very self-annihilation and devotion to public service. Thus, if he claims the necessity of inventing what he himself alleges has existed for a long time, it is because he himself engages in the project of establishing a Japanese national subjectivity that continues from the past to the future, while at the same time he invents the tradition whose epitome provides the norm for this subjectivity. Carrying out this project inevitably requires the double gesture of emphasizing the actuality of something and, at once, trying to effectuate this very actuality. To this extent, entering this circle and moving within it is a prerequisite for this project. For those who actively engage themselves in this project, throwing themselves into this circle and making it work is a kind of trial to pass through, rather than a mere contradiction to avoid.

An act of creating what does not exist in the present, by following the norm found in the past, is not exactly the same as simply returning to the previous state. Here, creating what does not exist entails an act of shaping a better future with the intent of ameliorating the present condition. Nishitani describes the complication in this act as follows: "[T]he movement of going forward comes to take the form of returning to the origin for the moment, and then from this backward flow emerges the movement in the forward direction" (SN 171).

But, indeed, this complication does not merely concern the involvement of the future. Given that the origin or tradition to which people should return cannot but be retrospectively reconstructed from arbitrarily selected elements, the return to the origin or tradition cannot exist as what was supposed to be, according to those who exhort this return. What seemed to be a movement forward into the future, through the movement backward to the origin, is in fact an act of drawing a continuous flow of history from the past to the future, as well as redefining what "the actual" is in the present situated between them. When the narrative of this history is initiated and shared on a national scale, this act of initiation and sharing coincides with an act of creating a national subjectivity, which has supposedly existed for a long time and will live in this history, thus confirming the quasi-eternal subsistence of this subjectivity.

In fact, the *Bungakukai* symposium on "overcoming modernity" shared this concern about the creation of national subjectivity with the *Chūōkōron* symposia on the philosophy of world history. As we have seen, Calichman observes that Hayashi Fusao, a literary figure who participated in the *Bungakukai* symposium, attempted to assimilate "Japan in its actual existence" to "Japan in its essential being" (OM 2). Calichman also refers to the appeal commonly made by symposium participants to the subject formation that should be carried out in the way that could restore Japanese people's original identity:

> Clearly, this return to original identity on the part of the Japanese people could not be achieved directly given its absence or obscuration in modern society. The return could only be effected, therefore, by introducing a process of subject formation whose telos of producing Japanese citizens who fully embody their essential identity was to be reached sometime in the future. (OM 7–8)

This process of subject formation is isomorphic to the process in which the Japanese national subjectivity envisioned by Nishitani and his three colleagues should be created. For, in both cases, the return to the supposed original condition of Japaneseness, which is lost in the present, is conceived to be achieved through the movement forward into the future to create this condition. In both the *Bungakukai* and *Chūōkōron* symposia, participants recognized this creation of national subjectivity as the task for the Japanese to tackle. While in the *Bungakukai* symposium the subjectivity to be created was not systematically addressed, in the *Chūōkōron* symposia the four Kyoto thinkers gave a clearer formulation to this subjectivity and situated it in a significant position within their view of the world and its history.

When the four Kyoto thinkers engaged in the project of establishing Japanese national subjectivity that could assume world-historical responsibility, the subjectivity of other people was not the only thing that mattered. These thinkers took themselves as the practical subjects who acted upon world history through their philosophy of world history. Likewise, Nishitani's attitude concerning his claim of the necessity to realize Japanese traditional virtues is the same as that of the practical subject of world history the four thinkers envisioned: the subject who, through their action, at once follows and realizes world-historical necessity qua ethicality. In his project of creating Japanese national subjectivity, Nishitani's entry into the circle of the already realized ethical state and the ethical state to be realized shows that he is trying to assume this task as a Japanese person and as a practical subject of world history.

Chapter 3

The Unity between the Subject and the Substratum of the State

The First Characteristic of Japanese National Subjectivity

Given the four thinkers' project of creating Japanese national subjectivity and their attitude as practical subjects consistent in this project, there arises a possibility of reconsidering Nishitani's arguments regarding Japan and the Greater East Asia Co-Prosperity Sphere related to the *Bungakukai* symposium. That is to say, rather than presupposing the ethicality or morality inherent in Japan and its military policies, his arguments might be intended to constitute a practical act through public discourse in order to effectuate such ethicality or morality in Japan, and to produce a moral or ethical subjectivity that can act properly to fulfill its world-historical responsibility. Certainly, the ethics of selflessness and no-mindedness was not in fact effectuated among contemporary Japanese. Nevertheless, he may have thought that if it were to come true by the creation of their national subjectivity, the status quo of the Greater East Asia Co-Prosperity Sphere would change because of the moral energy this subjectivity would produce and transmit within Japan's sphere of domination. Even though the Greater East Asia Co-Prosperity Sphere was founded through colonial aggression and rule, once permeated by this energy, it would really be turned into the international communality faithful to the above ethics. Then, the sequence of events that brought it into existence would no longer matter. Whether this defense is convincing enough, in light of the philosophy of world history, Nishitani's arguments may be interpreted as the means for the ethical transformation of the state of Japan and its policies. Considering the common concern about, and attempt at creating, Japanese national subjectivity shared by both the *Bungakukai* and *Chūōkōron* symposia, Williams's qualification of the latter as "providing perhaps the most testing examples of criticism from within the Japanese academic establishment of the military policies of the Tojo regime" (*Defending Japan's Pacific War* 63) may be also applicable to the arguments related to the former.

Still, questions remain of whether this view holds true and, even if it does, whether the idea of the Japanese national subjectivity shared by the four thinkers and the project of creating this subjectivity, the project on which this ethical transformation depends, deserve to be highly appreciated. In order to answer these questions, a further critical examination of what this Japanese national subjectivity is in reality is needed.

To carry out this examination, I will proceed by inquiring into the logics and ways of thinking that operated in the Kyoto philosophers' arguments regarding this subjectivity. Here, I will discern the three notable characteristics present in their formulation of this subjectivity. After uncovering what these characteristics actually mean beneath the façade, I will reconsider what kind of national subjectivity is to be shaped by combining these characteristics. I will then question whether the creation of this subjectivity could really contribute to offering ethical instruction to Japan and its military policies to transform them.

Exploring the reality of this subjectivity will also enable us to cast light on the problems involved in the philosophy of world history. It will also reveal what aspects the project of overcoming modernity—to be achieved by this subjectivity once it was successfully created—lay hidden behind these four thinkers' professed ideals.

In the three chapters that follow, I will critically examine what the Japanese national subjectivity envisioned by the four thinkers truly was by investigating its three notable characteristics. As a first step, this chapter observes Kōyama's arguments in the symposia concerning the norm and ethics for the Japanese national subjectivity to be created anew. The four thinkers called this "new Japanese." Next, I will turn to Nishitani's essays written around the same time as the symposia, and look into his arguments concerning Japanese national subjectivity, developed relevantly to those of Kōyama. I will cast focus upon Nishitani's vision of the ideal state and its challenge to Western modernity, both of which he believed to be realized based on this subjectivity. Then, after discerning the first characteristic of this subjectivity, I will reveal its problems by explicating the contradictions present in Nishitani's arguments.

Section 1: The Norm and Ethics for Japanese National Subjectivity

Let me start by observing the kind of human type and morality the four thinkers found to be the epitome of Japanese indigenous tradition and the norm for the national subjectivity to be created. What condenses these thinkers' ideas, here, are Kōyama's arguments about the samurai and their ethics. Following Kōyama's reasoning, we will see how it may have buttressed Nishitani's aforementioned claim that self-annihilation and devotion to public service are the Japanese people's traditional virtues, and those which the state should demand of its members.

As the ideal human type, which has its roots in Japanese tradition and after whose example contemporary Japanese people should cultivate their subjectivity, Kōyama invokes the samurai. This epitomization of the samurai seems typical, as it simply repeats the cliché of the samurai as the incarnation of Japanese spirit. But the meaning Kōyama assigned to the samurai way of life is slightly different from that which is generally accepted. This difference first appears in his understanding of the Edo period, which is particularly represented as the age of the samurai, and as being in strong continuity with the medieval period before it.

In medieval Japan, wars occurred frequently, and samurai, who had to fight in them, always ran the risk of losing their lives. In this situation, Kōyama remarks, "in the face of the absolute fact of death, there was duly the consciousness of absolute individuality, that is, the existence, or *Existenz* in the sense of contemporary philosophy" (SN 167). In his view, when a matter of life and death was at stake, only honesty and trust could be the principle to maintain stable social relationships. In order for one to be honest and trustworthy, the "self-awareness of subjectivity that one is the subject of absolute responsibility" (SN 166), comparable to *Existenz*, was required. What Kōyama finds important in this mode of existence is that "human relationship was built through the mediation of the absolute" (SN 166). The absolute appeared to humans in the shape of death, and confrontation with this absolute enabled an ethics of responsibility, backed by the awareness of individual subjectivity. When the samurai is the vassal, his service to the lord is not mere servitude. Kōyama goes so far as to say, "even though [the samurai] throws his life away for the lord, the fact of throwing it away itself at once comes to have an absolute significance" (SN 166). That is, the samurai's self-sacrifice ethically means the fulfillment of his absolute responsibility, which reveals itself in the face of death, insofar as he voluntarily takes charge of this act rather than blindly following orders. Even in the Edo period, in which peace predominated and samurai did not need to confront the risk of imminent death, Kōyama asserts that *bushidō*, in the sense of the ethics of responsibility, remained in each individual samurai. Although the samurai's attitude is often mistaken as blind submission and servitude to social hierarchy, here it is not. What actually matters is something inherent in these behaviors, which is the voluntary assumption of responsibility by each individual. In this argument, by seeking the essence of true Japanese spirituality outside of what is typically regarded as "tradition," Kōyama tries to give Japanese spirituality a sense of responsibility and subjectivity, while rescuing it from the inertia of submission or servitude taken for granted in the clichés of this "tradition."

Kōyama also brings up the subjectivity of responsibility in the subsequent discussion. In analyzing this subjectivity independently of a specific historical context, he describes this ethics in more general terms and clarifies a definition of the absolute, which has a key role in this ethics:

> Needless to say, the standpoint of the subject of responsibility is the standpoint of freedom, and it must entail spontaneity. In turn, spontaneity or freedom designates the state of being unconstrained by others. Of course, people can realize this state when they give orders or follow them in their workplace organization. Even when they are ordered to do a certain act, if they do it on their own responsibility, then they have put themselves in a position of freedom. It is precisely because they are free that they are not allowed to shift their responsibility to others. By the way, the state of freedom unrestrained by others is "nothingness." That is to say, if we truly take full responsibility for our act, we face absolute nothingness. Only in the face of this nothingness, do we become selfless [*muga*]. The self, or the I, disappears into absolute nothingness. Where we are thoroughly faithful to our true subjectivity of responsibility, we necessarily become selfless. (ST 104)

The point Kōyama raises here is that people make themselves subjects of responsibility when they take sole responsibility for their own acts. Being unable to shift their responsibility to others means being restrained by none of them—that is, in Kōyama's view, true freedom. Freedom in this sense is equal to the state of nothingness, in that nothingness is never determined by or bound to anything else, while all beings are determined by and bound to something else. The awareness that humans, in this sense, become nothingness and, as such, become free, makes them attain a state of selflessness. It is in this state that they devote themselves fully to the act for which they are responsible, so as to annihilate themselves. Insofar as their attitude of taking full responsibility for their acts constitutes freedom, they can be not only moral, but also free, even when performing an ordered act.

Articulated as such, the ethics of the subjectivity of responsibility Kōyama has in mind is not exclusively that of the samurai, nor does it necessarily require people to constantly face the risk of imminent death as the samurai did. Rather, he conceives this ethics as able to suggest a way in which ordinary people can face the absolute and make themselves ethical subjects by engaging themselves even in the most banal activities in their daily lives. The absolute, which samurai confront in the form of imminent death, reveals itself as absolute nothingness that people face as their freedom in taking full responsibility of their own acts and devoting themselves to carrying these out so as to annihilate themselves.

Given that the subjectivity of responsibility, which is a specific mode of existence, is enabled in confrontation with nothingness, it is inseparable from a kind of paradox. Indeed, it is in itself a paradox, which Kōyama formulates as follows:

> In this way, from the standpoint of the subjectivity of responsibility, when we pursue the being of the self [*yūga*] to the extreme, this being necessarily turns into the absence of the self/selflessness [*muga*]. And at the apex of this absence of the self, my act is indeed at once not my act. (ST 104)

The paradox here is that people no sooner make themselves subjects by taking full responsibility for their acts than they efface themselves as such subjects in fully dedicating themselves to these acts. Therefore, from the standpoint of the subject of responsibility, the self exists and does not exist; my act is not my act, simultaneously. Although this ambiguous state seems contradictory, Kōyama asserts that it is not. If it appears to be, it is insofar as people observe it from the outside and logically contemplate it. When they assume their responsibility and devote themselves to their acts, there is no contradiction between the existence and non-existence of their subjectivity.

Furthermore, Kōyama declares that it is the Japanese who have thus lived the paradox between the existence and non-existence of their subjectivity, and resolved the contradiction in their practice:

> But, isn't it typical "Japanese" who have sophisticated that state [in which the being of the self is equal to the absence of the self, and the act of the self is the act of the other] and put this state into

> practice docilely, without fussing about that contradiction? I have a feeling that the Japanese, referred to when we say "Thou shalt be Japanese,"—the ideal Japanese, who actually existed in history and still appeal to us as traditional norms—are the people who have attained this state beyond reason or logic. (ST 104)
>
> Japanese civilization [*nihon bunmei*] is a little different. I think I may safely say that it is composed of the spirit equating the self and the absence of the self. Therefore, to be truly faithful to the idea of responsibility, to stick to the standpoint of the subjectivity of responsibility, in thoroughly doing so, to turn oneself selfless, and to train oneself so as to recall this state everyday anew, here is a sort of way or maxim to arise moral vitality, I think. (ST 105)

Kōyama not only attributes the attitude of equating the existence and non-existence of subjectivity peculiarly to Japanese people, but also ascribes this peculiarity of theirs to Japanese culture. Based on the equation between the existence and non-existence of this subjectivity, he could formulate the principle of the ethics of the subjectivity of responsibility, conspicuously personified in the samurai, and also applicable to ordinary Japanese people.

Kōyama's arguments about the samurai's ethics of responsibility, and the Japanese people's peculiar disposition that fits this ethics, naturalize conformity to it. Such arguments, combined with the four thinkers' emphasis on the necessity of creating Japanese national subjectivity, worked to buttress Nishitani's double claim that, first, self-annihilation and devotion to public service are Japanese people's traditional virtues, and that, second, the state of Japan should demand of its members such "virtues." His argumentation works to blur the gap between these two facets.

Aside from the credibility of these thinkers' narratives in themselves, expressing them in public has some meaning for the four thinkers. Delineating Japanese people as those who, in their own cultural peculiarity, have a disposition to assume world-historical responsibility may work to promote self-awareness as such a people, as well as inspire them to really become so. Encouraging the Japanese to become subjects of the responsibility of creating the new world order by following the ideal type found in their tradition also calls on them to organize themselves into a collective national subject that is continuous from the past to the present, in view of the world's future. In other words, the four thinkers' discussions about questions such as who the Japanese are, what their cultural peculiarity is, and what their ideal human type based on this cultural peculiarity is, constitute in themselves an act of creating "new Japanese." As these thinkers lamented the lack of such "new

Japanese" in their time, this act is an indispensable part of their practice of the philosophy of world history.

Section 2: The Vision of the State in View of Overcoming Western Modernity

While Kōyama's arguments thus back up Nishitani's claim, in his essays around the time of the symposia, Nishitani explores the possible outcome of the subjectivity formation as argued by Kōyama. More concretely, keeping Japan in mind, Nishitani discusses what the ideal state should be and bases it upon a similar subjectivity as that which Kōyama envisioned. As such, Nishitani's vision of this state is permeated by the same question the four thinkers addressed in the symposia, namely who the "new Japanese" should be. In responding to this question through this vision, Nishitani also gives a prospect as to how such "new Japanese" could contribute to the state of Japan. These interlacing themes exemplify the close connection between these philosophers' thoughts.

As it relates to state power, Nishitani explains that the Japanese people's self-annihilation and devotion to public service should be realized, even through state coercion. His arguments in "My View on Overcoming Modernity" suggest the reason underlying this explanation. On the one hand, he writes:

> To take matters a step further, then, why must the state demand of its citizens such self-annihilating service in their work? Needless to say, this is because the state must strengthen, as much as possible, its own internal unity. Such unity is necessary for it to concentrate its aggregate force as an individual totality and act with great energy. Moreover, this concentration of aggregate force would be fundamentally impossible without a profound ethicality, in which each and every citizen is reduced to the state qua totality by annihilating his or her self. (OM 57)

Nishitani maintains that the state needs its members' self-annihilation and identification with the state in order to strengthen its internal unity and accumulate its force to act. Due to the ethicality this force takes on in being produced through this self-annihilation, Nishitani equates this force with moral energy. Then, on the other hand, he writes:

> As I have stated, moral energy realizes a popular or national ethics by having each and every citizen annihilate their selves in their

work and serve the state, while at the same time making the state qua community of the people itself ethical and furnishing a high degree of concentrated energy to the state. (OM 60; translation modified by referring to Kawakami et al. 33)[1]

Here, Nishitani suggests that this moral energy leads citizens to annihilate themselves in their work and serve the state. Again, he emphasizes that doing so gives the state intensified moral energy along with strengthened internal unity. In other words, he conceives of the cycle between two movements in opposite and complementary directions. In one of these movements, citizens' self-annihilation and devotion to public service produces moral energy; in another, this very moral energy leads them to assume self-annihilation and devotion to public service. In this cycle, once the state succeeds in having citizens annihilate and devote themselves to public service, the moral energy produced by these acts would urge citizens to do so continually, while reproducing this energy itself. If Nishitani encourages the state's compulsory measure to demand of citizens such acts, it is also for the creation of the circuit of reproduction of moral energy in this cycle of the two movements outlined above. Stable reproduction of moral energy in this circuit would, above all, ensure continual amplification of the unity and force of the state.

Here again, it is not without reason that Nishitani attaches importance to the reproduction of moral energy. We can find this reason in his essay, "Worldview and Stateview" (*Sekaikan to kokkakan*), from 1941. In it, Nishitani also emphasizes the necessity of citizens' voluntary acceptance of the state's compulsory policy: "The state, out of its demand for high politicality, needs to control the field of freedom even to its foundation on the one hand, and to have this control justified with the consent out of this very fundamental freedom on the other" (NKC IV 278). The state in pursuit of its stronger unity must take control over the freedom of its members, yet this control must be accepted of their own free wills without coercion, even if this control itself is coercive. Only with its members' voluntary acceptance can the state justify its coercive control over their freedom. Moreover, when this happens, Nishitani goes so far as to say, "the very source of the inclination toward the intensive control over the field of freedom has at its own basis the root of freedom, and makes the ideal of freedom a driving force of its own existence" (NCK IV 273). That is, the state taking coercive control over the citizens' freedom is not synonymous with the state suppressing their freedom, insofar as the citizens freely and willingly agree to this control. For, if this is the case, their freedom becomes sublimated at a higher level, so that the opposition between freedom and control is sublated, so to speak. Nishitani finds the reproduction of moral energy to be important, because once the circuit of this reproduction is made, citizens come to voluntarily accept the state's compulsory policy, even if it is as a result of the state's demand. The justification of coercive control by this voluntary acceptance also contributes to the amplification of the state's unity and force.

In "Worldview and Stateview," Nishitani also provides theoretical considerations for the kind of collective national subjectivity citizens come to organize themselves into through their voluntary acceptance of state control, and further clarifies what is at stake in it:

> Therefore, that intensive control is the state's will to bind individuals within the unity of a collectivity that is the substratum of the state, and therefore also the desire of this collectivity itself. To thus bind individuals is to turn them into the substratum in their relation to the state. In turn, the necessity that state control must be justified by the consent out of fundamental freedom is the demand that all individuals must respectively put themselves in the position of the subject without merely immerging themselves in the natural substratum of the state. Put another way, the state demands turning the substratum into the subject and turning this subject into the substratum again. That is to say, the subject, rather than falling down to mere substratum, subjectively turns to the substratum and puts itself in a position of the substratum while remaining the subject. This circle between the substratum's becoming subject and the subject's becoming the substratum is nothing but a movement of a collectivity remaining the substratum and yet turning itself into the subject. (NKC IV 278–79)

Nishitani asserts that, whereas state control is the expression of the state's will to unite citizens and make them its foundation or substratum, when they accept this control willingly, they can become subjects with their own agency rather than remaining mere substratum. In other words, by taking the state's will to control as their own will, citizens integrate into the state's substratum and simultaneously retain their subjectivity, which is indiscernible from the state's subjectivity. In this way, the national subjectivity, which Nishitani believes Japan should create through state control, incessantly moves between the status of the substratum and that of the subject. It is this circular movement itself that constitutes this subjectivity.

It is not a coincidence that Nishitani's emphasis on citizens' voluntary acceptance of state control reminds us of Kōyama's reference to the samurai, who willingly follow orders at the risk of their lives, as the ideal type for the creation of "new Japanese." Nishitani's idea of the national subjectivity citizens organize themselves into through this voluntary acceptance, and Kōyama's idea of the subjectivity of responsibility the samurai realized by willingly following orders, share the same logic that true subjectivity resides in spontaneous subjection. The "new Japanese," who the four thinkers believed to be modeled upon samurai, are nothing but those who voluntarily accept state control and annihilate themselves to carry out the state's orders. In other words, they attain their subjectivity only by turning themselves into the substratum of the state.

For Nishitani, the way in which the "new Japanese," who organize themselves into such subjectivity to contribute to the state of Japan, is not limited to the reproduction of moral energy and the amplification of the state's unity and force. In his conception of the subject qua substratum of the state and the intimate unity between the state and its citizens, as built upon the unity between their status of subject and that of substratum, Nishitani's concern persists regarding overcoming Western modernity. Following the above citation in which he discusses the union of the subject and substratum of the state, he continues:

> At this point, the state (and therefore community) reflects its will in the interior of individuals, and thus brings its own unity to a higher dimension, while individuals see in the will of the state the will of community, and therefore their own will, and become aware of themselves being in the state. This situation is fundamentally different from that of the absolutist state in which the citizens are mere substratum without subjectivity, and from that of the liberal state in which they were mere subjects disengaged from the substratum. (NKC IV 279)

What Nishitani has in mind as the absolutist state is that of early modern Europe—the state that had unified ruling power over all the people divided within the class system that had persisted from the Middle Ages. He thinks of the liberal state as the modern Western state, in which the citizens liberated from the class system have gained individual freedom that has increased, until colliding with state power. When Nishitani maintains that the state, whose subject and substratum are one, is different from these states, he denotes this is a third type in addition to the first two.

> The principle that enables the sublation of complete state control and complete spontaneous freedom, and the unity between the state's high politicality and openness comprehending the world,

is actually given only in the state structure of our country [*waga kuni*], whereas to do so is to resolve the problem posed by the way existing modern states are grounded. (NKC IV 291)

"Complete state control" designates the characteristic of the absolutist state, while "complete spontaneous freedom" is characteristic of the liberal state. In claiming that these two characteristics occur in the state structure of Japan, Nishitani also suggests that the state that synthesizes these two types is precisely what Japan should become, where subjects and substratum are one as the result of the citizens' voluntary acceptance of state control. In this way, for him, the creation of the Japanese national subjectivity he tries to promote is inseparable from the establishment of the new state of Japan that can overcome Western early modern and modern states by resolving the problems inherent in them. Just as the four thinkers, in conceiving the philosophy of world history, kept in mind overcoming Western modernity, Nishitani's intention of doing so permeates his project of establishing the new state of Japan and create a Japanese national subjectivity based on this philosophy. His idea is that Japanese citizens who organize themselves into this subjectivity and become united with the substratum of the state will contribute to it by sublating the opposition between individual freedom and state power, and by regenerating this state as that which can overcome Western modernity.

Nishitani's phrase, "The principle . . . is actually given . . . in the state structure" has subtle connotations. Even though he uses the term "actually," the situation that this principle is supposed to enable has not been actualized. Just the principle is given, not in the actual state but allegedly in its structure. The pattern of logic here is the same as that which he uses when he asserts that self-annihilation and devotion to public service are the Japanese people's traditional virtues, yet that the state of Japan should demand them to practice these virtues. Needless to say, this pattern of logic was at the *Chūōkōron* symposia in the four thinkers' insistence that the ideal human types, like the samurai, illustrate a Japanese spirit particular to the Japanese, all the while also emphasizing the necessity of creating new Japanese who bear a Japanese spirit modeled after these types. That said, the state of Japan with the ability to overcome Western modern states, as well as unite Japanese national subjectivity with its substratum, as conceived by Nishitani, is to be established or created anew from now on. Pursuing the narrative as to what they are, or indeed should be, is a practical act to promote this creation. This act also exemplifies the attitude that Kōyama found to be typically Japanese, namely that of living the paradox between the existence and non-existence of the self, and thus—if we take "the self" mentioned here to be that of the Japanese national subject—resolving their contradiction.

Section 3: The Illusion of Greater Autonomy and Freedom

The noticeable characteristic of Japanese national subjectivity, which is articulated in Nishitani's arguments so far, is the unity between its statuses as the subject and substratum of the state of Japan. This characteristic undergirds the idea that Japanese national subjectivity should be created by the state's coercion of Japanese people into self-annihilation and devotion to public service. The state's demands of, and compulsory measures against its citizens force them to continuously practice these virtues and, through this repetition, constantly reproduce moral energy. By virtue of this energy, the state can strengthen its unity and acquire power to take action against rival states; in other words, the state can attain strong subjectivity. The citizens, by annihilating themselves and devoting themselves to public service, become the substratum of the state. It is only in doing so that they can contribute to taking part in the subjectivity of the state. Thus, in the Japanese national subjectivity, Nishitani tries to create the status of the subject and that of the substratum as inseparable.

Now, I will investigate the problems involved in this first characteristic of the subjectivity in question. Given that Nishitani bases the possibility that the new ideal state of Japan can overcome Western modernity upon this characteristic of Japanese national subjectivity, the following examination entails the evaluation as to whether this overcoming is successful.

In order to critically examine this characteristic, let me review some of Nishitani's statement, previously quoted from "Worldview and Stateview":

> In turn, the necessity that state control must be justified by the consent out of fundamental freedom is the demand that all individuals must respectively put themselves in the position of subject without merely immersing themselves in the natural substratum of the state. (NKC IV 278)
>
> That is to say, the subject, rather than falling down to mere substratum, subjectively turns to the substratum and puts itself in a position of the substratum while remaining the subject. (NKC IV 278–79)

Careful inspection of the usage of the word "subject" in these passages reveals something strange. When Nishitani asserts that individuals can put themselves in the position of the subject of the state if (and only if) they subjectively turn to its substratum, he declares that their subjectivity consists merely in putting themselves in the position of the substratum out of their own free will. In this statement, Nishitani deprives the word "subject" of its agency to act, and limits the meaning of this word to the agent of volition. In this limited sense of the word "subject," Nishitani's purport is that, even if individuals are in the position of the substratum, they are in the position of the subject insofar as they have the will to be the substratum. He also implicitly suggests that all individuals should have the will to be so and the possibilities of other wills or of other subjectivities are precluded.

Nishitani would object to this criticism, which is made evident in "Worldview and Stateview": "This circle between the substratum's becoming subject and the subject's becoming substratum is nothing but a movement of a collectivity remaining substratum, and yet turning itself into subject" (NKC IV 279). This passage tells us that what Nishitani refers to as the subject qua substratum is, strictly speaking, the collectivity of Japanese national citizens. If he talks about each citizen's status as subject or substratum, it is on the assumption that each is, or will be, part of this collectivity. Regarding the construction and maintenance of such a collectivity, disparate individuals should be tightly united and their unity should not be disturbed. In this respect, individuals' personal freedom, which may give them room to diverge from or disturb this unity, is merely an obstacle. If Nishitani thinks the control over, and the negation of, this freedom is mandatory, it is for the purpose of supporting this collectivity of citizens, which will be the substratum of the state, as he himself confesses: "[T]hat intensive control is the state's will to bind individuals within the unity of a collectivity that is the substratum of the state, and therefore also the desire of this collectivity itself" (NKC IV 278).

Nishitani's stance is also manifested in his following statement on the autonomy of national citizens in one of the *Chūōkōron* symposia:

> I believe that the autonomy and inventiveness of citizens or civilians would not be authentic, unless such autonomy and inventiveness rise from the depths of the situation in which so-called freedom is completely negated by the thorough enforcement of such control, or unless they come out through the meshes of control spread across the whole state (ST 71).

What matters for Nishitani is not the private freedom of separate individuals, but the autonomy of national citizens in their collectivity. He thus insists that they must be brought under the control of this collectivity itself, which for him is equal to the state, or more precisely, the nation-state, in order to be integrated into it. In his view, insofar as this control comes from the will of this collectivity to establish and sustain itself, this control is the autonomy of citizens as one nation. Given that they, as the members of this collectivity, control themselves by themselves, their autonomy is authentic. Only by being controlled in this way can they cultivate their collective inventiveness as potential for massive achievements, something that would be impossible if everybody acted separately. Nishitani allows citizens only the freedom of accepting state control or finding their subjectivity in turning to the substratum of the state, because he always thinks from the standpoint of the collectivity of national citizens—indeed, for the benefit of the state.

Still, it is undeniable that there is something dubious in this "autonomy." If the state imposes control upon citizens in order to incorporate them into it, it must preexist this incorporation. That is to say, at the point of this imposition, there is a gap between what controls and what is controlled, or in other words, between the subject and substratum of the state. To this extent, this is not exactly autonomy in the sense of people giving themselves law and controlling themselves by themselves. If Nishitani does not hesitate to call this state "autonomy," it is again because he assumes that all citizens should be incorporated into the state, and will be so subsequently. For, once this happens, the gap between the controller and the controlled disappears, and they will become one and the same. Autonomy, as Nishitani asserts it to be, is that which will be reconstituted only retrospectively, in the prospect of the future unity between the controller and the controlled, between subject and substratum, based on a certain moral postulate.[2]

One reason Nishitani does not mind disregarding the gap between subject and substratum, and his supposing that becoming substratum is immediately becoming subject, can be discerned in the idea of the subject of responsibility shared by him and his three colleagues, and epitomized by the samurai, as Kōyama argued. These thinkers discuss the idea that people can attain their subjectivity of responsibility as their true subjectivity only when they devote themselves to assuming their responsibility and annihilate themselves. In this self-annihilation, the disappearance of their banal subjectivity becomes at once the appearance of their new subjectivity. Indeed, the being of their new subjectivity is equal to the nothingness of their own subjectivity. Based on this logic of the unity of the being and nothingness of the subject whose existence resides only in its absence, it is possible to claim that abandoning personal subjectivity, will, and freedom is attaining higher subjectivity, will, and freedom. When all citizens' acts of putting themselves under state control are regarded as their responsibility, their higher subjectivity thus attained is easily merged with the collective subjectivity of the people who similarly abandon their individual subjectivity and accept state control. Higher will, here, is equated with the will of this collective subjectivity, and higher freedom with autonomy, in the sense of this collective subjectivity wielding its power of control over itself.

Thus, the logic of unity of the being and nothingness of the subject of responsibility operates behind Nishitani's bridging the gap between subject and substratum, and naturalizing the absorption of the individual subjectivities of citizens into the collective subjectivity of the state. The logic that authentic subjectivity exists only in the absence of banal subjectivity permeates and buttresses his claims that citizens can attain their subjectivity only by being integrated into the substratum of the state, that their individual wills should be united into the collective will of the state in order to control them, and that their true freedom comes from the suppression of their personal freedom under state control.

However, to say that the subject and its will or freedom exist only insofar as it is negated is to confess that room for the subject that is not integrated into the substratum of the state, out of the refusal to accept state control, and for unsuppressed freedom, is rejected from the outset. The absence of these things can be covered up for the ostensible reason that the subject integrated into the substratum of the state and the will to accept state control and suppressed freedom are authentic, become superior through being negated. While the logic of the unity between being and nothingness and the existence and absence of subjectivity may support this argument because of the very ambivalence it upholds, this logic also discloses that such an authentic or superior subject, will, and freedom do not exist as what they are.

Nishitani praised the state with which citizens identify and, thus, whose subject and substratum are united, and regarded it as the sublation of both the absolutist states of early modern Europe and the liberal European states of his time. But, given that room for individual freedom characteristic of the liberal state is precluded in the state he envisions, it cannot be said that the latter sublates the former in the sense of both negating and preserving. The same applies to the absolutist state, characterized by its unified ruling power over all citizens. However, it applies in a different sense: this power is preserved in the state Nishitani has in mind, but it is now regarded as the power of the citizens insofar as they identify with the state as its substratum qua subjects. The excuse that this change is the negation of the unified ruling power, and that this power's exercise over citizens constitutes their autonomy in which their freedom is preserved, is hardly convincing. For, what happens in the state whose subject and substratum are united is the endorsement of its unified ruling power over citizens by themselves on the condition that they lack individual will or freedom to refuse to subject to the state. In spite of Nishitani's praise of this state, it has not sublated the absolutist state and the liberal state, nor does it overcome either of them. Just as the "higher" autonomy or freedom that should result from the first characteristic of Japanese national subjectivity is illusory, so is the overcoming of Western modernity.

Chapter 4

The Interpenetration between the National and the International

The Second Characteristic of Japanese National Subjectivity

In his complete works, compiled in the postwar period, Nishitani made "Worldview and Stateview" the second part, and "Philosophy of World History" the first part of a section named "Philosophy of World History and Historical Consciousness" (*Sekaishi no tetsugaku to rekishiteki ishiki*). This fact suggests that he considered his view of the state, presented in the former essay, as relevant to Japan in the world-historical position based on the philosophy of world history, which is argued in the latter. This is only natural given the four thinkers, including Nishitani, pondered how the state of Japan could assume the responsibility imposed by world-historical necessity qua ethicality, and thus conceived a Japanese national subjectivity that would make this possible. What remains unaddressed is what these thinkers believed could make this subjectivity, to be formed according to the norm found in Japanese indigenous tradition, capable of assuming this world-historical responsibility.

Regarding Kōyama's recourse to the samurai as the norm for this subjectivity, one might question whether the samurai—usually regarded as representative of Japanese indigenous tradition—can be a suitable ideal type for cultivating such a subjectivity to assume the world-historical responsibility. To this, the four thinkers would answer that even though the samurai are a type of human that appeared in Japanese history and are representative of Japanese indigenous tradition, the subjectivity of responsibility they epitomize is not necessarily so. Then, the question is, why did these thinkers believe this subjectivity, while having its origin in the national, could go beyond to suitably become the practical subject of world history? The four thinkers' discussions concerning this question certainly include something that is irreducible to sheer, exclusivist nationalism. However, this does not necessarily mean this "excess" constitutes a resistance to ethnocentric nationalism.

In this chapter, I will investigate the second notable characteristic of Japanese national subjectivity concerning its internationality. First, I will look to how, according to the four thinkers, following the norm of the samurai enables Japanese people to cultivate their subjectivity of responsibility and, at the same time, makes this subjectivity both national and international. Second, I will observe these thinkers' discussions of the "center" and the new world they envisioned resulting from it. As they conceived this subjectivity as both national and international at once, I will demonstrate how this undergirds their discussion that Japan is the center that yields other centers that constitute this world order. Third, by explicating the ambiguities of the above discussions, I will illuminate the gap between the ideal and reality of Japanese national subjectivity and the new world it sought to establish. In the course of this investigation, I will disclose what the interpenetration between the national and the international in this subjectivity actually means.

Section 1: Internationality Involved in a National Spirit

Let me address how the four thinkers would answer the question as to how the Japanese national subjectivity, modelled after the norm that is representative of Japanese indigenous tradition, can assume the responsibility of realizing the necessity qua ethicality of world history. To do so, I will start by looking to the context in which these thinkers promoted the idea of the samurai as the norm.

When the subject of responsibility of the samurai in the face of death was at issue in the four thinkers' discussion, Kōyama broached this topic after Kōsaka had proposed the prospect of "resolv[ing] a problem of the soul of an individual person by thinking of this problem in relation to the course of the history of the ethnic group [*minzoku*]" (SN 164). Rather than confining this prospect to a nationalistic scope, Kōsaka equates it with the prospect of "giv[ing] life to Oriental nothingness in history" (SN 164). Claiming that "the East has a principle different from that of the West in understanding history" (SN 174), he refers to absolute nothingness. However, he has no intention of restricting the scope of this principle merely to the East: "Although the world itself is now somehow divided into the Western world and Eastern world, if we pursue historicism to the extreme, isn't it the case that we come to see at the bottom of the world its absolute ground, what should be called absolute nothingness?" (SN181). Kōsaka here announces absolute nothingness as the ground for the entire world, including the West and the East. He believes this ground should direct the way the world operates, as the principle of world history, even though it was discovered in Oriental culture and has been so far neglected in the Western-centered world.

Considering these descriptions of absolute nothingness, it turns out that the subjectivity of responsibility is, with respect to its condition of possibility, related to the ground of the world and the principle of its history. That absolute nothingness is the principle of world history means that some ethical subjects of responsibility, realized in the face of absolute nothingness, can by their act decide the direction in which world history goes at its crucial moment, while emanating moral energy through this act. In this way, world history has essential ethicality. Therefore, according to these thinkers, making samurai the ideal type for present-day Japanese people to follow does not necessarily amount to making them narrow-minded and concerned only with their own country. Rather, this ideal type, insofar as following it enables Japanese people to confront absolute nothingness as the ground of the world and the principle of its history, is the best medium through which they can cultivate their subjectivity in order to meet the responsibility imposed by world-historical necessity qua ethicality.

In light of the four thinkers' idea of absolute nothingness, Japanese national subjectivity has the implication that what is qualified here as Japanese and national is at once international and open to the entire world. An expression of these thinkers' stance of seeing the national and the international as compatible, or even as one, is articulated in the following statement by Kōsaka: "Although people speak as if being global somehow severely contradicted being national [*kokkateki*], these two things never contradict. Being global is not being anti-national, but rather being national. There is no need to think that being global and being national contradict each other" (SN 177). The second notable characteristic of the Japanese national subjectivity the four thinkers envisioned is this interpenetration between the national and the international within this subjectivity. By presupposing this characteristic, these thinkers can claim this subjectivity, to be created by Japanese people according to the norm found in their indigenous tradition, could carry out the world-historical mission. These thinkers anchor this characteristic in absolute nothingness as the ground for the world and the principle of its history.

The four thinkers' rationale that aims to make the national and the international compatible is reflected in their discussion of another human type they viewed as a potential norm for the "new Japanese" along with samurai. This other type is usually regarded as a personification of chauvinism. Both Kōyama and Nishitani discern this type in the young Japanese soldiers who participated in the attacks on Pearl Harbor and off the east coast of Malaya, and sacrificed themselves in their suicide attacks. Kōyama even calls them "true Japanese, in whom a type of modern hero resides" (TRR 160). The attitude of these soldiers bears a stark similarity to that of samurai delineated by the four thinkers in that both consist in accepting an order on their own free will, and having no regrets about dying to complete the order. Although I have discussed the problems entailed in the first characteristic of the subjectivity manifested in such attitudes, what I pay attention to here is this subjectivity's second characteristic as aforementioned. Referring to these soldiers as paragons of Japanese spirit, Kōyama and Nishitani assign a different meaning to their attitude from that which is typically given to it, just as Kōyama did regarding the samurai.

First, Kōyama and Nishitani celebrate the Japanese spirit of these soldiers, not because it excluded all outside influences in order to be purely "Japanese," but because, in Nishitani's words, it "clearly showed how science and spirit can harmoniously unite into one" (TRR 159–60). The recourse to Japanese spirit in this sense is intended as an objection to a common formula that emphasized how intellectual education is against Japanese spirit that claimed to require no imported Western science. This intention is also expressed in Kōyama's statement that "Japanese spirit, rather than excluding scientificity or rationality, pursues it to the end, breaks through it and finally returns to an absolute fact of the unity of reason and fact" (TRR 160). What these two thinkers highly appreciate in the Japanese spirit thus conceived is that it can harmonize or unite itself with the modern—indeed Western—civilization. Regarding the young soldiers who threw themselves into suicide attacks, if Nishitani and Kōyama see in these soldiers the Japanese spirit in this sense, it is due to the fact these soldiers had received a modern education in Western science and yet did not hesitate to sacrifice themselves for their state.

In other words, these two thinkers see in these soldiers the exemplary specimens of Japanese spirit, and a human type that could harmonize this spirit with the Western science they had learned through modern education. The reference to these soldiers as the personification of Japanese is undeniably and absurdly cruel, even though this type of discourse was quite common in wartime discourses. Still, notable here is the two thinkers' gesture toward reading internationality into a certain nationalistic mentality. These thinkers redefined this as distinct from its vulgarized idea, prefiguring the second characteristic of Japanese national subjectivity.

When thus presenting the samurai and young Japanese soldiers as ideal human types to the public, the four thinkers reconciled their being Japanese and having a global mind. This was done to provide a way out of the indirection these characterizations suffered from, as they were both imported from modern Western civilization and of Japanese indigenous tradition. As such, these thinkers' idea of Japanese national subjectivity, modelled after such types, was also intended to make contemporary Japanese people aware of their world-historical responsibility, inseparably connected with their responsibility of being Japanese.

Section 2: A Center that Yields Many Centers

For the four thinkers, Japanese national subjectivity's thus having internationality, and supposedly being open to the world and able to act upon it from a global perspective, crucially determines the nature of the new world order this subjectivity should establish by fulfilling its world-historical responsibility. Their discussion of this new world order's "center" provides an illustration of its intended nature. Kōsaka comments on this center as follows:

> When history moves, there is a central point, which moves it; there is an absolute center of historical actuality. From this center, the movement of history spreads and construction extends itself. Speaking in regard to that *moralische Energie*, this center is the center through which moral power manifests itself. This center is Japan. . . . (ST 70)

The center, here, refers to a point through which moral energy manifests itself. As such, it is a point where the practical subjects of world history who emanate this energy through their acts appear. Kōsaka's description of his own country as this "center," and his qualification of this center as "absolute," seems self-centered and self-righteous. However, in light of his and his colleagues' other comments on this point, they do not seem to take these expressions as applicable exclusively to Japan as the one and only center.

First, when the four thinkers call this center "absolute," they do not mean that there was/is no other center in the world. Kōyama speaks of what the "absolute" means from the standpoint of the philosophy of world history. In the course of history, innumerable things appear periodically and disappear as time goes by. In this respect, everything in history seems to be relative. However, Kōyama insists, some points may be of absolute significance:

> Carrying on one's back the tendency of world history in the capacity of subject resolutely—Such an ethical vitality itself is not merely relative, but at once has an absolute significance because of which

one can throw one's life away without regret. This is what I mean [by absolute ethics]. This is, after all, what it means to transcend history within it, so to speak. (TRR 158)

The "absolute" Kōyama speaks of here concerns ethical vitality as the driving force of world history, insofar as it reveals itself in the act of the subject who grasps the direction in which world history should move, and who also acts to make world history move in this direction. Although this act is merely one of many events that appear and disappear in world history, insofar as it suits and effectuates the necessity qua ethicality of world history, it is fundamentally distinguished from other events or acts. As such, it touches something beyond empirical reality while at the same time being in it. It is to this extent that it can be said ethical vitality, or more precisely, its revelation through the act of the practical subject, is relative, and yet has an absolute significance. Therefore, to be absolute in the context of world history means to take part in the necessity qua ethicality of world history inherent in this ethical vitality.

Considering this meaning of the term "absolute," when Kōsaka refers to Japan as the absolute center through which such ethical vitality manifests itself, he does not mean Japan is the only center throughout world history. That the center is absolute means that the act of the practical subject carried out in that center accords with world-historical necessity qua ethicality. That is to say, the act is what should be happening at that very moment in view of the course of world history. As such, this act may happen anywhere when the time comes; there is no necessity that it happen only once in world history and in only one place. In other words, the center as the place where this act happens can be multiple, emerging anytime, anywhere.

Besides, even though these philosophers' assertions—that Japan is the center which moves world history and through which moral power manifests itself—sound pretentious, they have their reasons and are based on their view of world history and grasp of the world-historical situation in their time. If they called Japan the "center" in the above sense, it is because Japan, at their time, was the only state that was forced to confront the Eurocentric world and could struggle to change it into the true world. As such, for Japan, this meant following and realizing world-historical necessity qua ethicality at that time. That Japan's status as the center is thus determined by its world-historical situation at a certain moment means that the country is not necessarily the only permanent center of the world.

When the four thinkers criticize "the Eurocentric world," they implicitly admit the existence of another center preceding Japan. However, when the notion of the "world" was first shaped in Europe, it was positioned as the only center of this world. Positing such a totality, and allegedly integrating all peoples and countries into Europe's sphere of domination and influence, was certainly the first step in the direction required by the necessity and ethicality of world history. Now, carrying this move further, another center emerged in non-European areas through Japan's rise to rival the great powers of Europe. According to these philosophers, this should have cleaved a way for the emergence of other centers in these areas. Therefore, Nishitani says, "we should think about many centers in the present world" (SN 178). There can be many centers located in various places, either at different points in time or within the same period. Along this line, and in correspondence to his pluralistic view of history, Suzuki states, "[N]ow Japan assumes the task of constructing a new world order," that is, a "pluralistic world order" (TRR 123). We can understand this world order as that in which many centers coexist, in opposition to a monistic Eurocentric world order.

For the four thinkers, Japan's fulfillment of its world-historical responsibility means constructing this pluralistic world order that has multiple centers. Strictly speaking, what they assert in principle is not simply that Japan is one center among multiple centers. Rather, they view Japan as a center that enables the emergence of many others and that which initiates the construction of the pluralistic world order. What undergirds this assertion is these thinkers' idea that Japanese national subjectivity, as the agent of this construction and as formed in confrontation with absolute nothingness, has internationality in precisely being national. Because of the inseparability between being national and being international, this subjectivity emanates moral energy through its acts. Thus, Japan becoming a center cannot be limited to a matter of national interests. Rather, this should entail promoting the cultivation of similar subjectivities elsewhere, so to allow the emergence of other centers for the sake of global goodness. Here, the interpenetration between the national and the international in Japanese national subjectivity, derived from its confrontation with absolute nothingness, supposedly guarantees the pluralistic nature of the new world order that this subjectivity could and should establish.

Section 3: National Desire for Global Hegemony in the Guise of Internationality

So far I have discussed the interpenetration between the national and the international in Japanese national subjectivity as its second characteristic. In order to become a practical subject of world history that follows and realizes the necessity qua ethicality of world history, Japanese national subjectivity must not merely have a pure and exclusive Japanese nature isolated from the world. Rather it must be at once national and international, with its roots in Japanese indigenous tradition while also interacting with the entire world. If the internationality of this subjectivity can be claimed, it is insofar that self-annihilation is the way to achieve the task of emulating the ideal human type for Japanese people in order to attain this subjectivity. Absolute nothingness, which they face upon self-annihilation, and which enables them to attain this subjectivity, is not only the essential element of Oriental culture, but is also the absolute ground of the world and the principle of world history. Thus, the recourse to absolute nothingness, which allegedly determines the quintessence of Japanese culture and tradition, lends Japanese national subjectivity an internationality open to the world. Ultimately, it is through the mediation of absolute nothingness that the national and the international interpenetrate this subjectivity. Due to this characteristic, the four thinkers asserted the new world order established around the center of this subjectivity could give birth to many other centers within this world order.

However, with good reason, doubts can be cast upon such arguments. First, while the four thinkers assert the interpenetration of the national and the international in this subjectivity, the coexistence of the two natures—namely "being global and being national" (SN 177), in Kōsaka's words—raises a question concerning the relation between them. The possibility of this question was already foreshadowed in Kōsaka's previous statement, in which he claims, "[T]here is a central point, which moves [history]." He adds, "From this center, the movement of history spreads and construction extends itself" (ST 70). Here, whereas he certainly speaks of the spread of the historical movement in which multiple centers emerge, he also emphasizes this movement itself arises from one specific center. Put in another way, the question raised is whether these thinkers' idea of the pluralistic world order to be initiated by the Japanese national subject entails the ethnocentric privileging of this subject. If this is the case, one must ask whether these two elements contradict each other. Looking further into the four thinkers' discussions and exploring the answers to these questions will reveal what the interpenetration between the national and the international in Japanese national subjectivity actually means. Furthermore, it will reveal the reality of the pluralistic world order to be constructed by the agent with this characteristic.

Surprisingly, the four thinkers assume the ethnocentric privileging of Japanese national subjectivity and try to make it compatible with the pluralistic world order. While acknowledging the plurality of the centers, the points from which the ethnic self-awareness of each ethnic group arises to counter the monocentric world order under the hegemony of the West, Nishitani maintains elsewhere that Japan's leadership is indispensable to achieving this state of affairs. But he, and his colleagues, are not unaware of the difficulty making the pluralistic world order, and the leadership of one of the members of this order compatible, carry with it:

> On the one hand, [Japan] arouses the ethnic self-awareness in each ethnic group and makes them have autonomous active power. On the other hand, in doing so, Japan retains its leading position. While these two sides are connected to each other, their relation implies a contradiction, if we think them on the same plane. How we can think their relation without contradiction? That is a fundamental problem. (TRR 143)

While formulating the difficulty in making seemingly contradictory things compatible, Nishitani also alludes to a key to its solution: put Japan's leadership on a higher level than that of the plurality of centers. This would seem to show that Japan, and only it, enables the plurality of centers, and does not disturb it.

The subsequent challenge for the four thinkers is to explain the reason why Japan's leadership can enable the pluralistic world order in which many centers coexist. Suzuki states, "as the most familiar reason of Japan's leadership, isn't it necessary to take into account the fact that Japan had 'modernity'?" (ST 94). However, given this leadership is to be attained in rivalry with Western hegemony, Japan's mere modernization cannot be a sufficient reason for it to have this leadership. What is more important is Kōsaka's statement, which succeeds Suzuki's: "By positively participating in the modern world, Japan grasped the truth of this world and perceived its error" (ST 96). Coming to terms with this error, in the eyes of the four thinkers, may enable Japan to avoid constructing the monocentric world order under its leadership, comparable to the existing one under the hegemony of the West.

Throughout the roundtable discussions, the four thinkers vehemently condemn the hypocrisy of the Western moral ideals of equality and freedom, which they perceived to be a major problem in the current world order. Kōyama's arguments, in particular, follow a consistent line of thought on this topic. In the West, he declaims, people advocate for these two ideals together, as if they were realizable simultaneously. In reality, though, there are the strong and the weak, and if both are treated equally and set free so that they can do whatever they want, the strong come to subjugate and exploit the weak. Paradoxically, in reality, the ideals of equality and freedom give rise to domination and oppression. This is the case not only in relations between humans within one state, but also relations between different states or ethnic groups. In this way, Western powers, professing the ideals of equality and freedom, ended up colonizing non-Western countries (TRR 144–45). After pointing out the contradiction between these ideals and their actual consequences, Kōyama goes on to discuss the fundamental cause of this inconsistency:

> In short, the source of error resides in the thought that starts with the supposition of the person [*jinkaku*] or ethnic group that has been completed from the beginning, I mean, in individualistic thought. The ideas of freedom and equality, whether they are those of an individual human or an ethnic group, result from this supposition. This supposition utterly ignores human reality. It does not include at all the notion of the state in which each is put in the right place [*tokoro wo eru*], or of the act of putting each in the right place [(*tokoro wo*) *eshimeru*]. I wonder how to put it into words, but [in the case of the above two ideals] thinking that everything has been completed from the outset has amounted to thinking that each has been put in the right place from the beginning. And yet, this situation is somehow taken as that in which everybody is equal and there is no distinction between the one and the other. So there is no "place" proper, and what seems to be a "place" does not make sense as such. In this way of thinking, there is no idea of history at all. Not only the idea of "time" but also that of "place" is lacking. Here is the source of error in the first place. As people invent ideals on such a supposition that has nothing to do with reality at all, ideals do not have the least moral power to lead reality, and ethics and power, ideal and reality are left in opposition. Therefore, even if such people think of ethnic states [*minzoku kokka*] and try to establish their international relations according to this way of thinking, the abstractness and error entailed in its first supposition reveal themselves everywhere. There is no way that a truly peaceful order of the world is constructed. (ST 84)

Provided that the four thinkers found the modern Western world to be built on the ideals of equality and freedom, the source of the error discussed by Kōyama overlaps with what Kōsaka called the source of the error of the modern world. Kōyama tracks it in an atomistic view of humans, states, and ethnic groups, by regarding them as complete and independent individual entities. If the ideals of equality and freedom allow the strong to subjugate and exploit the weak, as he discussed earlier, it is because these ideals derive from, and therefore presuppose, a view that disregards the differences and relations among humans or groups and sees them as similar individual and independent entities. When all humans or groups are treated equally in spite of their differences and are allowed to have their own way, their inequality and unfairness are aggravated. To counter this view and tackle the problems consequent upon it, Kōyama proposes the idea of "being put in the right place" or "putting each in the right place." He is convinced that respecting the differences among humans or groups and giving them appropriate positions in appropriate relations is necessary to construct a peaceful world order. In other words, the principle of "putting each in the right place" is the key to the pluralistic world order.

A careful reading of Kōyama's statement reveals the respect of difference supposed to be realized by "putting each in the right place" denies not only the contradictory consequence of the ideal of equality, but also this ideal itself. This denial is obvious from Kōyama's attitude of seeing the ideal of equality as derivative from the atomistic view he criticizes. He states that thinking everybody is equal and without distinction is equivalent to thinking that each person has been put in the right place from the beginning; yet there is no "place" proper in such a way of thinking. If "putting each in the right place," in his eyes, is an ideal to be achieved, it follows that the state of equality, in which he sees no "place" proper, neither fits reality nor makes sense as an ideal. Moreover, if there is no "place" proper where everything is equal, the "place" is a matter not only of the difference, but also of the hierarchy among the things that occupy it. More precisely, the "place" in which each should be put means the position of each, to be determined in its distinction and discrimination from others and assigned to each in relation to them.

Thus, in association with the motif of "place," Kōyama has in mind a kind of naturalized ideal order that reflects the actual differences and hierarchy among humans or groups, and situates them suitably according to their respective natures. He characterizes the ethics expressed in this order as rooted in the Oriental tradition:

> Rather than the ethics of person, which results from the position that all humans are equal and free from birth, a different ethics, which should be called the ethics of "ethical life" [*jinrin*], holds true. This is the ethics that results from the position that each human should be put in the right place. I think that such an ethical thought had been hitherto alive in the East. (TTR 145)

Kōyama seeks the archetype of this Oriental ethics in the structure of the family system: "The ethical structure of the family system [*ie*], in the sense of a system in which the parent raises and guides the child, forms the most fundamental archetype of the ethics of ethical life" (TRR 149). While parents raise and guide children, the former's acts of raising and guiding the latter bind them together and give them a sense of identification. Even though parent and child are neither equal, nor independent, they love and respect each other, as they are different. In this way, in the family, Kōyama explains:

> [. . .] each different skill, duty, gift and ability are given to each member, and yet all the members harmonize each other so as to accomplish a total unity. Rather than the same things simply gathering together like atoms and making up an additional sum, different members connect and complement each other so as to shape a harmonized totality. This is the fundamental principle of the "family system," properly speaking. (TRR 152)

Against a simple sum of similar entities equated to individual and independent humans or groups in the atomistic view, Kōyama contrasts a harmonized totality in which different members are put in the right places, and seeks the principle of this totality in the family system. Given that he apparently takes this totality to be the model for the pluralistic world order, he thinks the family system, indeed its ethics, can resolve the problems resulting from the ideals of equality and freedom and can thus correct the errors of Western modern world.

Unexpectedly, carrying this argument one step further, Kōyama comes to base Japan's leadership on this ethics of family:

> [. . .] I think it can be said that the "family system" has always lived in the historical fact of Japan. Of course this "family system" is factual and not an empty ideal. Far from the empty ideal of so-called person [*jinkaku*], the "family system" is the foundation of ethical life and, as such, factual. And yet it is also at once the social ideal of Japan. Exactly as ideal and fact, as fact and ideal at the same time, the "family system" or its spirit has been living in Japan. I wonder if it is okay to say this. This said, based on the spirit of this family system, we can think about an ethics whose foundation is education or enlightenment. Although this is the ethics of family, it works at once as the ethics organizing society outside family. The idea of aristocracy under the rule of the wise [*kentetsu seiji*] is deduced from this ethics. Furthermore, what the leader means today comes to be understood as the extension of the ethics in the sense I have just said. Then, I think we will be able to say that a new principle or spirit of world order is also connected with Japanese spirit. (TRR 150)

Kōyama insists that, although the ethics of the family system is peculiar to the East, its factual realization in people's lives throughout society finds its completion exclusively in Japan. Since this ethics provides the principle of the harmonious totality, in which each is put in the right place, he continues, the pluralistic world order modeled after this totality can be achieved only under Japan's leadership.

The compatibility between the leadership and the pluralistic world order is likened to the indispensability of the parent, who raises and guides the child. While parents and children are different in their duty and ability, all fulfill their duty as is suitable to their ability, and thus live harmoniously as if they were one. Children alone would not be able to live in this way, because they do not know what their duty or ability is—therefore, guidance by the parent, who knows it is necessary, is needed. This is comparable to "the aristocracy under the rule of the wise" (TRR 150). In Kōyama's view, given that the existent Western-centered world order is far from the harmonious totality of the family system, there is no way that the countries satisfied with that world order could take the initiative to create a new world order as per such a totality. Only the country in which the ethics of the family system has been thoroughly realized can take the initiative to do so and guide others to cooperate, just as parent does to child. In this way, Japan's leadership and the pluralistic world order would be compatible with the former, enabling the latter.

By introducing the distinction between the knowing and the not-knowing, allegedly between Japan and other countries, Kōyama responds to Nishitani's request to establish another level, different from that of genuine multiplicity and on which Japan's leadership can be situated. And yet, when the four thinkers speak of the harmonious totality putting each in the right place or the world with plural centers creates, they invoke both the hierarchical relations between the knowing and the not-knowing, and the non-hierarchical relations among those of the latter, just as the family system includes both the relations between parent and children, and the relations among children.

Hence the ambivalence illustrated by Nishitani's statements, in which he admits the coexistence of "many centers" (SN 178) from which the ethnic self-awareness of each ethnic group arises, and yet infamously encourages other ethnic groups in the Greater East Asia Co-Prosperity Sphere to "Japanize" (ST 78) or "half-Japanize" (TRR 161). If Nishitani, as well as his three colleagues, sees no contradiction in these statements, it is because they assume the aforementioned two kinds of relations among plural centers, and believe it impossible to maintain both harmoniously without Japan's guidance.

Kōyama's emphasis on the parent's responsibility "to raise children so that they will grow into those who equal or even surpass the parent, at least the persons equal to the parent" (TRR 154) may be taken as a message that the leader is replaceable once other ethnic groups grow up. But, as the terms "Japanize" and "half-Japanize" illustrate, insofar as the model of the grown-up or the criteria of growth is given by the parent, children can never be equal or surpass the parent, for their very differences would be unilaterally judged as signs of their immaturity from the standpoint of the parent. Speaking of the two kinds of centers, multiple centers outside of Japan would never attain the same status as the single "center" equated with Japan.

Considering this paternalistic authority presupposed in the pluralistic world order, it is impossible to take Kōyama's slogan, "the plurality of historical worlds," at face value. The gist of this slogan is not the affirmation of genuine multiplicity of different historical worlds, as is often professed, especially given his claim that Japan's leadership, based on its incorporation of the ethics of the family system, serves as the principle of the new world order.[1]

In "The Ideal of World History," Kōyama states, "I have no intention of simply sticking with the pluralism of worlds. There is no room for the pluralism that does not anticipate monism in a certain form to exist" ("*Sekaishi no rinen*" (1) 347–48). He further expresses his wish that multiple historical worlds be united. To unify them without negating their plurality, he proposes, "We must take seriously the fact that respective historical worlds have their own completeness and incompleteness based on the differences among regions or ethnic groups, and deeply acknowledge that the development and construction of world history takes place in the interrelations of these worlds" ("*Sekaishi no rinen*" (2) 581). In his idea that these worlds should be connected considering their "completeness" and "incompleteness," there are echoes of the harmonious totality comparable to the family system, in which the supposedly inferior is put in the right place under the guidance of the supposedly superior. Certainly, Kōyama is confident his conception of monism is completely different: "[T]he monism mediated by the awareness of the pluralism of worlds can no longer be the same as the existent monism of the world without such awareness, the monism from whose standpoint people extend the principle of their own particular historical world directly to other worlds, regarding this principle as universal" ("*Sekaishi no rinen*" (1) 348). But, when he takes the ethics of the family system, which he believes is unique to the East and fully incorporated in Japan, as the principle of the new world order, he ends up doing the same thing as the advocates of the existent monism he himself criticizes. Sakai's criticism of the philosophers of world history—that the "[p]luralistic world history proves itself to be another version of monistic history" ("Modernity and its Critique" 113)—surely has reasoning in their own texts. Given that these philosophers believe the respect for hierarchical differences requires paternalistic authority, the existence of an aspiration for monistic unification in these philosophers' idea of the pluralistic world order is undeniable.

When Kōsaka speaks of the Greater East Asia Co-Prosperity Sphere in the last of the three symposia, he betrays this aspiration for the unification of multiple centers through praising the power of the single one, which is his own country:

> The ethics of the Greater East Asia Co-Prosperity Sphere is the ethics of "place," which puts each in the right place. Likewise, I think we can also take the logic of this sphere as the logic of place. It is the logic of the mediation by place, the logic through which subjects are mutually mediated exactly according to the purposeful plans on "things." Of course, mediation has its center, which is Japan. All subjects converge upon this center, are represented by, guided and organized from it. . . . (ST 101)

The logic of place mentioned here originates in the philosophy of Nishida Kitarō, founder of the Kyoto School and mentor of all its thinkers. Place, as he conceives of it, is that in which there can be anything, and yet which in itself is nothing. As such, place can be the mediator, making all things in it relate to and act upon each other. In this sense, Kōsaka likens Japan to place, insofar as it supposedly guides and organizes all the ethnic subjects in the Co-Prosperity Sphere. When he states that each subject is "put in the right place" through the mediation of "place," as equated with Japan, he distinguishes two kinds of place: the multiple places simply related to each other, and the single privileged place that mediates all of them. By making this distinction, he discloses that the ideal situation for the four thinkers, in which each is put in the right place, is possible only if all places are related to the single privileged place, just as the harmony of the family system is possible only under paternalistic authority. The ambiguity in the four thinkers' use of the term "place" corresponds to that of the term "the center," as illustrated by their statements that, on the one hand, there are many centers in the world and that, on the other, Japan is the center. Just as the coexistence of multiple centers depends upon the single privileged center, for these thinkers the situation in which all ethnic subjects are respectively put in the right places depends upon one single privileged place that is exceptional.

Nishida's equation between place and nothingness, tacitly assumed in Kōsaka's aforementioned remark, has significant implication considering that the four thinkers regarded nothingness as the principle of world history and the source of the moral energy driving it. When likening Japan to place,

Kōsaka gives it the role of nothingness. He thus equates Japan with the source of moral energy, rather than one of the points from which it manifests itself. The single, privileged "center" is synonymous with this source. As we have seen elsewhere in the four thinkers' discussions, the confrontation with absolute nothingness, as the ground for the world and the principle of its history, was supposed to give Japanese national subjectivity a global character. However, equating Japan and place qua nothingness, as Kōsaka does, amounts to confining absolute nothingness within the national, and thus ruins its allegedly global character. As a result, the second character of this subjectivity—the interpenetration between the national and the international—is itself undermined, while the latter is subordinated to the former in order to buttress it.

Another consequence of the equation between Japan and place as nothingness is the creation of the illusion that Japanese national subjectivity is not an agent of action. Or, if it is, the agent is one of selfless action devoted to its mission and annihilating itself. Yet, Kōsaka's remark that Japan is the center upon which the subjects of other states or ethnic groups concentrate, and through which they are represented, guided, and organized, alludes to the existence of strong, centralized power. As a matter of fact, the construction of this sphere was the outcome of Japan's invasions of other Asian countries, and the maintenance of this sphere required the oppression of the peoples living there. Nevertheless, Kōsaka reduces the strong centralization through such violent measures to the function of mediation of interaction among other states or ethnic groups, and delineates this centralization as a natural and peaceful matter of course without invasion or oppression. The equation of Japan and nothingness enables him to behave as if neither the subject of this state, nor its positive actions, existed. Combined with the idea of the ethical subject of responsibility, which is rooted in Japanese tradition and whose existence and absence are united, this equation results in the assertion that the deeds of the Japanese national subject, as the subject of responsibility, are ethical. The thought of place as nothingness cooperates with the logic of unity between the being and nothingness of the subject of responsibility in order to disguise the reality of Japan's deeds in the war.

No matter how much high-flown language is used, just as the world order constructed under the paternalistic authority of a single state cannot respect the genuine plurality of different worlds, the national subject that struggles for the construction of such a world order under its own authority cannot have a profoundly international perspective. This consequence becomes more understandable given the isomorphism between the way in which Kōyama carries his argument and the logical structure of the four thinkers' discussions concerning the internationality in Japanese national subjectivity.

First, Kōyama argues that the ethics characteristic of Oriental tradition can resolve the problems and correct the errors resulting from the moral ideals of Western modernity. In doing so, he maintains the superiority of Oriental tradition over Western modernity. Finding the best embodiment of these ethics in Japan, he then claims its leadership of the East and of the world. In turn, as I discussed previously, the four thinkers treat Oriental nothingness as the absolute ground of world history, encompassing the East and the West, and insist that its ideal embodiment could be found in Japanese people's way of life, as epitomized by the samurai's ethics of responsibility. In both cases, the first step is to argue that Oriental tradition surpasses Western modernity and influences the entire world. The next step is to argue that Japan is the epitome of this tradition and therefore should have a special status in the world. This line of argument is reminiscent of Nishitani, who in his contribution to the *Bungakukai* symposium claimed that Japan could overcome Western modernity by resolving its defect by virtue of Oriental religiosity epitomized in Japanese spirit and tradition.

This isomorphism indicates the consistency of the logic or way of thinking common among the four thinkers. In light of this, their idea of the interpenetration between the national and the international in Japanese subjectivity does not necessarily lead Japanese people to broaden their horizons to the world, nor to make a neutral community for all its members. Rather, it tends toward convincing them of Japan's privileged status in the world because the global is concentrated in Japanese culture and tradition. The interpenetration between the national and the international in this subjectivity becomes merely an appearance of the former's subjection to the latter in order to legitimize Japan's authority in the international sphere. The world-historical mission to be assumed by Japanese national subjectivity, as the four thinkers conceive of it, is after all the establishment of Japan's international hegemony on the pretext of respecting the differences among those living under this hegemony. Even though these thinkers brought the world into view and spoke a great deal about it, Sakai is right in perceiving "what they wished to realize was to change the world so that the Japanese would occupy the position of the center and of the subject which determines other particularities in its own universal terms" ("Modernity and its Critique" 113).

Chapter 5

The Reciprocal Determination between the Virtual and the Actual

The Third Characteristic of Japanese National Subjectivity

As discussed in the previous chapter, the pluralistic world order with many centers, which the four thinkers claimed to be constructed by Japanese national subjectivity, turned out to be the integration of plural states or ethnic groups under Japan's hegemony. This subjectivity's alleged global character, which should define this world order's pluralistic nature, turned out not to exist as such, insofar as this character was reduced to the national in order to serve it.

Nevertheless, the four thinkers still ventured to legitimize this hegemony itself, without camouflaging it as pluralistic. They did so by further developing their discussions on Japanese national subjectivity in the *Chūōkōron* symposia. To buttress their arguments, they asserted the virtual subsistence of what was to be created and its inherent righteousness. This assertion, or indeed the invention, of the virtual not only enabled one to see the actual differently in light of the supposedly virtual. But, by asserting the necessity of the actualization of the virtual, it also enabled one to solicit the creation of this subjectivity.

The assertion or invention of the virtual does not always allow for the reinterpretation or alteration of the actual—nor vice versa. The assertion or invention of the virtual that should be necessarily actualized often bases itself upon what actually exists as alleged proof of this actualization. This assertion or invention of the virtual entails the reinterpretation or reconstruction of the actual. Besides, when the goal is to justify an already established state of affairs, it is the reinterpretation of the actual that calls for the invention of the virtual that can give the actual a new meaning. The invention of the virtual that should be actualized can be either a cause or an effect of the reinterpretation of the actual into which the invented virtual should have been effectuated. As such, the invention of the virtual is inseparable from and complementary with the reinterpretation of the actual. To this extent, it is not only the virtual that determines the actual, but also the actual that determines the virtual. The third characteristic of Japanese national subjectivity conceived by the four thinkers is this reciprocal determination between its virtuality and actuality—it is posed sometimes as what virtually subsists, and sometimes as what should be actualized, while both aspects uphold each other.

In this chapter, I will inquire into this third characteristic of the Japanese national subjectivity envisioned by the four thinkers. First, I will provide an overview of how this reciprocal determination between the virtual and the actual had been already operative in these thinkers' discussions about Japanese national subjectivity and the philosophy of world history. Second, I will inspect one side of this reciprocal determination perceived in these thinkers' discussions, that is, the aspect in which the assertion or invention of the virtual potential of this subjectivity requires the reinterpretation or alteration of its actual state of affairs. I will focus upon how this aspect of the thinkers' argumentation works to buttress their arguments to legitimate Japan's hegemony to be established. Third, I will inspect the other side of this reciprocal determination, that is, the aspect in which the reinterpretation of the actual deeds of this subjectivity requires the invention of its virtual potential that should have been actualized through them. Here, I will focus upon how this approach works to buttress their arguments to justify the warfare Japan had carried out until then, and would continue. This inquiry will elucidate the nature of the Japanese national subjectivity that would result from its third characteristic. Thereby, the determination of the actual by the virtual, and the determination of the virtual by the actual, are coordinated to work together and promote each other.

Section 1: Entering the Circle, Resolving the Contradiction

Let me start by overviewing how the reciprocal determination between the actual and the virtual was already operative in the four thinkers' discussions on Japanese national subjectivity and the philosophy of world history.

When discussing the first characteristic of Japanese national subjectivity—that is, the unity between the subject and substratum of the state—I sought to draw out the reason Nishitani does not hesitate to disregard the gap between them in the logic of the unity of being and nothingness of the subject of responsibility. This should coincide with Japanese national subjectivity. Another reason, which is not unrelated, could lie in the assumption of the reciprocal determination between the actual and the virtual in this subjectivity. Provided that Nishitani thinks from the standpoint of a national collectivity and its autonomy, drawing upon the unity of the state and citizens to be reconstructed retrospectively, he is in the circle between what is supposed to virtually subsist and what should be actualized. By relying on this reciprocal determination between the virtual and the actual, he could also easily ignore the gap between the state and citizens.

Thus, the reciprocal determination between the actual and the virtual supplements and enforces the logic of the unity of the subject's being and nothingness. Strictly speaking, what allegedly subsists virtually and nothingness are not the same. However, both the logic of the unity of being and nothingness of the subjectivity at issue, and the reciprocal determination between the virtuality and actuality of this subjectivity, can create the appearance that what is actually not there somehow exists on another level. The logic of unity between being and nothingness can buttress the claim that citizens' subjectivity exists in their abandoning individual subjectivity and becoming the substratum of the state. The idea of the reciprocal determination between the actual and the virtual can buttress the claim that a national collectivity, even if it has not properly organized in the present, has been and will always be there. Combined, these two conceptual devices cooperate to disguise the gap between the state and its citizens that is entailed in the Japanese national subjectivity conceived as the substratum of the state.

The effect of thus creating an appearance is not just a matter of appearance itself. For, by professing itself as reality, the appearance thus created can realize the state of affairs it corresponds to. Once this happens, the gap between what is actually there and what should be virtually there disappears, as if it had not existed in the first place. In the reciprocal determination between the virtual and the actual, the gap between what is supposed to be virtually there and what is actually there can be resolved by actualizing the supposedly virtual. Speaking from Nishitani's standpoint, even if there is a gap between the controlling state and controlled citizens, it will disappear through the creation of a national collectivity in which citizens completely identify with the state. Or, when Japanese people enact self-annihilation and devotion to public service, even if through the state's compulsory measure, there will be no gap between these people's actual lives and the alleged Japanese traditional virtues that are believed to have subsisted since ancient times.

It is not only in Nishitani's thought that we can find the circularity between what has allegedly existed for a long time, what should be virtually there all the time, and what is not there in the present and should be actualized. The same circularity also manifests itself in his and his three colleagues' discussions about how to conceive a new collective Japanese subject in the *Chūōkōron* symposia. The four thinkers assert that the ideal human type and the virtues to be practiced by it have already been realized in Japanese tradition, yet they also call on contemporary Japanese, viewed as not actually fulfilling this type, to model themselves on these ideals. From the standpoint of the project to produce this subjectivity's advocates, this circle between what should be virtually there and what should be actualized is not a contradiction between these two opposites, but a process to go through so as to overcome their contradiction in the very production of this subjectivity.

This stance toward the circle between the actual and the virtual coincides with the stance of the practical subject of world history. Such a subject discerns and follows the necessity qua ethicality of world history on the one hand, while on the other, it realizes this necessity qua ethicality and directs the course of world history. When this subject, by its moral acts, concretizes moral energy as the driving force of world history, it makes itself an agent of this energy and, as such, moves and creates world history. Viewed from the standpoint of this subject, world-historical necessity qua morality, which allegedly has been "actual," is now potentially there, waiting for its actualization. Yet it cannot be verified as actual necessity or morality unless it is realized in history through the acts of the subject.

This circle between the actuality and virtuality of world-historical necessity qua morality corresponds to the circle taken for granted by the four thinkers between the persistence of ideal human types or traditional virtues throughout Japanese history and the need to realize them by people's practice in contemporary Japan. If the characteristics of the Japanese national subject to be created and those of the practical subject of world history coincide as above, it is because these thinkers believed that the former should become the latter. In either case, these thinkers enter the circle between the virtuality and the actuality of the subjectivity they envision and try to overcome their contradiction by creating this subjectivity. Given this, it is natural the virtuality and actuality of this subjectivity determine each other.

However, this way of resolving the circularity is vulnerable to the risk of arbitrarily inventing the virtual to which the actual should adjust itself, or of perceiving actualization to be that of the idealized virtual. The four thinkers' framing of Japanese national subjectivity as a practical subjectivity of world history is not immune to this risk. Next, I will look into how this risk affects these philosophers' thoughts about Japanese national subjectivity with regard to the two directions of the reciprocal determination between the virtual and the actual—one in which the virtual determines the actual, and the other in which the actual determines the virtual.

Section 2: Ancient Spirituality and Eternal Subjectivity

I will now turn to the reciprocal determination between the virtual and the actual, that in which the former determines the latter. In tracking the four thinkers' arguments to legitimate Japan's hegemony, I will survey how these thinkers ended up arbitrarily inventing the virtual to which the actual should adjust itself.

In the four thinkers' discussion to establish Japan's leadership, or its special position that necessitates it to assume the world-historical responsibility, Suzuki stated that "as the most familiar reason of Japan's leadership, isn't it necessary to take into account the fact that Japan had 'modernity'?" (ST 94). Kōsaka stated that "[b]y positively participating in the modern world, Japan grasped the truth of this world and perceived its error" (ST 96). In the previous chapter, I examined the contradictions entailed in the countermeasure these thinkers had proposed to "correct" this error. However, their presupposition for this proposal that seeks the reason for Japan's special position in its modernization was a double-edged sword.

First, these thinkers judged that Japan could become a practical subject of world history and would follow and realize the necessity qua morality of this history, because Japan rivalled Western powers and challenged their hegemony as the only non-Western country that could achieve modernization through Westernization. This method of judgment, however, puts the four thinkers in a dilemma as they try to make this practical subject and the Japanese national subject correspond. On the one hand, the Japanese national subject must be compatible with modernization, for the denial of modernization would undermine its capacity to be a practical subject of world history. However, this alone is not enough. To challenge Western hegemony, Japan must have its own unique subjectivity invulnerable to Western influence. Otherwise, Japan would become a mere imitator and follower of the West.

In response to such ambivalent requirements, the four thinkers give a picture of the virtually subsisting national subjectivity underlying Japan's modernization. Suzuki states, "it is not that Japan was subjugated to European modernity because it did not have its own modernity, but that Japan actively and subjectively modernized itself, and we can find Japan's subjectivity in the fact that it has undergone this process" (ST 95). Kōyama subsequently comments, "the fact was that because Japan was autonomous, it could freely adopt European stuff" (ST 95). Suzuki and Kōyama emphasize that Japan was able to adopt Western things and modernize itself due to its active, free and autonomous subjectivity. In doing so, they explain Japan's modernization, not as the result of dependence on or the subjugation to the West, but as the result of Japan's inner nature. They complement the external determination of Japan's capacity to become a world-historical subject with its internal determination. Going one step further, Nishitani tracks the source of Japan's subjectivity back to its antiquity:

> It is a fundamental fact that Japan possessed modernity in the global sense. At the same time, behind this fact, there is another fundamental fact that Japan possesses "antiquity." Paradoxically, we can also say that Japan could have modernity by having antiquity. (ST 96)
>
> In short, something ancient or older had been alive and active in Japan until the present, and consequently Japan could become modern. Here is a characteristic not seen in other countries. This is, after all, I think, the flexibility of the Japanese spirit. (ST 97)

By seeking the cause of Japan's successful modernization in its spirit, which has persisted since ancient times in this way, Nishitani claims the persistence of the subjectivity both peculiar to Japan yet compatible with modernization. It was by extending this line of thought that Kōsaka goes so far as to say: "By positively participating in the modern world, Japan grasped the truth of this world and perceived its error" (ST 96). He continues, "This is thanks to the clean and right spiritual power that has existed in Japan from the ancient times" (ST 96). He invokes the Japanese spirit from ancient times as the reason Japan can accomplish modernity and go beyond it. Thus, it is in this persistent ancient spirituality that Japanese national subjectivity finds the grounds for its capacity to become a practical subject of world history, to rival Western powers, and to challenge their hegemony.

Then, what did these Kyoto scholars believe this ancient Japanese spirituality was like? Kōsaka, above, refers to this as "the clean and right spiritual power." Kōyama once described the spirit that constitutes Japanese civilization as "the spirit equating the self and the absence of the self," which consists of "turn[ing] oneself selfless, and train[ing] oneself so as to recall this state everyday anew" as "a sort of way or maxim to arise moral vitality" (ST 105). Elsewhere in the *Chūōkōron* symposia, Kōsaka insists that during the Nara period, around the time when *Man'yōshū*, the oldest collection of Japanese poetry, was compiled, ancient Japanese people had an "awareness of individuality, which is close to the vigorous life of a natural person" (SN 168). Immediately following this, Kōyama delineates a distinctive feature of the mentality he believes Japanese people had in the Nara period, an ancient era in which *Man'yōshū* was complied: "[T]here is no consciousness of schism or opposition between the state and individuals, but both are directly in harmony, so that for them to live for the state is to live for themselves, and vice versa" (SN 168).

The different points raised in these statements may seem to have no connection with each other. However, as formulated in Nishitani's essay contribution to the "Overcoming Modernity" roundtable, they do. What Nishitani describes as "clean and bright mind" (*seimeishin / kiyoki akaki kokoro*) (OM 61; translation modified by referring to Kawakami et al. 35) overlaps with what Kōsaka refers to as "the clean and right spiritual power" (*kiyoku tadashii seishinryoku*). Nishitani asserts citizens of the state of Japan acquire clean and bright minds "in their efforts at professional mastery and self-annihilation," and in doing so "they can merge with the fountainhead of state life that runs throughout national history" (OM 62; translation modified by referring to Kawakami et al. 35). Following this line of thought, what Kōsaka describes as the "clean and right spiritual power" that enabled Japanese people to accept modern Western civilization and perceive its error, was, in words, cultivated by "turn[ing] oneself selfless, and train[ing] oneself so as to recall this state [of mind] everyday anew." This is a way of emptying and purifying one's mind. This state of mind coincides with what Kōyama describes as ancient Japanese people's consciousness—individuals and the state as their society "are directly in harmony." In Kōsaka's eyes, this state of mind of the ancient Japanese "is close to the vigorous life of a natural person" who lives in harmony with nature.

Despite the affinity between Kōsaka and Kōyama's statements on the one hand, and Nishitani's on the other, there is a slight gap between them. However, this disparity is not an issue for these thinkers. Rather, this very gap works to facilitate the achievement of their goal, which, once achieved, will also bridge it.

On the one hand, Nishitani discusses how he believes contemporary Japanese people should behave in line with his argument about Japanese national subjectivity as the substratum of the state. On the other hand, Kōsaka and Kōyama discuss ancient Japanese spirituality, which they idealize and regard more natural than modern (Western or Westernized) consciousness.

What is to be noted is that Kōsaka and Kōyama describe the features of this ancient spirituality almost in the same way as Nishitani describes the elements of what he thinks is the ideal discipline for contemporary Japanese. In other words, between both sides, there is a gap between what should virtually subsist all the time and what should be actualized in the present; yet, these two things are equated with each other.

Given that the four thinkers shared the task of creating a certain type of national subjectivity and sought the suitable norm for it in Japanese history, it is natural that the ancient Japanese spirituality they invoke is modelled after the discipline they view as ideal to cultivate this subjectivity among contemporary Japanese people. Here, what should virtually subsist from the past is invented so it can determine what should be actualized in the present. To undergird this invention, the actual in the past—in this case the ancient Japanese consciousness in the Nara period—is reinterpreted, or even reconstructed, as the proof of the actualization of the virtual. Once the virtual is thus invented, it works to lead people to appreciate or solicit certain acts regarded as actualizing this virtual. This is how the Kyoto scholars' ideas of ancient Japanese spirituality naturalize and necessitate Japanese people's self-abandonment for, and identification with, the state. These thinkers present such behaviors as rooted in these people's inherent disposition from ancient times. When citizens are disciplined properly to organize themselves into the national subjectivity united with the state's substratum, ancient national spirituality will be incarnated in contemporary discipline, and there will be no distinction between them. In this way, once the supposedly virtual is actualized, the gap between what should be virtually subsistent all the time and what should be actualized will disappear as both become one in actualization.

The reciprocal determination between the virtual and the actual in the four thinkers' position on Japanese national subjectivity was the circle they inevitably entered. They did this as they worked to carry out their project to create this subjectivity in the capacity of practical subjects that should at once discern and realize the necessity qua ethicality of world history.

These thinkers sought the essence of ancient Japanese spirituality, which should still subsist as Japanese people's inherent disposition, in the aptitude for dedication to and identification with the state. However, naturalizing and idealizing such behaviors as proper to "Japaneseness" tended to prompt these people to effectuate such behaviors faithfully to this invented "spirituality" and "disposition." Here, the four thinkers arbitrarily invent the virtual to which the actual should adjust itself, and in doing so let the virtual take over and lead the actual in a certain direction.

This invention of the virtual culminates in these thinkers' idea of a transcendent structure that guarantees the subsistence of this subjectivity. Ironically, Kōyama broaches this when he discusses the idea that Japanese subjectivity is not an eternal Form:

> When advocating Japan's subjectivity, I think it is really important that this subjectivity is not apart from time, but proved in history. If we think subjectivity to be non-historical, it stops being subjectivity and turns into objectivity like [Platonic] Forms or Ideas. This point seems hard to understand. Japan's leadership today comes from the fact that it has accomplished modernity. Japan's subjectivity,

which has accomplished modernity and passed through it, and the spirit of moral subjectivity fundamentally different from that of Europe, have appeared today "by seizing an opportunity" [*toki wo ete*]. An eternal truth proves to be a truth by itself. For this to happen, history is necessary as the scene in which this truth proves itself. (ST 95–96)

By saying that Japanese subjectivity is not like Platonic Forms or Ideas, Kōyama means that this subjectivity cannot be reduced to an abstract, permanent, and invariable form of objectivity. Rather, it is a temporal being that should be concretely verified in history, when the time comes, through its practical acts. Given his criticism of Europe's "anti-historical power of taking solely the Anglo-Saxon world order as super-historical, and thinking the existent order to be the eternal order" (TRR 147), his intention in emphasizing the historicity of Japanese subjectivity is to counter European subjectivity, which is abstractly represented as permanent and unchangeable by Westerners to themselves and others. At first glance, he seems to claim something contrary to the persistence of Japanese subjectivity. Given that he still assumes the existence of an eternal truth and regards Japanese subjectivity as an agent proving this truth, however, this first impression turns out to be disappointing.

The question may arise as to whether or not an eternal truth deserves the name if it proves itself only at a certain point in time, as Kōyama states. As in contradiction, he then says that this truth has actually proved itself so many times throughout Japanese history, although it did not attain its authentic realization in world history. He describes this realization as something crucial that occurs "by seizing an opportunity:"

> The truthfulness of Japan has existed for eternity from ancient times. We can say that Japanese history is composed of the traces proving this truthfulness. However, for this truthfulness to realize itself authentically as the eternal truth, it must manifest itself by seizing an opportunity, both in the scene of Japanese history and in that of world history. (ST 99)

Kōyama insists that Japanese history is full of traces of facts that prove Japan's truthfulness. These, he argues, date from ancient times, while similar facts should also appear in world history when the time comes. This truthfulness originates in Japanese people's confrontation with absolute nothingness as the ground of the world and the principle of its history. The facts that prove Japan's truthfulness represent the way of life of these people, who annihilate themselves while facing absolute nothingness in order to accomplish their responsibilities, as epitomized by the samurai. When Kōyama declares that Japan's truthfulness, thus proven throughout its history, will also prove itself in world history, he expects that this proof will appear when Japan undertakes its world-historical responsibility and becomes a practical subject of world history. Describing the manifestation of Japanese subjectivity's truthfulness in world history as the authentic realization of the eternal truth accomplished by "seizing an opportunity," Kōyama contrasts this "eternal truth" to false ones, such as Platonic Forms or Ideas that serve as a model for European subjectivity and are represented as permanent, invariable, and without historicity.

In discussing the eternal truth that would "authentically" manifest itself when Japan establishes its world-historical subjectivity, Kōyama uses two different logics. When discussing the emergence of Japan's subjectivity in world history and the verification of the authentically eternal truth, he underlines, on the one hand, the historicity of "seizing an opportunity," in contrast to the eternity falsely represented as permanent and unchangeable. On the other hand, when it comes to the verification of this truth within Japanese history, he underlines the recurrence of innumerable facts proving this truth. Asserting that, "[t]he truthfulness of Japan has existed for eternity from ancient times" and gathering disparate "traces" of facts in Japanese history as attesting to this truthfulness, he affords this truthfulness a likeness to permanent and unchangeable Forms or Ideas underlying various appearances. If this truthfulness is thus eternalized, the subjectivity in which it is inherent will follow. The latent Japanese national subject appropriates the eternal truthfulness to be verified in world history. Thus, despite his criticism of the eternalization of European subjectivity, Kōyama himself eternalizes Japanese subjectivity differently. After all, Kōyama's criticism of the "anti-historical power of taking solely the Anglo-Saxon world order as super-historical and thinking the existent order to be the eternal order" (TRR 147) backfires on his own nation once the term "Japanese" replaces "Anglo-Saxon." When he maintains that Japan's truthfulness that has been proved in Japanese history will also attest itself in world history, he bases the historicity of Japanese subjectivity upon its eternity, which he establishes on another level. In doing so, he undermines his own emphasis on the historicity of Japanese subjectivity, which distinguishes it from European subjectivity.

Kōyama tried to oppose Japanese subjectivity—which he viewed as based on historicity and believed would appear on the scene of world history through opportunity—to European subjectivity represented as an eternal form. However, Japanese subjectivity had not appeared in his time even in Japan, and had yet to be created. To claim that what had not yet appeared would necessarily appear, his strategy was to assert its virtual subsistence, while seeking its alleged actualization in the past on a smaller scale through reinterpreting the actual. Hence, he turned to the idea that Japanese subjectivity and its inherent truthfulness, both of which quasi-eternally subsist, have proved themselves in national history, and will eventually be proved in world history. Based on this invention of the virtual, he related that actualizing this virtual subjectivity and proving its truthfulness in the scene of world history is a world-historical necessity. By abandoning themselves for the state, Japanese people could contribute to this mission, which would amount to establishing Japan's privileged status in the world. By maintaining the virtual had designated the direction in which the actual should go, his narrative tended to urge Japanese people into this self-abandonment, just as the naturalization or idealization of such behaviors through recourse to ancient Japanese spirituality did. Here again, the invented virtual takes over the actual, while the scope of the invention of the virtual expands further.

Section 3: The State that Is Always Right and Does the Right Thing

In the previous section I outlined one side of the reciprocal determination between the virtual and the actual operating in the four thinkers' approach of Japanese national subjectivity, namely the side in which the virtual takes over the actual. In this section, I will look into another, complementary side of this determination, namely that in which the actual takes over the virtual. Exemplifying the inseparability of the two sides of this reciprocal determination, these thinkers' invention of the virtual that determines the actual—that is, their assertion of the quasi-eternally subsisting Japanese subjectivity and its eternal truthfulness—drew upon the reinterpretation of the actual that determines the virtual at the level of national history. Likewise, as we will see, when the actual arbitrarily determines the virtual, the virtual thus invented also determines the actual in order to uphold it.

There is a moment in which these thinkers themselves justify the actual taking over the virtual when discussing the world-historical mission of Japan as a practical subject of world history. As we have seen, becoming this subject requires entering the circle between what should virtually subsist all the time and what should be actualized in the present, and thus revolving in this circularity between the virtual and the actual by effectuating the former into the latter. What throws the practical subject of world history into this circle is this subject's dual task of "responding to the call from world history and constituting the world itself" (TRR 145). On the one hand, the subject discerns in the course of world history its necessity qua ethicality and follows it, and in doing so, constitutes the world in which this necessity qua ethicality is realized and directs world history on the other. The world-historical necessity qua ethicality appears to this subject at once as what should virtually subsist and as what should be actualized. This subject's task consists of making these two elements coincide, and turning their circularity into a matter of fact through the actualization of the supposedly virtual. However, while rephrasing the description of this task, Kōsaka diverges from its original conception in a way that seems contradictory:

> In this time of upheaval, where will be the center of the world? Although, of course, economic or military power is also important, it must be given such a principle as a new worldview or new moral energy. Whether a new worldview or morality is established or not decides the direction of world history. Isn't it that the ones who can create such a worldview or morality come to lead world history? Now Japan is required by world history to find such a principle in the aforementioned sense. Japan is urged to do so and bears world-historical necessity, I feel like this. (SN 190)

Kōsaka's phrase, "the ones who create a new worldview or morality come to lead world history," describes something other than the aforementioned dual task. It suggests the creator of the worldview or morality can lead world history. In saying this, Kōsaka no longer cares whether this newly created worldview or morality accords with the world-historical necessity qua ethicality, which should be discovered before the act of creation, according to the original conception of the practical subject of world history. In light of this attitude, Suzuki's thesis that "historical necessity is subjective or indeed practical necessity" (TRR 122) appears in a different light. When a certain subject determines what historical necessity is, whatever it is, what is thus determined can become actual historical necessity. The world-historical necessity that is supposed to be virtually there, and be discovered, succumbs to the act of actualizing this very necessity, so that this act can determine and create this necessity. Here, the actual takes over the virtual, and the subject of actualization appropriates the world-historical necessity. When the four thinkers equate the act of creating a new worldview or morality with the realization of the world-historical necessity, they run the risk of asserting whatever actualization is to be that of the idealized virtual. Whereas the act of actualization, or even what is actualized by it, is given the power to determine what the virtual thus actualized is, this newly determined virtual, fabricated in adjustment to the actual, gives a convenient justification for the actual and the act of actualizing it. When the determination of the virtual by the actual is thus complemented by the determination of the actual by the virtual, this reciprocal determination between the virtual and the actual is reduced to the banal excuse, "First come, first served."

Reviewed from this perspective, the four thinkers' argument that Japan is qualified to seize global leadership because it is the only non-Western country that achieved modernization in their time betrays itself as a variant of this excuse. The fact that only a certain country among similar others could achieve something depended upon various kinds of factors which cannot be reduced merely to that single country's peculiar attributes. Inferring from this fact the necessity qua ethicality of world history that only that country can realize is nothing but asserting whatever actualization is to be that of the idealized virtual. Claiming the legitimacy of this country's efforts to seize global leadership with recourse to this necessity qua ethicality is nothing but giving a convenient justification for whatever further acts by professing them to be similar actualizations of this virtual. As such, the four thinkers' argument that connects Japan's modernization and global leadership "reveals a certain complicity between truth and forms of hegemonic power" in Kimoto Takeshi's words (113), in the sense that the one who first exercises power can claim to possess truth and in the name of this truth can further wields power over others.

The logic inherent in the above excuse "First come, first served" finds another expression in the four thinkers' arguments about the war. Regarding *Shina jihen*, the old name for the first phase of the Second Chino-Japanese War that spanned from the Marco Polo Bridge Incident to the launch of the Pacific War, Kōyama states:

> We should not ask whether the significance of the incident existed at the beginning. Rather we should newly create this significance and give it to the incident by our actions from now on. Waging the war comes to create its true significance. Whether we let the past live or die depends on present acts. (SN 191)

By saying that present acts may give life to the past incident, during which Japan launched the war against China, Kōyama is not suggesting amelioration of the cruel situations created by the incident. What matters to him is to "create" its "true significance," and to do so is by waging the war—this is what "present acts" are all about.

Following Kōyama, Kōsaka claims that the creation of this true significance is left to the very state that caused the incident:

> Of course, we cannot find the problem of history as we wish, for this problem appears through the mediation of the past. However, the meaning of history reveals itself where we voluntarily resolve

> this problem and develop a new world. The subjects of this solution are the national citizens. It is through the state that a new world opens itself. (SN 191)

Considering Kōyama's previous statement, the problem that appears through the mediation of the past, according to Kōsaka, is the incident whose ethicality was dubious, and yet whose occurrence was unchangeable fact. The resolution of this problem is to create a new meaning of this incident. The claim that this new meaning reveals itself where a new world is developed is in line with the aforementioned claim that the people who create a new worldview or morality come to lead world history and decide its necessity qua ethicality. In this light, if they develop a new world subsequent to the problematic incident of the past and assert the doctrine of this world to be a new world-historical necessity qua ethicality, they can change the meaning of this incident retrospectively, as if this new necessity qua ethicality had required this incident. Here, it is not just that what actually happened presides over the way in which the virtual is fabricated on the one hand, and that the virtual thus fabricated gives a justification to the actual on the other. To reinforce this justification of the actual and solidify the credibility of the virtual, these thinkers solicit further acts of actualizing the virtual in sequence. Here, they are mired in the vicious circle between the actual and the virtual and continue to reproduce this circle themselves.

Kōsaka regards the state and its citizens identifying themselves with it as the subjects of the development of a new world and the creation of the new meaning of the past. In doing so, he puts his trust in the goodness of the deeds of his own state and in the direction in which, through its deeds, it tries to lead world history. This conviction in the acts of actualization of the virtual is complementary to the conviction in the agent of this act. What exemplifies the latter is Nishitani's argument about the Asia-Pacific War near the end of the third roundtable discussion. Referring to Nietzsche, Nishitani relates, "people usually think that a good *Sache* [cause][1] makes a war holy; in other words, a war is called a holy one when its objective or motive is good, but in fact a good war makes a *Sache* holy" (ST 106). He continues by saying that the goodness of the war comes from the goodness of its subject:

> For example, the political guidance of a certain state is respectable, drawing upon a keen insight into the direction in which world history should proceed, and full of passionate moral spirit leading the citizens. And the citizens keep in mind the same spirit and comply with the guidance of the state—the war waged by such a state and citizens is, so to speak, a "good war" in Nietzsche's

sense, because the subject of the war is good and has a good standpoint. (ST 106)

Nishitani claims that the act of war in and of itself is neither good nor bad; if a state as the subject of an act is good, the war it wages is a good one. The war's goodness, derived from that of its subject, defines the goodness of the war's cause, and not the reverse. By this "good subject," he means Japan, and by the "good war," the Asia-Pacific War. At first glance, when he describes a good subject as the state having "a keen insight into the direction in which world history should proceed" and "passionate moral spirit leading the citizens," he does not seem to presuppose the goodness of the subject. However, considering that the philosophers of world history came to speak of the creation of world-historical necessity qua ethicality by the practical subject, "the direction in which world history should proceed" is, after all, the direction in which the state as such a subject tries to lead world history. Following this, the morality by which the state leads its citizens is the morality the state establishes. As such, these descriptions cannot provide sufficient criteria of a good state. The consequence is the assertion that the state that tries to lead world history in the direction it wishes is good.

Proceeding from this thesis, these thinkers fall into a tautological circle: they claim the state is good because the deeds of the state are good, which also works to confirm that the state is good, and so on. Yet, the subjectivity of this state has not been produced, nor have its creative deeds been achieved. If these thinkers nevertheless continue to rely on such absent subjectivity and its unaccomplished deeds, it is because they take for granted the reciprocal determination, indeed the confusion, between the actual and the virtual in the subject and its practice.

I have examined the reciprocal determination between the virtual and the actual in the four thinkers' ideas of Japanese national subjectivity with an eye to the two sides of this determination—that is, one in which the virtual determines the actual, and the other in which the actual determines the virtual. On the one hand, these thinkers' position on the virtual determining the actual culminates in their assertion of the virtual subsistence of Japanese subjectivity and its eternal truthfulness, and of the necessity for Japanese people to devote themselves to the state as proof. On the other hand, their arguments on the actual determining the virtual uphold the belief in the inherent goodness of the actually existing state. They thus viewed Japan's deeds as also inherently good, as if no matter what it does would meet the necessity or ethicality of world history. The combination of these assertions constitutes the dogmatic conviction in the righteousness of the state of Japan and its deeds both in terms of reality and potential. While the first side of the reciprocal determination enables one to give what does not exist the appearance of existence and the power to move people, the second side enables to give what exists or what has happened excessive meaning beyond the real state of affairs. The two sides' complementing each other works to intensify this dogmatic conviction, while magnifying it in the light of eternal truthfulness.

Chapter 6

The Outcomes of the Two Projects at Stake in Japanese National Subjectivity

So far, I have examined the three notable characteristics of the Japanese national subjectivity the four thinkers attempted to create, as articulated in their discussions in the *Chūōkōron* symposia and their relevant works published around that time. Through this examination, I have elucidated the problems involved in these characteristics. In this last chapter of part 1, I will proceed by reflecting on the kind of subjectivity that is shaped by these characteristics. I will then return to the two issues raised in relation to not only the *Chūōkōron* symposia, but also to the *Bungakukai* symposium. The first is the possibility of the ethical transformation of Japan and its policies through these thinkers' discourses. The second is the question of "overcoming modernity," broadly considered.

First, I will consider whether the Japanese national subjectivity thus envisioned could theoretically contribute to the ethical transformation of the Japanese empire and its military policies from within. I will also clarify what significance it has to thus elucidate the problems involved in the four thinkers' thought articulated in their discourses, rather than presuming their "real" intentions behind the texts. Second, I will assess the four thinkers' project of "overcoming modernity" to be carried out through this subjectivity, as it surfaced in their discussions in the *Chūōkōron* symposia and in Nishitani's works around that time. In reference to some postwar and contemporary scholars' reflections upon the defects of projects of overcoming modernity broadly carried out in wartime Japan, I will illuminate the problems of the four thinkers' project in a wider perspective.

Section 1: The Impossibility of Ethical Transformation from Within

Thus far, I have examined the three characteristics of the Japanese national subjectivity envisioned by the four thinkers and their characteristic problems. Now, after reviewing the result of this examination, I will return to the question of whether the creation of this subjectivity could contribute to the ethical transformation of the state of Japan from within.

At first glance, the four thinkers' conception of the three characteristics of Japanese national subjectivity might seem to provide a balanced position that synthesizes the opposites, allegedly expressed in their concept of this subjectivity. This, however, turns out not to be. In terms of the first and second characteristics, the two aspects that are to coexist and interrelate equally in fact do not—instead, one of them dominates and appropriates the other. The unity of the subject and substratum of the state is possible through the reduction of the former with respect to the latter, and the interpenetration between the international and the national in Japanese subjectivity is an appearance given to the former's subjugation to the latter. In terms of the third characteristic—the reciprocal determination between the actuality and the virtuality of this subjectivity—it is not necessarily the case that one of the two terms dominates and appropriates the other. However, this reciprocal determination amounts to confusion between them, to the translation of one to the other in a self-serving manner, and lends itself to the firm belief in this subjectivity existing continually from the past into the future.

If each of these three characteristics had produced a proper synthesis of the two opposites, the Japanese national subjectivity bearing these characteristics might have been that which the four thinkers claimed it to be. The unity between this subjectivity's status as the subject and substratum of the state might have brought about the situation in which citizens dedicate efforts to reforming their state, and the state dedicates efforts to improving citizens' lives. The interpenetration between the national and the international in this subjectivity might have given it the aptitude for succeeding national tradition without being caught up in national egoism. Instead, it might have led to a position concerning itself with the international situation, thus pursuing the construction of fairer international relations in cooperation with other peoples across national borders. The reciprocal determination between the virtual and the actual in this subjectivity might have urged it into unremitting efforts to realize ethicality in the state and its international relations without indulging itself in the dogmatic belief in the state's inherent goodness. If this had been the case, this subjectivity might have become worthy of a practical subject of world history. If so, the four thinkers' discourses on the ethicality of Japan and its military policies might have been perceived as intended for the ethical transformation of the very things whose ethicality is discussed, enabled by the creation of this subjectivity.

However, given that the three characteristics of this subjectivity turn out to be not what they seem, this subjectivity cannot but reveal itself differently. The confusion between the virtual and the actual allows for the assumption of the existence of essentially truthful national subjectivity, which has not actually existed in the present and yet should be virtually there in order to be actualized. The assumption of the collective subjectivity, subsisting from the past into the future, makes it easier to urge citizens to identify with this subjectivity. The belief that this subjectivity has traditionally consisted of annihilating oneself in accomplishing one's responsibility justifies the state's demand that citizens should abandon their personal subjectivities and be integrated into the substratum of the state. The internationality, which this subjectivity is supposed to attain in the face of Oriental nothingness as the ground of the world and the principle for its history, is used to qualify Japan to represent the East in its challenge to Western hegemony and to establish another hegemony under the pretext of creating a better world order. This subjectivity then produces the collective imagery that citizens' accomplishment of their responsibility of devoting themselves to the state contributes to the state's accomplishment of its world-historical responsibility, thus promoting their further self-annihilation.

Here, the third characteristic of this subjectivity—the reciprocal determination between the virtual and the actual—in giving what does not exist the appearance of existence and what exists excessive meaning gives life to the first and second characteristics while camouflaging their deceptions. The idea of absolute nothingness, the confrontation with which plays a key role in the first and second characteristics, bridges them and provides a conceptual link between citizens' devotion to the state and the state's world-historical mission. At the same time, it charges them with an aura of holiness. The same aura shrouds the third characteristic, due to its affinity with the logic of the unity between the being and nothingness of the subjectivity formed in the face of absolute nothingness. Here, the confusion between the actual and virtual is sanctified. Thus, the idea of absolute nothingness underlies the three characteristics and undergirds their cooperation.

The Japanese national subjectivity, shaped by the combination of the three characteristics, draws upon the dogmatic belief in the truthfulness of the state of Japan and its actions. This belief is derived from the third characteristic and permeates the other two. This belief, once accepted, lends an appearance of legitimacy to the subjugation of Japanese citizens to their state and the subjugation of other ethnic groups to the Japanese empire, promoting the integration of all these people into this subjectivity. The logic of the unity of the being and nothingness of the subject of responsibility, identified with this national subject, obscures the existence of a subjugating power and its agent and disguises the deeds of this subject as ethical. The discourses that call on people for creating such subjectivity can hardly promote the ethical transformation of Japan and its policies from within. For, they presuppose the truthfulness of the state and its deeds and, based on this presupposition, insist on the reinforcement and expansion of the state's power, whether over its citizens or over other states and ethnic groups.

In the afterword to his "Worldview and Stateview," added in 1946 following the Asia-Pacific War, Nishitani retrospectively explains the intention of this essay as "cleav[ing] a path in thought that, in confrontation with ultranationalism that was becoming prominent at that time, might overcome it from within" (NKC IV 384). However, considering the nature of the Japanese national subjectivity the four thinkers tried to create, presumably dovetailing with the intention of this essay, their project does not seem to provide even an attempt at overcoming ultranationalism from within. For, aside from the façade of their internationalism, the philosophers who engaged in this project seem neither to reject a nationalistic assumption, nor to free themselves from ethnocentrism, both of which they share with ultranationalists.

There can be disagreement within nationalism or ultranationalism, but dissenting viewpoints do not necessarily prove themselves to be a true resistance to either position. A position that confronts one form of ultranationalism or nationalism can prove to be just another form of it. A position that professes to be more "open" to the world, thus "overcoming" ultranationalism, might still keep intact the ethnocentrism at the core and facilitate the integration of other ethnic groups under that nation's hegemony. In fact, such a position can more suitably support imperialism than exclusivist ultranationalism does. What matters here is the ideological affinity between the four thinkers' discourses in the *Chūōkōron* symposia and the *Bungakukai* symposium on the one hand, and wartime ideologies on the other. The problem is that such discourses currently tend to be presented as anti-war, pacifist, or cosmopolitan discourses that resisted such ideologies with the goal of overturning the wartime regime.

Of course, given the wartime censorship and control over speech at the time, we cannot completely deny the possibility that the four thinkers might have attempted to dignify the Japanese people through such discourses, that they had no choice but to obey the government to avoid arrest and imprisonment.

Finding "higher" freedom and autonomy in citizens' forced obedience to, and self-sacrifice for, the state; discerning in the state's brutal expansionist policies, which they were forced to support and participate in, the seeds for a better, ethical world; seeing reality in light of ideals beyond it and conferring upon reality the potential to effectuate these ideals. All these might have been done out of the concern for the people who could not find significance in what the government did, and yet obliged them to. In the situation in which all resistance to the state was supressed, even if it was almost impossible for civilians to change the status quo, the four thinkers might at least have tried to give different meanings to it so as to make it bearable. Their idea of a subjectivity whose being is one with nothingness and is created through self-annihilation might have implicitly alluded to their wish for a small possibility to change the unchangeable status quo through enduring it.

It is impossible to know these thinkers' intentions as they *really* were, especially given doubt has been cast onto the sincerity of their own retrospections. For example, Kobayashi Toshiaki perceives a marked gap between Kōsaka's postwar vindication of his and his colleagues' position during the wartime, namely that they exhorted "Japan's self-negation, the state's self-negation," and these thinkers' actual wartime statements (*The Melancholy of Nishida Kitarō* 263–64). If we were to suppose these Kyoto thinkers had "real" intentions of resisting the wartime regime through their discourses in whatever way, from the standpoint of present readers there remains a large gap between two issues. The first is the existence (or at least the possibility) of such intentions behind their wartime discourses, and the second are interpretations of such discourses as constituting a resistance, including the parts that significantly overlap with wartime ideologies. If the confusion of these two things goes unchallenged, invoking (even without proving) the existence of "real" intentions of resistance would be a good enough excuse to treat the commonalities between such discourses and wartime ideologies as constituents of alleged "pacifism" or "cosmopolitanism" of the thinkers in question. Even though such pacifism or cosmopolitanism, as expressed in their discourse as a whole, is permeated by ethnocentrism, this point would not be problematized. As a result, ethnocentrism would succeed in infiltrating into, and becoming disguised as, pacifism or cosmopolitanism. The claim of this pacifism or cosmopolitanism would be that a certain country's seizing global hegemony, by whatever means, should bring peace to the world and therefore should be approved. This was in fact a central dogma of wartime ideologies in tune with governmental propaganda. Presenting such discourses as expressions of pacifism or cosmopolitanism is not so different from reviving and promoting these very same wartime ideologies.[1]

In effect, and as much research has shown, when the transcripts of the roundtable discussions "Overcoming Modernity" and "Philosophy of World History" were published, they were accepted by general readers as constituting or even representing jingoistic ideologies. Even though these discussions alone did not drive people into war, the fact remains that a large majority of Japanese people enthusiastically supported Japan when it launched the Pacific War and found their own voice expressed in these discussions.

To oppose apologists of Japan's war efforts, who claim they were made for the sake of the independence of Asian countries under Western colonialism, Tsurumi Shunsuke, a representative of postwar Japanese liberal intellectual thought, makes the following comments in his *An Intellectual History of Wartime Japan 1931–1945*:

> "Greater East Asia" was an expression coined in response to the military needs of the Japanese Government in the 1940s. Towards the end of the war, when it became apparent that victory was impossible, the Japanese Government decided to give independence to the Asian nations, an action which cost them nothing because they took no measures to change the reality of situation. (40)

Tsurumi emphasizes the fact that many Asian countries achieved independence as the result of the war. However, he notes this does not mean the Japanese government waged the war for that specific purpose. For, as far as Japan retained military control of these countries, their independence was impossible. Therefore, Tsurumi insists, "the result was in fact liberation and independence, gained not through the intention of the Japanese Government but through the efforts of the people of Asia" (41). Incisively, Tsurumi quotes a remark on Japanese militarists famously made by Ba Maw, a Burmese political leader who became a prime minister of the independent state of Burma under Japanese occupation during the World War II:

> As for the Japanese militarists, few people were mentally so race-bound, so one-dimensional in their thinking, and in consequence so totally incapable either of understanding others, or of making themselves understood by others. That was why so much of what they did during the war in Southeast Asia, whether it was right or wrong, always appeared to be wrong to the people there. The militarists saw everything only in a Japanese perspective and, even worse, they insisted that all others dealing with them should do the same. For them there was only one way to do a thing, the Japanese way; only one goal and interest, the Japanese interest;

only one destiny for the East Asian countries, to become so many Manchukuos or Koreas tied forever to Japan. These racial impositions—they were just that—made any real understanding between the Japanese militarists and the peoples of our region virtually impossible.

The case of Japan is indeed tragic. Looking at it historically, no nation has done so much to liberate Asia from white domination, yet no nation has been so misunderstood by the very peoples whom it has helped either to liberate or to set an example to in many things. (Ba Maw 185: quoted in Tsurumi 38–39)[2]

While showing some compassion for Japanese people, who upheld the ideal of liberating Asia from Western colonial rule during the war, Ba Maw illustrates here the large gap between this ideal and the reality of Japan's military and colonial rule in Asia. Certainly, it is undeniable that some Japanese seriously believed in and lived according to this principle. Some even lent their support for Burma's independence movement. However, one-sidedly imposing this ideal with a high-and-mighty attitude, backed up by military force, and disregarding the people who are supposed to be liberated, does not necessarily help them—nor does it really amount to respecting or realizing their independence. We should think about how much arrogance is hidden in the assumption that they should naturally accept this imposition and understand its value. This is not only the case with "Japan's" military and colonial rule or the aforementioned "Japanese" philosophers who enthusiastically supported it.

"If the peoples in other countries accept our authority and obey our rule, they will live a peaceful, happier life, and the attitude of thus minding the world beyond the national borders is altruistic and cosmopolitan"—this kind of deceitful logic was, is, and can be used in any country at any time to instigate certain people to attack and subjugate others, while at the same time justifying this violence. This is not limited to wartime Japan. One of the objectives of my argument is to reveal the deception of this logic through the examination of the four philosophers of the Kyoto School in wartime Japan. It was necessary to focus on analyzing these philosophers' thoughts as articulated in their discourses, and the problems involved, so as to demonstrate how far from pacifism or cosmopolitanism they are. If one's ideal of a peaceful world carries with it a desire to dominate others, upholding it would easily amount to approving the exercise of violence against others in the name of this ideal. When this happens, it is unlikely the façade of pacifism or cosmopolitanism is enough to stop or prevent such violence. For it is this very façade that is (ab)used to promote and justify such violence.

Section 2: The Question on Overcoming Modernity

An examination of the three characteristics of Japanese national subjectivity reveals the four thinkers' efforts to criticize the political system, collective subjectivity and colonialism characteristic to Western modernity, and propose alternatives. Reflecting on these ideas provides us with a perspective from which to evaluate these thinkers' attempt to overcome modernity, their ongoing task in crafting their idea of Japanese national subjectivity and their philosophy of world history. But, seen from this perspective, the outcomes of their attempt are disappointing.

First, although Nishitani asserts that the state in which the subject and substratum are united could sublate absolutist states in early modern Europe and liberal states in modern Europe, the state in question preserved the unified ruling power over its people, which had been established in former states, and suppressed the freedom that had been attained in the latter. To celebrate this state as he does is to claim that the ideal state should reestablish the unified ruling power over its people, as in the absolutist states of early modern Europe, by rejecting personal freedom which characterizes the liberal states of the modern Europe of Nishitani's time.

Second, through recourse to the international in the essence of Japanese tradition, the four thinkers insisted on Japan's potential to construct a new world order with many centers, freed from colonialism under the rule of Western powers. However, since this new world order centered upon Japan and presupposed its authority, these thinkers fell into the contradiction of reproducing the same kind of hegemony of a specific group of humans over others as that which they criticized.

Third, the four thinkers criticized Europeans for eternalizing their subjectivity as if it were permanent and unchangeable. However, these thinkers at once historicized and eternalized Japanese national subjectivity by conveniently translating its actuality into virtuality and vice versa, and ended up allowing themselves to create a variant of the subjectivity they criticized others for constructing.

In terms of the first characteristic, the ideal state envisioned by Nishitani did not sublate the two state types he took as representative of Western modernity, but succeeded the power structure that he took as peculiar to one of them, supposedly overcome by the other. In terms of the second and third characteristics, these thinkers appropriated the detrimental mechanisms they found in the collective subjectivity and colonialism of Western modernity *mutatis mutandis*. Thus, their attempt at overcoming modernity amounted to circumventing what they professed to overcome. In other words, this allowed it to survive under a different guise.

The contradiction of criticizing others as evildoers, while perpetuating the same evildoings as them, was already evident in the "Overcoming Modernity" symposium. Many commentators have discussed this contradiction so far, and have found it not only in this symposium, but also in the discourses concerning the theme of "overcoming modernity" in a broader sense. Takeuchi Yoshimi, in his landmark 1959 essay "Overcoming Modernity," draws our attention to "[t]he Pacific War's dual aspects of colonial invasion and anti-imperialism" (124–25). He points out that these dual aspects constituted the war's double structure, which "involved the demand for leadership in East Asia on the one hand and a goal of world domination by driving out the West on the other hand" (Takeuchi, "Overcoming Modernity" 125). Takeuchi insists the symposium should have confronted this double structure and resolved its contradiction. If it had done so, he states, it might have been able to create an influential current of thought that could have led people to understand the war differently, and could have changed its nature, or even stopped it completely. Yet this was not the case:

> In sum, the "Overcoming modernity" symposium marked the final attempt at forming thought, an attempt that, however, failed. (Takeuchi, "Overcoming Modernity" 145)
> That the symposium produced such poor results . . . stems from the symposium's failure to dissolve the war's double nature, that is to say, its failure to objectify the aporias of modern Japanese history *qua* aporias. (Takeuchi, "Overcoming Modernity" 146)

In Takeuchi's eyes, the reason for the symposium's failure was that the contradictions, or aporias, to be tackled, including that of the war's double nature, were not even taken as such. Thus, the two contradictory aspects of the war were conveniently held together as if there was no conflict between them in the first place. Unsurprisingly, Takeuchi remarks, the consequence of ignoring the contradiction was the confirmation of common wartime ideology, and in this sense, "the disappearance of these aporias prepared the intellectual ground for Japan's colonization" ("Overcoming Modernity" 146).

Sharing Takeuchi's concern about the aporias in the war, Hiromatsu Wataru offers another viewpoint in his *Theories on "Overcoming Modernity"* (*"Kindai no chōkoku" ron*), originally published in 1980, followed by a re-edited version in 1989. Against Takeuchi's view that the symposium failed to achieve "its status as war and fascist ideology" ("Overcoming Modernity" 113) due to its failure to construct a decent theory, Hiromatsu insists that the Kyoto School's concept of overcoming modernity nevertheless constituted "a respectable form of 'war and fascist ideology' in its own way" (170). He suggests the Kyoto School's theories of overcoming modernity, rather than being unable to dissolve the war's double nature, "objectified the double nature by making it stand for-itself, 'united' the two aspects into one ideology and gave the aporia a 'solution' in the form of ideology." This is why "these theories gave the 'theoretical' basis for intellectuals' assistance for the wartime regime" (Hiromatsu 171). In fact, this comment does not mean what we think it means upon first reading. Hiromatsu's use of quotation marks for several words casts doubt on whether he used these words in their literal sense or not. His following remark clarifies what he really meant by these words.

> The theories of "overcoming modernity" ideologically embodied and articulated the world-historical "position" and "situation," in which "the ethnic Japanese" [*nihon minzoku*] put themselves, and their desire concerning a matter of life and death in such a position and situation—without sufficient scholarly analysis and grasp. (Hiromatsu 178)

In other words, theories lacking a "sufficiently scholarly analysis and grasp" cannot "unite" the contradictory double nature of the war, nor can they give its aporia a "resolution" or a "theoretical basis" for anything. Hiromatsu thus suggests the theories of "overcoming modernity" merely presented the double nature as united, and its aporia as resolved, but without really uniting or resolving either, in response to the collective desire of the people. His remark alerts us to the risk that even an ill-formed thought or an attitude of ignorance toward existing aporias can be capable of influencing reality, if the situation demands it or the people desire it.

Whether Japanese intellectuals who engaged themselves in wartime discourses of overcoming modernity succeeded in constructing a decent form of war and fascist ideology or not, the fact remains that these discourses neither resolved this aporia, nor articulated it clearly. This very unresolvedness and obscurity helped them support Japan's Asia-Pacific War. The same applies to the four thinkers' arguments concerning "overcoming modernity" in the *Chūōkōron* symposia. Koyasu Nobukuni, in his 2008 book *What Is "Overcoming Modernity"?* (*"Kindai no chōkoku" towa nani ka*), insists on the pertinence of the concealment of this aporia in these symposia to the justification of the war:

> These theories of "overcoming modernity" from beginning to end conceal the fact that the modernity to be overcome through the war is also but oneself who wages the war. The theories concerning "overcoming modernity" at the time of the war in the Shōwa period were constructed based on the concealment of the state of affairs

that Japan had undoubtedly achieved modernity as an imperialist state. (. . .) Such theories of "overcoming modernity" that are developed by concealing this modern state of Japan carrying out an imperialist war as one of great powers in the world, therefore, cannot but turn into a logic that advocates Japan's war." (248)[3]

Naturally, if it is accepted to turn one's eyes from one's own evildoings and to attack others for their wrongs, the result would be the selective and one-sided advocacy of these evildoings, without questioning what their evilness is and what is wrong with oneself. That is why, as Koyasu claims, the roundtable discussions that left the aporia between the dual aspects of Japan's war unresolved amounted to self-centered advocacy of the war from the side of the agent that waged it. This self-centeredness, which excuses one from the critical reflection upon one's own acts, derives from what I discuss as the dogmatic conviction in the righteousness of the state and its deeds. Through the lens of this conviction, there should be no aporia and, even if it appears, it should be dissolved over the course of time through the state's deeds.

However, given the aporia of the war at issue was unresolvable in the first place, the war efforts to resolve it would have to be extended and expand its scope indefinitely. What is more, the arguments to glorify such efforts should have been complemented by the arguments about the absolute, privileged uniqueness of the state and its people, who were the only ones qualified to carry on such interminable efforts toward the resolution of the unresolvable aporia. From this perspective, Takeuchi identifies principal constituents of wartime Japanese thought as follows: "Although mutually contradictory, total war, eternal warfare, and the ideals instituted at the 'nation's founding' united to form the official system of war thought ("Overcoming Modernity" 129). Takeuchi summarizes the Kyoto School's contribution to this system of thought as follows: "The Kyoto School did the most to logically explain the relations among total war, eternal warfare, and the ideal of 'nation founding'" ("Overcoming Modernity" 131).

Kimoto Takeshi, in his 2009 essay "Antinomies of Total War," more comprehensively understands total war, which by definition "exceeds all distinctions, determinations, and boundaries" (108), as encompassing eternal warfare. What Kimoto finds significant is that in the *Chūōkōron* symposia (especially the third symposium), the four Kyoto thinkers' "philosophical language systematically developed the implications of total war to the limit thereby revealing its internal contradictions" (98), such as "anticapitalism intensified exploitation and mobilization, anti-imperialism concealed domination and hierarchy, universal truth contained hegemonic power, war possessed an end but was endless, and war was peace and peace was war" (120). What

Kimoto pays attention to in these thinkers' discussions is "the performative meaning" (121) of exhibiting (neither tackling nor concealing) these contradictions in a specific way in association with the idea of total war that was supposed to resolve them if waged infinitely. Kimoto discusses the effect of this performance as follows:

> All-inclusive total war annihilated any oppositional logic and thus was absolute rather than relative. Thus it performatively produced a sense of the sublime, which was, in actual fact, realized through the operation of the wartime regime. War was to be expanded throughout all society in order to effect the mobilization of every social domain. (121)

The idea of total war that should undo any distinction or opposition concerning warfare had the effect of positioning the actual war as having the power to dissolve its contradictions—which it, of course, did not. This helped dignify the war and drive people to dedicate their efforts to it in all aspects of their social lives. Thus, according to Kimoto, the aporia, which had betrayed itself as unresolved and obscured in the *Bungakukai* symposium, found another articulation in the *Chūōkōron* symposia in the form of antinomies that were turned into "the driving forces behind total mobilization and subjection" (122) in the very capacity of unresolvable contradictions. The antinomic nature of the aporia is thus exploited to promote the war rather than disclose its dysfunctionality, while leaving almost no room to face or tackle the aporia as such. Along with the total mobilization outlined and facilitated by the idea of total war, Kimoto also emphasizes the significance of "the project of developing a productive subjectivity as one of the war's decisive conditions" (121). In his words, the subjectivity to be developed should have been "measured and defined by their resolution vis-à-vis the war efforts taking place in every social field," and also "disciplined through a sublime state of mind, as affected by the antinomic infinity of total war" (Kimoto 121).

Although from a different perspective, my argument so far thematized is that a similar project, carried out by the four thinkers of the Kyoto School, to create Japanese national subjectivity could serve the state and dedicate itself to its war with ardor. In scrutinizing their idea of this subjectivity, I focused on how they based this subjectivity upon the ethos and logic they found in Japanese indigenous tradition—or rather invented along with this tradition itself—to naturalize Japanese people's service to the state and dedication to the war. In doing so, I read in the *Chūōkōron* symposia on the philosophy of world history a line of thought that had developed an attempt at subject formation discerned by Calichman in the *Bungakukai* symposium on the theme of overcoming modernity. In examining the problems involved in the Japanese national subjectivity as conceived by the four Kyoto thinkers, I also elucidated the contradictions it harbors, including the aforementioned aporia concerning the war at issue, which many scholars have discussed, and yet which continues to be disregarded today.

The four thinkers' move of basing the national subjectivity, envisioned in view of the state's war, upon Japanese indigenous tradition in an essentialist manner raises further questions in light of the idea of total war. Here, war and peace become indistinguishable and the state's mobilizing force permeates all social domains and all aspects of citizens' lives. Although national subjectivity that is conceived based on alleged indigenous tradition or culture independently of war tends to be taken as "natural," is it freed from the violence against other kinds of people? Does this kind of subjectivity not have any structural similarities to the subjectivity intended for the agents of war? Here again, these questions do not exclusively concern Japan and Japanese people.[4]

It may be possible that the logic of total war, in whatever guise it appears, still determines our thoughts and actions to mobilize our lives to generate the antagonism between "us" and "them," even in peacetime through the seemingly "natural" idea of national subjectivity.[5] If this is the case, our vigilance for, and critical examination of, such determinations will have to be incessantly called for. While total war presents itself as permanent, efforts to make it fail, or at least to disclose its inherent dysfunctionality, will be endlessly needed.

Part 2

A Political Dimension of Nishida Kitarō's Philosophy of Nothingness

Chapter 7

Questions Concerning Nishida and Japanese Subjectivity

Naturally enough, the thought of the philosophers of world history, who belonged to the second generation of the Kyoto School, was greatly influenced by the thought of Nishida Kitarō, the four thinkers' mentor and founder of the Kyoto School. For example, the idea of absolute nothingness, which the four thinkers regarded as the ground of the world and the principle of world history in the *Chūōkōron* symposia, originally came from Nishida. We have seen how this idea cast a shadow upon these thinkers' discussions of Japanese national subjectivity. Qualifying a Japanese national subject as the subject of responsibility established in the face of absolute nothingness, these thinkers claimed that the being and nothingness, the existence and absence of the former subject, are united. Going so far as to equate Japan and nothingness, these thinkers asserted that Japan could also transform other nations or ethnic groups into similar subjects, so that they could cooperate harmoniously. The logic of unity between the being and nothingness of the subject, as well as the idea of absolute nothingness from which this unity derives, generated the appearance of Japan and its deeds actually being ethical. The paradox drawn from the logic that the Japanese national subject at once exists and does not exist obscured the fact that this subject shared the same detrimental mechanisms as other collective subjects it was supposed to counter. Thus, this logic not only undermined the possibility of the ethical transformation of Japan and its military policies, but also foiled their attempt at overcoming Western modernity.

Although such failures seem to be primarily the outcome of applying the idea of the subject established in the face of nothingness to a certain collectivity in a certain historical-political situation, it may be the case that the causes behind these failures are, among other notions, also inherent in the very idea of such a subject and the nothingness that enables it. An investigation of Nishida's philosophy with an eye to its relationship with his disciples' ideas of Japanese national subjectivity may offer a chance not only to further study the causes of these failures but also to explore the problems within this very philosophy.

However, before undertaking this investigation, I need to explain why I believe that an exploration of the affinity between Nishida and his disciples' philosophies in the prewar and wartime periods is legitimate, as well as to clarify from what standpoint I will carry out this exploration. There are divergent views about the relations between Nishida and his four disciples' prewar and wartime philosophies. This divergence overlaps with disagreements about Nishida's political stance at that time. Specifically, with regard to ideas of Japanese national subjectivity, there is a common claim that Nishida (different from his disciples who upheld their philosophy of world history), negated Japanese subjectivity, which he associated with imperialism. Therefore, exploring the affinity between Nishida and his disciples' philosophies around Japanese national subjectivity requires offering a counterargument to this claim. Proposing this counterargument will also involve specifying my own standpoint toward the ambiguity about Nishida's political stance.

In this chapter, I will first give evidence against the claim that Nishida negated Japanese subjectivity. By looking into the presuppositions of the scholars who disregard this evidence, I will show the overlap between positions that insist upon Nishida's negation of Japanese subjectivity, and the positions that assert the incompatibility of his philosophy with wartime ideologies. Second, I will give an overview of the controversy surrounding his political stance during the wartime period and show that a defense of Nishida as a liberal intellectual underpins the above two positions. With consideration of several scholars with different views about this, I will articulate my position and explain the reasons why I regard the exploration of his philosophical affinity with wartime ideologies as important. In doing so, I will show the pertinence of addressing the continuity and overlap between Nishida and his four disciples' philosophies.

Section 1: The Ambiguity in Nishida's Position toward Subjectivity

The four thinkers did not simply accept their mentor's ideas, but developed them in their own ways. Thus, doubts may arise as to whether or not we can trace the source of the problems with the four disciples' thought back to their master. This is especially relevant in terms of the motif of Japanese national subjectivity, and even in terms of subjectivity in general, as some scholars see a decisive difference between Nishida and his disciples. For example, in his short commentary on the Tōeisha version of *Theories of World History* (*Sekaishi no riron*), Mori Tetsurō comments that, around the time of the original publication of Kōbundō's book, Nishida "has deep misgivings about reducing history to a matter of the subject = substratum [*rekishi no "shutai-ka = kitai-ka"*]," while "Nishida's disciples launch a new attempt emphasizing 'subjectivity'" (SR 406). As for textual evidence of his stance, Mori refers to Nishida's statement in "The Problem of Japanese Culture" (*Nihonbunka no mondai*), which was published in 1940 and based on his 1938 lecture series: "What we should above all caution ourselves against is making Japan a subject" (NKZ XII 341).

Yet, this is just one side of the matter. Mori somehow disregards another statement made by Nishida soon thereafter, in which he qualifies Japan as a subject. In reference to his remark, "We should contribute to the world by finding the principle of the self-formation of the contradictorily self-identical world itself at the bottom of our historical development" (NKZ XII 341), Nishida continues, "That we demonstrate the principle of world formation lying at the basis of our [Japanese] history does not mean that Japan stops being a historical subject or stops being Japan" (NKZ XII 341–42). In these two cases, Nishida does not use the term "subject" in the same sense. The meanings behind Nishida's statements that Japan should not be made a subject, and that Japan continues to be a subject, need to be elucidated. It is noteworthy that Nishida took an ambiguous attitude toward subjectivity by negating and affirming its existence at the same time, before his disciples did the same. Given this, tracing the source of the problems with the four thinkers' ideas of Japanese national subjectivity, characterized by the unity of its being and nothingness, back to the thought of their mentor who first elaborated the concept of nothingness is not a pointless move.

Mori is not the only scholar who brings forward solely aspects of Nishida's philosophy that negate Japan subjectivity. Ueda Shizuteru and Yusa Michiko are among scholars who adopt a similar stance. Ueda quotes Nishida's above caution against making Japan a subject[1] together with the following passage in "The Problem of Japanese Culture": "To take a position as one subject vis-à-vis other subjects, and thereby to negate the others or try to reduce them to oneself, is nothing other than imperialism" (Ueda 84; quotation from NKZ XII 349: translated by Jan Van Bragt). Ueda then insists that "[t]hese words ... are unambiguous public criticism" (85) of the Japanese government's expansionist policies at that time:

> *In* [Nishida's] *opinion* the nation must not think of itself as a *subject* because this would be tantamount to *imperialism*. The words are as clear as the noonday sun, and nothing in the context can leave room for misunderstanding. It is hard to see how later critics can have overlooked them or misrepresented their intent. (85)

Strangely, Ueda disregards Nishida's aforementioned affirmative remark on Japan's subjectivity that, Nishida himself insisted, should be attained paradoxically when Japan negates its own subjectivity in the usual sense, although the existence of this remark in the same essay is "clear as the noonday sun" as well. In the words of Ueda wondering about later critics: "it is hard to see how [he could] have overlooked" these words from Nishida.

Yusa also emphasizes Nishida's negation of Japanese subjectivity with the admonishment that "[Japan] cannot afford to become a subjectivistic power unto itself" ("Nishida and Totalitarianism" 126). Although Yusa refers to "the principle of the self-formation of the contradictory self-identical world itself" ("Nishida and Totalitarianism" 127), a concept Nishida discussed in "The Problem of Japanese Culture," she does not refer to the Japanese subjectivity he affirmed in relation to this principle. In the words of Nishida's statement: "To make Japan 'subjective' is in effect to turn the 'Way of the emperor' into a form of hegemony and imperialism" ("Nishida and Totalitarianism" 126; quoted from NKZ XII 341; translated by Yusa). From the same essay, Yusa, like Ueda, perceives "direct and harsh criticisms of current military policies" ("Nishida and Totalitarianism" 127) of the Japanese wartime government in Nishida's words.

Considering that Japan waged war under the banner of the Emperor, Yusa's claim that Nishida believed the Way of the Emperor or the Imperial Way (*kōdō*: the characteristic way in which the Emperor governs the country) to be opposed to militarism and imperialism may sound strange. However, in thus claiming Yusa intends to challenge the very assumption that "the emperor system had been the willing vehicle for colonial expansion and military aggressions, and the idea of supporting the imperial household was enough to bring the thought of Nishida and others in the Kyoto school under suspicion of fascist ideology" ("Nishida and Totalitarianism" 108).

According to Yusa, Nishida believed that the emperor-ruled system ran contrary to such things. It is sometimes said that throughout Japanese history, while "[t]he controls shifted hands with the passage of time ... the imperial family was always present in the background" ("Nishida and Totalitarianism" 126). Yusa insists that for Nishida, the Way of the Emperor was the Imperial Family's mode of existence that ensures their "ongoing presence amidst the changes of history" ("Nishida and Totalitarianism" 127), and it is this presence that in turn constitutes the aforementioned principle of the self-formation of the world. Since Nishida relayed this as "a principle aimed at realizing a global unity of independent countries" ("Nishida and Totalitarianism" 127–28), Yusa argues that what Nishida discussed in reference to the Imperial Way is different from what the Japanese military government did under the banner of the Emperor (that is, the negation of the independence of neighboring countries). Hence Yusa's claim that Nishida—through recourse to the Imperial Family—meant to criticize the government's military policies rather than to support them.

There are some problems with Yusa's above argument, which also concern Yusa's disregard for Nishida's affirmative remarks on subjectivity. Nishida equated the Imperial Way with the principle of the formation of the world. Nishida himself formulates this equation more clearly as follows: "The principle of the formation of Japan must become the principle of the formation of the world" (NKZ XII 341). Here, he asserts that the Way of the Emperor, a way of governing through a particular political system in a particular country, is universal so therefore the entire world should be formed in conformity with to it. Yusa does not question this universalization of the particular. Rather, Yusa states that Nishida's claim is that "[w]hat Japan has to bring to the international community is a heritage of continuity symbolized in the way of the emperor" ("Nishida and Totalitarianism" 127). Here, Yusa accepts this claim and endorses Nishida's universalization of the particular. However, this universalization, which gives one particular political system of a particular country a privileged status as an overarching principle for the formation of the entire world, obviously implies a form of ethnocentrism—one which nationalist and ultranationalist agendas of the day also shared. As such, this universalization is not just a matter of a certain country's contribution to the world.

When offering reasons for why Nishida should be taken as "a thinker who resisted fanatic nationalism" ("Nishida and Totalitarianism" 107), Yusa emphasizes his position that "Japan is no longer a string of secluded islands lying in the eastern seas. It is 'in' a larger world and must open up itself to that world" ("Nishida and Totalitarianism" 126). However, even if Nishida considered Japan as needing to be open to the world, it does not mean that further exploration of the nationalistic aspects of his discourse and its affinity with wartime ideologies is unnecessary or pointless. As I discussed in part 1 while examining the wartime discourse of his four disciples, what matters is how one placed Japan in the world. An attitude that considers one's own country as the center of the world seems far from an attitude that is contrary to nationalism. Thus, opposition to a certain kind of nationalism does not prevent one from upholding another kind of nationalism. In terms of Yusa's above argument, it is possible that she means that ethnocentrism invoked for the purpose of "realizing a global unity of independent countries" should be exempt from blame, whereas an ethnocentrism intended "for colonial expansion and military aggressions" should not be exempted. Curiously, and despite Japan's actual colonial expansion and military aggressions, Japanese wartime ideologies held up the realization of a peaceful world and the harmonious coexistence of different countries or peoples in it as an ideal, asserting that Japan's hegemony (the route toward enabling this realization) was different from Western imperialism and colonialism. Given this, regardless of Nishida's real intentions, his discourse presents a likeness to wartime ideologies, with similarities based on shared ethnocentric beliefs.

What seems problematic is that certain scholars take it for granted that such an affinity can be justifiably ignored, either by invoking the fact that Nishida opposed certain kinds of nationalists of his time, or by invoking the fact that he conceived of the Imperial Way as the opposite to imperialism. These scholars' disregard for Nishida's affirmative remark on Japan's subjectivity can be explained in a similar vein: Nishida opposed imperialism so if the subject for Nishida is a symbol of imperialism then only his negation of subjectivity is important to their work, and his remarks affirming subjectivity are not. Therefore, there is no problem in neglecting the latter and highlighting the former. Here, it seems to be that Nishida's specific position is accepted as undoubtable, and based on this assumption, the manner in which his discourse should be approached and the questions regarding which parts of it should be taken seriously is determined. This is not uncommon when it comes to the interpretation of philosophers' texts. However, while a re-examination of these texts may require changes to understandings about philosophers' positions, here the prescribed position of the philosopher is prioritized, to the extent that even the parts of Nishida's texts that can disprove this (established) position are taken as negligible.

Section 2: The Controversy about Nishida's Political Stance

This matter can be situated within the broader context of the controversy surrounding Nishida's wartime political stance. In her survey of this controversy, Arisaka Yōko classifies different views on Nishida's position into three categories ("The Nishida Enigma" 88–99). Nishida's critics see his philosophy's complicity with ultranationalism and support of imperialism as problematic; his defenders claim that he was a liberal thinker opposed to nationalism and imperialism; between these two groups are moderates whose opinions vary. Arisaka summarizes the disagreement between Nishida's critics and defenders as stemming from the opposition between a position that highlights "the relative importance of Nishida's personal agenda and beliefs" and a position that puts emphasis upon "the objective role of his philosophy within the ultranationalist political milieu" ("The Nishida Enigma" 94). Yusa and Ueda are counted by Arisaka as representative defenders. Since their concern centers upon "Nishida's intent," Arisaka comments that "[t]heir general strategy is to focus on the historical circumstances and Nishida's personal writings—letters and diaries—to show his antipathy toward the military government" ("The Nishida Enigma" 91). This strategy explains why Yusa and Ueda (and perhaps some other defenders of Nishida) might justify any disregard for certain parts of Nishida's public discourse. In wartime Japan, free speech was suppressed, and censorship and restraint were imposed upon publications. In such circumstances, there is a high probability that printed and published texts were not precise expressions of the author's true intentions. Hence, a good way for scholars to approach such texts afterward would be to read the author's true intentions from his personal writings (such as letters and diaries) and then interpret his public discourse from the standpoint of such intentions. Doing so would allow for the precise expressions of the author's intentions to be sorted out from his public discourse, also allowing other parts that were seemingly written against his intentions, most likely forced by his historical circumstances, to be disregarded.

In her 2002 *Zen & Philosophy: An Intellectual Biography of Nishida Kitarō*, Yusa gives a detailed account of the historical circumstances that surrounded Nishida during wartime, as well as his life as a philosopher faced with such circumstances (262–335). The military intervened in politics and controlled speech. When fascist ideologies became dominant, liberalism and individualism came to be denounced. The intellectuals who publicly expressed opinions that explicitly opposed governmental policies or ultranationalist agendas were sued, arrested, or imprisoned. These intellectuals were also vulnerable to harassment or attacks by fanatic ultranationalists. In such a situation, Nishida tried his best to resist the status quo. Hoping to influence government policies, he met government officials and wrote an essay at their request. Using words and phrases that (during wartime) were typically employed in line with fascist ideologies, he tried to give such terms different meanings grounded in his philosophy to awaken people's rationality. Ueda famously called Nishida's efforts a "tug-of-war over meaning." As Nishida's remark that "These days, apparently the word 'world' is a dirty word, which we are not even supposed to use!" (quoted from NKZ XIV 396 and translated by Yusa in *Zen and Philosophy* 293) suggests, just using the word "world" at that time might provoke accusations, assaults, or penalties. In this situation, merely using this word would have implied an act of resistance, a risk which required courage.

I have no intention of denying the worth of Nishida's resistance efforts in such difficult circumstances or being disrespectful toward his good intentions and conscience as an intellectual. However, whether these efforts should be reason enough to negate the necessity or relevance of critical examinations of Nishida's public discourse is another matter. In his 1997 book *Nishida Kitarō: The Writing of Otherness* (*Nishida Kitarō tasei no buntai*), Kobayashi Toshiaki makes a pertinent comment on this matter:

> The real problem for us does not reside in such personal circumstances. I admit that Nishida was a liberal thinker, and that from the standpoint of such a thinker, he tried to make efforts of resistance *in his own way*. However, what matters to us is the ideological nature essentially entailed in that very liberal discourse, or the historical and paradigmatic ideology, so to speak, that eventually drags even what this liberalism professes to oppose onto the same horizon. (*The Writing of Otherness* 129)

In terms of an effect of this "ideology," which is understandable as a set of beliefs, conscious or unconscious, that directs people's thoughts and acts, Kobayashi draws our attention to one fact: that once Nishida's wartime discourse is posited with recourse to his personal circumstances or the political situation that pressured him, "one 'philosophical' discourse is shifted onto another dimension. Then the responsibility of the discourse *itself* is no longer questioned" (*The Writing of Otherness* 120). Kobayashi continues:

> This kind of generosity was a habitual practice of Nishida's disciples. In a sense, it was also precisely characteristic of the mentality of "Japanese nothingness." However, if we are going to show our respect for Nishida as a "philosopher," shouldn't we rather examine this matter as a problem entailed in his discourse itself, even if the outcomes of such examinations are a disgrace to him? (*The Writing of Otherness* 120)

Insofar as philosophers are philosophers, their philosophies are destined to undergo scrutiny and criticism; they are always vulnerable to this kind of "disgrace," which has nothing to do with their personalities or ways of life. Even if they have a great personality or live a conscious life, this does not mean that their philosophies are impeccable or exempt from critical reflections, which is impossible in principle. Philosophers' works, in whatever situation they are written, exist long after being written. Detached from such contexts, these works continue to be read by many people, and to influence their opinions. Given this enduring nature, critically examination of the thoughts and problems articulated in philosophical works themselves is crucial and indispensable, and just as necessary as keeping records of philosophers' lives and the situations in which they created their works.

It is from this standpoint that I will critically examine Nishida's philosophy as articulated in his texts with an eye to its affinity with wartime ideologies. As such, according to Arisaka's classification, I am in the group of critics who inquire into the role of the philosophy in question within a given milieu. I think it still meaningful to carry out this inquiry independent of Nishida's personal agenda as interpreted by defenders, while I do not necessarily deny the significance of their inquiries into this agenda in and of itself.

For the purpose of exploring and clarifying the problems in Nishida's philosophy, I also place importance upon some insights offered by moderates such as Andrew Feenberg, who finds it problematic for Nishida "to treat the imperial house—a 'particular,' because it is a historical entity—as if it were a metaphysical universal" (Arisaka, "The Nishida Enigma" 97). In raising this point, Feenberg practically indicates the defect within "Yusa and Ueda's strongest defense of Nishida" that "stresses the universalist implications of his philosophy" (Arisaka, "The Nishida Enigma" 92). This defect overlaps with the problem inherent in Nishida's aforementioned claim that the Imperial Way as the principle for the formation of Japan should be the principle for the formation of the world. The exclusive universalization of a specific particular taking place here implies this particular's incomparable superiority to other particulars. When this particular refers to a certain country or the people living in it, the implications of this universalization are far from innocuous. In her 1997 essay "Beyond 'East' and 'West': Nishida's Universalism and Postcolonial Critique" Arisaka argues that in Nishida's case, "Japanese philosophy's claim of universality became entangled with the imperialist regime" (560), and rebuts his defenders' claims that his universalist philosophy excludes nationalism (551). What is problematic is not the fact that Nishida pursued universality per se but the manner in which he pursued and formulated it, and how that pursuit and formulation of universality worked both in his philosophy and in the given social, historical and political context.

Paying attention to this universalization of the particular in Nishida's philosophy also enables us to turn our eyes to a similar operation inadvertently generated by his defenders' claims. The universalization of the particular is completed when the particular origin of the alleged universal is forgotten, and when this universal comes to be recognized as the genuine universal that is neutral to any particular, including this specific particular, which (however tacitly) retains a special tie with that universal. When Nishida's defenders highlight the universal dimension of his philosophy, they advise the readers to ignore ultranationalist jargon used in it as well as the Japanese particularism infused into the jargon and philosophy. For the defenders insist that he was forced to use these terms due to the social, historical, and political situation at his time. If we read his texts according to the defenders' advice, (even though his discourse may universalize a specific particular in front of us), we put the particularity of this particular between parentheses and leave it out of consideration. This way of reading urges us to forget the particularity of the particular and to recognize the universal that this particular has become as the genuine universal, unbound to any particularity. As a result, the defenders' tendency to stress the universalist implications of Nishida's philosophy bears the same effect as the universalization of the particular in this philosophy, endorsing the universalization operation and reinforcing its effects. Therefore, the defenders, even if they claim that Nishida's philosophy is incompatible with wartime ideologies, and even if they are against these ideologies, ultimately present both his philosophy and these defenders' own claims as complicit with these ideologies by virtue of their common gesture of universalizing the particular. It seems that this could be a possible cause of what Kobayashi referred to above as "the ideological nature essentially entailed in that very liberal discourse" of Nishida: the mechanism "that eventually drags even what this liberalism professes to oppose onto the same horizon."

I will return to the theme of the universalization of the particular in Nishida's arguments about "*kokutai*," something Kobayashi associated with this ideological mechanism (*Writing of Otherness* 129). But before doing this, I will explore the affinity between Nishida and his disciples' philosophies with regard to Japanese national subjectivity. The investigation of his thoughts related to this subjectivity will indirectly help to cast light upon his idea of *kokutai* as playing a crucial role in forming this subjectivity.

Chapter 8

Nishida's Political Thoughts Concerning Japanese National Subjectivity

In this chapter, I will elucidate the overlap between the thought of the philosophers of world history and that of Nishida during approximately the same period as the three symposia on the theme of Japanese national subjectivity, upon which his four disciples put so much emphasis. In this elucidation, I will use the three characteristics of this subjectivity as my points of reference. First, I will discuss Nishida's ideas regarding the endorsement of the unity between the subject and the substratum of the state. Second, I will explore his ideas about naturalizing the reciprocal determination between virtuality and actuality of the state. Third, I will discuss his ideas suggesting the interpenetration between the national and the international in Japanese subjectivity. Through the investigation of such elements from his ideas that correspond with these three characteristics, I will highlight Nishida's idea of Japanese national subjectivity as something that is significantly continuous or overlapping with his four disciples' ideas.

In this chapter, I will consult the following texts by Nishida: "The Problem of the Reason of the State" (*Kokkariyū no mondai*), in which his view of the state is conspicuously articulated, first published in 1941 and included in *Philosophical Essays* vol. 4 (*Tetsugaku ronbunshū daiyon*) in the same year; "On Traditionalism" (*Dentōshugi ni tsuite*), in which he thematizes his view of tradition, inseparably connected with his view of the state, published in 1935 and based on Kōsaka Masaaki's transcripts of his lecture; the aforementioned "The Problem of Japanese Culture," published in 1940 and based on his lectures at Kyoto University in 1938; the "Supplement (*hoi*) to *Philosophical Essays* vol. 4" and the three appendixes (*furoku*) to this supplement (the supplement and first appendix were written and published in 1944. The third appendix, titled

"The Principle of the New World Order," was written and mimeographed in 1943, and the second appendix was discovered later and added to the old version of *Nishida Kitarō zenshū* XII).[1] In order to elucidate Nishida's notion of active intuition, which crops up in his discussion, I will also refer to "The Standpoint of Active Intuition" (*Kōiteki chokkan no tachiba*), first published in 1935 and included in *Philosophical Essays* vol. 1 in the same year.

The *Chūōkōron* symposia took place between November 1941 and November 1942, while the discussions and transcripts from it were published between January 1942 and January 1943. Some of Nishida's texts listed above, namely the supplement to *Philosophical Essays* vol. 4 and its appendixes, were written or published after these symposia, while others were written or published before. Although the terms "supplement" and "appendix" in the titles of these materials indicate their annexation to this philosophical anthology, the editors of NKZ see a strong connection with "The Problem of Japanese Culture," in terms of content. For this reason, they include them in the same volume as this essay (NKZ XII 470). I will likewise treat these texts as the continuous extension of Nishida's thought from before the symposia, and address how his thought is logically and theoretically interconnected with that of his four disciples, rather than tracking how they influenced each other chronologically.

Section 1: The State as Embodying the Morality of Absolute Nothingness

With regard to the first characteristics of the Japanese national subjectivity conceived of by the four thinkers, their thought explicitly shows close similarity to that of their mentor. This characteristic was, as previously mentioned, the unity between the subject and substratum of the state, meaning that in order for citizens to attain this subjectivity they had to become the substratum of the state by devoting themselves to the state. In turning themselves into its substratum, citizens' devotion to the state is taken as the morality they observe. By imposing this morality upon them, the state sustains itself and enforces its unity.

One of the four thinkers, Suzuki, briefly commented upon the relevance of the thought of their mentor, Nishida, to their idea of the unity between the state and its citizens as well as the moral implications of this unity. In the roundtable discussion, "The World-Historical Position and Japan," Suzuki refers to Nishida's "The Problem of the Reason of the State," and mentions that this essay explains, "in the ethics of the polis in ancient times, there is no radical contradiction between the state and the individual" (SN 168). In this essay, Nishida writes that in the ancient Greek polis "the individual and the state were still one" and "the reason of the state and morality agreed" (NKZ X 275). These statements show that Nishida places great importance on the unity of the state with its individual citizens and insists that the morality, implied in this unity, is the reason of such a state. Thus, Nishida's thought on the state around the time of the *Chūōkōron* symposia shows affinity with his disciples' thought on the subject qua substratum of the state. To elucidate further the affinity of Nishida's thought with that of Nishitani and the other three disciples' in this respect, I will explore how, in his "The Problem of the Reason of State," Nishida argues that the state could be united with citizens and its raison d'être could be morality.

As a preliminary step to this exploration, let me start with Nishida's idea of humanity, which forms the basis of his idea of the state. A classical definition of humanity includes *homo poieticus* as creative maker of things. However, for Nishida, humans do not exist as such from the beginning. As living things, humans have physical existence and, to this extent, are made and determined by the external environment, which includes the things in it. Nevertheless, humans have come to determine who they are, and to make things by themselves. This transition, which Nishida formulates as "from the made to the making," occurs as a result of the interaction between humans and environment. Therefore, humans being born to determine themselves is equivalent to the world determining itself so that humans are born from it: "[T]hat the individual determines itself is that the world determines itself, and that the world determines itself is that the individual determines itself" (NKZ X 282). Nishida uses a Japanese term for "individual," "*kobutsu,*" which, generally speaking, not only means the individual human, who is independent and substantial as implied in individualism, but can include both the human and the non-human, the living and the non-living. However, as it is only humans who have come to determine themselves rather than simply being determined, it is only they who can truly determine themselves as individual. For Nishida, the individual proper in its most advanced state is the human.

Thus conceived, paradoxically, the individual's self-determination is not an individual, but rather a collective, phenomenon. Human transition from the made to the making—that is, self-determination being a result of the interaction between subject and environment—occurs commonly among people who live in the same environment, enabling them to shape their collective identity as beings of the same kind. In this sense, Nishida writes, "Our selves are born as the individuals of the world, historically, and as species, in other words, socially" (NKZ X 293).[2] Humans determine themselves as individuals while identifying themselves and the people living with them as the same species and members of the same ethnic society. Synonymous with ethnicity, species does not designate biological race, but rather a historically and socially formed human group bound by a sense of identification as the reason to share the same geo-cultural environment, and the folkways and mores formed within it.

Strictly speaking, Nishida specifies that in order for individuals to truly become individual, being members of such an ethnic society is not enough—their society must establish its own law and legal system, with institutional forces beyond mere habits and customs of the ethnic group. For Nishida, this is how society develops into the state. Law and a legal system, which make the state what it is, incline people to comply by virtue of their moral ideality, rather than letting people blindly follow, as is the case with habits and customs. The respect for individuals with regard to their intrinsic values is possible only in a state in which its members conform to its law and legal system. To this extent, individuals as singular beings can truly become individual and live together only in such a state. Thus, for Nishida, the state develops from and builds upon ethnic society as a collectivity of people of the same species. He concludes that the true individual, respected for the sake of its very individuality, is ineluctably national: "[T]hat our selves work historically and formatively as the individuals of the historical world should mean that they do so through the mediation of the state" (NZK X 308).

Now we can understand how Nishida believed the state is united with its citizens, and its raison d'être is morality. If morality is the raison d'être of the state, it is because the state, by virtue of its law and legal system, makes citizens practice morality. Here, the state itself becomes the embodiment of morality. If the state and its citizens are united, it is because citizens' individual beings are one with their being the members of the state, to the extent that they can truly live as individuals only if they practice morality by living in the state. Hence, Nishida's statement: "To be national [*kokkateki*] should be the way in which the individual self exists. Being and morality become one in the state" (NKZ X 327). This is the clearest articulation of what Kevin M. Doak describes as the Kyoto School's "modern and progressive beliefs about the ability to construct institutions that would be 'good' and would of themselves induce people to act morally" (157–58).

Although Nishida distinguishes the state from the ethnic society through the existence of the law in the former, it is in the latter that law has its roots. It is from the law's rootedness in the ethnic society that he derives the law's authority over citizens in the state:

> We can locate the foundation of the law in the self-formation of ethnic will. Our selves are born from a certain ethnic group and live as its members. In this regard, it can be said that the law has authority over our selves as such, neither for the sake of a certain ethnic group, nor for the sake of a certain class, and that we must admit the authority of the law in our selves as such. (NKZ X 299)

In the first place, Nishida remarks, to form an ethnic group and give order to it is the will of the people who belong to this group, and therefore of this group itself. Although this will realizes an ethnic society and is materialized in it, insofar as this will involves the ideal of order beyond the interests of a specific human group, whether it is a class or ethnic group, it surpasses the limits of an ethnic society, prepares its transition to a state, and subsists within the state. As such, the will of an ethnic group provides the foundation of the law, which subsequently constitutes a state. If the law of the state has authority over its citizens, it is because this law has come from the will of the ethnic group on which the state is based and, therefore, from the depth of its citizens.

The implication here is that an ethnic society naturally turns into a state if this society is healthy enough. In the supplement to his *Philosophical Essays* vol. 4, Nishida presents this very view: "[T]he historical world is thoroughly actively state-formative. The ethnic group, as historical and formative, already has in itself the nature of the state" (NKZ XII 411). Given that all humans are members of ethnic societies, the law derived from the will of such groups is internal to the self of each individual citizen of that state and has authority to dictate to each self from within. For the members of the state to observe its law is to discipline themselves of their own collective will, which is rooted in their ethnicity. The reason for this observance is not merely that disciplining themselves in this way amounts to maintaining the order of the state as willed by the ethnic will. In "The Problem of the Reason of the State," Nishida states, "the individual person's compliance with the law of one's society must make the individual person as such" (NKZ X 329). In Nishida's view, only by living within this order are people able to truly become individuals worthy of respect. Thus, the observance of the law of the state by its members is an act of their own will for their own sake.

Moreover, from the equation of the individual's self-determination and that of the world, it follows that the observance of the state's law is postulated, not only by the way in which the individual exists, but also by the way in which the world exists. In this sense, Nishida states, "The law is the command that the world itself gives our selves, the command that reveals itself where our selves as the individuals of the historical world practically form this world" (NKZ X 302).

As the law of the state realizes morality among citizens, this morality also takes on a character of similar command or compulsion. As such, Nishida states, "I think that we should not consider morality merely as the internal 'ought' of our selves, as conventionally considered, but it originally takes on a character of command or compulsion, the character which I think is the essence of morality" (NKZ X 328). When Nishida states morality as a command or compulsion is not merely internal to our selves, he means that it primarily comes from within the world itself and, only in this capacity, comes from within our selves, determined as such in this world. He claims the observance of this law and morality as obedience to their command or compulsion is required from the depths within individuals and is that which makes them truly individual.

Nishida assumes that the ethnic society evolves into the state, and that individuals become truly individual only in the state. Based on this assumption, he claims the inseparability of the individuality of humans from their membership in the state. Since the self-determination of individuals is at once that of the world, the establishment of the state in which individuals determine themselves as such is postulated by the world through its self-determination. Therefore, the citizens' obedience to the state's command or compulsion is their response to the call from both the world and their own individual selves. Thus, Nishida provides an explanation for the unity of the state and its citizens, and for the citizens' acceptance of the state's command or compulsion of their own will in a wider context. He also takes into account how the world and individuals exist, while necessitating the development of the state from the ethnic society. Substantially, Nishida's view of the state, situated within his broader view of the world and history from which the state emerges, dovetails with Nishitani's idea of the state, whose subject and substratum are one, and provides a milieu in which this idea can live.

Concerning the unity of the subject and substratum of the state, there is another continuity between Nishida's thought and that of his four disciples at a deeper level. Nishitani appreciated citizens abandoning their personal subjectivity and turning themselves into the substratum of the state as their achievement of higher subjectivity. Tacitly assumed in this appreciation was the idea of the subject of responsibility, modeled on the philosophers of world history's conception of Japanese national subjectivity. This subject was established through self-annihilation in accomplishing one's responsibility and confronting nothingness. As such, the being of this subject was one with nothingness. Confronting nothingness as the ground of the world and the principle of world history has thus guaranteed this subject the ethicality and necessity of its acts. Nishida not only presented the idea of nothingness, which his disciples developed in their own ways, but his thought is also in line with theirs in seeking the ultimate source of morality or ethicality in nothingness.

> The individual is the individual through the mediation of the single absolute, and therefore it can be said that the individual is the individual through the mediation of non-mediation, through the mediation of absolute nothingness. (NKZ X 321)

In this passage, Nishida indicates his belief that individual or world self-determination is mediated through nothingness, even though nothingness is the mediator, and therefore mediation is equal to the absence of mediation. If this is the case, it follows, as the command or compulsion originating in the ways in which the world and the individuals exist as the result of self-determination, morality has its ultimate source in absolute nothingness:

> But the fundamental standpoint of morality does not reside in the internal "ought" of the self. Rather it must be the standpoint of the awareness of place, the standpoint to see the self from the center of the world while the self becomes utterly nothingness. Therefore, I insist that moral "ought" at base has the character of command as the self-expression of the absolute. (NKZ X 330)

Nishida refers to nothingness as the absolute, the place that is in itself nothing and yet in which there is anything. In his view, all beings are created from the self-negation of absolute nothingness and should naturally return to where they were born through self-negation. Nishida describes the individual's arrival from, and return to, the movement from place to place as "from there to there." Since all beings move and should move in this way, this movement is at once the "is" and the "ought" for all beings. In particular, the moral "ought" for already existing individuals, after outward travel from absolute origin, is an act equivalent to homeward travel back to it. Such an act finds its moral endorsement in absolute nothingness, from which individuals were born and therefore to which they should return. Morality proper consists of such an act, insofar as it embodies the return to absolute nothingness and becomes its self-expression. Only as such does morality have the character of command ultimately grounded in this absolute origin of all beings.

Like Nishida, his four disciples, including Nishitani, also emphasized the morality or ethicality of self-annihilation and devotion to the state through recourse to the idea of nothingness as an ultimate metaphysical principle of the world of beings. Nishida, by establishing the direct link between absolute nothingness and the state, highlights the decisive significance, not merely of self-annihilation and devotion, but of self-annihilation for the state and devotion to it. Thus, Nishida presents a comprehensive cosmology around absolute nothingness to support his own claim, and also to reinforce that of his disciples. Nishitani's view of the state, whose subject and substratum are united, presents a possible form that the state Nishida had in mind can take. Likewise, the four disciples' idea of the subject of responsibility as this very subject = substratum delineates the agent that fits into, rather than diverges from, this cosmology. In turn, Nishida buttresses his four disciples' idea of this subject = substratum with this cosmology, in which citizens' serving the state is dignified as their observing the imperative of absolute nothingness.

Section 2: State as Tradition, Tradition as State

Based on the recognition of the lack of such a subject in Japan, the philosophers of world history insisted on the need to create it and tried to promote this creation through their discourse. For this purpose, these philosophers invoked the virtual subsistence of this subjectivity from ancient Japanese history. In the actual, they detected the symptoms of the virtual subsistence of this subjectivity. Once they assumed its virtual subsistence, they naturalized its actualization. Thus, through the attempt to create this subjectivity, it appeared as a subjectivity whose actuality and virtuality determined each other.

The third characteristic of the Japanese national subjectivity conceived of by these philosophers was this reciprocal determination between the actuality and virtuality of this subjectivity, between what is there *de facto* and what is *de jure*, and thus should come into existence. Although these philosophers struggled to resolve the gap between the actual absence and virtual presence of the Japanese national subject through their practice to create it, they ran the risk of asserting any actualization to be that of the idealized virtual, and arbitrarily inventing the virtual to which the actual should adjust itself.

With regard to this third characteristic, Nishida's thought also provides the theoretical support for that of his four disciples. In light of Nishida's view of history, the reciprocal determination between the actuality and virtuality of Japanese national subjectivity can be explained by the ineluctable course of history, culminating in the accomplishment of the state. If humans as social creatures cannot but form an ethnic society and develop it into a state for their self-realization, as Nishida believes, the state is the virtual in all ethnic societies in that each society has the potential to become a state. In turn, the state is the actual in all such societies in that each society is supposed to become a state in the future, if it is healthy enough. The gap between the virtual and the actual is bridged by his idea of the historical necessity of the passage from the ethnic society to the state. Supposing the virtual is necessarily actualized, the gap between the actual and the virtual will disappear over the course of time. As such, there is no problem in taking the virtual in the present to be the actual in the future. The assumption of the virtuality of the state throughout human history, and of the subjectivity of each state as that which should be actualized in the future, enables the four thinkers to jump over the gap between the actual lack and virtual presence of Japanese national subjectivity. Based on this assumption, it would be easy for them to profess the practice of creating Japanese national subjectivity, thrown into the circle between the virtual and the actual, follows and directs historical necessity.

Nishida's idea of tradition illustrates the virtual presence of the state even before its actual establishment, indirectly expressing itself in the ethnic society. If the state has been virtually present since the beginning of the ethnic society, the state manifests itself, albeit retrospectively, as if it had merged with the tradition of this society. This bond between tradition and the state appears when Nishida discusses the birth of the human self as inseparable from tradition in "The Problem of the Reason of the State":

> Our selves are born as the individuals of the world, historically, and as species, in other words, socially. They are not born into this world accidentally. That our selves are thus born historically, as species, that is, socially, means that they are born as part of tradition. Tradition is our selves' mirroring the past, and the past's determining our selves while expressing itself. However, living tradition must be the sense of what is eternal, as well as temporal, that is, something like the historical sense in Eliot's sense. (NKZ X 293–94)

As we have seen, for Nishida humans are the individuals determining themselves at the same time as the world determines itself. As essentially social beings, they are socially born; that is, they cannot properly live as humans without forming society. In addition, given that each society has its own history, the members of each society form their selves under the influence of this history. Tradition is the historical past of the society that thus constitutes an essential part of its members' selves, and expresses itself in these selves. Therefore, insofar as the human selves are socially born, they are also traditionally born.

Although, at first glance, it seems Nishida is simply talking about the tradition of society in general, he specifies in the subsequent passage that the society with living tradition, the society in which tradition acts vividly upon its members in that they are aware of this act, is the state:

> It can be said that our selves are born where historical tradition is, to put it in my own terms, active-intuitive, as the self-determination of the absolute present. Thus, that our selves thoroughly as individuals mirror the world of the absolute present in this way must mean that, at the same time as this mirroring, a society surmounts itself as merely subjective and becomes a world. Thus, this must mean, as I said above, that our selves become self-aware and rational, and that the society surpasses the mythical and becomes legislative and national. (NKZ X 294)

As we find here several different points intertwined with each other, I will unravel them one by one.

In the beginning, he states tradition gives birth to human selves when it is active-intuitive. The term "active-intuitive" is the adjectival form of Nishida's key concept, "active intuition [*kōiteki chokkan*]." He also states that if tradition is active-intuitive, it is as the absolute present's self-determination. The absolute present designates the temporality of absolute nothingness. Although there is no explicit mention in this passage, it is absolute nothingness that provokes active intuition and mediates the birth of human selves. In order to explain the unseen presence of absolute nothingness, for the time being, I will turn to his essay, "The Standpoint of Active Intuition."

In this essay, Nishida succinctly summarizes what he thinks this intuition is: "The fact that the subject determines the object, and the object determines the subject, is the fact that the thing acts; conversely, that we see things on the basis of action is active intuition" ("The Standpoint of Active Intuition" 99; translation modified by referring to NKZ VIII 155).[3] Active intuition is the intuition conceived to be in and of itself an action. Although intuition, as the direct apprehension of things, tends to be regarded as the subject's passive reception of the object, in Nishida's view, just intuiting the object is an action in the sense of actively determining what the object is. Moreover, if the subject thus intuits the object, it is because the object leads the subject to do so in the first place. This is yet another action, namely the action of actively determining the subject to be what it is. Thus, intuition is an action. In turn, the action is also intuition, given that the action occurs when what acts is affected by what is to be acted upon. Both action and intuition are interactions between two things, either of which becomes either the subject or the object.

For Nishida, precisely speaking, such an interaction originates in the object rather than the subject, and it does not occur by itself:

> Being born of things means that the subject is born of the object. That is intuition; that is truly seeing the thing. What I call

"determination without that which determines," or the "determination of the absolute nothingness," means nothing other than this [. . .]. ("Active Intuition" 107; translation modified by referring to NKZ VIII 166)[4]

When Nishida refers to the object of which the subject is born, he does not mean the already established object insofar as it is paired with the already established subject. The subject is not the subject from the beginning, but becomes the subject through a process similar to the birth of humans; that is, the transition from the made to the making. Before it becomes the subject, it is not the making but the made, just as the object is. What Nishida refers to as the object, of which the subject is born, is that which is in this state of being the made. Both the subject and the object, in order to become themselves, determine themselves as such through their interaction during this state of being the made. Active intuition emerges as such an interaction. In Nishida's view, this does not occur by itself, but requires that which mediates it. It is unknown whether the subject and the object, before becoming themselves and undifferentiated in the state of being the made, have commonality or continuity. What can mediate the interaction between such things, so that they determine themselves, should be that which is in and of itself empty and thus can contain whichever things. Nishida describes the determination of the subject and the object enabled in their interaction qua active intuition as the "determination of absolute nothingness"—that is, their determination through the mediation of absolute nothingness, even if this mediation is that of non-mediation. In essence, this description explains that where active intuition occurs, absolute nothingness lurks in it, mediating the interaction between what will become the subject and the object of this intuition, and enabling them to generate themselves as separate entities.

Returning to the previous quotation from "The Problem of the Reason of the State," I will explicate the absolute present, given that it is the temporality of absolute nothingness. If all beings come from and go back to nothingness, their movement makes a circle from nothingness to nothingness; even if the individuals move from the past to the present, and then to the future, as they go around in absolute nothingness, from its standpoint they stay in its eternal present. This eternal present is the absolute present, which underlies and comprehends all individuals' pasts, presents, and futures. Just as absolute nothingness, prior to all things, mediates the diversification in their interactions, the absolute present, prior to all empirical temporalities of individuals, mediates the differentiation in their interconnection. Just as the interaction of things through the mediation of absolute nothingness is active-intuitive, so too is the interconnection of the empirical pasts, presents, and futures through the mediation of the absolute present—that is, the self-determination of the absolute present qua the determination of such empirical temporalities.

If Nishida finds close ties between tradition and the absolute present, it is because tradition from the past, when it wields influence in present society and creates the future selves living in it, makes the past, the present, and the future coexist and incorporates the absolute present. To say, "tradition is . . . active-intuitive, as the self-determination of the absolute present" (NKZ X 294) implies tradition's act of giving birth to human selves and interconnecting the empirical past, present, and future makes these selves apprehend directly the interconnection in their immediate sense of unity with tradition, continuous from the past to the future. This is just as the subject directly apprehends the object in the midst of the interaction between them during active intuition. Naturally, the selves thus created also incorporate absolute nothingness and reflect in themselves the world as being in the absolute present. On the one hand, Nishida's conception of tradition, as one of the things created from absolute nothingness, rests in individuals' passing time. On the other, it participates in the eternal present of absolute nothingness, while also enabling the selves it creates to do so. Thus, in a reference to American-born British poet T. S. Eliot, he calls tradition that which is eternal as well as temporal.

Tradition and the state are the forms in which the absolute reveals itself in the earthly world, and so they make the entities upon which they act express the absolute in their own ways. Just as the state, by the force of its legislative system, leads its members to practice the morality of self-annihilation embodying absolute nothingness, by virtue of its incorporation of the absolute present, tradition creates the human selves that mirror the world of the absolute present. When Nishida states that, at the same time as the selves mirror the world of the absolute present, the society becomes legislative and national, he means the function of tradition and that of the state are correlative. To this extent, tradition and the state are complementary. In saying that our selves "individually mirror the world of the absolute present," Nishida suggests the selves created by tradition thus incorporate the absolute present only in the capacity of the individuals. Given that, in his view, the individual can truly become individual and live as such in the state, it is only in the state as the self-expression of absolute nothingness that tradition can be so influentially active as to make the selves it creates mirror the world of the absolute present. In that both tradition and the state are channels of the revelation of the absolute, the establishment of the state involves and reinforces the activation of tradition, and vice versa. In view of such correlation and complementarity, a consequence of the act of tradition is that the selves who are traditionally born are not merely socially born, but are ineluctably nationally born, and vice versa.

When tradition and the state are thus considered with respect to their correlation and complementarity, even though it is a product of the modern period, the state appears to take on traditional characteristics. The state, at least in its original form, is represented as if it had subsisted since ancient times and as if its establishment was destined from the beginning of history. Nishida's following statement (as quoted before) is again relevant here: "[T]he historical world is thoroughly actively state-formative. The ethnic group, as historical and formative, already has in itself the nature of the state" (NKZ XII 411). Nishida declares that the purpose of history is the formation of the state, and so the nature of the state implicitly resides in the ethnic group from which it develops. This formulation does not suddenly appear, but concisely summarizes his earlier ideas. Given that, for Nishida, the ethnic society is the most primitive form of society, and the state is the goal of all social forms, it follows that the nature of the state persists from the beginning to the end of that society's history. Thus, he assumes the virtual presence of the state throughout history. Or, more precisely, rather than the state itself, what is present throughout history is the essential structure of a state, which comes to define each specific state, and which, in terms of Japan, constitutes the so-called *kokutai*.

I will henceforth use the term "the structure of the state of Japan" to designate the concept Nishida invokes by using the term *kokutai*. Due to the complicated implications of this Japanese term, there are many ways in which it can be translated into English ("national polity," "national body," or "national essence," to name just a few). Naturally, the term "the structure of the state" does not entirely cover all such implications. While keeping in mind the limitations of this translation, I choose this term here given that my aim is to address *kokutai*'s structural aspects, upon which Nishida's philosophy seems to have put great emphasis, in agreement with his rational standpoint. I will discuss the significance of his stance through bringing forward such structural aspects of *kokutai* as well as the historical backdrop wherein it had such significance in the subsequent chapter. Before doing this, I shall look into how he conceived of this structure of the state.

Based on Nishida's idea of the structure of the state of Japan as aforementioned, it becomes easier to allege the consistent existence of Japan as a state since the beginning of history and to encourage the creation of Japanese national subjectivity through the return to tradition, as is done by the philosophers of world history. Supposing the essential structure of the state persists throughout history as a crucial part of tradition, there would be no problem in seeking a model of this subjectivity in tradition, so that it would be formed in a manner true to the professed permanent essence of their state. Once tradition and the state are considered with respect to their correlation and complementarity, and the persistence of the essential structure of the state is taken for granted, it would seem natural to see the ideal form of the state in tradition, and the accomplished form of tradition in the state.

The ideal form of the state for Nishida—one that is composed of a single ethnic group, namely, the nation-state—is a product of modernity. Likewise, tradition, which is activated for the establishment of this state and also needs establishment for this activation, is an invention of modernity. Eric Hobsbawm argues " '[t]raditions' which appear or claim to be old are often quite recent in origin and sometimes invented" (1), and points out such invented traditions' relevance to the nation and its associated phenomena, such as the nation-state (13). Hobsbawm remarks that "modern nations and all their impedimenta generally claim to be the opposite of novel, namely rooted in the remotest antiquity, and the opposite of constructed, namely human communities so 'natural' as to require no definition other than self-assertion" (14). Paradoxically, the traditions that modern nation-states invoke to claim themselves to be rooted in history and therefore "natural" are often modern inventions. This paradox also applies to the tradition conceived by Nishida in terms of its correlation and complementarity with the nation-state. This raises doubts as to whether the tradition that is activated for the establishment of the nation-state and which needs this establishment to be initiated is nothing but a similar invention of modernity.

However, if this is the case, it does not matter to Nishida. In "On Traditionalism," he states, "as the constitutive principle of the historical world, tradition should exist in the beginning and at the end at the same time. It should develop infinitely. The new is guided by the old and at once changes it" (NKZ XIV 384). While insisting on the persistence of tradition from the beginning to the end of a society, Nishida suggests that persistent tradition does not remain unchanged but is changeable and develops infinitely. Even when people try to restore past tradition in the present, it is precisely in doing so that they will change, not only the future, but also this tradition itself by reconfiguring it in relation to the present situation. Therefore, the persistence of tradition is inseparable from its continual renewal in the process of being handed down. It is no wonder that, whenever people try to restore it, tradition is a product of the time.

Nishida goes so far as to say that tradition would not be tradition proper without the act of its renewal, or indeed that of its creation. In "The Problems of the Reason of State," he explains his idea of tradition in reference to Eliot's historical sense that tradition is eternal as well as temporal. In "The Problem of Japanese Culture," again in reference to Eliot, Nishida specifies what he means:

> T. S. Eliot says that tradition is not to be inherited, but to be obtained by effort; that it contains historical sense and that this sense, in which time and what is beyond time are united, makes humans belong to tradition. Tradition is that in which the past and the future are united into the present so as to create things as the self-determination of the eternal now. It is a sort of catalyst, so to speak. Otherwise tradition would be a mere relic of the past. It would be no different from the fossils of ancient creatures. In creation, humans thoroughly belong to tradition, and yet add something to that which coexists with the past and the future—that is, to the eternal. What is newly created emerges while coexisting with the past things. Here resides the true freedom of humans. (NKZ XII 378–79)

For Nishida, that tradition is at once temporal and eternal does not mean it is unchangeable and, as such, continues to manifest itself in the temporal world in the same way throughout history. If humans live in the present simply by repeating life in the past, it is not only the present, but also the future, that will not be different from the past for them. Moving from the past to the future in this way will not incorporate the eternal temporality of the absolute present in which the past, the present, and the future coexist as three different earthly temporalities, while keeping continuity in their discontinuity. For the temporalities to be different, the future must have something radically new that did not exist in the past; the present must be the moment in which the act of creating this new thing begins, modeled upon the past. Only through such an act does the absolute present reveal itself in the historical world, and only through the succession of such acts is tradition established as "living" tradition, in which the past, the present, and the future vividly interact while being in touch with the eternal. Tradition will not persist unless it is continually recreated, and such creative acts are constitutive of tradition.

Nishida's idea of tradition enables the philosophers of world history to see the risk they ran in their project to generate Japanese national subjectivity differently. Assuming the reciprocal determination between the virtuality and actuality of this subjectivity, these philosophers ran the risk of arbitrarily inventing the virtual to which the actual should adjust and asserting whatever actualization to be that of the idealized virtual. While professing to return to Japanese tradition in search of the model of this subjectivity, they invented this tradition in a manner suitable for their purpose as the virtual to be actualized. With recourse to this tradition, they gave arbitrary meanings to reality, as the actualization of this virtual, with the intention of leading reality in a certain direction. In short, they invented a tradition to which people should return, and tried to guide them to open a new epoch under the banner of the revival of this tradition.

However, based on Nishida's idea of tradition, constituted by repetitious acts of renewal, his disciples' gesture can be appreciated as the act of creating tradition in order to extend it and transform the present into the new future in the wake of this tradition. Even though these thinkers loaded tradition with fictitious virtualities of what they believed should be actualized, and justified any actualization as that of these alleged virtualities, their having done so is acceptable given that reviving and succeeding tradition is inseparable from creating it. By carrying out this act of creation and making the past, the present, and the future coexist, the four thinkers also came to practice exactly what Nishida theorized as the act through which tradition acts upon human selves and the absolute reveals itself. Once again, Nishida's thought has provided the theoretical support for that of his disciples by constructing a framework through which the defects of their project to create Japanese national subjectivity could be interpreted as its creative strengths.

Section 3: The Structure of the State Encircling a Being of Nothingness

The motif of the structure of the state, coming to the fore in the examination of the affinity of Nishida's thought with his four disciples' in terms of the third characteristic of Japanese national subjectivity conceived by the latter, also concerns its second characteristic: the interpenetration between the national and the international. By invoking the structure of the state of Japan, Nishida asserts what his disciples did through recourse to the second and third characteristics: the persistence of Japanese national tradition and Japan's leadership in the world. Since the motif of this structure ranges over these two characteristics, I will look into it further before moving from the third to the second characteristic. In this process, it will be revealed that Nishida held the idea that Japanese subjectivity is decisively shaped by the structure of the state of Japan.

Undoubtedly, the state has a special status in all existing things for Nishida. As we have seen, the state is not only determined by the world to be one of all existing things, but also determines the humans living in the state so that they determine themselves as truly individual insofar as they are its members. To this extent, the state is not only formed by the world, but also becomes a particular world, thus determining the humans living in it in a particular way. Hence, in the second appendix to the supplement to his *Philosophical Essays* vol. 4, Nishida states, "[A] state is established when a certain ethnic group, as a species of the historical world, forms a particular world" (NKZ XII 421). Since the self-determination of these individuals is possible based on their membership in this particular world, it also enables them to determine themselves as one collective subject of this state with its own sovereignty. Nishida thinks that national spirit works in the formation of this collective subject, and closely associates this spirit with the structure of the state:

> When a national spirit [kokuminteki seishin] is formed by the heroic efforts of a certain ethnic group at a certain point of time and place, a state is established. National spirit is nothing but a historical and corporeal formative force formed as the reciprocal determination between subject and environment. The form thus forming itself is the structure of the state. (NKZ XII 420)

A state is established when a human society, formed in the interaction between subject and environment, attains the power of self-formation beyond the extent of this interaction. For this to happen, the people living in this society must form themselves into one collective subject that determines itself by itself. Nishida defines national spirit as the force of this self-formation. This definition is not alien to the national spirit in the general sense of the word—the mentality peculiarly ascribed to a nation. To the extent that such a mentality not only gives the people of this nation a sense of solidarity but also inclines them to physically act together in unity, it is a force of the self-formation of a national collectivity that binds and urges them to build and maintain a state. For Nishida, the shape of national polity configured in the work of this formative force is *kokurai* as the structure of the state.

Once formed, this structure comes to form itself by itself, so as to model national spirit as its original formative force. Insofar as this self-formation is crucial to the establishment and maintenance of the state, its essential structure should reside not in a certain fixed form, but in the force and the form of this self-formation. Nishida often refers to such a form as "a form without form." Then, the persistence of the structure of the state does not necessarily mean the permanence of a specific concrete form of the state. Rather, it denotes the subsistence of the force and form of its self-formation throughout the changes of its concrete form. This line of thought concerning the structure of the state is in keeping with his understanding of tradition, supposedly correlative with and complementary to this structure, constituted by continual renewals.

The idea of this structure as the formless form seems to be applicable to any structure of any state, accepting any form without restriction. Surprisingly, in the supplement to his *Philosophical Essays* vol. 4, Nishida says bluntly, "Strictly speaking, it can also be said that the structure of the state does not exist outside our country [*waga kuni*]" (NKZ XII 410). Immediately prior to making this statement, Nishida explains its reason: "the view of the structure of the state that is equal to morality has developed only in our Japan" (NKZ XII 410). Given his view that the ethnic society has its own will to order and maintain, any ethnic society should have the germ of morality to be realized by force of the state's law. Nevertheless, why does Nishida say that only Japan has the structure of the state equal to morality? The reason resides in his idea of the uniqueness of the Japanese state's structure:

> In the history of our country, at whose basis the myth of the establishment of the state lies, the country that is historical and generative, as the absolute nothingness' self-determination that takes place in such a way that the transcendental is the immanent and the immanent is the transcendent, the awareness of the structure of the state that is equal to morality arose for the first time. As I once stated in "The Problem of Japanese Culture," in the structure of the state of our country [*waga kuni no kokutai*], the Imperial Family is the beginning and the end of the world. The quintessence of the structure of our state [*waga kokutai*] is that the Imperial Family envelops the past and the future and that, as the self-determination of the absolute present, all vigorously develops around the center of the Imperial Family. (NKZ XII 409)

It sounds odd that Nishida claims the state of Japan has, at its base, the myth of its establishment. It is unlikely that the state at issue here existed in the same way as it was during the era of myth. However, his meaning becomes clear in the text that follows, in which he seeks the quintessence of the structure of the Japanese state in the Imperial Family. He means that, although the modern state of Japan was constructed around the Emperor and his relatives, Japanese myth tells that the country possessed this very structure—the state—from the beginning, and that this structure has subsisted even though Japanese society has undergone many changes over the course of time. The Japanese myth, usually understood as is laid out in *The Kojiki* and *The Nihon Shoki*, the oldest official books on Japanese ancient history, describes how the descendants of the gods (who created heaven, earth, and the land of Japan), came down from the heavens to become the rulers of Japan, thus establishing the Japanese Imperial Court. If this myth is taken into account, Nishida's idea of the correlation between tradition and the state as best expressed in Japan, as Japanese tradition contains the original form of the state since the beginning of society, compliments the establishment of the state as inseparable from the activation of this tradition. Moreover, supposing that tradition and the state persist throughout Japanese history, it follows that the Imperial Family, in its alleged subsistence from the beginning of Japan in spite of changes in society, personifies the absolute present in which the past, the present, and the future coexist, and which conditions the possibility of tradition. The structure of the state, when it is thus constructed around the center of this personification of the eternal present of absolute nothingness, spontaneously comes to conform to morality, in which this nothingness expresses itself. Therefore, Nishida's belief that the structure of the state of Japan is equal to morality lies in the consistent centrality of the Imperial Family to this structure, since the country's beginning.

His recourse to Japanese myth in claiming that the Imperial Family has been consistently central since the dawn of Japanese history, suggests a lineage that predates even this beginning. This raises the question as to whether Nishida confuses myth and historical fact. However, contrary to first appearances, he does not necessarily insist that the Japanese myth contains literal truth. We should remember Nishida once noted that a society becomes a state by surpassing the mythical. For him, the mythical is something to be overcome for the state to be established and, to this extent, myth itself cannot be the foundation of the state. However, this does not mean that he perceives myth and legend to be useless objects we should completely disregard.

In "On Traditionalism," in which he emphasizes the value of tradition, he remarks, "[A]ncient mythology and legend should contain deep significance concerning the composition of the historical world" (NKZ XIV 383). Myth and legend are created by an ethnic society at the premier stage, and usually include the narratives of the origin of this ethnic group and the world it exists in. As such, myth and legend represent, even if naïvely and crudely, the way in which the world and humans as social beings were born through the self-negation of absolute nothingness. Consequently, the myth and legend of an ethnic group not only bond its members spiritually, but also make them understand in significant ways, even if indirectly, how they and the world to which they belong came to exist. For Nishida, the unreasonableness of myth and legend must be overcome for the state to be established with reasonable law and morality. But when a state is completely separated from the myth and legend of the ethnic society from which it developed, its members lose contact with absolute nothingness as their true origin that is hidden under the naïve and crude representations of its folklore. As a result, the morality to be realized in that state is not a self-expression of absolute nothingness.

From this standpoint, Nishida's claim appears in a different light: the Japanese myth in which the descendants of the gods who created heaven and earth came down from the heavens can be understood as a primitive representation of the creation of all existing things through the self-negation of absolute nothingness. Combined with this myth of the alleged ancestors of the Imperial Family, the narrative of the consistent centrality of the Imperial Family throughout Japanese history can be understood as an illustration of the persistence of absolute nothingness in history as the condition of its possibility. In short, if Nishida adopts the narrative straddling Japanese myth and history, it is insofar as this narrative contains a suitable expression of his cosmology centering on absolute nothingness. Although he does not necessarily swallow myth, he admits its irreplaceable value, because he tracks the source of the state's true morality in the traces of the primal revelation of absolute nothingness in ancient legends.

The deeper reason for his claim that only Japan has a structure of the state equal to morality resides in Nishida's belief that this structure, or its representation by the Imperial Family, retains continuity with the primal revelation of absolute nothingness, which expresses itself later as morality in the state. This belief manifests itself more clearly in his explanation as to why he thinks there is no structure of the state, in the exact sense of the word, in European countries, in contrast to Japan. In the supplement to his *Philosophical Essays* vol. 4, he states, "The states in the West today were environmentally formed after all that was ethnic and religious had been once destroyed by the unification by the Roman Empire" (NKZ XII 410). As a result, he continues, in those states "abstract morality must have been introduced as the reason of the state," and "the view of the divine state as that of our country did not develop" (NKZ XII 410). Aside from the factuality of this observation, he means that the fabricated morality, separate from ethnic religion succeeding from ancient times, cannot be a true expression of absolute nothingness. Even though new morality was introduced in the name of the God of Christianity, it was an abstract morality severed from the origin of the ethnic group. Therefore, the state established after the destruction of ethnic religion lacks the structure that makes this state equal to the morality of absolute nothingness. When he describes European countries as "environmentally formed," that is, formed through the forces of their external environment, he implies that even if the formation of the state is motivated by the national spirit born at a later time, this formation is not truly intrinsic. He qualifies this by arguing it does not derive from the ethnic will born in and subsisting from the oldest ethnic society. Without the contact with absolute nothingness operative in the origin of the ethnic group, it would be impossible for the state to become the embodiment of the morality of absolute nothingness.

Considering the importance of absolute nothingness for Nishida, the question remains as to why Nishida reduces the structure of the state in the exact sense of the word to a specific concrete structure. Given his description of the state's structure as the form of self-formation—the formless form—the absence of a fixed model seems more suitable for the expression of absolute nothingness. Examining Nishida's arguments with respect to the Imperial Family, and the structure of the Japanese state formed around the Family, will provide an answer to this question.

Surprisingly, in "The Problem of Japanese Culture," Nishida describes the Imperial Family as a "being of nothingness [*mu no yū*]" (NKZ XII 336). Along the same lines as common observations of the Imperial Family, Nishida states that the members of the Imperial Family never became subjects who wielded power and moved Japanese history, and yet the Family has subsisted behind the scenes of history while having authority over these subjects, as Yusa mentioned before. Thus, the Imperial Family inherited an uninterrupted lineage independent from the rise and fall of men of power. As such, Nishida comments, "I think that the Imperial Family, transcending these subjective beings, was in the position of the world that determines itself as the contradictory self-identity between the one as subjective and the multiple as individual" (NKZ XII 335–36). In other words, although the Imperial Family does not have its own subjectivity, it allows for the subjectivities of many others, just as the world determines individuals so that they determine themselves. Besides, just as the world envelops individuals as they are, the Imperial Family accepts others' different subjectivities and makes them coexist. Nishida calls the Imperial Family a being of nothingness because, in the absence of its own subjectivity, the Imperial Family puts itself in the position of the world and takes on the function of absolute nothingness to create and envelop the subjectivities of others, as if the Imperial Family were absolute nothingness incarnate.

Nishida's views that the state is a particular world, and that the Imperial Family is in the position of the world, entail the corollary that the Imperial Family is most representative of the Japanese state and its structure, representing itself as equivalent. Needless to say, this corollary is a natural consequence of his idea of the Imperial Family's centrality in the structure of the Japanese state. However, for Nishida, this centrality means more than the Imperial Family's influence, exerted from behind the scenes of history, upon the subjects of power in every era.

In the appendix to "The Problem of Japanese Culture," Nishida says, "[Japan] has sustained its self-identity thoroughly around the center of the Imperial Family, and Japanese spirit has resided in this attitude" (NKZ XII 386). The national spirit of Japan—the force binding citizens into one collective subject and urging them to build or maintain their state, the force forming and formed by the structure of the state—resides in its attitude of centering the Imperial Family. The centrality of the Imperial Family in the structure of the Japanese state also confirms its centrality in the organization of Japanese people into one collective unity, sustaining their common self-identity by sharing the same center.

If the people calling themselves Japanese, and these people's culture, have certain natures, Nishida concludes that it is because the Imperial Family acts as the center, not only around which they identify with each other, but also with which they themselves identify. At this point, the Imperial Family is literally said to be the most representative of the structure of the Japanese state. Nishida sees the particularity of Japanese culture in the attitude of "thoroughly negating oneself and becoming the thing," or "emptying oneself and seeing a thing, immersing oneself in the thing" (NKZ XII 346). He equates this attitude with the quintessence of Japanese spirit, and explains where he thinks it originates:

> The quintessence of Japanese spirit must consist in being united into the thing or matter. To do so means to become one where there was neither the self, nor someone else in the first place. This would mean to center upon the Imperial Family in the manner of contradictory self-identity. (NKZ XII 346)

Nishida ascribes the particularity of Japanese culture, or the quintessence of Japanese spirit—the attitude of annihilating oneself and becoming one with an object—to the centrality of the Imperial Family, with which Japanese people are meant to identify directly. Important to remember is his description of the Imperial Family as a being of nothingness in that its members allegedly empty out their own subjectivities. Thus, as Japanese people identify with this being of nothingness, which serves as their model, the particularity of their culture, or the quintessence of their spirit, has come to consist of annihilating oneself.

Pursuing this line of thought, Nishida also sees annihilating oneself as a moral imperative of Japanese people. Hence his description of the national morality of Japanese as "thoroughly sacrificing ourselves and serving for the construction of a historical world in which our selves move from there to there" (NKZ XII 340). Japanese people centering on the Imperial Family as a being of nothingness and identifying with it not only determines the natures of their culture and spirit, but also requires them to practice the morality of self-annihilation, commanded by absolute nothingness, to complete the movement "from there to there." By practicing this morality, they are disciplined and organized into one collectivity suitable to constituting such a state, one that is essentially moral. In short, another reason for Nishida's claim that only Japan has the structure of the state equal to morality is his view that, as the result of the centrality of the Imperial Family in this structure, Japanese people are led to practice the morality of self-annihilation. Presenting the accord between this morality, on the one hand, and the particularity of Japanese culture, or the quintessence of Japanese spirit, on the other, Nishida emphasizes the unity of this "ought" and "is" for Japanese people.

Accordingly, Nishida prioritizes a certain form of the state's structure, formed around the center of the Imperial Family, and regards it alone as authentic. For him, the Imperial Family is a being of nothingness, a being in which absolute nothingness personifies itself exceptionally. Analogously, the structure of the state, constructed in the center of this being of nothingness, is a form in which absolute nothingness expresses itself par excellence, and as such is equivalent to a formless form, even though it is one of many concrete forms.

Moreover, the construction and maintenance of this structure is concomitant with the formation of a united and moralized human group. As previously mentioned, when people identify with and model themselves on the Imperial Family as a being of nothingness, they not only organize themselves into a collectivity, but also practice the morality of self-annihilation as if they made themselves into beings of nothingness. In a word, the structure of the state that centers upon the Imperial Family realizes the ideal state Nishida envisioned in "The Problem of the Reason of the State." Specifically, this is the state with which citizens are united, and in which they practice morality as the self-expression of absolute nothingness, so that the state itself embodies this morality.

With regard to the formation of a human group called the "Japanese" and the determination of their essence through the structure of the state of Japan, Nishida's arguments turn out to have significant relevance to his four disciples' arguments about Japanese national subjectivity. The Japanese discussed by Nishida, who practice the morality of self-annihilation by identifying with and modeling on a being of nothingness, are reminiscent of the ethical subject of responsibility conceived of by his disciples, namely the subject that annihilates itself in accomplishing its responsibility. Both attain their identities in the face of nothingness and realize the morality necessitated by nothingness. Although his disciples did not explore this further, while claiming the subject of responsibility is rooted in Japanese tradition and has proved its existence in Japanese history, Nishida provides an explanation as to why the Japanese, especially and exclusively, can be such people through recourse to the structure of the state of Japan correlative with and complementary to its tradition. The Japanese determine themselves by identifying with and modeling themselves on a being of nothingness at the center of this structure, thus making them especially capable of becoming subjects of responsibility who do not mind self-annihilation. Even though he does not put subjectivity at the center of his philosophy, his thought on the Japanese neither excludes subjectivity, nor contradicts his disciples' thought on Japanese national subjectivity. Rather, he buttresses it by inquiring into the conditions that make the production of this subjectivity possible.

Attaching great importance to the structure of the state of Japan, Nishida goes so far as to assert its worthiness not only for the Japanese, but also for the entire world. In the supplement to his *Philosophical Essays* vol. 4, he insists:

> Today we should not only be proud of the particularity of the structure of our state, but also have an eye to the global profundity of this structure and illuminate it, and then promulgate it in the world in both theory and practice, because now it is the time for global awareness. It is high time precisely for the essence of the state to be disclosed as the normative form of human actions to form the historical world. Then, consequently, a new world order will be constituted based on this form. (NKZ XII 410–11)

In short, Nishida argues that the structure of the state unique to Japan can be the norm for a new world order, which is in line with his statement quoted before: "[t]he principle of the formation of Japan must become the principle of the formation of the world" (NKZ XII 341). To disclose this norm in view of the construction of this new order, he exclaims that "we" should "illuminate the profundity of this structure" and "promulgate it in the world." Given his reference to "the structure of *our* state" after his assertion that only Japan has the structure of the state, it is obvious the term "we" designates the Japanese. When he states that once the essence of the state is disclosed, "a new world order will be constructed" under the guidance of this essence, it is unclear who he believes will construct it. However, in the same vein, in "The Problems of the Reason of State," he declares, "to embark on the formation of the world based on this structure of the state must be the mission of our nation [*waga kokumin*]" (NKZ X 334). The mission Nishida expects the Japanese to accomplish is not only to disclose the essence of the state, but also "to embark on the formation of the world based on [the] structure of the state" and to construct the new world order.

If it is to be successful, this mission cannot dispense with the subject who will succeed. Nishida's description of the mission is closely associated with this statement in "The Problem of Japanese Culture," quoted at the beginning of this chapter: "That we demonstrate the principle of world formation lying at the basis of our [Japanese] history does not mean that Japan stops being a historical subject or stops being Japan" (NKZ XII 341–42). Nishida states that Japan is still a subject in spite of his warning, "What we should above all caution ourselves against is making Japan a subject" (NKZ XII 341). The subject required for the above mission should be the former, historical subject that he has acknowledged. Aside from questions as to what this subject is and how it is different from that which Nishida admonishes against—which will be discussed in the next section—what should be noted is that in advocating for the construction of the new world order, he assumes the collective subjectivity of Japanese people as the agent of this construction. And if the structure of the state of Japan can be the norm of the new world order, as he asserts, this collective—indeed national—subjectivity formed by this structure would have global potential not limited to its local existence. At this point, the structure of the Japanese state described by Nishida finds its point of contact with the second characteristic of the Japanese national subjectivity conceived of by his four disciples: the interpenetration between the national and the international within it. I will now undertake the quest for overlap between his argument about the special mission of Japan and his four disciples' idea of the second characteristic of Japanese national subjectivity, followed by a comparison of the ways in which he and his disciples explain Japan's centrality in the world.

Section 4: The Subject Becoming the World and Enveloping Others

In the third appendix to the supplement to his *Philosophical Essays* vol. 4, titled "The Principle of a New World Order," Nishida discusses the themes of the new world order and its principle. In it he states, "It can be said that the principle of the structure of our state will give the resolution to today's world-historical task" (NKZ XII 434). This task is that "[e]ach and every state must constitute one *world-historical world, that is, the worldly world* by respectively becoming aware of its global mission" (NKZ XII 427). He further specifies:

> What I mean by the formation of the worldly world is that the world concretely becomes one, qua the worldly world, by each and every state and ethnic group's thoroughly accomplishing the world-historical mission on each their own historical basis, that is, by each living each their own historical life. (NKZ XII 430)

For Nishida, the constitution of one world does not entail the denial of the individualities of all states or ethnic groups for the oneness of the world. Ideally, he believes that only respect for the uniqueness of each state or ethnic group enables the unity of the world, and vice versa: "Just like in an organism, the whole's becoming one is each part's becoming itself, and each part's becoming itself is the whole's becoming one" (NKZ XII 430). The worldly world Nishida speaks of is the world that is one in this way, the world in which all states and ethnic groups are united, while their individualities are accepted. It is thus the world that truly deserves the name "the world," which includes all its members as they are. He uses a wartime slogan common in his day, "putting each and every country in the right place [*banpō onoono sono tokoro wo eseshimeru*]" (NKZ XII 430), to suggest the formation of this worldly world.

In keeping with the general current of thought at the time, Nishida and his four disciples conceive of the new world order as an alternative to the Western-centered world order. For Nishida, the question of how the worldly world is possible is inseparable from questions as to why this new world order is not another version of colonialism or imperialism, and how Japan's leadership or centrality in this order is different from Western hegemony. Before looking into Nishida's answers to these questions, we see here what Nishida thinks of Western imperialism and its causes:

> But the mere ethnicism, which consists of centering solely on one's own ethnic group that does not hold in itself true worldness and thinking of the entire world from the standpoint of this group, is ethnic egoism [*minzoku jikoshugi*]. As the consequence of ethnic egoism, an ethnic group could not but give oneself up to aggressive policy or imperialism. Anglo-American imperialism today is based upon nothing but their ethnic egoism. (NKZ XII 432–33)

Nishida refers to ethnic egoism as the cause of imperialism. Although he does not discuss its meaning here, he hints at it in "The Problem of Japanese Culture." As his defenders such as Yusa and Ueda highlighted, Nishida observes imperialism with regard to its subjectivity and states, "the behaviour of facing other subjects in the capacity of the subject, of trying to negate them and make them one's self, is nothing but that of imperialism" (NKZ XII 349). Supposing that the subject is either the state or ethnic group, Nishida says that imperialism emerges when one state or ethnic group negates the subjectivity of others and imposes its subjectivity upon them, either by integrating them into it or subjugating them to it. This means that "one subject tries to become a world" and one ethnic group or one state "tries to dominate the world." Further, he states, "Imperialism is a consequence of such a tendency" (NKZ XII 373). Imperialism is caused by the tendency of a certain state or ethnic group to adhere to its own subjectivity and try to expand this subjectivity all over the world, regardless of the subjectivities of other states or ethnic groups. This is what Nishida calls ethnic egoism.

Although, at first glance, Nishida's argument with respect to what causes problems for the hegemony of Western powers may seem different from what his four disciples argue, all address the same thing in different ways. The four disciples sought the cause of these problems in the atomistic view of humans underlying the ideals of freedom and equality and asserted that once the ethnic groups that determine themselves according to such a view are set free, ineluctably the strong will conquer and exploit the weak. Nishida seeks the cause of these problems in ethnic egoism, which he sees as the tendency of the ethnic group to expand its own subjectivity while negating the subjectivity of other ethnic groups, and traces the origin of this tendency to the attitude of the subjects of different ethnic groups facing and opposing each other. If ethnic groups cannot but oppose each other, it is because they determine themselves to be completely separate and independent, just as with the atomistic view of humans that sees the negation of others as not harming but profiting oneself. What the disciples describe as a certain view of humans seeming to influence the behaviours of ethnic groups, Nishida describes as a typical mode of the subject's existence as he understands it.

While Western countries succumbed to ethnic egoism and were drawn into imperialism because of this mode of existence, Nishida stresses, Japan would never follow in their footsteps for it has a capacity to exist beyond such a mode. Nishida ascribes this disparity to the cultural difference between the East and the West. Typically, he classifies Japan as belonging to the East, distinguished from and contrasted with the West, and explains the cultural difference as that of the dominant direction in the interaction between subject and environment, the interaction from which humans as social beings were born and whose dominant direction determines their cultural tendency. "Roughly speaking, Western culture is considered to go in the direction from environment to subject, and Oriental culture, on the contrary, from subject to environment" (NKZ XII 345). Western culture, because of the initial dominance of the act of environment upon subject, has a tendency to confront the environment and establish the subject solidly enough to counter it. Thus, the subject's typical mode of existence emerges and consists of facing and opposing other subjects so as to negate them. It expands itself, presupposed by ethnic egoism. Conversely, Nishida continues, Oriental culture, drawing mainly upon the movement from subject to environment, has a tendency in which "the subject negates itself and becomes environmental, becomes the thing" (NKZ XII 345). Determined by the movement opposite to that of Western culture, Oriental culture has a tendency to accord itself with environment and efface subject. As such, Oriental culture must have the potential to overcome the above mode of existence of the subject and ethnic egoism.

Strangely enough, in spite of this characterization of Oriental nature, Nishida suggests this potential did not develop in other countries in the East. He disdainfully asserts two major Oriental cultures, Chinese and Indian, "lacked the spirit of going toward truth to the end, and therefore were stiffened and fixed" (NKZ XII 280). In contrast to the spirit lacking in these cultures, he underlines the attitude permeating Japanese culture "to empty oneself and follow the truth of the thing" (NKZ XII 280). He means that Japanese culture pursued the movement characteristic of Oriental culture, according with environment and effacing subject, furthest. As a result, Japanese culture has "the subject qua world" as its essential form, that which "becomes the world by self-negation without going through numerous negations by environment" (NKZ XII 348). Nishida distinguishes this subject qua world from the subject he found in Western culture—the subject that confronts and conquers not only environment, but also other subjects, in order to become the world. Whereas the latter subject adheres to its own subjectivity and expands itself to include the world, the former forsakes its own subjectivity and merges with the world. Therefore, while the latter negates other subjects, leading to ethnic egoism and imperialism, the former accepts other subjects and establishes another kind of relationship among different ethnic groups. Thus, Nishida sees in Japanese culture the full development of Oriental culture's potential to overcome ethnic egoism and imperialism.

Based on his view of this potential in Japanese culture, Nishida specifies one of its tasks to be "enveloping other subjects as a world, rather than facing them in the capacity of the subject" (NKZ XII 349). For Nishida, "enveloping other subjects as a world" is different from "facing other subjects in the capacity of the subject" and "trying to negate them and make them one's self" (NKZ XII 349), so as to become a world. If different subjects attempt this negation, they clash with each other when trying to expand themselves. Once the strongest among them expand themselves beyond the others and integrate the others into themselves, the result will merely be the conquest and exploitation of the weak by the strong. In contrast, if one subject envelops other subjects, there will be no clash. Since enveloping is possible only by emptying one's own self, the enveloping is not opposed to the enveloped. Rather, the enveloping one can change the enveloped ones, so that they no longer oppose each other. Nishida expects the worldly world he envisions to be constructed through this envelopment. Thus, the task of Japanese culture mentioned above, "enveloping other subjects as a world," is tantamount to constructing this worldly world based upon the essential form of Japanese culture, so that "the principle of the formation of Japan must become the principle of the formation of the world" (NKZ XII 341).

In "The Problem of Japanese Culture," Nishida attributes this capacity in Japanese culture to the Japanese geopolitical condition: "Japan has been located on an isolated island in the sea in the East for thousands of years (NKZ XII 348). What he refers to as the antipode to this situation is "the European world, formed environmentally in the direction from environment to subject" (NKZ XII 349). Here, he refers to a continent on which the shared borders of the lands of different ethnic groups forced them to undergo innumerable negations and establish solid subjects to rival or even defeat others. Conversely, if surrounded by the sea and isolated from others, an ethnic group does not need to oppose such negations and establish a solid subject. It can easily negate itself as a subject and merge with the world. Aside from the fact that there have historically been numerous minority ethnic groups within Japan, and that other ethnic groups have come from abroad during the course of Japanese history, Nishida invokes a kind of environmental determinism, as if the geopolitical conditions of Japan, distinguished from those of other countries, had predestined it to cultivate a special culture and concentrate within itself the potential of Oriental culture to overcome Western culture and its harmful consequences.[5]

However, if Japan simply indulges itself as being determined by its geopolitical condition in its primal state of affairs, the state in which the subject completely immerses itself in the world where it was born, Japan would never be able to envelop other subjects or other ethnic groups outside the island. Enveloping them, whatever this involves, at least means putting itself in a special position that distinguishes itself from other subjects and wields certain influence over them. Doing so requires a shift from this primal state of affairs, which Nishida hints entails the emergence of certain subjectivity, although it is supposed to be different from that which he found to be characteristic of Western culture. Nishida remarks, "For the ethnic Japanese [*nihon minzoku*], who have inhabited an isolated island in the sea in the East and developed uniquely in an almost closed society for thousands of years, Japan was immediately the world," followed by his comment that, "Japan was not a historical subject" (NKZ XII 341). He contrasts the Japan of the past to that of the present: "However Japan today is no longer that which has rested on an isolated island in the sea in the East. It is no longer a closed society. It is the Japan of the world, Japan standing in the face of the world" (NKZ XII 341). This is followed by his statement on Japan as a historical subject, as quoted earlier: "That we demonstrate the principle of world formation lying at the base of our [Japanese] history does not mean that Japan stops being a historical subject or stops being Japan" (NKZ XII 341–42). Nishida suggests that Japan now must step out of its primal unity with its own world and become a subject while attaining its unity with a wider world, the worldly world he envisioned. This suggestion means that Japanese people, rather than merely living according to their natural disposition or following the structure of their state from force of habit, must resolutely uphold this structure and demonstrate that it can embody the principle of world formation. This act consciously exerts their capacity to self-negate, as cultivated by Japan's geopolitical condition and state structure, so that Japan can envelop other countries in the world and promulgate this same structure there. This means that although both Japan's geopolitical condition and state structure contributed to fostering Japanese people's subjectivity in conjunction with aspects of their living environment, the crucial determinant for the development of this subjectivity on the global scene is the state structure itself.

For Nishida, the subject that Japan should become by upholding a state structure centered upon the Imperial Family is not one that adheres to its subjectivity and extends it over the world, but one that empties its subjectivity and merges with the world. Only such a subject is capable of "enveloping other subjects as a world" (NKZ XII 349), just as the Imperial Family does. Certainly "enveloping other subjects" is impossible if that which envelops is of the same kind as that which is enveloped. But the adjective, "other," added to the noun, "subjects," implies that what envelops them is still a subject, albeit of another kind. In Nishida's view, only this subject, which remains after it empties its subjectivity, or more precisely, which forms itself through the emptying of its subjectivity, is true to the authentic structure of the state of Japan as an expression of absolute nothingness. As such it is qualified to promulgate this structure in the world. When this subject does so it would subsequently realize the worldly world by enveloping other subjects as they are, differently from the subjects of ethnic egoism or imperialism.

Nishida's attitude toward Japan's subjectivity is ambiguous; he negates subjectivity on the one hand and affirms another subjectivity that should result from this negation on the other. Although he does not clearly formulate this ambiguity as such, his four disciples' logic of the unity between the being and nothingness of the subject of responsibility—the subject for which, they believed, the Japanese have a great aptitude—provides an equivalent to such a formulation. Given that he presents, albeit implicitly and intricately, the notion of the subject that can be affirmed only through self-negation, he has substantially prepared this logic, which his disciples give a definite and clear shape.

While these disciples simply describe the paradox wherein Japanese subjectivity is affirmed through self-negation (that it both exists and does not exist), as a peculiarity of Japanese people or culture, Nishida seeks an explanation for this paradoxical peculiarity through considering the centrality of the

Imperial Family in the structure of the Japanese state. That is, if Japan can become a subject without subjectivity, it is within a context where Japanese people not only live following this structure of the state formed around the center of this being of nothingness, but also where they resolutely uphold this structure. It was in the same vein that Nishida takes this structure as equivalent to a formless form, which is parallel to its center's being without being. Thus, he grounds the formation of Japanese national subjectivity in the structure of the state of Japan, and bases the unity of the being and the nothingness of this subjectivity upon the Imperial Family as a being of nothingness at the center of this structure.

Moreover, according to Nishida, by negating its own subjectivity, Japan's subjectivity becomes the world, which in turn anticipates the interpenetration between the national and the international in the Japanese national subjectivity conceived of by his four disciples. Nishida's discussion of Japan becoming a global subject and promulgating its state structure to the entire world dovetails with his four disciples' discussions around Japanese national subjectivity proving its truthfulness in world history. Common to both is also the assumption that the capacity to be international, whether by becoming the world and enveloping other subjects or facing the ground of the world and the principle of world history, is exceptionally fostered in Japan, due to Japanese culture's special inclination toward nothingness. In this interpenetration between the national and the international, Nishida and his four disciples ground Japan's centrality in the new world order, yet to be constructed.

Nishida once described ethnic egoism as "centering solely on one's own ethnic group that does not hold in itself true worldness, and thinking of the entire world from the standpoint of this group" (NKZ XII 432). At first glance, this description seems to apply to any ethnic group. However, supposing there is an ethnic group that "hold[s] in itself true worldness" thanks to the interpenetration between the national and the international in the subjectivity of that group as its cultural specificity, this ethnic group's centering upon itself and thinking the entire world from its standpoint does not fall into the category of ethnic egoism. Combined with his assertion that the Japanese, by negating their subjectivity, become the world and envelop other subjects, Nishida's description of ethnic egoism has allowed him to make Japan the sole exception and unconditionally absolve it of any accusation of ethnocentrism or expansionism.[6]

Even though Nishida argues that Japanese subjectivity is without subjectivity and as such evades ethnic egoism or imperialism, his insistence that only Japan can attain such subjectivity suggests that this subjectivity is, in fact, not really international or cosmopolitan. An additional overlap between Nishida and his four disciples confirms his point. The latter's intention to establish

Japan's centrality in the world by invoking the interpenetration between the national and the international in Japanese national subjectivity is illustrated in the logical structure of their discussions concerning this characteristic. First, Oriental tradition has something surpassing Western modernity and influencing the entire world; second, Japan is the epitome of this tradition and should therefore have special status in the world. Apparently Nishida shares this argument, as he ascribes the potential to overcome ethnic egoism and imperialism resulting from Western culture to Oriental culture, and finds in Japanese culture the full development of this potential. Even if the Japanese subjectivity he has in mind, by negating itself and merging with the world, has enough true worldness to envelop other subjects, insofar as this worldness is thus invoked to legitimate the single subject's envelopment of others, the internationality of Japanese subjectivity is subjugated to the national to confirm its privilege.

Graham Parkes describes the stance of the Kyoto School philosophers, including Nishida and Nishitani, as "a 'rooted cosmopolitanism,'" using Kwame Anthony Appiah's terms (180). As his reasoning for applying this appellation to these philosophers, Parkes refers to their assertion regarding "the compatibility of nationalism with internationalism" (179). However, this compatibility, discussed by them in the form of the interpenetration between the national and the international, appears to conceal a national desire for hegemony in the guise of internationality, as in Nishida's and Nishitani's cases. As such, their stances seem to exist far from an ideology of "rooted cosmopolitanism." As a matter of fact, "the internationalist stance of the Kyoto School thinkers" that Parkes claims to distinguish from "particularistic nationalism" (179) is inseparably connected to it in order to buttress it in the name of this very internationality.

In following the same argument, Nishida and his four disciples seem to differ in what they perceive as Oriental culture's peculiarity, which has the potential to overcome Western culture and is epitomized in Japanese culture. While Nishida sees this peculiarity in the tendency to negate subjectivity and become the thing or the world, his four disciples see it in the ethics of the family system. However, this tendency permeates this ethics as its fulcrum. Their inseparability has been alluded to, as the four thinkers base the pluralistic world order they conceived of as analogous to the family system upon Japan's central position as place qua nothingness. This equation between Japan and nothingness has an anchor in the four disciples' idea of the subject of responsibility, defined by self-annihilation, rooted particularly in Japanese tradition and realized in the lives of Japanese people. The four disciples claimed that Japan in the capacity of place qua nothingness should guide other subjects to put themselves in the right places and harmonize each other in this world order just as the parent raises the child. Thus, putting oneself in the position of nothingness affords paternalistic authority over others. That is to say, this authority resides in allegedly negating one's own subjectivity, and comes closest to nothingness qua place, so as to know the "places" of others. This is viewed as pursuing the dominant tendency of Oriental culture the furthest, as Nishida believed Japan did. In this respect, the four thinkers are hand-in-hand with their mentor, who argued the subject that negates itself and becomes the world can envelop other subjects. The same logic has also appeared in Nishitani's argument that, insofar as it fully realizes the ethics of selflessness or no-mindedness as Oriental tradition, Japan should be the leading state of new international communality established upon this ethics.

In discussing the problems with the thought of Nishida's four disciples, I have mentioned the risk of assuming morality or ethicality as inherent to the essence of a certain group of humans or a political body, and justifying its authority on this assumption while wrapping this authority in a moral or ethical appearance. Even if that morality or ethicality sounds respectable or innocuous, once it is assumed to be inherent to the essence of a certain group of people, it produces not only a hierarchy between them and others, but also an impression that the hierarchy is part of this morality or ethicality. Here lies the problem with the four thinkers' arguments about the Japanese morality or ethicality; the same applies to Nishida's arguments. He insists the ideal of self-negation not only belongs to Japan's cultural particularity as determined by its geopolitical condition, but also is fully developed through its state structure. When he grounds Japan's centrality in the new world order or authority over other countries in this essentialism, his gesture is far from the ideal of self-negation. Nevertheless, this gap is hidden by the excuse that the ground for this centrality or authority is a moral or ethical ideal. Likewise, the desire for global hegemony is disguised as the aspiration for a non-imperialistic, peaceful world order.

This disguise is supported by Nishida's ambiguous stance toward subjectivity. By affirming the subject through appeal to its essence that allegedly involves self-negation, Nishida reintroduces the same old egoistic subject greedy for centrality or authority under the guise of the new moral or ethical subject. This problem affected not only Nishida's idea of Japanese subjectivity, but also that of his disciples. In the latter's case, in a way reminiscent of the former's, the unity between the being and nothingness of the Japanese national subject obscures the existence of any subjugating power or any related desire for domination, as well as its agent, and disguises this subject's deeds as ethical.

In the discussion so far, Nishida's thought, dating from the time of the *Chūōkōron* symposia, is seen to have significant overlap with the four participants' thought on Japanese national subjectivity in terms of its three notable characteristics. Both sides had a quite similar thought at times, but sometimes both addressed the same thing differently. While the former's thought theoretically supported the latter's in a wider perspective at times and gave it a solid basis or a suitable milieu, sometimes the former's anticipated or prepared the latter's.

Along with such overlaps, all the thinkers also shared common problems with their ideas of Japanese subjectivity, and with the morality or ethicality they ascribed to this subjectivity. While asserting that this subjectivity can realize a peaceful world order by virtue of the selfless morality it embodies, all these thinkers insisted that the privileged status of the state (to which this subjectivity belongs in this world order) must remain indispensable for this world order to be realized. Here, the claim of ethnocentrism that is central to and complicit with ethnic egoism or imperialism takes on the appearance of the claim that Japanese subjectivity can help lead toward the realization of morality or peaceful world order. These thinkers' conception of the Japanese national subjectivity, whose being is united with its absence, works to help this disguise.

Certainly, as evidenced by his letter to Kōsaka around the time of the *Chūōkōron* symposia, Nishida found the four disciples' discussions in these symposia to be so outrageous that it led him to advise these thinkers to stop engaging with the journal and its editors (NKZ XIX 257; Letter No. 1815). However, the continuity and affinity between his philosophy and that of his four disciples, expressed in both parties' texts as a matter of fact, cannot be lightly dismissed. In his 1980 book *Theories on "Overcoming Modernity,* Hiromatsu Wataru commented that "the great part of the theories of 'overcoming modernity,' advocated by the philosophers under Nishida's care, and their philosophy of history and view of society or the state, all of which undergirded such theories, already had its precedent in the thoughts of the great master Nishida Kitarō himself" (211). This view has not lost its validity.

Nishida's defenders, who emphasize his intentions to protest against the military government, may want to distinguish between his philosophy and that of his disciples, given the fact that (unlike his disciples) he did not eloquently advocate for the Greater East Asia War. For example, Christopher Goto-Jones remarks, "Nishida's closest colleagues [other members of the Kyoto School], variously disfigured by the pressures of intellectual life in a totalitarian policy, pushed his thought further in the direction of imperialism and ultranationalism" (*Political Philosophy in Japan* 125). Goto-Jones argues that because of its idealism or utopianism, Nishida's philosophy was "routinely exploited as justifications for violence directed at revolution" (*Political Philosophy in Japan* 129).

In his essay "Nishida Kitarō 'The Problem of Japanese Culture'" (*Nishida Kitarō "Nihonbunka no mondai"*), Kobayashi argues that defenders who distinguish Nishida as pacifist (in contrast to his belligerent disciples) neglect the "crucial point" that Nishida "does not negate the struggle and war between ethnic groups but regards them as the necessity of history" (57). Drawing on Nishida's "The Problem of Japanese Culture," Kobayashi ("Nishida Kitarō 'The Problem of Japanese Culture'" 61) quotes a passage that exemplifies this perspective on the struggle: "There are only struggles between species interminably. In the manner of the contradictory self-identity, the historical world is a world of struggle in which species oppose and fight each other interminably" (NKZ XII 334). When Nishida subsequently states that "From today's global struggle, a new form of humans would have to be born" (NKZ XII 334) without concretely specifying the meaning of this statement, Kobayashi remarks that, regardless of Nishida's real intentions, his claim appears as similar to that of the military ("Nishida Kitarō 'The Problem of Japanese Culture'" 63).

Kobayashi's remarks are one more reminder of the necessity of critically examining thoughts as expressed in the texts of the philosophers in question, rather than avoiding this examination on the basis of those philosophers' intentions to protest, or the apparent sublimity or innocuousness of their ideals. As I discussed in part 1, if we present an ideal or utopian vision on the one hand, but build a narrative as if this vision has already been realized on the other, neither idealism nor utopianism continues to be the force to radically criticize and transform reality. Instead, it lends itself to the dogmatic conviction in, or unconditional celebration of, the rightness of the existing regime in its status quo, that which this vision was supposed to contest. Unfortunately, this seems to be the case not only with the four thinkers, but also with their mentor, as they all go around between the virtuality and actuality, or the being and nothingness, of the Japanese subjectivity they advocated for. There are particular cases of what Yonetani described as "the complementarity between ideal and reality" (229) that merit consideration. Here again, what happened in these cases cannot be reduced to a matter of misunderstanding or ignorance from the masses. Regardless of Nishida's intentions, the problem is that his texts inherently presented ideals in a manner where they may appear to justify the realities of colonial rule and aggression of the time, while simultaneously fostering this very kind of "misunderstanding" from the masses. To understand how these ideals and reality interacted to create problematic effects, a critical examination of Nishida's texts and an inquiry into the textual elements that mediate and facilitate this interaction is absolutely necessary.

Chapter 9

The Significance and Problems of Nishida's Arguments about *Kokutai*

In the previous chapter, the exploration of the continuity and overlap between the four thinkers' ideas of Japanese national subjectivity and those of their mentor Nishida led us to the discovery that his ideas posited a similar subjectivity conceived in a more comprehensive way, as well as suggestions that the structure of the state of Japan is what would determine the formation of this subjectivity. It was also revealed that Nishida asserts not only that the Imperial Way is the way in which the Japanese Emperor should govern the country, but also that the structure of the Japanese state, formed around the Imperial Family, should to be the principle for the formation of the entire world.

The Imperial Way and the structure of the Japanese state as Nishida conceived of them are not separate, but are indispensably complementary to each other. According to Nishida's arguments, the Imperial Way consisted of the Emperor exerting influence over subjects of power from behind the scenes of history, without becoming such a subject, with the Emperor thus enveloping them as a being of nothingness. The structure of the state of Japan was constituted by the Japanese people modelling themselves upon and identifying with the Imperial Family, thus practicing the morality of self-annihilation in the face of this being of nothingness. While the Imperial Way forms the core of the Japanese state's structure, without this structure, the Imperial Way does not function, just as the Emperor does not (or cannot) play a role at the center without people who organize themselves around him. Therefore, what Nishida construed as the principle for the formation of Japan and for the entire world is precisely the structure of the Japanese state, complete with the Imperial Way at its core. If this structure can be the principle for world formation, it is because it enables the formation of subjects who are in turn capable of enveloping other subjects in line with the model of a being of nothingness at the structure's center. Thus, for Nishida, the privileged status that Japanese national subjectivity would occupy in the new world order stems from this structure that determines the formation of this subjectivity and guarantees the ability of that subjectivity to subsequently envelop other subjects so that they can peacefully coexist and live morally.

Although his arguments that universalize a particular state structure seem to simply echo the Emperor-worship that pervaded wartime ideologies, they have factors that cannot be simply explained away as elements of such worship. For example, these arguments addressing the structural aspects of *kokutai* elaborate how *kokutai* is formed, sustained, and grounded; how it determines the characteristics of the people living in that state and their culture; and what kind of subjectivity it cultivates among them (and so forth). Simply put, Nishida's arguments provide a systematic explanation of *kokutai* in a rational manner, different from a mere manifestation of worship, thus explaining the universal implications of a particular state structure. Seen alongside the backdrop of the historical context in which he wrote and published these arguments, certain significance can be attached to them, although, despite this significance, these arguments still have their own problems.

In this chapter, I will first give an overview of the historical context in which Nishida wrote and published his arguments about *kokutai*, with a focus upon an incident that exemplifies this situation, called the Minobe incident (or the Minobe affair), which was provoked by Minobe Tatsukichi's theory regarding the Emperor. I will then explore the significance that Nishida's arguments addressing the structural aspects of *kokutai* and the function of the Imperial Family could have in this historical context, by comparing these arguments and Minobe's above theory. Second, I will reflect upon the role that Nishida's arguments inadvertently ended up playing in this context through consideration of the similar roles that Minobe and Miki Kiyoshi's theories played. Third, I will show that a cause of what made Nishida's arguments work in this way was contained within these very arguments and that this very facet undergirds his arguments universalizing one particular nation-state. Thus, by clarifying the significance and problems of Nishida's arguments about *kokutai*, I will highlight the importance of further exploring the matter of the universalization of the particular in his philosophy, as well as associated concepts that also support this universalization.

Section 1: The Stakes of Nishida's Theory Concerning the Imperial Family

To understand the significance of Nishida's arguments about *kokutai*, which is often credited to his rational way of formulating them and its illumination of the structural aspects of *kokutai*, an overview of the historical situation for Japanese intellectuals at that time, as well as some details on an incident that epitomized that situation, is necessary.

In 1925, the Peace Preservation Law (*Chian iji hō*) was enacted to suppress political movements scheming to alter the Japanese *kokutai*. Although its initial targets were communism and socialism, the law's later targets came to include liberalism, individualism, and a broad range of non-political activities. The military wielded its influence and promoted militarism and Emperor-worship, both of which found fanatic support among civilians. Military radicals and their civilian auxiliaries waged violent attacks against people who they judged as disrespectful to the Japanese *kokutai* or disloyal to the Emperor. To carry out this agenda thoroughly, the military also put pressure on the parliament to influence policymaking in the military's favor.

In 1935, Japanese scholar of law Minobe Tatsukichi was denounced in both houses of parliament and charged with lese-majeste because of his theory known as the emperor organ theory (*Tennō kikan setsu*; sometimes simply called the organ theory), which defined the Emperor as a national organ. Although the prosecution was suspended, Minobe was forced to resign all of his public posts, and the teaching of his emperor organ theory at universities was banned. This series of events is called the Minobe incident. In 1936, Minobe was shot by a right-wing zealot and wounded. In the aftermath of the Minobe incident, the military's increasing power over the government, politics, and society led to the negation of liberal constitutionalism and the eradication of freedom of speech. Although the Minobe incident is an exemplary case, he is not the only intellectual who was persecuted on account of his scholarly inquiry.[1]

Minobe's emperor organ theory claims that governmental power pertains not to the Emperor as a person but to the Emperor as the head of the state. To this extent, governmental power ultimately resides in the state, and the Emperor is the supreme national organ through which this power can be exercised in the interests of the state and its members. Therefore, the parliament representing these people can bind the Emperor's will in terms of his exercise of this power. This theory is an interpretation of the Meiji Constitution (the Constitution of the Empire of Japan). As such, it did not intend to subvert the state or destroy its system. In fact, before the incident, this theory had been largely accepted as a reasonable constitutional interpretation for decades. Nevertheless, fierce attacks against it started. Since the enactment of the Peace Preservation Law, a trend had emerged in which any thought labelled as "contrary to the Japanese *kokutai*," whether the thought was Western, liberal, individualistic, scientific, or otherwise, was denounced. Along with this rising trend, the qualification of the Emperor as an "organ," which was superficially understood only at the level of terminology, fueled the rage of patriots. Under such circumstances, simply treating *kokutai* as an object of scholarly inquiry could put a scholar in danger of being harmed. Given this context, Nishida's arguments about *kokutai*, formulated rationally so as to illuminate its structural aspects, especially after Minobe incident, may be understandable as a form of resistance to the suppression of freedom of thought and expression, at least in a situation in which even the intellectual basis for resistance had been destroyed and where liberties were very limited.

Various attempts have been made to interpret Nishida's arguments as intended to resist the very state or *kokutai* they address. For example, in his 2007 book *Nishida Kitarō and the Question of the State* (*Nishida Kitarō to kokka eno toi*), Kado Kazumasa discerns an implicit criticism of the state of Japan in its status quo and the commonly accepted theories of *kokutai* in Nishida's arguments about the state and its raison d'être. Kado suggests that Nishida's arguments contain an implicit potential to undermine the vision of the totalitarian state, comparable to, or even more radical than the threatening potential that Minobe's emperor organ theory had toward these theories of *kokutai*. Kado takes the motifs that Nishida's arguments share with the common theories of *kokutai* as mere representations. Rather than understanding his arguments as literal addresses toward the existing referents of these representations, Kado inquires into how these representations work and deciphers what they express beneath the surface.

In Kado's view, the representation of the state in Nishida's arguments expresses the absoluteness of law in the sense that law precedes all individual entities, obliging them to act morally in compliance with law, thus making them persons to be respected in their own right. This absoluteness of law, which turns these entities equally into sovereigns, can be rendered as sovereignty itself, which is distinguished from any sovereign as a specific individual entity. The function of sovereignty in this sense (of articulating the relations between at least two entities while making them individual and sovereign) is described as "the third term." Kado insists that "the sovereignty, abstracted as the function of the third term, cannot be found in any individual entity and should be a nothingness ("being of nothingness") that cannot be substantialized" (218–19). Consequently, if sovereignty resides in the state it only resides there in terms of the state's upholding of the absoluteness of law understood as this being of nothingness. According to Kado, this is what Nishida meant when he emphasized the state's basis within nothingness, as exemplified by the phrase that the state is the self-expression of absolute nothingness. The implication here is that a state that professes to be sovereign must not only require its members to act morally in compliance with the law and respect each other as individuals, but it must also behave in the same way toward those individuals and toward other states, if it wants to ensure the legitimacy of its sovereignty. Therefore, Kado claims:

> Nishida's objective was not to rationalize actions of power but to secure the subjectification of the individual through recourse to "the absoluteness of law" or the absoluteness of [the] conformity [with this absoluteness], and to demand from the state "what is general or universal [*ippanteki na mono*]" as the norm for this [subjectification]. (207)

The crux of the above argument concerning the state can be found by locating the ultimate whereabouts of sovereignty (equated with the absoluteness of law) within nothingness, which supposedly cannot be appropriated by any individual entity. Reconsidering the state in light of sovereignty existing as such a being of nothingness suggests an argument in favor of putting all entities, including the state itself, under the control of the law of morality and forbidding the monopolization or arbitrary exercise of power by anybody.

We have seen that Nishida used the phrase "being of nothingness" to refer to the Imperial Family. Kado's choice of this phrase to describe sovereignty, conceived of as the absoluteness of law, is not random. In Kado's view, the implication of this terminology is not that the Imperial Family is a single supreme sovereign who occupies power, something that for Kado would be impossible given his conception of sovereignty. Rather, the implication is, as mentioned, that the sovereign state should be formed around the center of the absoluteness of law (described as a being of nothingness), if it wants to ensure the legitimacy of its being sovereign, as this sovereignty then cannot be appropriated by any individual entity. Here, the Imperial Family is invoked merely as a representation of the function of rendering the state, and its members, sovereign in conformity with the absoluteness of law, while regulating the relation between persons or states. For Kado, this is what Nishida meant in his argument about the Imperial Family as a being of nothingness.

> Here "the Imperial Family" is the guarantor of the institution. In that sense, it is not that "the Imperial Family" itself is public, but that it has the *function* to guarantee "subjects" to be public. Therefore, "the Imperial Family" is not a subjective entity but merely a name for a *function*. So, it is a "being of nothingness" and a contradictory self-identity. It is a place where subjects are established, and is in itself "nothingness." (187)

Here again, by investigating how representation works rather than what it refers to, Kado reads Nishida's implicit claim that Japanese citizens' individuality should be affirmed in the name of the Imperial Family into his argument which instead seems to assert the Imperial Family's centrality to the state of Japan. Nishida's equation of the Imperial Family with a being of nothingness enables the detachment of the representation of the Imperial Family from the absolute power granted to it by common theories of the *kokutai*, using this representation for the purpose of establishing citizens as sovereign subjects to be individually respected, contrary to the totalitarian assertions of theories that attack individualism.

Considering this conception of the Imperial Family as the guarantor of institution, it becomes understandable why Kado compares Nishida's arguments about the Imperial Family to Minobe's organ theory. The similarity between Minobe's claim and that of Nishida as interpreted by Kado is that both focus upon the function that the Emperor or the Imperial Family serves in the state, and that both define this function as restricting the arbitrary exercise of power, making state systems work in a way that can contribute to the good of the citizens.

In the context in which Minobe's organ theory was denounced, there was a risk that any scholarly inquiry treating the state or the Emperor as research objects and inspecting their functions would face similar accusations, and all the more so if the scholar was perceived as a scholar of "Western" philosophy, a supposed enemy of the "Japanese" spirit. However, even rightwing zealots would not have attacked someone's argument that the Japanese *kokutai* is formed around the center of the Imperial Family, even if they might still complain about the way it is argued. According to Kado's interpretation, Nishida under the guise of claiming the Imperial Family's centrality in the state of Japan implicitly claimed the necessity of respect for people's individuality in conformity with the absoluteness of law by invoking the Imperial Family as the guarantor of this conformity. Given that this conformity also applies to the state and binds it to respect any person or state beyond exclusivism, Kado insists that Nishida's arguments about the state have the potential to challenge it by "relativiz[ing] the fiction of the modern state or nation-state that constitutes the identity absorbing individuals" (222).

Section 2: The Thin Line between the Protest against and Advocacy of the Japanese *Kokutai*

Undeniably, Nishida's struggle to oppose commonly accepted theories of *kokutai* at that time by giving it different meanings has certain significance, and so do the explorations of the philosophical implications in this struggle. Still, whether this struggle contained any potential to challenge the state or *kokutai* can be questioned. Again, the fact that ultranationalists accused a certain theory of running counter to the Japanese *kokutai* based on its deviation from their agenda does not mean that this theory really challenged the *kokutai* and the state that possesses it, or that the theory could work to protest against them in the given situation.

Speaking of Minobe's organ theory (which Kado compares to Nishida's arguments about the state and the Imperial Family), Kawamura Satofumi in his 2014 essay "The National Polity and the Formation of the Modern National Subject in Japan" offers a fresh view of the role that Minobe's theory played in Japanese society precisely around the time that this theory was denounced, by taking into account the theory's initial reception in the preceding time period, and its subsequent impact.

According to Kawamura's account, after its first publication organ theory became a dominant constitutional interpretation and boosted democratic tendencies in the Taishō period. In the 1930s, when movements glorifying Japan's *kokutai* and attacking liberalism became stronger, this theory was suppressed alongside the democratic trends that had welcomed it. Against this backdrop, organ theory is usually construed as criticizing or opposing the Japanese *kokutai*. However, in Kawamura's view, this very theory actually "helped create the framework in which the 1930s and 1940s *kokutai* discourse was articulated" (27) so that this discourse could exploit the outcomes of the Taishō Democracy despite the former's opposing gestures toward democracy.

At first glance, Minobe's organ theory seems incompatible with the typical advocacy of the Japanese *kokutai*. This is because the former defines the Emperor as the organ through which the state's governmental power is exercised for the good of the citizens, whereas the latter claims that only the Emperor has this power, and citizens must thoroughly obey it regardless of how it would be exercised. To gain insight into the reality beneath the façade of this apparent incompatibility, Kawamura invokes Michel Foucault's notion of pastoral power. Pastoral power is power exercised over people to direct them so that (or on the pretext that) they could achieve wellbeing, just as a shepherd guides sheep to salvation. In order to direct people, it is crucial to convince them that this direction is rational and is worth following for their own sake. In Kawamura's view, Minobe's organ theory, precisely because of its rationality, could provide an effective explanation convincing Japanese people to obey any state power exercised in the name of the Emperor.

> In fact, according to Minobe's logic, if governmental "power" is exercised according to the "social" purpose or interest, each individual should voluntarily accept and follow the government as the way to achieve his/her own purpose: this is the exercise of power according to the rational mechanism of society. Hence, Minobe's logic could work as a limitation of the absolutised sovereign power, but, at the same time, could legitimise the exercise

of the governmental power. Thus, from the Foucauldian perspective, Minobe's organ theory should be understood as a theory, not to limit power per se, but to suggest another rational (and sophisticated) way to exercise power. (36)

Here, Kawamura notes the ambiguity in Minobe's organ theory. Although this theory restrains the arbitrary exercise of state power so that it can be used for individuals' wellbeing, this theory can also legitimize the exercise of state power, once a pretext is made that the power is used for their wellbeing. According to Kawamura, the discourse on *kokutai* in 1930s and 1940s took over the latter aspect and, by turning it against the former, succeeded in canceling it out. More concretely, by emphasizing people's wellbeing, the *kokutai* discourse around that time legitimized total mobilization, and consequently absolutized state power exercised over citizens. Even though Minobe's organ theory and the democratic movement that had originated in the Taishō period were suppressed in the Shōwa period, because of their previous large social impact, any state or *kokutai* that disregarded people would no longer hold any appeal to the masses. So the *kokutai* discourse in the 1930s and 1940s adopted a rationale of exercising state power for the sake of the people, an ideal upheld by organ theory. Ironically, once integrated into such discourse, this rationale turned into a pretext to rationalize their obedience to state power. To this extent, Minobe's theory inadvertently contributed to realizing the state of affairs promoted by ultranationalist advocates of the very *kokutai* who attacked him.

As the paragon of the 1930s *kokutai* discourse that appropriated the stance of Minobe's organ theory, Kawamura refers to the theory of cooperativism as elaborated by Miki Kiyoshi, one of Nishida's disciples. Although Miki placed importance on each person's individuality, he asserted it to be realizable only within fruitful social relationships, which could be cultivated through individual cooperation in view of the public interest of society. If people separately pursued their personal interest as opposed to social interest, they would conflict with each other and would neither cooperate nor attain their true individuality. In order to attain their true individuality, Miki maintained that a leader who guides and organizes them is indispensable so that their personal interests would be in accord with society's interests, and so they could cooperate appropriately. In Miki's view, only the Emperor can be such a leader. The ideal *kokutai* for Miki was one of unity between the Emperor and people, in which the Emperor's leadership enables both people's dedication to this society *and* their true self-realization to become one and the same.

Thus, Miki envisaged a harmonious ideal in which the leader and individuals created "society" cooperatively, and he thereby tried to direct the individual subjects to devote themselves to such an ideal. For Miki, the ideal of cooperativism was that the Emperor as the leader would direct the individuals to the point at which the specific interest of each person and the universal interest of society could be compatible. In this sense, Miki's Emperor was parallel with Minobe's Emperor who must care for "society." . . . (Kawamura 42)

Kawamura finds another formulation of pastoral power in Miki's theory of cooperativism. Miki's claim that citizens' devotion to society, practiced under the guidance of the Emperor, is what enables their true self-realization can be easily used to validate their obedience to state power exercised in the name of the Emperor. And, in fact, this is how Miki's theory of cooperativism worked in practice. Miki published this theory as a member of the Shōwa Research Group (*Shōwa kenkyūkai*), which contributed to the policies of the Konoe government, the Tōjō military government's predecessor. The outline of Konoe's policy, written in line with Miki's theory, advocated for the total mobilization of Japanese people. This resulted in the formation of the Imperial Rule Assistance Association (*Taisei yokusan kai*), which was created by uniting all political parties in Japan, making the country a one-party state that could unanimously support and cooperate with government policy (Kawamura 40).[2]

Miki's theory of the Japanese *kokutai* depicted the Emperor as a beneficent leader who could guide people toward wellbeing, and thus rationalizing their obedience to state power exercised under his leadership. This theory is different from the ultranationalist *kokutai* theories, which sanctified the Emperor as the one by virtue of whom the state of Japan exists, and which attributed absolute governmental power to him, to which citizens should be thoroughly obedient. Nevertheless, and precisely because of this difference, Miki's theory effectively promoted thorough obedience to state power exercised in the Emperor's name, and contributed to the absolutization of this power, as envisioned in the ultranationalist theories of *kokutai*. This is similar to what happened in the case of Minobe's organ theory.

Nishida began to treat the themes of the state, society, history, and politics following criticism from Marxists including Miki and Tosaka Jun. While Miki's two treatises on cooperativism were published in 1939, Nishida's "The Problem of the Reason of the State" was published in 1941, and "The Problem of Japanese Culture," which includes related arguments about *kokutai*, in 1940. Thus given their almost contemporaneous publication, Miki and Nishida's essays concerning the state and *kokutai* tackled the same problematic pertinent to Japan's situation at that time. Naturally, the ways in which the two philosophers tackled it differed. Still, Nishida's implicit claim as interpreted by Kado—that the state centered upon the Imperial Family as the representation of the absoluteness of law is obliged to respect citizens' individuality—has a similar ring to Miki's claim that the people who follow the Emperor's guidance can realize their true individuality in harmony with society. Similarly to Miki's claim, Nishida practically echoes claims that submission to the Emperor and his Family is indispensable for the realization of respect for individuality. If Nishida's claim can be understood in this way, the rendering of the Imperial Family as the representation of the absoluteness of law does not necessarily result in a moral binding for the state formed around this center. Rather, it can create the appearance that people should absolutely obey this state, just as they obey law, and that doing so is the sole way for them to attain their true individuality.

The notion of pastoral power offers a useful perspective for considering the danger implicit in claims of Miki and Nishida. As previously mentioned, for this power to function it is crucial to convince people of the rationality of their obedience to power with regard to their own wellbeing. In other words, once people are successfully persuaded to accept obedience as rational, they will no longer question whether the story told to persuade them is true, or whether this obedience is really rational, as they are convinced that it is indeed the case, even if in fact it is not. Seen in this light, giving rational explanations to a state of affairs wherein people have no choice but to obey can work as an effective method for persuading people to accept such a state of affairs as rational. Viewed through this lens of pastoral power, invoking an ideal far from reality does not necessarily constitute a resistance to it, but can instead justify it while covering up its actual taints.

Even though it may be argued that, in Nishida's case, the Imperial Family is a mere representation, that which is supposedly represented (sovereignty itself as the absoluteness of law, or whatever) does not inherently entail the power that subordinates certain people to others—that is, the power that the representation's referent (as a specific person or group of people) has over others in reality. Nevertheless, when the representation is superimposed upon the represented, a rationalization of the compliance with the represented can easily amount to a rationalization of the subordinating power of the representation's referent. Even if a certain ideal is sublime, or simply innocuous, when it is projected onto a certain entity as a professed representation of an ideal, that projection can produce harmful effects, with the ideal being used to disguise the iniquity of the power exercised in the name of the entity.

As such, regardless of his intention, Nishida's arguments about the state and the Imperial Family could work to rationalize and thus promote individuals' obedience to state power exercised in the name of the Emperor. Given the similarities between Nishida's arguments and Minobe's organ theory, his arguments are apparently not free from the ambiguity of pastoral power exemplified by organ theory. In part 1, I referred to Doak's observation that, precisely because of its rationality, the Kyoto School's discourse around the time of the "Overcoming Modernity" symposium, played a crucial role in integrating ethnic nationalists who were opposed to the Kyoto School into the modern state of Japan. Likewise, and also in the case of Nishida, the rationale of the philosopher's discourse does not necessarily work as a weapon of protest against the state and its status quo, but could adversely serve as a means to advocate for the status quo, even if this is against the philosopher's intentions. Back then, Nishida certainly could not publish anything contrary to the stance of the state or the Japanese *kokutai* and yet did his best to resist this state of affairs. That being said, whether doing so constituted an effective act of resistance in the given context is another matter.

Section 3: The Perplexities Caused by the "Being of Nothingness"

Furthermore, Nishida's arguments themselves are not without responsibility for their consequences. Even if Nishida (as interpreted by Kado) struggled to bind the state of Japan to respect the individualities of its members and of other states through recourse to the Imperial Family, Nishida's very arguments thwart any semblance of this struggle. A stumbling block here is Nishida's equating of the Imperial Family with a "being of nothingness." Aside from questions about whether this phase is an oxymoron (which, however, may have philosophical implications worth exploring), Nishida's gesture of specially qualifying the Imperial Family is perplexing with regard to the principle of the absoluteness of law, which he might have sought to uphold.

As discussed, Kado takes the Imperial Family as the representation (or more precisely, the symbol) of the absoluteness of law, a principle which cannot be incarnated within any individual entity and which for this reason he believes to be qualified as "being of nothingness. However, when what in principle cannot be incarnated is equated with a specific entity through a qualification of both as "being of nothingness," this equation may be taken as a suggestion that a principle which cannot be incarnated can in fact be incarnated exclusively in a certain entity, which is inherently contradictory. Through this equation, the entity in which the absoluteness of law is exceptionally incarnated appears as the absolute sovereign without parallel. Kado is well aware of this possibility:

> Even if [one] introduces the notion of the "symbol" and thus is able to distinguish between the Emperor and absolute nothingness,

> a new conundrum emerges as to whether the Emperor is the "incarnation" of absolute nothingness, that is, whether he is *the* sovereign. (Kado 202)

Particularly in "The Problem of Japanese Culture," Nishida's arguments construing the Imperial Family as if it were the incarnation of absolute nothingness are conspicuous. It is through such arguments that Kado discerns the inconsistency of Nishida's arguments. Kado insists that because of this inconsistency, Nishida's arguments could not overcome the framework of the state that existed at that time (194), despite their potential for "relativiz[ing] the fiction of the modern state or nation-state that constitutes the identity absorbing individuals" (222). If the absolute sovereign exists as the sole incarnation of the absoluteness of law, everyone would be obliged to obey this incomparable person, or the state which wields him or her as the leader. The existence of the absolute sovereign in that state would forge an exclusivist and totalizing national identity among citizens. The principle of the absoluteness of law would end up authorizing any exercise of power by this sovereign or state over others, resulting in the loss of the force which morally binds all persons.

Although Kado does not further explore the problems inherent in Nishida's gesture allowing the incarnation of nothingness, Kobayashi draws attention to the serious harms here:

> That an entity that has evident substantiality is identified as "nothingness," or that the Imperial Family as such an entity is sublimated into the ideal of a movement that does not have substantiality, and is "reinterpreted," this is an obvious metabasis. If we qualify this with regard to the "authenticity" of "nothingness," this is a "falling into inauthenticity (*Verfallen*)." . . . Besides, when this falling arises in the form of an "interpretation" of a substantial entity through the lens of "nothingness," which cannot be such an entity in the first place, this interpretation, far beyond being a mere interpretation, can sometimes create demagogic legitimation. (*The Writing of Otherness* 120–21)

In the sense that nothingness incorporated within a certain entity is not an authentic nothingness, Kobayashi describes the substantialization of nothingness as a fall from authenticity to inauthenticity, using Heideggerian terms. Kobayashi argues that this substantialization is problematic not only in itself but also in terms of its consequences. When a specific entity equated with nothingness attains substantialization, the attributes that are arbitrarily ascribed to nothingness (imagined in superempirical ways), such as eternity, are also ascribed to this entity. Then, idolization or worship of this entity is naturalized, dramatically distinguishing it from other earthly entities and causing it to inspire awe among people. Kobayashi summarizes this as follows: "Feelings of awe do not arise from mere nothingness. They arise when this 'nothingness' is substantialized and also turned into a fetish being given the attribute of 'eternity'" (Kobayashi, *The Writing of Otherness* 121), associated with the mythical imagery of the Imperial lineage's perpetuity. Because of this sanctifying effect of the substantialization of nothingness, arguments that the structure of the state is formed around a being of nothingness, as Nishida made, results in citizens kneeling down to the being in awe and obeying the state which centers upon it. Such arguments lend themselves to an organization of people around this center and solidifying their identities as members of a nation-state, rather than relativizing it.

It is not only that Nishida's arguments about the state and the Imperial Family worked to promote obedience to state power exercised in the name of the Emperor within the given situation and context. His arguments themselves contained the elements that allowed them to operate thusly, by metaphysically sanctifying the Imperial Family at the center of the Japanese state. Regarding this outcome, Kobayashi argues, again using Heideggerian terms:

> Nishida might say that this is "misunderstanding." However, in the first place, this "misunderstanding" came from his own "falling" in terms of his theory [his move of degrading the authenticity of nothingness into inauthenticity, corresponding to the aforementioned *Verfallen*], the "falling" that consisted of confusing "being (*Sein*) = nothingness (*Nichts*)" and "entities (*Seiendes*)." (*The Writing of Otherness* 121)

Contrary to Kado's emphasis that "Nishida's theory of sovereignty ... is not a theory that can establish the unconditionality of power in the name of obedience to the Emperor" (117), Kobayashi's remarks tell us that Nishida's philosophies ultimately turned into such a theory. It is Nishida's own process of substantializing nothingness (which derives from the inconsistency of his arguments about the state and the Imperial Family) that turned these arguments against themselves and made them serve a purpose he did not intend.

Furthermore, insofar as this substantialization of nothingness was limited to a specific entity deemed to represent a specific country, another question is raised concerning the universalization of the particular. If it is argued that the Imperial Family is the exclusive incarnation of absolute nothingness as the groundless ground for all reality, this means that this particular entity takes on universality by virtue of its own particularity, and hence so does a particular state constructed around the center of this entity.

In Kado's view, Nishida's pursuit of Japanese particularity is a mere façade, a means to eschew the confrontation with ordinary theories of *kokutai* (113). Rather, Kado insists that "the essence of Nishida's theory of sovereignty" resides in the "possibility of universalization beyond any peculiarity [*koyūsei*]" (114), expressed in his concept of absolute nothingness, or sovereignty as the third term that mediates and regulates the relation between sovereigns without being incarnated by any of them in principle.

However, even if Nishida's thought has this dimension of the universality beyond any particularity, the problem is that this dimension coexists and merges with the idea of the specific particular professed to be *the* symbol of the universal in his very thought. Even if the universal may be conceived of as independent or neutral to any particular, if a specific particular is constantly presented as the symbol of this universal and even though the impossibility of such incarnation may be stated elsewhere, this particular then appears as a privileged incarnation of the universal. Certainly, the importance of Nishida's pursuit of a universal that is unbound to particularity should not be neglected. But what equally must not be neglected is the existence of elements within his thought that associate the universal exclusively with a specific particular against the tenets of his pursuit.

As discussed before, the universalization of the particular is completed when the particular source of the universal is forgotten and the universal manifests itself as genuinely neutral to any particular, while in fact this universal implicitly retains a special tie with a specific particular, allowing it to subjugate other particulars. If only Nishida's pursuit of the universal is underlined, and the tie he establishes between the universal and the specific particular is disregarded, this would amount to endorsing or even promoting, rather than nullifying, the universalization of the particular in his thought. To avoid this, when Nishida's pursuit of the universal is foregrounded, special attention also should be paid to the harmful effects of his process of associating the universal with the specific particular, presenting the latter as the epitome or incarnation of the universal. Even if this pursuit of the universal may have some positive outcomes, this association would undo such outcomes and undermine this pursuit itself.

As a case that exemplifies this, in subsequent chapters I will explore a project to overcome modernity which is discernible in Nishida's philosophy at a more fundamental level than in that of his four disciples. This exploration will elucidate how the substantialization of nothingness and the universalization of the particular affect Nishida's views of the state and the world more broadly than aforementioned, interrupting his own line of thought in pursuit of the universal in a way that could affirm all particulars without privileging a specific one among them.

Chapter 10

Nishida's Criticism of Hegel with an Eye to Overcoming Western Modernity

Jürgen Habermas appreciates German philosopher George Wilhelm Friedrich Hegel as "the first philosopher to develop a clear concept of modernity" (4). In his note, "Hegelian Dialectic Seen from My Standpoint" (*Watakushi no tachiba kara mita hēgeru no benshōhō*), first published as a journal essay in 1931 and then included in the book, *Thinking and Experience Continued* (*Zoku shisaku to taiken*) in 1937, Nishida states, "Hegel taught me a lot so that I could develop my thought that I have today, which is closer to his more than anyone's. At once, I have a lot to say to him" (NKZ XII 84n). While admitting his great indebtedness to Hegel, Nishida also expresses his intent to contest Hegel. Although Hegel is not the only philosopher who influenced Nishida, Nishida's criticisms of Hegel and his attempts to go beyond Hegel's philosophy cast a shadow on crucial parts of Nishida's philosophy. It is due to this that I claim to discern in Nishida's confrontation with Hegelianism a line of thought that constitutes an attempt to challenge modernity as it is understood philosophically. As such, my reading is a retrospective interpretation. Although this approach cannot completely avoid the projection of external schema, it can enable one to cast light upon the potentials and limits of Nishida's philosophy.

In this chapter, I will first introduce what Habermas interprets as the original formulation of the concept of modernity in Hegelianism (specifically Western modernity), and will posit its detrimental effects. Second, I will observe how Nishida criticized the Hegelian dialectic as the logic which characterizes Western modernity, and how he conceived of an alternate dialectic to avoid the former's defects. Third, I will look at how Nishida criticized Hegel's views of the world and the history that should result from the Hegelian dialectic.

Fourth, I will elucidate how Nishida criticized Hegel's view of the state that should likewise follow from this dialectic. And finally, I will explore how Nishida, based on his own dialectic, offered alternative views of the world and the state to resolve the problems he found in Hegelianism. Within such views, I will argue that Nishida's project to overcome Western modernity is in line with his criticism of Hegel's universalization of the West as a specific particular and with Nishida's pursuit of a different type of universality.

Section 1: Modernity According to Habermas and Its Detrimental Effects

It is Habermas's understanding of modernity that provides a guiding thread to explore Nishida's challenge to Western modernity. According to Habermas, the essence of the historical consciousness of modernity is the tendency to distinguish itself as the most recent stage of advancement in relation to the past, or even from the modern (6). Modernity thus understood consists of the distinct differentiating movement from old to new. However, since the most recent quickly becomes less new over time, for modernity to sustain itself as such it must continue to differentiate itself from itself. This generates what Habermas refers to as "a *continual renewal*" (7). This untiring urge toward incessant progress is for Habermas the principle of modernity. Habermas remarks that if Hegel could conceptualize the principle of modernity as such, it is by his concept of "an absolute that [. . .] retains as unconditional only the infinite processing of the relation-to-self that swallows up everything finite within itself" (36).

The absolute mentioned here is absolute spirit as Hegel conceives of it. In the preface of *The Phenomenology of Spirit*, Hegel calls this spirit "the living Substance," and explains:

> Further, the living Substance is being which is in truth *Subject*, or, what is the same, is in truth real only in so far [sic] as it is the movement of positing itself, or is the mediation of its self-othering with itself. This Substance is, as Subject, pure, *simple negativity*, and is for this very reason the bifurcation of the simple; it is the doubling which sets up opposition, and then again the negation of this indifferent diversity and of its antithesis. Only this *self-restoring* sameness, or this reflection in otherness within itself—not an *original* or *immediate* unity as such—is the True. (10; translation slightly modified by referring to HW VII 23)[1]

In Hegel's thought, absolute spirit is the substance that posits itself as the subject, while at once making its object diverge from it. This subject, by cognizing the object, negates the opposition between the subject and the object, and restores the sameness of the subject while enriching itself by incorporating the object. The logic operative in this movement, the logic that consists in posing the opposites and resolving their contradiction through their synthesis, is the so-called "dialectic." By infinitely repeating this movement, Spirit creates all existing things in the entire world and its history and then integrates them into itself, while seeing its realization in all of them. For Hegel, the dialectic is the logic of Spirit's development in which it enlarges itself through the creation and recognition of reality. While continually diverging from and returning to itself, absolute spirit realizes and comprehends itself through itself, also enriching itself and its self-knowledge. In the course of this movement, rationality is gradually realized and attained in the world and its history.

According to Hegel, absolute spirit's self-cognition, carried out dialectically, is not only the realization of rationality, but also that of freedom, in the actual world. Hegel believed the dialectical movement of the spirit that goes toward this goal moves the world and carries history forward: "[W]orld history is the necessary development, out of the Notion of spirit's freedom alone, of the moments of reason and so of the self-consciousness and freedom of spirit. This development is the interpretation and realization of the universal spirit" (*Philosophy of Right* 216; translation modified by referring to HW VII, 504).[2]

In Hegel's view, it is not that an object comes first and then is grasped by the Notion, but that the Notion precedes the object and makes it emerge: "the Notion is what truly comes first, and things are what they are through the activity of the Notion that dwells in them and reveals itself in them" (Hegel, *The Encyclopedia Logic* 241; translation slightly modified by referring to HW VIII 313).[3] If the Notion precedes the object, it is because absolute spirit creates its object through the Notion, or indeed, because this spirit itself is the Notion: "It is essentially only spirit that can comprehend the Notion as Notion; for this is not merely the property of spirit but spirit's pure self" (*Science of Logic* 618). As such, the Notion has a power to realize what it conceives. That world history develops "out of the Notion of spirit's freedom" means absolute spirit, through understanding itself as freedom, leads humans to work on realizing it in the actual world. Through this process of realization, world history is created. While the spirit in developing its self-cognition repeats bifurcation and integration, humans having different positions face and surmount their oppositions or conflicts, so as to attain greater truth and freedom.

As understood from Hegel's above thoughts, when Habermas finds the principle of modernity in the movement of absolute spirit thus conceived, what is at stake is not only incessant innovation articulated by this movement, but also the advancement of the human knowledge and spirit, and the acquisition of freedom, all of which should occur concomitantly. For Hegel, various manifestations of absolute spirit through this movement culminate in the concretizations of reason as the highest human faculty in social and historical reality. Certainly, Habermas does not entirely agree with Hegel's idea of absolute spirit. Still, Habermas shares with Hegel the belief that the gradual actualization of reason corresponds to the progress of humans and the achievement of freedom. Hence, Habermas's qualification of modernity, the project of Enlightenment, is an eternally unfinished project that should be pursued endlessly toward ever-further improvement of human conditions. Looking on the bright side of Habermas's project, Bernard Stevens optimistically remarks that, "[M]odernity in the political sense is the still-incomplete effort to emancipate humanity from what oppresses it, including Western imperialism," and as such is "a project that [. . .] has yet to be achieved either in the West or in the East" (235).

This, however, is not so simple. The complexity resides in the inseparability of the emancipatory aspect of modernity and its oppressive aspect that implicitly endorses Western imperialism. When Peter Osborne claims, "modernity is a Western concept, inextricably linked to the history of European colonialism" (13), he draws our attention to the inextricability of modernity from the sociopolitical conditions of its emergence. In his view, the sources of the time-consciousness of continual renewal are "the temporalities of capital accumulation and its social and political consequences" (Osborne 13), generated against the backdrop of incessant concentration of wealth at the expense of the exploitation of others. As an act that propels this concentration of wealth, Western imperialism is a crucial factor to the formation of Western modernity. Western imperialist ideologies cast a shadow upon the time-consciousness of Western modernity, especially upon the characteristic manner by which this consciousness deals with its others. The time-consciousness of Western modernity, which consists in differentiating itself as the "newest," cannot but regard non-Western others who live elsewhere as corresponding to different moments in its past, simply because they are different. Osborne describes this operation as follows:

> [T]he results of synchronic comparisons are ordered diachronically to produce a scale of development which defines 'progress' in terms of the projection of certain people's presents as other people's futures, at the level of the development of history as a whole. (17)

Western modernity's time-consciousness projects a diachronic temporal order, professed to be linear progress, onto a synchronic spatial order as the relation of different regions and peoples belonging to the same time, while transcribing the former onto the latter. The others of Western modernity, regarded as its pasts, are meant to arrive at its stage in the future. Here, they are regarded as different stages of development simply integrated into one and the same historical process—into the universal history whose forefront and standard are Western modernity. The West's consciousness of the "backwardness" of non-Western others, attained in view of this alleged universal history, provides pretext for the West's domination over them, often in the name of enlightenment and rescuing them from their "backwardness." Thus, Western modernity's time-consciousness, in an encounter with non-Western others, turns into a mechanism of hierarchically subjugating them. This, in turn, lends itself to the justification of Western imperialism. What complicates this is the logic that formulates continual renewal and supposedly promises progress and liberation of all the humans at the same time contributes to legitimating certain people's oppression of others, thus breaking this promise.

By considering modernity as Habermas construes it in Hegel through the lens of Osborne, it is revealed that modernity is not a neutral formulation of continual renewal and the progress that comes from that renewal. The modernity at issue here tacitly presupposes that, from the beginning, the West would be situated at the forefront of human progress and identified as the single privileged agent that could unfalteringly continue this renewal while others stopped it on the path to progress.[4] Considering this, the modernity formulated as above was also a conceptual device for universalizing a specific particular: the West. Insofar as modernity is formulated in such a way, it constitutes a device that could work to subjugate various others of the West. What is at issue here is no longer a conception of modernity that is neutral to any region and people in the world, equally guaranteeing them the possibility of progress and emancipation. Rather, it is a particular kind of modernity formed in the West and then universalized as the standard and as applicable to the entire world, while legitimating the West's hegemony over other regions and people.

Sakai, in his insight into the self-consciousness of the West, illustrates how a particular, called the West, universalizes itself and subjugates others as particulars:

> In short, the West must represent the moment of the universal under which particulars are subsumed. Indeed, the West is particular in itself, but it also constitutes the universal point of reference in relation to which others recognize themselves as particularities. And, in this regard, the West thinks itself to be ubiquitous. ("Modernity and Its Critique" 95)

It is because this self-consciousness of the West as universal and ubiquitous is somehow largely shared by (or rather imposed upon) other non-Western entities that Western modernity is generally referred to as "modernity" without adjectives, as if it were neutral. Given this, questioning such modernity must entail questioning its dubious neutrality and the procedure through which it takes on its appearance of neutrality, that is, the universalization of the West as a specific particular.

Therefore, to discern the lines of thought that challenge Western modernity in Nishida's philosophy, it is necessary to address not only how Nishida tackled the Hegelian dialectic as the logic of modernity but also how Nishida confronted Hegel's universalization of the West and his ideas of the universal that undergird this universalization and other associated concepts. Let me start by looking into Nishida's criticisms of the Hegelian dialectic.

Section 2: Nishida's Criticism of the Hegelian Dialectic

Nishida expresses his dissatisfaction with the Hegelian dialectic many times throughout his works. In "The Hegelian Dialectic from My Standpoint," he gives an account of how he perceives the Hegelian dialectic, as well as what its insufficiency is. In the note to this essay, which was added when it was included in a compilation, he admits his indebtedness to Hegel. Immediately thereafter, Nishida summarizes what he thinks the shortcoming is:

> If you ask me, the Hegelian dialectic is still subjective [*shugoteki*] and noematic. At least, I cannot help but say that it puts stress on that direction. On the contrary, however, I think that true dialectic must emerge where we break away from such a standpoint. (NKZ XII 84n)

Noema is the object or the objective aspect of thought, and as such is something that can be the grammatical subject (*shugo*) to be predicated in the proposition. Given that the Hegelian dialectic characterizes the movement of absolute spirit cognizing the object and integrating it into itself, this dialectic cannot but be understood with regard to the object that is grasped by absolute spirit, as illustrated by the pivotal role of the Notion in this movement. This dialectic is noematic, which means it is the movement of the permanent subject (*shutai*) of consciousness grasping the object and making it the grammatical subject (*shugo*) of the proposition. Whereas Hegel believes the production of reality consists in this noematic movement, for Nishida, being noematic means not only falling into the category of the grammatical subject (*shugoteki*), but also being subjective (*shukanteki*) in the sense of depending on and solely deriving from the subject of consciousness. Thus, he comments in the essay: "Hegel [. . .] thought reason [*risei*] behind the fact instead of thinking the fact behind reason. It can be said that the subjectivity [*shukansei*] of his dialectic resided in this point" (NKZ XII 80). By the subjectivity of Hegel's dialectic, Nishida is referring to its lack of true objectivity.

In order to escape this confinement within subjectivity and recover true objectivity, Nishida insists that the Hegelian dialectic should be complemented by what he conceives of as a true dialectic: the dialectic based on nothingness, rather than absolute spirit.

> [. . .] I think that what is regarded as the Hegelian dialectic can be also understood by putting at its beginning what I call the self-awareness of nothingness. What is regarded as true dialectic must genuinely signify the self-aware determination of nothingness. (NKZ XII 76)

What is this dialectic of nothingness, claimed to be the true dialectic that precedes the Hegelian one and complements it? Nishida proceeds:

> However, if we can think dialectical movements behind [the world of subjective (*shugoteki*) beings], it must be because being is, immediately as nothingness, one with its other. Furthermore, we should keep in mind that this happens only in the self-awareness of nothingness, and only in this sense we can think that self-identity is self-contradiction. Dialectical mediation does not mean that something mediates itself by something else. Dialectical mediation occurs because the self is the other, because self-affirmation is immediately self-negation, and self-negation is immediately self-affirmation. Dialectical mediation emerges from the equation between nothingness and being. (NKZ XII 81)

The dialectic of nothingness described here resides in the process in which beings are created through the self-negation of nothingness. When nothingness negates itself and becomes beings, it also mediates the self-affirmation of beings. Nothingness and beings are united, while the former completely negates itself and becomes the latter. In this process, not only nothingness and beings, but also the self-negation and self-affirmation of both, become equal, while remaining different. The self-identity of either is nowhere but in this self-contradiction.

Claiming to find in this process the true dialectic, Nishida has in mind a common formulation: "the negation of the negation." This is equated with affirmation and used to describe the Hegelian dialectic in which the subject is first negated by the object, negates the opposition between the subject and the object, and finally affirms both in their synthesis.

One of the major differences Nishida finds between his thought and Hegel's is that, as suggested in Nishida's description of Hegel's "reason behind the fact," Hegel sees absolute spirit as the permanent subject underneath all realities, whereas Nishida sees absolute nothingness there. In the Hegelian dialectic, the object, which is supposed to mediate the subject by negating it, is posited by it, and is destined to be incorporated into it when it cognizes this object. The object does not really negate the subject. The mediation by this object simply serves to enlarge the permanent subject and enrich its self-knowledge. If the subject is not truly negated, the synthesis between the subject and the object, supposed to be the affirmation achieved by the negation of this negation, is not truly what it is supposed to be—that is, the synthesis of the opposites, which is different from one's integration of the other into itself. Thus, the Hegelian dialectic is not the dialectic proper. Nishida states, "the true dialectical movement begins with nothingness' becoming beings" (NKZ XII 74). From this standpoint, only nothingness is the radical negation of all beings. Therefore, the true dialectic can be conceived only by starting from this nothingness as the radical negation, and by reaching the affirmation of beings through the negation of this negation. Only in this dialectic of nothingness can extreme opposites be synthesized without submitting one to the other, while true affirmation results from the self-negation of the true negation.

Naturally, one may ask how Nishida can claim that nothingness, something that does not exist, negates itself in order to generate beings in the first place. In the same vein, the question remains, how can he claim nothingness as such becomes aware of itself when he also says the self-awareness of nothingness precedes the Hegelian dialectic? Nishida does not develop the idea of the self-awareness of nothingness randomly, but draws it from the exploration of the conditions surrounding the possibility of knowledge.

The Hegelian dialectic, following a classical tradition of Western philosophy, bases knowledge on the unity between the knowing subject and the known object. On this basis, it explains the movement of absolute spirit, enlarging itself and enriching its self-consciousness. The concept of knowledge as unity between the subject and the object fits Hegel's noematic dialectic that proceeds through the subject's incorporation of the object. However, for Nishida, knowledge is not possible in this subject-centered way:

> Against the conventional idea that self-awareness is the unity between the knowing and the known, I take self-awareness as seeing the self in the self. All that is regarded as the so-called phenomenon of consciousness can be taken as existing in this

> way. What is regarded as noetic must have the meaning of self-awareness [. . .] However, the self's seeing the self in the above sense of self-awareness must mean the self's becoming nothingness, the self's becoming what determines itself while itself being nothingness. Insofar as the self sees itself in conformity with the object, in other words, insofar as it is conscious of itself, it cannot be said that the self is truly aware of itself. The self of which it is conscious is not the true self. (NKZ XII 66–67)

In Nishida's view, if knowledge is possible, it is not because the knowing subject and the known object are united. If this were the case, knowledge would be possible only if the subject imposes its unity upon the object in cognizing it. In that way, the subject could not actually know the object as it truly is. Instead, if the self can know the object as such, it is because the self has emptied itself so that it can envelop the object as it is without assimilating it. In other words, knowledge is possible because the self has already become nothingness. Only by being nothingness can the self determine the object as such, while at once determining oneself as the subject knowing it, of which the self is conscious as another object. This is how the true dialectic for Nishida works in the field of knowledge: nothingness, through its self-negation, achieves the self-affirmation of beings. The self-awareness of nothingness is the immediate intuition in which the self feels itself as nothingness, on the basis of which the self sees both itself and its object as beings. At the same time, it perceives the emergence of the latter self from the former as the act of nothingness determining itself in negating itself and affirming beings. This is why Nishida describes this self-awareness of nothingness as noetic instead of noematic, stressing the act or function of thinking.

His usage of the term "noetic" may be confusing and reminiscent of the binary opposition between the noetic and the noematic presupposed in the usual usage of this term, according to which the noetic refers to subjective consciousness opposed to its objects. However, Nishida does not use the term "noetic" in this way. In a note added later, he further specifies what he means: "When I say noetic here, I do not take it abstractly as opposed to noematic. The same is true of self-awareness. I do not have in mind merely subjective self-awareness" (NKZ XII 84n). When he describes the self-awareness of nothingness as noetic, he does not mean that this self-awareness is the counterpart to noema, and as such reducible to the act of subjective consciousness. Rather, the noesis at issue here, as shown in his explanation of the self-awareness of nothingness, underlies and generates noema, including not only the object, but also the subject conscious of itself. The term "noetic" that Nishida uses to qualify the dialectic of nothingness in contrast to the Hegelian noematic dialectic should be understood in this sense. In Nishida's view, given that the Hegelian dialectic proceeds through the subject's knowledge of the object, his own dialectic that underlies and generates both the subject and the object can be regarded as the Hegelian dialectic's precondition, in preceding such knowledge and conditioning its possibility. That is why he claims that his "noetic" dialectic reaches "the fact behind reason" (NKZ XII 80) and addresses the way in which "fact determines fact itself" (NKZ XII 76). This is in contrast to the Hegelian "noematic" dialectic that puts reason behind the fact and confines reality within the scope of subjectivity.

One may object to Nishida, saying that Hegel also speaks of nothingness and its unity with being. Nishida knows this fact. His dissatisfaction is that Hegel, in doing so, does not do justice to nothingness. For example, at the beginning of his *Science of Logic*, Hegel states:

> [Nothing] is empty intuition and thought itself, and the same empty intuition or thought as pure being. Nothing is, therefore, the same determination, or rather absence of determination, and thus altogether the same as, pure *being.*" (82)

Here Hegel equates pure being and pure nothingness, because what they are cannot be determined either by intuition or thought. Nishida comments, "However undetermined we think what we take as a subjective [*shugoteki*] being, it does not become nothing" (NKZ XII 72). For Nishida, being is what can be the grammatical subject (*shugo*) of a proposition, that is, what is noematic as the object of consciousness. As such, being is radically different from nothingness, which is noetic in his sense. By equating both because they are undetermined, Hegel disregards this difference and puts nothingness in the same category as being.

Hegel's similar disregard for nothingness also manifests itself in his idea of the unity between being and nothingness. Elsewhere in the *Science of Logic*, after speaking of the fleeting realization of this unity through becoming, Hegel describes what this process ends up with as follows: "[The result] is the unity of being and nothing which has settled into a stable oneness. But this stable oneness is being" (106). Hegel calls this being "determinate being," or the being determined as a result of the sublation of pure being and pure nothing in their becoming. About this outcome, Nishida asks, "[W]here is the reason why [the being in becoming] undergoing a complete change must positively determine itself as a determinate being, that is, a certain thing?" (NKZ XII 74). He questions whether the result of the unity between the opposites can be one of these opposites in a determined state, without one being favored over the other.

We can find the reason for Hegel's predilection for being over nothingness in his idea of beginning, in which being becomes from nothing:

> The beginning is not pure nothing, but a nothing from which something is to proceed; therefore being, too, is already contained in the beginning. The beginning, therefore, contains both, being and nothing, is the unity of being and nothing; or is non-being which is at the same time being, and being which is at the same time non-being. (*Science of Logic* 73)

Hegel explains how beginning as the becoming of being from nothing is possible. In his view, it is because being is contained in nothing in the first place. If becoming is the unity of being and nothing, it is because this becoming occurs from the nothing that contains being. However, nothing thus conceived is not genuine nothingness. Nishida equates this nothing that contains being with "latent being" (NKZ XII 74), and criticizes Hegel's idea:

> We cannot utterly take being and nothingness to be one as noematic. If we assume something at the bottom of nothingness, it is a being that determines another being, and not nothingness that becomes being. If this is the case, there is neither true beginning, nor any contradiction. Therefore, no dialectical movement arises from there. (NKZ XII 74)

Even though one may insist Hegel thinks about the dialectical synthesis between being and nothing in becoming, if nothingness is latent being, and this is the way in which the unity between nothingness and being is conceivable, then from Nishida's standpoint nothingness and being would not really be opposites. Their synthesis does not entail true contradiction between them. Therefore, this synthesis cannot be truly dialectical. Furthermore, to posit the unity between nothing as latent being on the one hand, and being on the other hand, is to assume the latter as the appearance of the former, and to allow the determination of the latter by the former, or more precisely, to confer on latent being a capacity to prescribe what emergent being will become.

The presupposition of latent being Nishida detects in Hegelianism is related to the Hegelian dialectic's subject-centeredness. For the latent being whose presupposition Nishida criticizes here is ultimately that of absolute spirit, of this single true subject that recognizes its own being in all the objects it posits. In the above citation in which Hegel describes absolute spirit as the living substance and the true subject, he describes the process in which Spirit posits the object that opposes it, and then negates this opposition as follows:

"Only this *self-restoring* sameness, or this reflection in otherness within itself—not an *original* or *immediate* unity as such—is the True" (*The Phenomenology of Spirit* 10). Hegel admits the movement of the spirit sublating its opposite is, after all, the return to the same self and the comprehension of the other within it. He continues: "It is the process of its own becoming, the circle that presupposes its end as its goal, having its end also as its beginning; and only by being worked out to its end, is it real" (*The Phenomenology of Spirit* 10; translation slightly modified, referring to HW III 23).[5] This circle would not be made if the beginning and the end were not one and the same. When this circle is completed—which would only be possible from the standpoint of the goal that has not actually been attained yet—it is already presupposed that the end was there from the beginning, though only implicitly. Therefore, to say there is a circle is the same as saying that what is to be actualized in the end is latently there from the beginning. In other words, absolute spirit, which should realize itself in the course of history, subsists in it from the beginning to the end. Thus, the entire process in which this spirit opposes its objects and synthesizes them presupposes its latent being. Only based on this presupposition, can it be said that this single true subject departs from itself and returns to itself in its dialectical movement. The Hegelian dialectic, as the synthesis of the opposites centering upon the subject of absolute spirit, is possible by presupposing the latent being of this spirit.

The cause of the lack of absolute negation in the Hegelian dialectic, as Nishida points out, can ultimately be sought in this presupposition of the latent being of the subject of absolute spirit, attested by the circle in which Spirit moves, departing from and returning to itself. If the subject subsists and remains the same based on its latent being, the objects that detach themselves from this subject and confront it never radically negate it, but degenerate into the means for its expansive development by being integrated into it.

Taking into account his criticism of the Hegelian dialectic, Nishida's conception of his dialectic of nothingness does not presuppose the latent being of the permanent subject, but introduces absolute negation between nothingness and the beings it engenders. Speaking from Nishida's standpoint, wherein nothingness is the absolute ground for all beings, producing them only through its self-negation, nothingness cannot impose its unity upon beings as is the case with absolute spirit, as conceived by Hegel. Certainly, Nishida has his own idea of the circle in which beings are born from nothingness and return to it. But, in this circle, there is no permanent subject that evolves through the integration of its object; therefore, this circle would not result in integrating all the objects at the respective stages of the evolution of this subject.

Section 3: Nishida's Criticism of Hegel's Views of the World and Its History

Nishida's criticism of the Hegelian dialectic is not just a matter of questions regarding thought on the ontological or epistemological principles. Given that Hegel conceived of his dialectic as the logic of the movement that produces all reality in the world and its history, this dialectic inevitably puts forward views as to how the world and its entities exist, and how its history unfurled. Through observing Hegel's views of history and the world, and Nishida's criticism of them, it will become understandable how Nishida's criticism of the Hegelian dialectic constitutes a line of thought that challenges Western modernity.

When Osborne argued that the Hegelian dialectic could serve as a logic for hierarchically subjugating others of the West, he did not so without reason. We can see that Hegel himself, in his texts, links dialectic and universal history, in which different regions or peoples are hierarchized. In *The Philosophy of History*, he articulates his concept of such a history:

> For that history is the exhibition of the divine, absolute development of Spirit in its highest forms—that gradation by which it attains its truth and consciousness of itself. The forms which these grades of progress assume are the characteristic "National Spirits" of World History; the peculiar tenor of their ethical life, of their Government, their Art, Religion, and Science. (53; translation modified by referring to HW XII 73)[6]

Hegel here asserts that the development of absolute spirit proceeds through stages, and that the form in which this spirit appears as a human spirit at each stage corresponds to each national spirit. In doing so, he reduces the difference between various nations in the world to the difference in the degree of the progress of human spirit and establishes a hierarchy among these nations while integrating them into one and the same universal history. He continues: "To realize these grades is the boundless impulse of the World-Spirit—its irresistible urging; for this division into organic members, and the full development of each, is its Notion" (Hegel, *The Philosophy of History* 53; translation modified by referring to HW XII 73).[7] Hegel insists the differentiation of various nations as gradations of progress is the impulse of World Spirit—absolute spirit realizing itself in history in the ways that have significance for the entire world and revealing itself as a principle to explain the world and its history. He further posits that the development of these nations as the division according to the degrees of progress is the Notion of Spirit. Given Hegel's idea that Spirit, through its Notion, creates all realities throughout the entire world and its history, the above passage suggests that the establishment of a hierarchical order of different nations corresponding to their degrees of progress is a necessity for world history as destined by Spirit and its Notion. Here, Hegel justifies the hierarchy that is produced as an outcome of the essence of Notion and absolute spirit.

The dialectic also plays a role in this justification. Elsewhere in *The Philosophy of History*, Hegel qualifies the nature of the Notion as essentially dialectical, explaining the consequence of this dialectical nature as follows:

> The logical, and—as still more prominent—the *dialectical* nature of the Notion in general, viz. that it is self-determined—that it posits in itself determinations which it successively sublates; and by this very process of sublating its earlier stages, gains an affirmative, and, in fact, a richer and more concrete determination [. . .] . (63; translation modified by referring to HW XII 86)[8]

Given the dialectical movement of absolute spirit sublating the opposition between itself and the object it posits through cognition, the Notion the Spirit has of itself and all its objects also bears a dialectical nature. Hegel draws from this dialectical nature of the Notion the hierarchical order among the objects that absolute spirit posits one after another. Hegel's description of the Notion becoming richer and more concrete every time absolute spirit cognizes and incorporates its object as the Notion's "sublating its earlier stages" attests to his sense of hierarchy between earlier stages and later stages in the movement of Spirit. Insofar as the dialectic is the process through which the absolute spirit (as the single substance) enlarges itself and its Notion enriches itself, the stages of their dialectical movement cannot avoid being hierarchized along a single path of progress. As such, the dialectic, when applied to relations between nations, serves as a logical device that necessitates this hierarchy.

It is not only in his general view of history that he expresses his opinion on the hierarchy of different regions or peoples. His sense of hierarchy manifests itself more bluntly when he refers to the concrete others of Europe, as exemplified by Hegel's infamous disdain toward non-European regions and peoples. For example, he states Africa "is no historical part of the World; it has no movement or development to exhibit" (*The Philosophy of History* 99). Excluding certain regions or peoples from history in this way means refusing them the possibility of progress, which he himself claims should reside in all human beings. Looking down upon them works to regard them as not a part of humanity proper. He also states, "Europe is absolutely the end of History, Asia the beginning" (Hegel, *The Philosophy of History* 103). In his view, Europe is at the forefront of progress, and Asia is the least advanced, or at the starting point of progress. Then he declares, "[I]t is the necessary fate of Asiatic Empires to be subjected to Europeans" (Hegel, *The Philosophy of History* 142). Strictly speaking, Hegel sees the most advanced stage of humanity not in the idealized image of the Westerner in general, but in that of the German in particular: "The German Spirit is the Spirit of the new World. Its aim is the realization of absolute Truth as the unlimited self-determination of Freedom" (*The Philosophy of History* 341). That is, absolute spirit and freedom find their highest realization in the national spirit of the German, which is in the forefront of the dialectical movement of this realization. Germany, meant to represent the new world at the latest stage in universal history, is in a stark contrast with Africa and Asia, which are situated outside or at the beginning of this history. Naturally, theorizations of a hierarchy among different regions or peoples can easily lead toward rationalizing that the allegedly superior should wield power over the allegedly inferior. When one professes certain people correspond to the most advanced stage of the development of absolute subject, this could mislead them into believing that their treatment of others who are allegedly at less advanced stages as mere "objects" is authorized. Needless to say, such a thought cannot be unrelated to the exercise of that power, whichever precedes or succeeds it.[9]

Nishida is bitter about such a view of world history in which Europe or a specific part of it is situated at the most advanced stage and other regions at less advanced stages. For example, in "The Problems of Japanese Culture," he critically mentions the Eurocentric idea of universal history:

> As a consequence of the conflicts and frictions among various cultures for thousands of years [in Europe], a theoretical archetype [of European culture] was formed. [European people] regard it as the single cultural archetype. According to this archetype, they conceive of the stages of cultural forms and situate Oriental culture at an undeveloped stage. They believe that Oriental culture, if it develops, should necessarily become the same as their culture. Even such a great thinker as Hegel had a similar thought. I think here is the problem. (NKZ XII 284)

According to Nishida, the "theoretical archetype" of European culture, taken for granted by Europeans, is itself a product of history, formed at a certain point in time as a result of a particular course of events. He describes this as "conflicts and frictions among various cultures."

Nevertheless, once it is formed, people come to mistake such an "archetype" as the single cultural archetype, which then becomes the standard according to which they judge other cultures as undeveloped and inferior. Hegel's aforementioned idea of universal history—in which Asia is situated at the beginning, Europe at the end, and from which Africa is excluded—comes from the imposition of a similar single standard of progress upon regions other than Europe. This imposition allowed him to one-sidedly judge cultural others as less advanced. Nishida believes this mentality of assuming the single standard and imposing it upon others is not specific of Hegel, but common to contemporary Europeans. Naturally, a philosopher's thought cannot but reflect the collective consciousness of his time and place, more or less.

Furthermore, for Nishida, Hegelianism is not just one example among many to express this consciousness, but rather its very epitome. Along this line, Nishida perceives Hegelianism's affinity with European imperialism, which was a dominant and accepted ideology in Europe during Hegel's time. Nishida also sees overlaps between the problems of Hegelianism and those of the dogma that advocates European imperialism. Nishida criticizes Hegelianism for being complicit with this dogma based on its subject-centered ways of thinking originating from Hegel's concept of absolute spirit. In "The Problems of Japanese Culture," he presents his opinion that, when "people came to think that the center of human action is in the subject" in Europe, "the imperialistic human form in the nineteenth century" appeared (NKZ XII 376). He continues:

> Hegel's ethical philosophy would express the morality of such a time. Behind the historical subject as he conceived of it was absolute spirit [. . .] However, absolute spirit conceived by Hegel was still subjective [*shutaiteki*], to put in my own terms, in the category of the grammatical subject [*shugoteki*]. It could be said that thinking the world to be environmentally one is the culmination of a way of thinking characteristic of Western culture, a way of thinking in which the world is taken to be subjectively one. (NKZ XII 376–77)

In Hegel's philosophy, since absolute spirit is the permanent subject of world history, there is ultimately only one world corresponding to this single subject that produces, cognizes, and identifies with that world, and thus carries history forward. Absolute spirit as this ultimate subject expands itself so as to swallow the whole world far beyond being the center of it. In this concept, Nishida sees the culmination of the subject-centered way of thinking, and takes this extremity of subject-centeredness as coordinated with "the imperialistic human form" at Hegel's time. Supposing that absolute spirit is the only subject equal to only one world that is the true reality, the idea that all other things, regarded as its objects, should be integrated into and subjugated to this subject would easily follow. When one likens Europe and the peoples living there to this ultimate subject qua world, and other regions and the peoples living there to the objects of this subject qua world, one would be led to use this idea to justify European imperialism. Thus, Nishida connects the acceptance of the dogma of European imperialism with the extremity of subject-centeredness in Hegelianism, and locates the epitome of this dogma as being within Hegel's idea of absolute spirit.

Naturally enough, Nishida thinks the extremity of the subject-centered way of thinking can be discerned not only in Hegel's idea of absolute spirit, but also in his philosophy constructed around it.

> On the contrary, it could be said that Hegelian logic envelops humans' historical activities as objects. Nevertheless this logic has not gotten out of the stance of going from environment to subject. The subject still remains outside as ever. There is no absolute negation. Insofar as the subject remains, still [this logic] consists in thinking from the subject. It can be called subjective [*shukanteki*]. That is why Hegel's philosophy is called ideal. (NKZ XII 362)

In this essay, Nishida often uses the phrase, "from environment to subject," to describe Western culture and contrast it with Oriental culture. The stance of going from environment to subject is the stance of positing oneself as the subject through surmounting the confrontation with one's environment, and of continuing to be the subject by positing one's relation with others in the form of a similar opposition, and by resolving it in conquering them. Given Nishida's view of Hegelianism as the culmination of the characteristic way of thinking in Western culture, it is no wonder he uses this phrase to qualify Hegelianism. Specifically, Nishida states that Hegelianism deals with human historical activities as the objects of absolute subject. Insofar as Hegelianism assumes as its center such a subject that persists outside all objects and subsumes them, he regards Hegelianism as subjective and deprived of absolute negation. Qualifying Hegelianism as subjective in the same way as Hegel's concept of absolute spirit, Nishida implies that not only this concept, but also Hegelianism itself, epitomizes the dogma of European imperialism by centering upon the idea of the single subject qua the single world.

Although Nishida refers merely to Hegelian logic and does not specify what kind of logic it is, we can see the criticism Nishida raises here as also applicable to the Hegelian dialectic. In fact, negation, whose lack in this logic Nishida deplores, is an essential constituent of the Hegelian dialectic. Nishida's description of the subject-centeredness of Hegelian logic as the cause of its lack of true negation coincides with his description of the subjective or noematic nature of the Hegelian dialectic.

In fact, this salient characteristic of the Hegelian dialectic (which is criticized by Nishida as its defect) is an indispensable factor in making Western modernity's mechanism of subjugating and hierarchizing its others work as such, as illustrated by Hegel's views of the world and its history. If the Hegelian dialectic works by the logic defining this mechanism, it is insofar as this dialectic presupposes the latent being of absolute spirit, and the circular structure in which this spirit returns to itself, while gradually absorbing different others. It is the repetitious return to the self of such a subject, swallowing different objects in its path, that allows for the hierarchization of these objects. Allegedly, the degrees of progress in this hierarchy are decided corresponding to the stages through which this spirit passes by integrating into itself its objects one after another. If the subject does not keep its identity intact through these stages by consistently returning to itself, the progress could not be evaluated as such. Hegel could say that the realization of the grades of progress belongs to the nature of Spirit's Notion, based on the assumption that Spirit subsists throughout the process of progress and consistently returns to itself. Considering this, Nishida's criticism of the Hegelian dialectic tends to be aimed at disrupting the function of the above mechanism and surmounting the ill effects of Western modernity formulated by Hegelianism. Nishida's criticism of Europeans, including Hegel, for regarding their culture as the single archetype and judging another culture as undeveloped also point at this direction of thought.

Section 4: Nishida's Criticism of Hegel's Concepts of the Universal and the State

Naturally, dialectic as the fundamental principle of Hegelianism is inextricably associated with other Hegelian concepts. As such, Nishida's criticism of Hegelianism and the attempts of overcoming modernity implied in this criticism do not merely concern the Hegelian dialectic. Hegel conceived of the agent of all dialectical movements to be, in the end, absolute spirit. This spirit was supposed to manifest itself in the entire world and history and is, as such, the most universal. Since the latent being of this spirit is assumed throughout the Hegelian dialectic, Nishida's criticism of it cannot but extend itself to Hegel's concept of the most universal.

Furthermore, as illustrated by his famous phrase, "What is rational is real and what is real is rational" (Hegel, *The Philosophy of Right* 10; translation slightly modified by referring to HW VII 24),[10]" the absolute spirit as Hegel conceives of it is not isolated from reality. It ineluctably realizes itself in it. This realization reaches the concrete objectification of reason as the highest human faculty in the form of a certain human society beyond mere individual subjectivity. Hegel believes this objectification of reason, as the realization of absolute spirit, is the state, which is the concrete universal—i.e., the concretization of the most universal in reality. That is why he equates different appearances of absolute spirit with different national spirits, while hierarchizing them according to the degrees of the realization of absolute spirit. Then, presumably, Nishida's criticism of Hegelianism also entails Hegel's concept of the state as the concrete universal.

However at first glance, with regard to the concept of the state, and especially the state as an essentially moral polity, the similarities between Nishida and Hegel seem more conspicuous. Hegel believes by concretely objectifying reason, the state can realize the universal good that only reason can grasp. In doing so, the state will necessarily determine its members' ways of life as essentially ethical, as is succinctly summarized in his following statements:

> [. . .] the State is the actually existing, realized ethical life. (*The Philosophy of History* 38; translation modified by referring to HW XII 56)[11]
>
> Since the state is the objective spirit, it is only as one of its members that the individual oneself has objectivity, genuine individuality, and an ethical life. (*The Philosophy of Right* 156; translation modified by referring to HW VII 399)[12]

In this respect, Hegel's view of the state seems to show striking similarity to Nishida's. Nishida's statement cited earlier, "To be national should be the way in which the individual self exists. Being and morality become one in the state" (NKZ X 327), seems to endorse this similarity. Hegel sometimes distinguishes morality and ethicality: morality refers to the principle of good acts insofar as it is abstractly speculated about, while ethicality refers to the realization of such an ideal in people's actual lives. When Nishida emphasizes morality, what he has in mind is the morality thus realized, not that which is abstractly speculated about. In this context, the differences between ethicality, for Hegel, and morality, for Nishida, are negligible. Surely, both philosophers insist that the individual can realize ethicality/morality only insofar as one is a member of the state.

However, Nishida himself strongly disagrees with Hegel on his view of the state as personifying morality. In "The Problems of the Reason of State," Nishida expresses this disagreement as follows:

> From Hegel's standpoint of universal reason, even though he describes it as concrete, we cannot say that the state is equal to morality, nor can we truly resolve the problem of the reason of the state. The state cannot get out of the totalitarian standpoint negating the individuals. Starting from Hegelian logic, after all, we cannot think true, creative individuality. (NKZ X 331)

Against Hegel's assertion that the state personifies morality because absolute spirit concretizes itself in it as objectified reason, Nishida objects that the state conceived of in this way can never be equal to morality, insofar as it is nothing but the totality negating the individuals.

To clarify what Nishida means, I will look further into how Hegel thinks of the state as equal to morality. In *The Philosophy of History*, after affirming that, "the State is the actually existing, realized ethical life," Hegel continues:

> For it is the Unity of the general/universal [*allgemein*], essential Will, with that of the subjective; and this is "Ethicality." The Individual living in this unity has an ethical life. (38; translation modified by referring to HW XII 56)[13]
>
> [. . .] and the Universal is to be found in the State, in its laws, in its universal and rational arrangements. (39)
>
> For Law is the objectivity of Spirit; volition in its true form. Only that will which obeys law, is free; for it obeys itself—it is independent and so free. (39)

Here, Hegel refers to Jean-Jacques Rousseau's term "general will," which is paired with and contrasted to particular will. The particular will is each individual's subjective will that guides personal interests, whereas the general will wills public good as the benefit of the whole society, as distinguished from the sum of personal, subjective interests of all individuals in the society. Although the universal will and the individual will seem incompatible, Hegel insists that their unity can be achieved in the state, and only in it. For Hegel, if the state is the concrete universal, it is to the extent that the law that founds the state, and thus represents its will in its rationality, objectifies universal and absolute spirit. As such, the state is itself universal, and the true form of the individual will should reside in the universal will. Therefore, when the individual obeys this law and unites individual will with the universal will of the state, the individual not only participates in the objective concretization of absolute spirit and lives an ethical life, but also acts faithfully to the true form of its own will and controls itself by itself to be independent and free.

Still, it seems difficult to ignore the similarities between Hegel and Nishida's thoughts. As cited earlier, Nishida states, "the individual person's compliance with the law of one's society must make the individual person as such" (NKZ X 329). Nishida insists the law and legal system of the state not only let its members practice morality, but also, in enabling them to respect each other, truly make them individuals. To this extent, obeying the law of the state and practicing morality are intrinsic to the individual. Nishida also writes, "Morality should not be the 'ought' stemming from abstractly being human, but the 'ought' of the citizen of the state as the self-expression of the absolute" (NKZ X 331). If Nishida regarded the practice of morality as intrinsic to the individual, it was ultimately because, for him, morality is the self-expression of absolute nothingness from which everything emerges. Insofar as the law of the state lets its members practice morality, the state itself becomes the self-expression of absolute nothingness. Nishida states, "from the standpoint of the state, law and morality become one." He goes on, "That is why the state is also called an ethical substance" (NKZ X 329). Nishida's use of Hegel's term, "ethical substance," seems to decisively attest to Nishida's acknowledgment of the overlap between his thought of the state qua morality and Hegel's thought of the state qua ethicality.

The cause of Nishida's disagreement with Hegel should be sought in that which grounds the equation between the state and morality, rather than in this equation itself. In one of the above citations, Hegel suggests that if morality is realized in the state, it is as the unity between the universal will of the state and the individual will. In doing so, he bases the equation between the state and morality upon this unity. In *The Philosophy of Right*, he explains how this unity is possible with recourse to the universality inherent in the essence of the will. The will can will anything, regardless of the determinacy of things. It thus contains "pure indeterminacy," that is, "the unrestricted infinity of absolute abstraction or universality" (Hegel, *The Philosophy of Right* 21) as its essential element. The freedom of the will, in principle, resides in this universality. Although the will cannot but will something particular in the existing order of things, and thus particularizes itself, this does not necessarily mean the will must abandon its universality and freedom. It is possible the will, by willing the particular, returns to its universality. This typically happens when the will wills public good. In this case, while willing something particular, the will exhibits universality that is not restricted to particular self-interests of the particular willing agent. Hegel defines the individuality of the will in such a situation as "particularity reflected into itself and so brought back to universality" (*The Philosophy of Right* 23), and sees in this return to universality through particularity the freedom of the will in reality: "Freedom is to will something determinate, yet in this determinacy to be by oneself and to revert once more to the universal" (*The Philosophy of Right* 229). If the will is free only insofar as it returns to universality as its essence, the will is, after all, the "self-determining universality" and "has for its object the will itself as such, and so the will in its sheer universality" (*The Philosophy of Right* 29). It follows from this that the individual naturally wills the universal will of the state, as well as the adherence to that which represents it—viz. the law. The identification of the individual will with the universal will of the state through the particular act of observing its law conforms to the universality as the essence of the individual will and enables it to attain freedom.

Hegel's concept of the unity between the individual will and universal will is backed up by his discussion of universality, particularity, and individuality as the three elements of the Notion. In *The Encyclopedia Logic*, which he frequently refers to in his *The Philosophy of Right*, he explains the relation between these three elements by giving the following example[14]:

> The individual [*einzeln*] human is what he is in particular, only insofar as he is, first of all, human as such, and within the universal. (Hegel, *The Encyclopedia Logic* 253; translation slightly modified by referring to HW VIII 327)[15]

If Hegel claims the individual is determined in its particularity only insofar as the individual belongs to the universal, it is because he presupposes "the universal is the ground and soil, the root and substance of the individual" (*The Encyclopedia Logic* 253; translation slightly modified by referring to HW VIII 327).[16] That is, the individual exists only based on the universal. He explicates what the universal in this case is:

> [T]he universal is not just something alongside other abstract qualities or mere determinations of reflection, but it is rather what permeates all the particulars and embraces them within itself. (Hegel, *The Encyclopedia Logic* 253; translation slightly modified by referring to HW VIII 327)[17]

His point is, given that the universal as the ground of all individuals permeates and embraces all their particular characteristics, subsuming the individual under the universal does not vitiate the particularity or individuality of the individual, but rather enables it to be truly defined as such.

Hegel's conception of the relation between the universal and the individual is based on his specific concept of the Notion, whose proper function consists in grasping the universal. In Hegel's view, as aforementioned, it is not that an object comes first and then is grasped by the Notion, but that the Notion precedes the object and makes it emerge so that it is recognized by the Notion, and thus accomplishes it. Put another way, the universal determinations of things, graspable only through the Notion, preexist things and concretize themselves in things insofar as these determinations are recognized by the Notion. To this extent, Hegel maintains, as above, that the universal, as the ground, permeates and embraces all the particularities of the individuals belonging to that very universal. Therefore, for him, to relate the individual to the universal, and subsume the former under the latter, is not only to more concretely and precisely understand both the individual and the universal in their inseparable connection, but also to bring the individual back to its own ground from which it emerges, and based on which it can exist and be recognized as such. Hence, Hegel's idea presented in *Science of Logic*, that the Notion of something is at first the simple determination of its abstract universality, proceeds to the determination of the particularity of this thing, and finally attains its determination in its individuality in which universality concretizes itself through particularity (598–622).

It is by following the same line of thought that Hegel insists the individual will's identification with the universal will conforms to the former's essence. In *The Encyclopedia Logic*, he likens the relation between the universal will and the laws that determine the individual will in particular ways to the relation between the Notion of the will and its particular determinations:

> The general/universal [*allgemein*] will is the *Notion* of willing, and the laws are the particular determinations of willing as grounded in this Notion. (241; translation slightly modified by referring to HW VIII 313)[18]

Although the laws in themselves are particular determinations of what individuals should and should not will, in their rationality they articulate the universal determinations of the will, and to this extent are grounded in the Notion of the will. Therefore, the will of the state, represented in its law, is ineluctably the universal will. It is the will in its true form grasped by the Notion, and only that can make all wills emerge. Then, for the individual will to obey the law and identify with the universal will of the state is to relate itself to the Notion of the will as the ground of the individual will. It thus recovers its authentic mode of existence in which the universal ground reveals itself. When Hegel insists the individual will's identification with the universal will conforms to the former's essence, his presupposition is that the Notion that comprehends universalities prior to individual things actually generates them. Therefore, for them to adjust themselves to the Notion, or to the entities that are supposed to embody it, is for them to be true to their own essence.

Nishida is not happy to accept Hegel's conception that underneath everything exists the Notion and the universality that it grasps. In "The World as Dialectical Universal" (*Benshōhōteki ippansha toshiteno sekai*), published in 1934 and included in *Fundamental Problems of Philosophy Continued: The Dialectical World* (*Tetsugaku no konpon mondai zokuhen: Benshōhōteki sekai*) in the same year, Nishida occasionally mentions and critiques the Hegelian concepts of the universal and dialectic, and presents his concept of the universal closely connected with his dialectic of nothingness. The following is an example:

> Hegel's "Notion" [*gainen*] also did not avoid being an organic unity. Even if it returned to itself by its own self-negation, it still did not avoid being a universal, or, if not that, a singular individual. This is the reason why the Hegelian dialectic cannot be thought to be a dialectic of true absolute negation. (Nishida "The World as Dialectical Universal" 167; translation modified by referring to NKZ VII 313)[19]

Hegel describes the movement of the Notion as that in which the negation of simple and abstract universality leads to the determination of particularity, whose negation and sublation in turn lead to the determination of individuality, as the particularity becomes one with universality. Thus, his concept of this movement pivots upon universality. Even if Hegel calls this movement dialectical, true negation is lacking in it in Nishida's eyes. Hegel regards particularity as that which is contained in universality and subsumed under it. He conceives of individuality as the unity of particularity and universality. Although the universal is supposed to be negated and then returned to itself, it subsists throughout this movement without being truly negated. That is how the universal's return to itself is possible, as is typically illustrated in Hegel's understanding of the will as the "self-determining universality," (*The Philosophy of Right* 29), and of its freedom as consisting in "revert[ing] once more to the universal" (*The Philosophy of Right* 229).

Nishida once located the cause of the Hegelian dialectic's lack of true negation in the subsistence of absolute spirit throughout this dialectic. In fact, absolute spirit is not unrelated to the movement of the universal returning to itself in the process of the Notion returning to itself. When Nishida states that the Hegelian Notion did not avoid being "a universal" and "a singular individual" ("The World as Dialectical Universal" 167; translation modified as above), he most likely had in mind absolute spirit. In a prior statement on dialectic, we can read an allusion to absolute spirit as the single authentic subject of the Hegelian dialectic:

> Even if, on the contrary, a dialectical process is conceived as an infinite dynamic unity, as long as a dynamic unity is conceived as spirit or as matter, it cannot avoid being one thing. It cannot avoid the monistic viewpoint. ("The World as Dialectical Universal" 167; translation modified by referring to NKZ VII 312)[20]

Even if one may say that a dialectical process is such a unity that is infinite in the sense of it being dynamic, open-ended, and constantly undergoing changes, insofar as this process itself is conceived as a unity, there should be something consistent in this process. If this unity itself is conceived as a certain entity, whether it is spirit or matter, then the consistency of the process is guaranteed by the subsistence of this entity. In this case, it is inevitable that this process ends up eradicating the differences of other things involved in it and unifying them from the standpoint of this entity. For Nishida, the absolute spirit conceived by Hegel, the spirit whose latent being predetermines all the beings emerging from it, is exactly such an entity described as "one thing" above. But, from Nishida's standpoint, such an entity, however it is conceived, is indeed one individual among many. Hence Nishida's above equation between Hegel's "universal" and his own "singular individual." When such a particular individual is professed to be the universal that should embrace and permeate all other individuals, it is given the status of the single authentic individual. As such, it ineluctably unitarily imposes its own particularity onto others in the name of universality.

Following Nishida's line of thought here, if the Hegelian universal returns to itself through the movement of the Notion returning to itself, it is because absolute spirit (equal to the Notion through which it comprehends itself by itself) moves in the circle going from and coming back to itself. The Notion's or the universal's return to itself derives from absolute spirit's *"self-restoring sameness"* or "reflection in otherness within itself" (Hegel, *The Phenomenology of Spirit* 10), integrating the objects it posits and synthesizing them with itself. However, if absolute spirit as the most universal is merely an individual entity professed to be universal, as Nishida insists, the universals in general conceived by Hegel, which are, after all, the provisional forms that the self-knowledge of absolute spirit takes at every moment, amount to unifying individuals and effacing their differences, just as absolute spirit does. The same applies to the individual will's return to universality as its essence. Although this return was supposed to legitimize the unity between the universal will of the state and the individual will, it turns out to be the movement of totalizing the latter and subjecting it to the former.

If the unity between the two kinds of will becomes possible through such a movement, so does the state, which Hegel equates with this unity as morality itself in order to buttress the equation between the state and morality. Now it becomes understandable why Nishida described how the state conceived by Hegel "cannot get out of the totalitarian standpoint negating the individuals" (NKZ X 331). This is because, in Nishida's eyes, the unity between the universal will and the individual will, equated by Hegel with the state itself, is ultimately the subjugation of the latter to the former.

In a sense, this subjugation is a natural consequence of Hegel's concept of the state as the concrete universal in which absolute spirit, as the most universal behind all universals, concretizes itself. In "The Problems of the Reason of State," Nishida also comments on Hegel's view of the state in reference to German historian Friedrich Meinecke's criticism of Hegel:

> In his philosophy of history, in which all individual things are subjugated to the universal, [Hegel] needed, in this world of empirical facts, the universal unifying them, that is to say, the power to rule the individuals, and therefore the state was deified. This is what Meinecke says. (NKZ X 274)

Hegel describes the state as "the shape which the perfect embodiment of Spirit assumes" (*The Philosophy of History* 17). As such, it is also "the rational freedom, recognizing itself in an objective form and being-for-itself" (Hegel, *The Philosophy of History* 47; translation modified by referring to HW XII 66).[21] If the purpose of world history consists in the realization of spirit and freedom, as Hegel believes, the emergence of the state in history marks a crucial moment that can decisively make history what it is. That is why he puts emphasis on the state in *The Philosophy of History*. With this in mind, what Nishida means by the above comment is, given that the dialectical movement through which absolute spirit realizes itself in history consists in subjugating the individual to the universal, the state resulting from this movement ineluctably amounts to it taking over and subjugating individuals to the universal.

Hegel himself also suggests the state's deed of doing so comes from absolute spirit's movement of subjugating the individual to the universal. In the *Science of Logic*, Hegel discusses how the state can be what it should be by contrasting it with the opposite case, in which the state is not what it should be:

But if an object, for example, the state, *did not correspond at all* to its Idea, that is, if in fact it was not the Idea of the state at all, if its reality, which is the self-conscious individuals, did not correspond at all to the Notion, its soul and its body would have parted; the former would escape into the solitary regions of thought, the latter would have broken up into the single individualities. (757)

Hegel conceives the Idea to be the adequate Notion, "the unity of *Notion* and *reality*," or already "the identity of itself and *reality*" (*Science of Logic* 758). But, given that he supposes the subsistence of the Notion that makes its object emerge and ideally coincides with it, every Notion is potentially the Idea and is to become it. If the Notion is the comprehension by absolute spirit, and this spirit also comprehends itself, then the Idea is the true self-knowledge of this spirit, the knowledge that it has by synthesizing the object it posits. Then, it is also this self-knowing spirit itself, insofar as it recognizes itself in its unity with the object. Hegel insists the state can be what it should be when it is one with its Idea, that is, when the Notion of the state has a corresponding reality. As this reality, he has in mind the self-conscious individuals who constitute the state. In contrast, he believes that if the state is not what it should be, separated into abstract thought of the state and isolated individuals, it is because these individuals do not correspond to the Idea or the Notion of the state. He describes this situation as that in which "the Idea has not completely leavened its reality, has imperfectly subdued it to the Notion" (Hegel, *Science of Logic* 757). To put it the other way around, for the state to be what it should be, the Idea of the state must completely leaven individuals and subdue them to the Notion of the state. That is to say, the true self-knowledge of absolute spirit, or this self-knowing spirit itself, must adjust individuals to the Notion of the state. It is absolute spirit's movement of subduing individuals to the Notion of the state, thus realizing its Idea that unites individuals with the state and makes the state what it should be.

Considering Hegel's claim, his definition of the Idea as the unity of the Notion and reality implies that the Idea, even in the situation in which reality does not correspond to the Notion, has the force to make them correspond by subduing reality to the Notion. In other words, just as absolute spirit is destined to synthesize the object it posits, the Idea, as the true self-knowledge of this spirit, is destined to realize itself by adjusting reality to the Notion. It follows from this that the Notion's priority to the object entails the truthfulness of the Notion to which reality should subject itself, and therefore that which is destined to become the Idea. That the Notion starts with comprehending universality, and ends with subsuming the individual under the universal, suggests the truthfulness of the Idea resides on the side of the universal supposedly preceding and permeating the individual. In *The Philosophy of History,* Hegel writes the "unity of the universal and the individual is the Idea itself, manifesting itself as the *state*" (46; translation modified by referring to HW XII 65).[22] If we take this passage and put it together with his former statement implying that the Idea of the state, in which individuals are in reality separated from the state, should subdue the individuals to its Notion, we can understand the manifestation of the Idea in the state, conceived by Hegel as the unity between universal will and the individual will, is possible through the subjugation of the individual to the universal.

Hegel is convinced that the authentic mode of existence of the individual—the way it should be—can be attained by adjusting the reality of the individual to the truthfulness that exists in the universal belonging to the self-knowledge of absolute spirit. Therefore, he believes the state can enable its members to live ethically, become constituents of an ethical substance, and objectify absolute spirit in the shape of reason by subjugating the individual will to the universal will. By virtue of this, people can grasp and share the universal good. However, from Nishida's standpoint, since this spirit is an individual entity professed to be universal, it cannot but impose its particularity upon other individuals. Therefore, the ethicality or morality to be realized in accordance with the self-knowledge of this spirit ends up disregarding the particularity, not only of each individual society, but also of each individual person. This is a natural consequence of assuming "reason behind the fact" (NKZ XII 80) and making fact fit reason. That is why Nishida insists the state conceived by Hegel, precisely because it is the embodiment of absolute spirit and the objectification of reason, cannot be equal to morality proper.

Section 5: Reformulating the Universal, Creating New Views of the World and the State

As discussed so far, in Nishida's view, the Hegelian dialectic is a process in which objects' differences are absorbed into the sameness of the permanent subject of absolute spirit, and the individual is subjugated to the universal. Consequently, this dialectic has a double effect in relation to Hegel's concept of the state as the concrete universal, in which absolute spirit as the most universal concretizes itself through this dialectic. On the one hand, different states or nations as the outcomes of this process are hierarchized, and likened to the objects that the subject posits and integrates into itself at different stages of its development. On the other hand, the individuals within each state or nation are unified, subjected to the allegedly universal standard of reason:

the manifestation of absolute spirit. Thus the Hegelian concepts of the most universal and the concrete universal suppress not only the individualities of different states or nations, but also the individualities of the members in each state or nation.

Nishida seeks the fundamental cause of the double effect of the Hegelian dialectic—characterized as that which suppresses the individualities of different states or nations and the individualities of the members in each state or nation—in the subject-centeredness of this dialectic and the assumption of the latent being of absolute spirit as the single subject throughout all dialectical processes. To counter this double effect, however, the reconsideration of the most universal in itself is not enough. The problems involved in the Hegelian concept of absolute spirit concern not only the relation between this most universal and its individual concretizations, but also the relation between each concrete universal and its individual members. To tackle these problems, Nishida's task would be to reconsider the universal and its relation with the individual at these two levels in order to retrieve the individual from its subjugation to the universal.

I will consider Nishida's project of overcoming Western modernity in light of this reconsideration of the universal at the two levels, exemplarily articulated in "The World as Dialectical Universal." It is the first aspect of the above double effect that constitutes Western modernity's mechanism of subjugating and hierarchizing its others concerning the relation between different states. However, Nishida saw this first aspect and the second aspect, concerning the relation between the state and its members, as both resulting from the same defect of the Hegelian dialectic. The project to overcome Western modernity as understood above, insofar as it tackles the defect of the Hegelian dialectic as the logic of this modernity, should ineluctably address these two aspects, corresponding to the above double effect and the two levels of the reconsideration of the universal. As Nishida identified the defect of the Hegelian dialectic as the cause of this double effect, an attempt to surmount this effect should draw upon Nishida's own dialectic of nothingness, which he intended to contribute to resolving this defect.

Based on his understanding that the subsistence of the latent being of absolute spirit in the Hegelian dialectic deprives it of true negation and makes it subjugate the individual to the universal, Nishida claims absolute nothingness, which he calls the "universal of all universals," as the agent of true dialectic. He thinks this nothingness negates itself to create beings so that they can affirm themselves. In this process, he sees true dialectic in which the true negation of its agency accomplishes the synthesis of the extreme opposites. Since nothingness creates beings only by negating itself, he insists that this universal would not subjugate individuals, but simply let them be themselves. Along with this ultimate universal, he also conceives the concrete universal that is compatible with this affirmation of individuals.

In "The World as Dialectical Universal," just after the passages in which he critically comments on the Hegelian Notion and dialectic, Nishida states: "When the universal truly negates itself, it must become a world of individuals" (167). Here, Nishida claims nothingness, through self-negation, not only creates individuals, but also becomes their world. The title of "The World as Dialectical Universal" indicates that the true universal, when it concretizes itself in reality through true dialectic, takes the shape of such a world. In short, Nishida conceives this world to be the equivalent to the concrete universal.

Nishida qualifies this world as "particular" and explains the self-determination of this particular world as the self-determination of nothingness qua place:

> The self-determination of the particular is conversely the self-determination of place. The self-determining particular always possesses the other in the determination of place. The self-determining particular is neither merely a particular as the determination of the universal, nor is it merely an individual. It must be solely a place where individuals face each other, a place of their mutual determination. It must be the particular of the universal, which takes the individual as extension. It must be the self-determination of absolute nothingness. ("The World as Dialectical Universal" 229; translation modified by referring to NKZ VII 419)[23]

Nishida's choice of the word "particular" to qualify the concrete universal has significant connotations. If the most universal is not Being, but nothingness, it would not impose its own unity upon the beings it encapsulates. Consequently, what becomes of this universal must be multiple concrete universals that are not unified or integrated into the single higher universal. This is why the self-determination of absolute nothingness cannot but lead to the self-determination of the particular, insofar as the particular designates that which is accompanied by other particulars and is distinguished from them by its genuine difference. For Nishida, each concrete universal is the particular in this sense. Thus, being as particular is the evidence that they are the outcome of the self-determination of absolute nothingness through its self-negation.

Nishida's idea of the particular presented here is different from Hegel's. Hegel believed the particular to be included in the universal in the first place, and was then to be subsumed under it. Due to this subsumption, the determination of the particular was ultimately, in Nishida's words above, "the determination of the universal," in the sense of the determination of the superordinate concept of the particular in question. One may wonder whether Nishida's equation between self-determination of absolute nothingness as the most universal, and self-determination of a world as a particular concrete universal, means the reduction of the self-determination of the particular to the self-determination of the universal, as is the case with Hegel. This is not what Nishida intends. Precisely, as the most universal that becomes the concrete universal is nothingness that negates itself, it does not subsume under itself all such concrete universals in order to unify them, but enables them to determine themselves as particular. The self-determination of the universal conceived by Nishida resides in the self-determination of each particular world as genuinely particular, which entails similar self-determinations of other particular worlds, without being reduced to the determination of the higher universal.

Explicating the implications of his concept of the concrete universal, Nishida claims each particular world, as the result of the concretization of absolute nothingness, participates in the work of this nothingness. If by negating itself, absolute nothingness creates beings, and itself becomes particular worlds, each of these worlds should appear to the individuals in it in the same way as absolute nothingness does. That is to say, just as self-negating nothingness does not unify these worlds, each of these worlds, as different concrete universals, should accept the individuals in it without subjugating their individualities to the universality of each concrete universal. It is to this extent that Nishida describes each particular world as "a place where individuals face each other," as "a place of their mutual determination," that is, a place where individuals mutually determine themselves to be individuals. Nishida's description of each particular world as "the particular of the universal which takes the individual as extension" ("The World as Dialectical Universal" 229) means that each particular world is a concretization of absolute nothingness from which individuals are born. This implies that this world enables the individuals in it to determine themselves as such, and allows them to be true to their individualities, just as absolute nothingness allows them to do so.

Such a world as a dialectical universal that is in itself an entity, and yet is also a place for individuals to live in, plays the same role as absolute nothingness. For this reason, Nishida describes this world as "a being-qua-nothingness [*yū soku mu*]" ("The World as Dialectical Universal" 169; NKZ VII 316).

Elsewhere, Nishida expresses more explicitly his idea that each particular world acts upon the individuals in it exactly in the same way as absolute nothingness does:

> At the same time, when the universal is self-determining, it must always envelop the individual. For if not, it would not be a universal. What I call the dialectical universal as the medium of individuals both envelops and determines individuals in such a sense. ("The World as Dialectical Universal" 169; translation altered by referring to NKZ VII 315–16)[24]

Throughout his works, Nishida frequently uses the word "envelop" (*tsutsumu*) to describe nothingness' acceptance of individuals the way they are, as a mirror that mirrors things without distorting the figure, or as mirroring without a mirror. Here, he uses this very word to describe the action of the concrete or dialectical on the individual, in which absolute nothingness dialectically concretizes itself upon individuals. What he means by the use of the word "envelop" is that the true universal, whether it is absolute nothingness or particular worlds emerging from it, should likewise allow individuals to affirm themselves, rather than negate them. This, for him, is what the true universal should be.

What should be noted is that the affirmation of individualities as conceived above becomes possible on the condition that the things whose individualities are affirmed (whether these things are concrete universals as states, or their members) are placed inside something more universal. A doubt arises as to whether this condition suggests that these entities are subjected to the unifying or totalizing function of that within which they are placed. As I will discuss later, this doubt is not without reason. Before looking at this point, it is important to consider what is at stake in Nishida's thoughts on the universal.

By conceiving the universal this way (whether it be the most universal or the concrete universal), Nishida intends to differentiate it from the Hegelian universal, which he understands as the individual that is professed to be universal and imposes its particularity upon other individuals. Consequently, on the one hand, Nishida conceives of the ultimate universal so that it does not subsume the individualities of particular concrete universals. On the other, he conceives of each concrete universal, which he calls the dialectical universal, so that it does not negate the individualities of the entities inside it. Leaving aside the aforementioned condition of being "inside" something for the affirmation of individualities in both cases, we can discern Nishida's countermeasure against the double effect of the Hegelian concept of the concrete universal in his thoughts on the two levels of the relation between the universal and the individual. Moreover, in further observing Nishida's thought concerning these aspects, we can also find his attempt to present another view of the world and that of the state.

On the one hand, what results from his reconsideration of the universal is the worldview in which many particular worlds coexist, while their individualities and particularities are not suppressed in the name of the higher universal. This is expressed in his statement: "[I]n the determination of place as the self-determination of the dialectical universal, innumerable worlds are possible" (Nishida, "The World as Dialectical Universal" 229–30; translation slightly modified by referring to NKZ VII 419).[25] In fact, if the self-determination of particular worlds occurs as the self-determination of place as nothingness, the place at issue cannot be the abstract place that can be anywhere, but multiple particular places, which are the only beings that can determine those particular worlds. This is how self-determination of absolute nothingness can be equal to self-determination of particular places, leading to the self-determination of the particular worlds in them. Then, concretely speaking, the self-determination of particular worlds is the formation of particular societies rooted in the particularities of their locations. Due to the absence of the single ultimate universal entity, such as absolute spirit, these particular societies are neither hierarchized according to the degrees to which this single ultimate universal realizes itself in these societies, nor subjugated to the single society in which this ultimate universal allegedly realizes itself at the highest degree.

What results from Nishida's reconsideration of the universal, on the other hand, is the view of the state in which the individualities of its members are not suppressed in the name of the totality of the state. This view is expressed in his idea of the immediate oneness between the individual and the universal in the dialectical universal:

> The self-determination of the actual world is the self-determination of the dialectical universal, which in turn means that the individual is the universal in the sense that the determination of the individual is immediately the determination of the universal and vice versa. ("The World as Dialectical Universal 193; translation altered by referring to NKZ VII 360)[26]

Equating the self-determination of the actual world and the self-determination of the dialectical universal, Nishida first repeats the aforementioned claim that each of many particular worlds is a concrete universal into which absolute nothingness dialectically concretizes itself. It is as a corollary of this claim that he broaches the accord of the determination of the individual and the determination of the universal within this particular world. As previously mentioned, the self-determination of beings through the self-negation of absolute nothingness occurs simultaneously and correlatively with the self-determination of this particular world that emerges within this nothingness. Nishida therefore claims, when these beings determine themselves as belonging to this particular world as concrete universal, their determination as individuals, as well as their determination as universal, do not conflict. Further, their determination as universal does not violate their determination as individuals; they simply merge together. The accord of these two kinds of determinations means that a person's individual identity and collective identity are one. Put in Rousseauian terms invoked by Hegel, the general/universal will and the individual will are truly united without subjugating the latter to the former.

Nishida's emphasis on the particularity of each world and society fostered in each particular place entails the emphasis on the particularity of the group of the individuals that are enveloped in such a world or society, and whose collective and individual identities are one. Referring to "a world in which individual determination and universal determination are dialectically opposed, and in which those opposites are one,"[27] Nishida adds, "presumably such a unity is the ethnic unity" ("The World as Dialectical Universal" 208; translation altered by referring to NKZ VII 383).[28] As aforementioned, Nishida defines the ethnic group not as race, but as the people who live together in the same place and who share the same mores and culture. In this sense, he suggests people's self-determination as individuals and as universal, and their individual and collective identities, can be one only for the members of the ethnic group.

Along the same line, he also finds it important for the ethnic group to be the basis for the state, but only insofar as such a group is understood properly. In "Prolegomena to Practical Philosophy" (*Jissen tetsugaku joron*), first published in 1940 and included in *Philosophical Essays* vol. 4 along with "The Problem of the Reason of State," Nishida remarks that the lack of the appropriate thinking of the ethnic group ruins Hegel's view of the state that is to be established based on this group:

> Of course, the universal, as Hegel conceives of it, is the concrete universal, and he would assume the ethnic group at the basis of the state. But he does not think of the ethnic group [*minzoku*] in the same way as I do, that is to say, he does not think that it becomes, as the contradictory self-identity between subject and environment, from the self-determination of the historical world in the manner of absolutely contradictory self-identity. I think the abstractness of his view of the state resides in this point [. . .] It seems to me that in the present, the essence of the state has disclosed itself ever more clearly as an individual life [*kotaiteki seimei*] based on ethnic spirit [*minzoku seishin*], rather than as concrete reason. (NKZ X 80–81)

The abstractness of Hegel's view of the state that Nishida points out here comes from Hegel's disregard for the particularity of each ethnic group or constituent nation rooted in each particular place, and whose self-determination is equal to the self-determination of absolute nothingness. Hegel understood different national spirits as different modes of the realization of absolute spirit and of the concrete objectification of universal reason. This is why he only saw the differences between multiple states or nations in terms of degrees, which corresponded to the stages of this realization and objectification, and which led to their integration into a unilinear hierarchy. When Nishida proposes to think of the state with regard to the particular ethnic group it is based on and the particular place it is located in, he does not merely present an alternative worldview to this unilinear hierarchization, which neglects the differences of states or nations according to the single abstract standard of concrete reason. By stating, "the essence of the state has disclosed itself ever more clearly as an individual life based on ethnic spirit" (NKZ X 81), he also suggests that if the state is based on the ethnic group in his sense, then the people's individual life and collective life, as the essence of the state, would be one without the latter's repressing the former. Thus, Nishida takes the ethnic group as he conceives of it to be the key to counter the double effect of the Hegelian concept of the concrete universal, which hierarchized different states and negated the individuals in each state.

Another reason why Nishida puts emphasis on the ethnic group is that it is the only basis on which the state can be truly equal to morality— or more precisely, morality can be truly realized in the state, as Hegel had wished but failed to consider properly. Nishida alludes to the importance of the ethnic group in this regard in a few short passages in "The World as Dialectical Universal." Nishida agrees with Hegel that morality should be realized in humans' communal life, thus existing as ethicality. He states, "[W]e may consider, with Hegel, that *Sittlichkeit* becomes the purpose of moral action" ("The World as Dialectical Universal" 225). But Nishida here agrees with Hegel only with reservation, which is actually more significant than the agreement itself: "*Sittlichkeit* must be the rationalization of the *gemeinschaftlich* [*Gemeinschaft tekinamono*]" ("The World as Dialectical Universal" 225; translation modified by referring to NKZ VII 411).[29] *Gemeinschaft* refers to a type of society that is naturally formed based on territorial connections and kinships, and in which social ties consist in personal or direct interactions. It is paired with *Gesellschaft*, in which social ties, organized in pursuit of interests and functionality, consist in indirect or impersonal interactions. By the term *Gemeinschaft*, Nishida designates the ethnic society as he conceives of it: the first human society composed of the people who live together in the same place and share the same mores and culture, the society whose particularity is determined by the particularity of its place. By using this term, Nishida insists that if ethicality as realized morality is rational, it is not because it is the objectification of universal reason or the concretization of absolute spirit as Hegel asserted, but because it is the rationalization of the mores of a particular ethnic society, which have been spontaneously born from within that society and thus reflect its particularity.

Hegel, as a consequence of his assumption of the truthfulness of the Idea and of the universal prior to reality, conceived ethicality as uniform rationality applicable to any society or person. In Nishida's view, since this abstract truthfulness disregards the particularities of various individual entities, the ethicality thus conceived would not fit each particular society. Even if such ethicality were somehow objectified as the universal will of a certain state, the individual will would not unite itself with the universal will without being forcefully subjugated to it. As such, the unity between the universal will and the individual will cannot be morality, nor can the state that realizes such "morality" be an ethical substance. This is how the Hegelian state ends up being a totality that negates the individual.

Instead, Nishida envisions that if morality were formed as the natural rationalization of the mores of the ethnic society, its members would certainly practice such morality of their own free will. If the state is constructed based on the ethnic group, then the universal will of the state and the individual will of its members would be spontaneously one, just as the individual identity and collective identity of the members of the ethnic group are so. Only in this way would the state be truly equal to morality as the unity between the two kinds of will, without subjugating the individual to the universal. Only such a state would deserve to be called ethical substance in Nishida's exact sense of the word. Nishida thus entrusts the ethnic group, as he conceives of it, the task of resolving the difficulties involved in the state theorized in Hegelianism, in which he sees the culmination of the Western way of thinking. Here, he expects that such ethnic groups would be the bases for different modes of state that could resist Western hegemony and develop in their own ways without being restrained by the norm of the realization of absolute spirit or of the objectification of abstract universal reason.

The Hegelian dialectic has an effect of hierarchizing different nations or states in the world in a way that prioritizes the West over the non-West. Nishida locates the problem of the Hegelian dialectic in its subject-centeredness and the assumption of the latent being of absolute spirit. Due to this problem, the Hegelian dialectic ends up being the logic of the movement of the permanent subject that continuously returns to itself, positing the objects and identifying with them one after another while enriching itself ever more. Thus, the Hegelian dialectic works as the mechanism subjugating to and integrating into this subject all the others it encounters, and then hierarchizing them according to the progression of its movement. Hegel's concept of absolute spirit as the most universal allows him to judge different particular states by the unilateral norm of the realization of the most universal. His concept of the state as the concrete universal, because of the totalizing effect of the dialectical movement of this realization, allows for the negation of the individualities of citizens for the sake of the totality of the state.

Nishida invents another dialectic based on absolute nothingness, rather than on Being, and reconceptualizes the most universal and its concretization. Consequently, on the one hand, he presents the worldview in which different states coexist as many particular worlds into which absolute nothingness concretizes itself in the absence of the single substance unifying all others. On the other, he presents a view of the state, which is one of such particular worlds, and accepts different individuals without totalizing them, just as absolute nothingness envelops beings the way they are. Nishida thinks that such a state is possible only based on the ethnic group whose particularity is rooted in its living place. This is one of the many particular places that determines itself as the self-determination of absolute nothingness. Thus, this place participates in the act of absolute nothingness. According to Nishida, the members of such an ethnic group, enveloped in their society just as in absolute nothingness, can naturally achieve the peaceful unity between their collective identity and individual identity.

Nishida's project of overcoming Western modernity can be discerned in his reconsideration of the universal as above, insofar as this reconsideration undermines the hierarchization of states with the West at the top, allegedly according to the degrees of progress. Nishida instead posits a worldview in which absolute nothingness as the most universal envelops all states as respective particular worlds. By presenting the stateview in which the concrete universal, rooted in each particular place, makes citizens' collective and individual identities coincide, this project also opposes the state's totalization of citizens in the name of a universal reason that tacitly presumes the West as the norm. In these two aspects of the project, Nishida resists Hegel's universalization of the West as a specific particular, with recourse of a universal conceived to affirm all particulars.

Chapter 11

Examining Nishida's Philosophical Project of Overcoming Western Modernity

Although Nishida's attempt to tackle the Hegelian dialectic and the world- and stateviews that result from it has a significance beyond a mere confrontation with Hegelianism, Nishida's attempt is not without its own problems. One of these problems concerns the aforementioned condition of being "within" something for the affirmation of individualities. Nishida would insist that absolute nothingness, as distinct from absolute spirit and its latent being that predetermines all other beings, neither unifies nor totalizes the entities it envelops. However, if absolute nothingness practically behaves in the same way as absolute sprit, this affirmation would not hold as professed. In that case, the condition of being "within" something may turn into a unifying and totalizing force similar to that of absolute spirit.

Another problem concerns the aforementioned universalization of the particular in Nishida's philosophy. If through criticizing Hegel's universalization of a specific particular Nishida himself universalizes another specific particular, a doubt arises that Nishida repeated the same error as Hegel, wherein Nishida's project to overcome the Western modernity formulated by Hegel collapses by contradicting itself. Alternatively, one may cast another doubt upon the way I am going to conclude Nishida's project (as above) to have failed.

As the criterion for assessing this project, this chapter will first insist on the importance of paying attention to the consistency between Nishida's criticisms of Hegelianism and the theory he elaborated to surmount Hegel's defects as well as his underlying philosophy. Second, I will look at the moments in which Nishida, in spite of his criticism of Hegel for assuming the latent being of absolute spirit, seems to assume the latent being of absolute nothingness as inseparably connected with the latent being of the state. Third, I will show how this assumption, which makes absolute nothingness behave like Being, affects Nishida's idea of the relation between the state and its members. Finally, I will turn toward the moments in which Nishida, again in spite of his criticism of Hegel for doing so, universalizes the particular.

These moves will be shown to have affected his idea of the relations among different states and to have destroyed his project to overcome Western modernity as well as his pursuit of another type of universality.

Section 1: The Criterion for the Assessment of Nishida's Project

I suggested above that Nishida's project to overcome modernity seemingly failed because of its own inconsistency. One may wonder why consistency matters. Or, one may understand this assessment to mean that Nishida was a bad imitator of Hegel, and that this caused the failure of the project, which is not what I mean. To avoid this misunderstanding and explicate the implications of this assessment, let me discuss the criterion for this conclusion.

Given the project was founded on Nishida's criticism of Hegel, and that the presentation of his new worldview, contra-Hegel's, is based on this criticism, such an examination is inevitably inseparable from an analysis of the validity of Nishida's criticism. Here, I have chosen to discount the typical defense of Hegel, wherein the Hegelian dialectic is structurally and theoretically supposed to have refuted all critics and defeated all opponents in advance by synthesizing all opposition. Certainly, the quest to find a way out of Hegelianism thus understood—i.e., without opposing it and thus being drawn into the synthesizing mechanism of the Hegelian dialectic—is an interesting one. In fact, explorations of it have produced much significant work in contemporary thought. However, to raise this defense without questioning from what standpoints and in what ways these criticisms have been made, as well as what is at stake in them and their possible results, seems to serve no other purpose than to prohibit all criticisms and objections in advance. This would presume the invincibility of Hegelianism from the outset.

Exemplifying this type of defense, Peter Suares excoriates Nishida's criticism of Hegel in many aspects. For one, Suares insists that, although Nishida criticized Hegel for assuming "the marginal status of the individual relative to the universal" and "unduly individualiz[ing] the universal" as "a single thing," "Hegel's actual beliefs are very different from those imputed to him by Nishida" (78–79). In Suares's view, Hegel has already formulated the determination of individuals as Nishida conceives of it. Furthermore, Suares suggests that "despite his philosophical dependence on Hegel," Nishida works at "downplaying Hegel's role in shaping his thought" (78). Aside from the question as to whether Suares's assertions that "Hegel defines the individual as *being by itself in its other*, that is, as identity through otherness" (78), and that "Hegel insists that spirit is the individual's *own* absolute aspect" (79) are convincing enough to prove Hegel did not negate the individual, or that Nishida imitated Hegel and blamed him for what he did not do, Nishida is not the only one who discerns in Hegelianism a totalizing tendency that amounts to the negation of the individual. When Suares nevertheless judges Nishida's criticism as groundless by comparing it with his own impeccable image of Hegelianism, he himself seems to downplay Nishida's thought and does not treat it on its own grounds.

In her overview of twentieth-century French interpretations of Hegel's *Phenomenology of Spirit*, Judith Butler comments:

> Although it was within the context of French theory, after all, that Hegel became synonymous with totality, teleology, conceptual domination, and the imperialist subject, the French appropriation of Hegel also puts the totalizing and teleological presumptions of Hegel's philosophy into question. (xii)

In the same period in which Nishida publicized his political thought, French intellectuals also started to discern in Hegelianism the totalizing presumptions that could support the imperial subject and domination over others. These intellectuals, in appropriating Hegel's thought and interpreting it differently, put such presumptions into question. Finding problems and creating such a reading that could resolve them, while neutralizing the totalizing effect of Hegelianism from within, is decisively different from elaborating a perfect picture exempt from all criticisms. The former attitude seems closer to Nishida's than the latter, regardless of whether the problems of Hegelianism are attacked from within or without. The kinds of problems one finds, where they are located, and how they are to be resolved, depends on each person. The ways in which one goes about inquiry naturally express how one's own thought differs from that of others.

As such, each philosopher's thought is worth being treated in its own right, rather than being discarded just because it is different from someone else's. When speaking of one philosopher's criticism of another, aside from the question of whether the former correctly understands the latter, what thought the former expresses or creates through this criticism is worthy of exploration. When philosophers criticize others, their reasons for doing so are closely connected to their own ways of thinking or their modes of existence. Ignoring connections between such philosophers' criticisms and their own thinking has resulted in accusations that declare defeat of the accused by simply differentiating their own thought from the "original" philosophy/ies under analysis. What becomes forgotten here is the fact that the allegedly "original" can only ever be reproduced from each individual's perspective.

How we might do justice to philosophers' critiques and their confrontations with each other is a difficult question with many possible answers. One helpful direction for this discussion can be found in Gilles Deleuze and Félix Guattari's idea of the plane of immanence, as presented in *What is Philosophy?*. Deleuze and Guattari insist that although what usually tends to draw people's attention to philosophers' thought are the singular concepts they create, "Philosophy is at once concept creation and instituting of the plane" (41). What they refer to here as "the plane" is their idea of the "plane of immanence," which they describe as "the image of thought, the image thought gives itself of what it means to think, to make use of thought, to find one's bearings in thought" (Deleuze and Guattari 37). It is "a nonconceptual understanding" (Deleuze and Guattari 40) of the presuppositions entailed by the creation of concepts, and which, as such, direct the ways by which concepts are created and arranged. Therefore, when philosophers create and arrange their respectively idiosyncratic concepts, they at once institute respectively unique planes of immanence underlying their creations and arrangements. If the thought of each philosopher, composed as such an arrangement of concepts, has its own unique continuity and integrity irreducible to that of the thought of other philosophers, it is because the plane of immanence instituted in this creation and arrangement gives their thought consistency. As such, Deleuze and Guattari also call this the "plane of consistency."

Given that philosophers often influence and criticize one another, their concepts cannot be completely unrelated. In view of the plane of immanence, however, even when one philosopher borrows a concept from another, it would be inaccurate to say the former's usage and understanding of that concept are right and true while evaluating the latter's as false, on the assumption that "the original" is superior to "the copy." For, since philosophers institute different planes of immanence, the concepts they arrange on these planes must inevitably have different significations and require different usage, even if they have the same names. Insofar as such differences in signification and usage constitute the uniqueness of the respective philosophers' thoughts, mere deviation from the "original" concept cannot be enough of a reason to depreciate the borrower's thought.

To illustrate this situation, Deleuze and Guattari give the example of Kant's usage of Descartes's concept of cogito, based on the former's criticism of the latter. Descartes regarded the cogito—that is, the "I think" that should demonstrate that "I exist"—as the truth beyond any doubt. Doubting this allegedly indubitable truth, Kant questioned why the thinking subject could thus conclude its existence. As Descartes had not allowed for time in the subject, Kant introduced the form of time into the subject as the necessary precondition for the thinking subject to determine itself as an existing subject. In Kant's philosophy, the cogito is connected with another component (time), and therefore has different significations and connotations than those in Descartes. It would clearly not make sense to say Kant's criticism of Descartes is invalid or pointless, simply because the former's understanding and usage of the concept of cogito deviates from the latter's. As Deleuze and Guattari explain, "The fact that Kant 'criticizes' Descartes means only that he sets up a plane and constructs a problem that could not be occupied or completed by the Cartesian cogito" (32). Viewed from Deleuze and Guattari's standpoint, when one philosopher criticizes another by using the other's concept, what matters is the plane of immanence the former institutes when connecting this concept with other components and using it differently from the latter. Given the critic's image of thought—which is essentially different from that of the criticized—is expressed in the critic's question, what matters is also what question the critic raises. It is only his or her thought that can properly respond to this question, while the thought of the criticized cannot. When the thought of the former, in response to this question, has enough continuity and integrity in itself, it can be said that the former succeeds in creating a new plane of immanence worthy of the alias of the plane of consistency, and that the former's criticism of the latter was raised in a meaningful way so as to be given a proper resolution.

With this point in mind, we now need to return to Nishida's criticism of Hegel. Speaking within the context of the discussion so far, there are two basic questions Nishida's philosophy raised with regard to this criticism of Hegel: first, how it is possible to think differently from the Hegelian dialectic, which Hegel intended to explain all the realities in world history with? And second, in thus thinking differently, how it is possible to avoid the problems Nishida himself finds in this dialectic? One way to evaluate the validity of Nishida's criticism of Hegel is to explore whether Nishida's thought has enough consistency so as to appropriately respond to these questions without reproducing the defects of Hegelianism that he himself pointed out. To do so, in other words, is to investigate whether Nishida's own thought, supposedly created to resolve these defects, can withstand this criticism when it is turned toward his own thought.

To sum up, the points of Nishida's criticism of Hegel are: (1) Hegel assumes the latent being of absolute spirit as the ground of all beings and gives it the power to prescribe what emergent beings will become; (2) Hegel professes absolute spirit to be the most universal, while also being merely an individual entity, and allows it to impose its particularity upon other individuals while disregarding their particularities. In light of these problems, the Hegelian dialectic does two things in particular: (1) it totalizes the members of each state in the name of the ethicality as the realization of absolute spirit; and (2) it justifies the hierarchization of different states according to the alleged degrees to which absolute spirit realizes itself in them, while prioritizing the West as corresponding to the highest degree of realization from the beginning. Nishida's project of overcoming Western modernity consists in challenging this double effect of the Hegelian dialectic corresponding to the harmful consequence of Western modernity. The goal of this project is to then open up another vista for understanding the relation among the different states and the relation between a state and its members through his own dialectic based on absolute nothingness, which he uses to counter the Hegelian one. What remains to be questioned is whether Nishida's thought of such a vista is constructed faithfully to and consistently with the main point of his criticism of Hegel and his challenge to the negative consequences of Western modernity corresponding to the double effect of the Hegelian dialectic.

Keeping this in mind, in the subsequent sections I will first look at the instances in which Nishida, in spite of his criticism of Hegel, did what the former himself had criticized the latter for doing. Through examining these moments, I will elucidate the problems with his philosophical project of overcoming Western modernity with regard to its faithfulness to and consistency with the principle of the project itself.

To reconsider the problems implied in Nishida's thought as discussed so far, I will return to some of his works I have already addressed in order to see them through a different lens that enables the discovery of these problems. In addition, to further elucidate the themes treated in these texts, I will consult two relevant essays: "Poiesis and Praxis: The Addendum to Prolegomena to Practical Philosophy" (*Poiēshisu to purakushisu: Jissen tetsugaku joron hosetsu*), published in 1940,[1] and "The Logic of Place and a Religious Worldview" (*Bashoteki ronri to shūkyōteki sekaikan*), which was Nishida's last essay, written two months before his death in 1945 and published posthumously in 1946. "The Logic of Place and the Religious Worldview" is generally regarded as the consummation of Nishida's thought.

Section 2: Absolute Nothingness Turned into Latent Being

As discussed above, Nishida criticized Hegel's assumption of the latent being of absolute spirit in his dialectic, insisting that this assumption affected his worldview and resulted from this dialectic. Whereas Nishida claims to present a worldview freed from this assumption by basing his dialectic upon absolute nothingness, a similar assumption is in fact not lacking in his very own worldview. This assumption has revealed itself in Nishida's idea of the state based on the ethnic group, in spite of his self-confidence that this is different from the Hegelian idea of the state. One of Nishida's statements, quoted before from the supplement to his *Philosophical Essays* vol. 4, reveals this assumption: "[T]he historical world is thoroughly actively state-formative. The ethnic group, as historical and formative, already has in itself the nature of the state" (NKZ XII 411). When Nishida thus asserts that history goes toward the formation of the state, and therefore the nature of the state has already resided in the ethnic group, he assumes the latent being of the state throughout history even before its actual establishment. This almost echoes Hegel's idea that the purpose of world history is the establishment and accomplishment of the state. Wilkinson emphasizes the difference between Nishida and Hegel's philosophy in this respect, and comments on the former that, "It is certainly not the case that history is a progress towards the formation of the state" (145) as is the case with the Hegel. Even so, it seems undeniable that Nishida pursued a line of thought similar to Hegel's, even though this may not be the single direction in which he carried out his philosophical pursuits.

Nishida's assumption of the latent being of the state does not only concern his thoughts on the state, but also affects his idea of absolute nothingness. This suggests the possibility that he might imply that absolute nothingness has the characteristic of latent being predestining the becoming of all beings. The connection between the assumption of the latent being of the state, and the assumption of absolute nothingness as quasi-latent being in Nishida's thought, becomes apparent when we look further into why he puts so much importance on the state within his worldview centering upon absolute nothingness. Observing how he believes the ethnic society crucially transforms into the state, and how he decisively distinguishes the latter from the former, gives us a hint to how we might further understand his reasons for regarding the state as so important.

In his last essay, "The Logic of Place and the Religious Worldview," Nishida writes, "I have touched upon the relation between states and religion from the fourth volume of my *Philosophical Essays*," and summarizes his idea of the transition from the ethnic society to the state:

> Each state is a world that contains the self-expression of the absolute within itself. Hence I say that when an ethnic society harbors the world's self-expression within itself—when it becomes rational—it becomes a state. Only such is the state. ("Nothingness and Religious Worldview" 122; translation modified by referring to NKZ XI 463)[2]

The world Nishida refers to here can be understood as the dialectical universal, that is, the concrete universal which absolute nothingness, as the most universal, becomes through its self-negation. His description of the world as "absolute being-qua-place [*zettai no bashoteki yū*]" in the same essay (NKZ XI 403),³ which designates the being that absolute nothingness becomes and which results in being one with place itself, endorses this understanding. As such, Nishida implies that the world in this sense envelops individuals in the same way as absolute nothingness does, and allows them to determine themselves as individuals. The ethnic society, when it becomes the state, harbors the world's self-expression within itself. This means the individuals become truly individual only when they are included in the state, just as the world as the dialectical universal, by enveloping individuals, enables them to affirm themselves as such. Interestingly, Nishida qualifies this shift not only as the society's becoming the state, but also as it becoming rational.

One may wonder if, according to the discussion in the previous chapter, the ethnic group as he conceives of it, when it is formed as the first human society, has naturally attained the unity between the members' individual determinations and universal determination, between their individual identity and collective identity, because absolute nothingness has been directly embodied in this first human society. In Nishida's analysis of the transition from the ethnic society to the state in "The Problems of the Reason of State," his description, which is similar to and yet slightly different from the above one, helps to untangle this perplexity:

> Thus, while the multiple as individuals is thoroughly what it is and so is the one as totality, the world forms itself in the manner of absolutely contradictory self-identity. Therefore society, as the self-determination of the absolute present, itself becomes the world in the manner of the contradictory self-identity between subject and environment. This is what the rationalization of society means. It can be also said that society returns to its ground, so to speak. The society taking on the character of the world is the state. (NKZ X 303)

Here, to describe the formation of the world in which both the one and the multiple exist as what they are respectively, Nishida uses the phrase, "the absolutely contradictory self-identity," by which he often qualifies the relation between the absolute and individuals. Here again, the world at issue is that of the dialectical universal. His statement that society's becoming the world is its rationalization is also in keeping with the previous citation. What is slightly different, here, is his explanation of this shift as that in which "society returns to its ground." This explanation, in line with his statement, "The ethnic group . . . already has in itself the nature of the state" (NKZ XII 411), suggests the ethnic society, as human society in its original condition, has contained the world in the sense of the dialectical universal, as a kind of undeveloped germ. Therefore, the ethnic society's becoming the world is its returning to what has been contained in this society from the start, through the actual development of the formerly undeveloped germ.

Nishida's following statement endorses this understanding: "At the beginning of the establishment of society, it must be promised that it harbors within itself a world as the life of a species [*shuteki seimei*] of the historical world and itself becomes a world" (NKZ X 293). The phrase, "A world as the life of a species of the historical world," can be taken as one of the particular worlds which absolute nothingness becomes through its self-negation, and in each of which a particular ethnic society is formed. It is because the ethnic society, as the result of the direct embodiment of absolute nothingness, already contains such a world—even if as a still undeveloped germ—that this society's members' individual determinations and universal determination, their individual identity and collective identity, are naturally united.

The explanation as to why the ethnic society in itself has not become the world in this sense can be found in Nishida's statements in "Poiesis and Praxis" that, "*Gemeinschaft* still does not have the nature of absolutely contradictory self-identity," and that in this collective society, "individuals are not truly independent" (NKZ X 161). In other words, for society to have this nature, being worthy to become the world, it is necessary that individuals once break away from their immediate primal unity with society, become independent, and then achieve their unity with it anew while retaining their independence. This occurs so that the contradiction between individuals and society is posed as such and then surmounted. This is what it means for the ethnic society to become the world and also the state, while the germ contained in the ethnic society develops itself. This society then comes to truly accord with what it has always contained. Now, what seems to be the assumption of the latent being of the state in the ethnic society in Nishida's worldview turns out to be, more precisely, the assumption of the latent being of the world that makes the state what it is.

Moreover, considering his discussion of the world that society should become, it also turns out that the world at issue cannot be a mere milieu that simply lets beings inhabit it. It instead entails a certain order that determines their relation to this world. Here lies the reason he refers to society's becoming the world as rationalization. His explanation as to what he believes is rationality in "The Problem of the Reason of the State" is accompanied by the explanation as to what this relation is like:

> That our selves as individual thoroughly express the world means that these selves in turn become the self-expressions of the world in a self-contradictory manner. It can be said that the more our selves become individual, we encounter in this world the absolutely infinite objective expression, that we touch what faces our selves as the self-expressions of the world of absolutely contradictory self-identity, as the absolute command of the absolute will, so to speak. Such a relation between the self and the world is rational, as aforementioned. (NKZ X 301)

Again using the phrase "absolutely contradictory self-identity," Nishida describes the relation between the world and the individuals in it. When individuals are truly individual while respectively expressing the world to which they belong, and yet identify with it so as to make themselves its self-expressions, it can be said that the world is in the relation of absolutely contradictory self-identity with the individuals it includes. In this relation, the one and the multiple merge together while also remaining contradictory to each other. Nishida's use of the phrase, "absolutely contradictory self-identity," to describe the relation between the world and the individuals in it suggests his view that individuals are to the world to which they belong as all beings are to absolute nothingness that created them through its self-negation. In other words, by thus belonging to that world, individuals follow the way in which everything is created from and enveloped by absolute nothingness. Nishida describes such a way as "the absolute command of the absolute will" in the sense of the imperative coming from absolute nothingness that creates everything, and as such determines how they exist. If he describes the relation between the world and individuals as rational, it is only insofar as this relation satisfies this imperative from absolute nothingness and accords with the relation of absolutely contradictory self-identity between absolute nothingness as the one, and all beings as the multiple. Thus, the rationality for him primarily resides not in a certain subjective faculty of humans, but in the objective order of things as a result of their creation from absolute nothingness. Only as such is this rationality taken to be the imperative, and only by observing this imperative can individuals become rational.

As his use of the phrase, "the rationalization of society," to describe the transition from the ethnic society to the state illustrates, Nishida emphasizes the essential rationality of the state as the criterion distinguishing it from the mere ethnic society. As we have seen in previous chapters, he finds the rationality of the state in its law, which makes the citizens obey it by virtue of its ideality, rather than by force of habit. But, given his view of rationality, it seems that the ground for the rationality of the state and its law seems to reside ultimately in the relation of absolutely contradictory self-identity between the self and the world—that is, the order of things resulting from their creation from absolute nothingness. Nishida repeats this point before the above citation:

> I think that the law should be based on the form of the expressive self-formation of the historical world, the form in which our selves thoroughly express the world and become the self-expressions of the world, as the self-determination of the world of absolutely contradictory self-identity. (NKZ X 301)

He repeats it again thereafter:

> The absolute authority of law should have its foundation in the absolute self-expression of such a world itself. (NKZ X 301)

In Nishida's view, if the law has the authority to make citizens obey it by virtue of its ideality, it is to the extent that the law in its nature has been based on the form of the formation of world—that is, the order of the things constituent of it, in which the self is individual and yet identifies with the world it belongs to in the manner of absolutely contradictory self-identity. In sum, if it can be said that people should obey the law, it is to the extent that the law has come from the rational order inherent in those people themselves. It thus decides their relation to the world where they live from the order according to which they were born. Nishida's previously quoted statement, "The law is the command that the world itself gives our selves, the command that reveal itself where our selves as the individuals of the historical world practically form this world" (NKZ X 302), is relevant here again.

Seen in this light, the state for Nishida, characterized by the rationality of the law it possesses, is a special polity in which the rational order inherent in everything explicitly manifests itself in the shape of the law to regulate the relation between citizens and the state in the same way as the relation between absolute nothingness and the individuals created from it. This is why, for him, the state can be the privileged medium for the self-expression of absolute nothingness.

From the discussion so far, it turns out that if the emergence of the state is historical necessity for Nishida, so is the effectuation of this rational order exclusively in the state. Therefore, there is another similarity between Hegel and Nishida's view of history. Instead of seeing "reason [*risei*] behind the fact," as Hegel did, Nishida pursues "the fact behind reason" (NKZ XII 80), and discerns rationality within the fact itself. However, when Nishida claims the rational order that has lurked at the bottom of everything from the beginning is necessarily to be effectuated in the shape of the state, his way of thinking comes close to Hegel's view that the Idea precedes reality and creates it so as to accommodate it to the Idea. Clearly, Nishida refuses to presuppose the permanent subject of absolute spirit behind all realities as Hegel does. But, when Nishida gives the rational order he finds in the creation of all entities from absolute nothingness the power to control the way they exist and to direct the course of history, he practically allows absolute nothingness as the ground of this order to work in the same way absolute spirit behind the Idea does. In a word, if the course of history and the way all entities should exist are thus predetermined because of the production of everything from absolute nothingness, absolute nothingness is not so much different from absolute spirit in Hegel, whose latent being prescribes what other emergent beings will become. In spite of Nishida's criticism of the Hegelian concept of latent being, absolute nothingness as he conceives of it behaves like this very latent being.

Section 3: The Individual Pressed under Totality

Given Nishida's assumption in his criticism of Hegel that latent being amounts to oppressing the individualities of the beings emerging from it, this very criticism may backfire on Nishida himself. One may object that, insofar as this rational order is inherent in all things, the assumption of the latent being of such an order would never distort the ways they are. One may also protest that, insofar as this order prescribes the relation of absolutely contradictory self-identity between the one and the multiple based on nothingness, it does not subjugate the multiple to the one, or individuals to the world or the state in order to achieve its ends. What can disprove such objections, however, is the compulsive character of this rational order. As we have seen, in view of the state as the privileged medium for the self-expression of absolute nothingness, Nishida regards the law of the state as "the command that the world itself gives our selves" (NKZ X 302), and the relation between the self and the world, the relation in which the state's law has its foundation, as "the absolute command of the absolute will" (NKZ X 301). Although he bases such commands upon the rational order allegedly inherent in everything, the term "command" here means more than the order or the maxim to follow it by. In "The Problem of the Reason of the State," in which he makes the above comments, he maintains not only that morality "takes on a character of command or compulsion," but also that this character is "the essence of morality" (NKZ X 328). His juxtaposition of the words "command" and "compulsion" suggests Nishida equates the two and gives the former the compelling force of the latter. His description of morality through this juxtaposition, along with his association of morality with law, has already made clear his view on the inseparability of morality and its practical enforcement.

Nishida may want to emphasize this compulsion would not vitiate the individual, but rather enable it to become what it truly is. In "Prolegomena to Practical Philosophy," he insists that the moral "ought" comes only from the one as totality that is in the relation of absolutely contradictory self-identity with the multiple as individual:

> Insofar as the one as totality is absolutely contradictory self-identity of the multiple as individuals, the one as totality, in the capacity of the universal, takes on the characteristic of the "ought" toward the multiple as individuals. (NKZ X 89)

Therefore, Nishida would say the individual's accordance with the "ought" coming from this totality should be compatible with the individual's being genuinely individual. Given his idea of the state as the society in which the rational order of absolutely contradictory self-identity between the one and the multiple is effectuated as the relation between society and its members, the phrase "the one as totality" in the above citation is replaceable with "the state." Once this is taken into consideration, the above passage can be read as a theoretical explanation of Nishida's claim that, since the state can enable its members to become truly individual, obeying its command does not negate their individualities.

Although Nishida seeks the justification of this command in the rational order inherent in everything, and tries to ground the "ought" in the "is," this move seems to fall into a literal self-contradiction. If this rational order is really rooted in the nature of everything, there is no need to compel individuals to do something so that they are true to their own nature. If there is a need to compel them in that way, this rational order reveals itself not to actually be rooted in the nature of things. Still, one can insist the character of command or compulsion that Nishida sees in this rational order resides in its strict regularity that nobody or nothing can escape or diverge from it. In this case, however, one ends up with admitting no room for individuality at all.

In fact, by seemingly insisting on such strict regularity of command, Nishida acknowledges the character of command basically in all societies, including those prior to the state in "Prolegomena to Practical Philosophy." This acknowledgment amounts to undermining his own claim that obeying society's command enables individuals to become truly individual, even if this command has its foundation in the rational order inherent in everything:

> What faces [our selves] as the one as totality expressively and formatively must be something like the objective will. It must have the characteristic of absolute command. It thoroughly presses [*appakusuru*] the multiple as individuals, which however has its body there [*soko ni*] and lives by working through this [*kore ni yotte*]. The organization of our society must be established with such a relation. (NKZ X 79)

Although, exactly what Nishida's phrase, "there [*soko ni*]" and "through this [*kore ni yotte*]," refers to is unclear, we can make a guess from context that "there" might be understood as "in the objective will or the one as totality that presses the multiple," and that "through this" might be understood as "through the body the multiple has in the one." By qualifying this pressure as absolute command, he implies the pressure that the one as totality puts on the multiple as individuals ultimately comes from absolute nothingness and is postulated by it. His description of this command as the objective will beyond the subjectivity of any member of society designates the validity of the compelling force of this command for all members. After writing that individuals as the multiple have their bodies only in totality as the one that presses them, and live only by working through such bodies under its pressure, Nishida states this is how human society in general is organized. After this passage, he suggests that even the primitive society is no exception.

Thus, if we understand that every society presses all its members, and this pressing is the command from absolute nothingness, Nishida's claim appears in a different light. The primal union in the ethnic society he imagines between the one and the multiple, between society and individuals, turns out to be the immersion of individuals in collectivity, or their formation fused with collectivity, realized under the pressure of this command. Even if the individual is said to acquire independence in the state, this command, as well as the compulsion to obey it, subsists regardless of the existence of the state. The change brought about by the emergence of the state is simply that the command comes to objectify rationality in the shape of law and the morality it realizes. In short, throughout the course of history, moving from the ethnic society to the state, individuals are consistently pressed by this command from society, which is equated with the command from absolute nothingness. Individuals are then compelled to obey this double command, whether doing so is compatible with respecting their individualities as such or not. Individuals have no other option than to obey this command. The difference between the ethnic society and the state is merely whether individuals do so in their natural and immediate union with society, or once they have acquired individual independence.

Thus, in Nishida's view of the world and history, there is no room for the ones who disobey this command in the first place. If all individuals are supposed to always uniformly obey this command, even in the state in which their individualities should be respected, a question arises as to what the individual as the multiple for Nishida is at all. To find his answer to this question, it will be helpful to reexamine his beliefs about how the individual becomes truly individual. The point to note here is the parallelism he sets up between this shift and the transition from the ethnic society to the state, as expressed in his statement, "To be national should be the way in which the individual self exists" (NKZ X 327). The presuppositions and implications of this parallelism also need to be explored.

As discussed previously, in "The Problem of the Reason of the State," Nishida discusses the individual's becoming rational concomitant with society's becoming the state. In the previous quotations, he describes this concomitance as follows: "that our selves thoroughly as individuals mirror the world of the absolute present . . . must mean that, at the same time as this mirroring, a society surmounts itself as merely subjective and becomes a world"; and "this must mean . . . that our selves become self-aware and rational and that the society surpasses the mythical and becomes legislative and national" (NKZ X 294). For Nishida, what undergirds this double becoming is tradition, more precisely, tradition in the second sense of his definition. The tradition in the second sense, which he qualifies as "living," is not the mere heritage of the past as the tradition in the first sense is. It is the continual renewal of the past heritage in each present moment toward a novel creation in the future. Although the tradition in the second sense also determines the selves in the present, they not only accept this determination by the past, but also come to determine the future by themselves. This makes this tradition "living" rather than dead as relic. When Nishida states "our selves are born where historical tradition is . . . active-intuitive, as the self-determination of the absolute present" (NKZ X 294), he implies that absolute nothingness lurks in this tradition. When the bearers of tradition not only passively inherit the past but also actively create the future and make this tradition "living," they participate in the temporality of absolute nothingness, that is, the absolute present in which the past, present, and future coexist. Thus, by mirroring in their selves the world of the absolute present, the bearers of this tradition, the agents of this renewal, face absolute nothingness.

It is this encounter with absolute nothingness that makes these selves truly individual. In the same essay, Nishida states that for the individual to become truly individual, the mediation of absolute nothingness is indispensable: "the individual is the individual through the mediation of non-mediation, through the mediation of absolute nothingness" (NKZ X 321). If the bearing of people's living tradition provokes their self-awareness as individuals, it is because the encounter with absolute nothingness through this tradition makes them recognize themselves as enveloped in absolute nothingness. Thus, the living tradition gives its bearers the intuition of absolute nothingness, the intuition that is in itself an act of recreating this tradition, as well as the individual selves of its bearers. This is how the living tradition is active-intuitive. To the extent that this self-awareness of being individual brings with it the awareness of the rational order of the absolutely contradictory self-identity between the one and the multiple, the individual's becoming individual and self-aware is at once its becoming rational.

This self-awareness of being individual, due to its recourse to tradition that is social and collective in nature, cannot but be accompanied by social and collective self-awareness. Attesting to the inseparability between the individual and social aspects of this self-awareness mediated by absolute nothingness, Nishida maintains that the society's becoming the state requires its self-awareness. He describes this in a way similar to the individual's self-awareness of being individual:

> In order for a society to become a state as the self-formation of the world, it must at first attain the self-awareness of being in the world of the absolute present that includes the past and the future, that is to say, in historical space. (NKZ X 304)
>
> That a certain ethnic society truly becomes a state must mean that it becomes a subject of the unique [*koseiteki*] self-formation of the historical world, as the self-determination of the absolute present that includes the past and the future. (NKZ X 304)

Here, by relating that a society, in order to become a state, must attain the self-awareness of being in the world of the absolute present, Nishida alludes to the close tie between this social self-awareness and the aforementioned individual self-awareness of being individual, which he explains as being attained by mirroring the world of the absolute present in the self. At the same time, he relates that an ethnic society becomes a state with the capacity of "the self-determination of the absolute present" by using the same phrase as he does to describe the living tradition, which likewise "includes the past and the future." In doing so, he suggests this transition, which should be accompanied by the above social self-awareness, occurs through recourse to the living tradition. What he thinks this social self-awareness is like, and what it means for him that an ethnic society passes into a state with this self-awareness, becomes understandable if we read the tacit implication of the living tradition between the lines of his statements.

Nishida describes an ethnic society's becoming a state as its becoming "a subject of the unique self-formation of the historical world." The world here designates the one or totality in the relation of absolutely contradictory self-identity with the multiple or individuals. A society's becoming the subject of the self-formation of such a world means it is forming itself as such a world and determining its own history by itself. Rather than simply being determined by history, it has sovereignty over itself to control its destiny. We can think that it is by bearing the living tradition that a society can become such a subject of the self-formation of the historical world, insofar as doing so is assuming the past of that society on the one hand, and creating its future on the other.

Given that the living tradition—by connecting the past, the present, and the future beyond their disparity—incorporates the absolute present, it is also by bearing this tradition that people attain the self-awareness that their society is in the world of the absolute present. Since the glimpse of the world of the absolute present involves the encounter with absolute nothingness underlying this temporality, this social self-awareness also entails that of this society enveloped in absolute nothingness as one of many particular worlds it becomes. Each of these particular worlds is individual, and as such unique. Moreover, because of the inseparability of this self-awareness of the society from the self-awareness of the individual who is likewise enveloped in absolute nothingness, the society attains the self-awareness of itself enveloping its members as individuals, just as absolute nothingness does. This self-awareness, that of being part of the rational order of absolutely contradictory self-identity between the one and the multiple, gives people an impulse to rationalize the mores of their society so as to realize this order in the relation between their society and themselves as its members. This is how people come to enact their law and establish a state to effectuate this rational order, while recognizing themselves as its members to be respected as individuals in it.

In this way, if Nishida takes the individual's becoming truly individual and the ethnic society's becoming the state to be concurrent, it is because of his belief both shifts are commonly led by the self-awareness attained in the face of absolute nothingness. In "Prolegomena to Practical Philosophy," he articulates the parallelism between these two shifts mediated by absolute nothingness:

> That our selves, as the points from which the absolute projects itself, from such standpoints, form the single historical world, this is what being national means. (Therefore, the state today must have the meaning of *Kirche* [church].) This means that our selves become rational as transcendent selves in their absolute relation to

> the absolute, and that our society faces us as the self-expression of
> the absolute. There the historical world comes to form itself in the
> manner of absolutely contradictory self-identity. (NKZ X 172–73)

By using the phrase, "the single [*yuiitsuno*] world," Nishida does not necessarily mean there is only one world for all humans. In his view, humans are essentially social beings, which he sometimes describes by using the term "species." Their collective, ethnic identity is provided through living together in the same society located in the same place. Then, naturally, each ethnic society is the only society for its members. As such, it becomes the only world with which they can be related in the manner of absolutely contradictory self-identity. Here, the phrase, "the single world," designates each of such worlds, which each of such ethnic societies is supposed to become. What Nishida means in the above passage is, at the same time as human selves become rational and individual in the face of absolute nothingness, the society to which they commonly belong appear to them as the self-expression of absolute nothingness, as the unique world enveloped by this nothingness and enveloping these selves as members.

What supports this parallelism is Nishida's concept of the world as the dialectical universal. The world in this sense (one of many worlds that absolute nothingness as the most universal becomes through its self-negation) affirms its own individuality in being enveloped by absolute nothingness. Furthermore, by taking over this act of enveloping as one of many concrete universals, it affirms the individualities of its members. This concept of the world was intended to be an alternative to Hegel's concept of the state, which in Nishida's eyes was simply a totality negating the individual. To Nishida, Hegel's assumption of the latent being of absolute spirit seems to be the common cause of the negation of the individualities of different states, and those of the members of each state. Replacing absolute nothingness for absolute spirit, and conceiving of the essentially multiple worlds born from this nothingness in the absence of the unifying or totalizing Being, Nishida aimed at affirming the individualities of different states, and those of the members of each state, at once. The parallelism he establishes between the individual's becoming truly individual and the ethnic society's becoming the state is an outcome of this double affirmation, which he expects should be possible in the world as the dialectical universal.

In spite of his underlying intention of affirming individuality, the review of Nishida's discussion as to how the individual becomes truly individual, while the ethnic society becomes the state, discloses that he actually does not treat the individual in its genuine individuality. This problem has revealed itself in his presupposition that the individual becomes truly individual only in relation to absolute nothingness, by facing it, and having the self-awareness of being enveloped in it. What matters in this process is not the individual in itself, but rather its relation to the absolute, which is supposed to make the individual what it really is. Strangely enough, Nishida's logic here is quite similar to Hegel's: the individual is determined in its particularity only insofar as the individual belongs to the universal. In both cases, it is supposed the individual does not exist as what it really is without being related to the universal as its ground.

Nishida might object that absolute nothingness, differently from any Being, neither unites nor totalizes beings. Therefore, the individual, as related to absolute nothingness, would be affirmed as it is, rather than being negated. However, against such expectations, the way in which he believes people can relate themselves to absolute nothingness and become truly individual opposes itself to their individualities. After all, he believes it is by bearing the living tradition of their own society and by assisting the sustenance of this society from the past to the future that ordinary humans encounter absolute nothingness and become truly individual. The individuality thus achieved is in fact the subjectivity of the act of shouldering the historical self-formation of that society. Such individuality merely consists in voluntarily taking part in this collective task, and can never go out of collectivity from the beginning to the end. That is why Nishida allows no room for the ones who do not obey the command from society. Just as his four disciples found authentic subjectivity in assuming the responsibility of following orders, he sees individuality in those who obey this command of their own free will. The way for individualization proposed here, by requiring humans to behave together uniformly in order to participate in the collective self-formation of a given society, vitiates the individuality it professes to realize. The state, whose establishment is parallel to this individualization, betrays itself as a cause and an effect of the unification and totalization of its members. Based on this parallelism, once the state appears as the privileged medium for human individualization, their individuality is reduced to a matter of their identification with and service to the state. Therefore, Nishida's idea of the state is not so different from that of Hegel, which Nishida thought "cannot get out of the totalitarian standpoint negating the individuals" (NKZ X 331).

Furthermore, perceived in this light, Nishida's claim that the most universal is absolute nothingness amounts to conferring upon each state the supreme authority over its members. For, because of the nonexistence of the higher universal as the single unifying instance, each state appears as the most universal entity on the earth to its members. This is also a natural consequence of how Nishida limits the way people can face absolute nothingness to bearing the living tradition of their society in order to make it a state. The view that different states are the essential multiple concretizations of absolute nothingness, and the privileged medium through which people can face it in order to become truly individual, allows for the cover-up of the negation of the individual in each state. This deifies it more than Hegel does. To the extent that Nishida thus makes absolute nothingness guarantee each state's divine authority over its members, he cannot escape from the criticism that he turned absolute nothingness into a quasi-latent being, inseparably binding it with the latent being of each state that regulates the behaviors of the citizens and negates their individualities.[4]

Section 4: Ethnocentric Universalization of the Particular

Nishida's project for philosophically overcoming Western modernity is twofold: one aspect challenges the hierarchy resulting from the Hegelian dialectic as the logic which characterized Western modernity; the other objects to Hegel's view of a state that totalizes citizens, similarly resulting from this dialectic. With regard to the second aspect, this project was flawed insofar as the state as Nishida conceived of it ended up being a totality negating the individual, as was the case with Hegel. With regard to the first aspect, again it is he himself who interrupts the line of thought that may provide a framework to affirm the individualities of different states as many unique worlds.

As I discussed earlier in my examination of his thought in close connection with his four disciples, Nishida also emphasized the necessity of the construction of a new world order in which the individuality of each state or ethnic group is respected. And yet, all these philosophers still insisted on Japan's authority over other countries in this world order. Nishida in particular buttressed this insistence by offering arguments that legitimized the universalization of the structure of the state that is particular to his own country as the principle of his proposed new world order. Thus, with regard to the first aspect, this project already appears to have fallen into contradiction. To elucidate the problems implicit in this self-contradiction, I will further investigate what is going on when Nishida universalizes a specific particular and how this operation functions alongside other elements of his philosophy.

Given the unbridgeable gap in nature between the particular and the universal, a discourse that universalizes the particular cannot avoid entailing self-contradictions. Nishida's assertion that the structure of the state that exists only in Japan can be the principle for the formation of the entire world is no exception here. In trying to bridge this gap, Nishida argues that absolute nothingness as the most universal is embodied in the structure of the Japanese state and thus tries to assert the inherent universality of this particular entity.

The thesis that the most universal is not Being but nothingness allows him to claim that it is the source of the true morality that can affirm the individualities of all entities, and that a particular state structure allegedly embodying this most universal par excellence should be justifiably rendered the principle of world formation for the realization of this morality. He argues that if the structure of a particular state is to be universalized like this, it is insofar as this structure is formed around a being of nothingness as an exceptional incarnation of nothingness. Here, it is the substantialization of nothingness that undergirds the universalization of the particular. However, once absolute nothingness is substantialized in order to universalize a particular entity that is professed to incarnate or embody it, the nothingness stops being what it was supposed to be. For, once substantialized, it no longer envelops all beings and affirms their particularities. Invoking absolute nothingness to bridge the gap between the particular and the universal amounts to denaturalizing what is thus invoked.

Looking at Nishida's arguments through a comparison with Hegelianism as he criticized it, it is revealed that at the moment when Nishida thus turned the particularities of his home country into the universal norms that all the other countries should observe, his criticism of Hegel again backfires. Whereas Nishida criticized Hegel for wrongly posing an individual entity as the most universal, and for allowing it to impose its own particularity upon other individuals to subjugate them, Nishida here does exactly what he himself insisted Hegel does. Certainly, Nishida replaces absolute nothingness for absolute spirit as the most universal so that there would be no single Being unifying or totalizing all beings. However, when Nishida asserts absolute nothingness finds its privileged embodiment in Japan, he turns his own country, an individual entity among others, into the epitome of the most universal, and concludes this individual entity's incomparable superiority to others, just as Hegel did. With respect to the ethnocentrism of one's own nation disguised as universalism, Nishida's claim that the quintessence of Japanese spirit consists in negating or emptying oneself, embodying absolute nothingness par excellence, is not so different from Hegel's claim that the national spirit of Germany is the highest realization of absolute spirit and freedom. By privileging just one state to exclusively represent absolute nothingness, Nishida not only interrupts his line of thought leading to the affirmation of different states and essentially multiple dialectical universals, but also limits the scope of his idea of absolute nothingness. As is the case with the state negating the individuals in it in the name of the self-expression of absolute nothingness, when absolute nothingness is used to guarantee the authority of a certain individual entity over others, absolute nothingness stops being what it literally is; it is turned into a quasi-latent being. Once Nishida stops being faithful to the main point of his criticism of Hegel and exempts his country from this criticism, Nishida ends up killing its potential.

Nishida's challenge to the hierarchy among different states or nations resulting from the Hegelian dialectic as the logic of Western modernity ends up replacing one hierarchy with another that centers upon his own country, rather than pursuing the relation among different peoples outside any hierarchy of domination/subjugation. In the case of Hegel, different nations or states are hierarchized in a unilinear order corresponding to the degrees to which absolute spirit progressively realizes itself in them through its dialectical movement. In the case of Nishida, among the different states as essentially multiple worlds affirmed through the self-negation of absolute nothingness, there is a hierarchical gap between Japan, which embodies absolute nothingness par excellence, and other states merely born from it. In Hegel's case, what determines the states' hierarchal order is the degree of advancement of the movement of the absolute. In Nishida's case, it is the subsistence of the same structure of the state from its origin and the perpetual presence of the exceptional incarnation of absolute nothingness at the center of this structure. The continuity with its origin and the possession of this being of nothingness at the center of its structure allows the Japanese state to exclusively participate in the absolute, and creates an unbridgeable gulf between it and all others. Although Nishida may want to give this gulf a non-hierarchical appearance by invoking his idea of absolute nothingness enveloping the multiple, the fact remains that, after all, in the hierarchy between two kinds of earthly entities, only one of them allegedly is especially blessed by the absolute.

One may still wonder why the production of another hierarchy to counter the existent one may not be considered a possible form of success of Nishida's project of overcoming Western modernity. Even though it might merely be as a pretext, Nishida, as well as the philosophers of world history, emphasized the construction of the new world order in which the individuality and uniqueness of each state or ethnic group is respected. Nishida's philosophical project of overcoming Western modernity was supposed to be the crucial step to achieving this objective. In light of the ideal he himself upheld, the replacement of a unipolar system of domination in the name of an Oriental tradition for a unilinear hierarchy of Western modernity cannot be taken as the success of this project.

Another reason for the failure of Nishida's project of overcoming Western modernity is that in trying to establish this unipolar system he performs an operation similar to that through which the unilinear hierarchy of Western modernity is established. As illustrated by Hegel's *Philosophy of History*, the time-consciousness of Western modernity distinguishes itself at the most advanced stage of the realization of absolute spirit from the previous, less advanced stages. It understands different others existing in the contemporary period as belonging to these stages of progress. In doing so, this time-consciousness projects the diachronic temporal order of unilinear progress onto the synchronic spatial order as the relation of different regions and peoples belonging to the same time; it transcribes the former order onto the latter. It is this operation of projection and transcription that gives the appearance of legitimacy to Western modernity's subjugation of others and establishment of its unilinear hierarchy.

The unipolar system of domination Nishida envisions with recourse to Japanese tradition also must undergo a similar operation in order to establish itself as such. To assert that absolute nothingness finds its best embodiment in Japan, he invokes the continuity of the structure of the state of Japan from the primal ethnic society into which absolute nothingness concretized itself at the origin of humanity. He then claims that Japan, as the best embodiment of absolute nothingness, should have the authority to provide the principle of the new world order in which the individuality of each state is respected as the absolute nothingness enveloping all individuals. In short, here he turns the historical continuity of the structure of a specific state into the proof of this state's capacity to preside over a certain synchronic relation between other states or ethnic groups. In doing so, he projects the diachronic order into the synchronic, and transcribes the former onto the latter, in order to ground the hegemony of his own country and its subjugation of others, just as the time-consciousness of Western modernity does. The commonality of this operation with Hegel's suggests Nishida's project is based on a twisted affinity with the very same Western modernity he wishes to overcome. The difference is merely whether the diachronic order to be projected and transcribed is that of progress or that of the perpetuity from the origin, while the vectors of both orders point in the opposite directions.

In fact, Nishida also invokes the operation of projection and transcription when he discusses the individual's becoming truly individual at the same time as the ethnic society's becoming the state through the people's act of bearing the living tradition. He insists that because this living tradition enables its bearers, who are also the bearer of the subsistence of that society, to face absolute nothingness enveloping individuals, they become truly individual. Their society also becomes a truly unique world along with others, just as both the individual person and society are enveloped in absolute nothingness. When he thus equates the prolongation of tradition from the past to the future with the affirmation of the individuality of a certain society along with others, and the affirmation of the individualities of its members, he projects a diachronic order onto a synchronic order, and transcribes the former onto the latter. Bearing the tradition of society does not necessarily let people step out of the social and collective, already given to them as the single milieu to which they belong. Yet, it is supposed that for them to stay within this social and collective milieu accompanied by the depth of tradition is at once to become truly individual and to constitute an individual world coexisting with others. The operation of projection and transcription between the synchronic and diachronic orders can be said to have fulfilled its purpose once this supposition has been accepted beyond a doubt.

The dazzling effect of this operation is the reverse side of Nishida's concept of the world as the dialectical universal, which he expected to enable the affirmation of the individualities of many different worlds, and those of the members of each such world. At the same time, this effect reveals a danger often involved in the move of returning to the tradition of a certain society or state in order to resist the global hegemony of Western modernity. For, even when this move is inseparably connected with that of establishing and justifying that group's domination over others, and aggravating the oppressions within this group, the appearance created by this operation—that the return to tradition would unconditionally guarantee the creation of an ideal space liberating everybody—easily puts out of sight what is actually going on.

Looking further into Nishida's views of the world and its history enables the discovery of deeper similarities with Hegel's, which disprove this appearance. As previously discussed, Nishida had the idea that the latent being of the state subsists from the beginning of history and directs its course toward the goal of the formation of the state as the realization of this latent being. In his view, the state is the privileged self-expression of absolute nothingness and as such can be united with its citizens in the manner of absolutely contradictory self-identity in the same way as nothingness envelops all beings it produces. The formation of this state was for Nishida the restoration of the original state of affairs in which beings are produced from nothingness and enveloped in it. Considering this view of history, when he talks about his country's perpetuity from its origin, what is at stake is not merely a matter of antiquity. By asserting that Japan has a state structure that is equivalent to morality and closest to this state of affairs, and that this structure should be the principle for the world's formation, he also situates his country as occupying the closest position to the goal of this history, equated with its origin, as providing the norm for the progress of other countries. That is why he can assert Japan's state structure to be the principle of world formation and put this state having the perpetuity from the origin at the top of hierarchy. Thus, the apparent opposition between the directions of history conceived of by Hegel and Nishida, with one going forward and the other backward, is insignificant. Nishida's idea of history as a return to the origin is superimposed upon the quasi-Hegelian idea of unilinear history in which state progress is judged by levels of the manifestation of the absolute, and in which historical courses are determined by its latent being.

It is not only the assumption of the latent being but also the substantialization of nothingness that plays a role in establishing a hierarchy between states based on their levels of this progress qua return. The state of Japan's perpetuity from the origin which Nishida has in mind derived from the continuity of the Imperial Family at the center of that state from the beginning of its history to the present. The Imperial Family as a being of nothingness allegedly upholds the original state of affairs in which nothingness envelops beings, and to this extent has already fulfilled the goal of history that should enable the reproduction of this state of affairs. As such, the existence of this being of nothingness substantiates the possibility that humans can attain this goal and can return to the origin at once, while betraying absolute nothingness' latent being-like behavior that determines how beings emerging from it should exist. The state of Japan's possession of this being of nothingness at the center of its structure gives it the normative status, closest to the origin and goal of history, legitimizing a world formation with Japan as the norm, as well as endorsing a course of history toward this formation. Thus, the substantialization of nothingness, which culminates in the idea of the Imperial Family as a being of nothingness, not only undergirds the universalization of a particular state and its structure. It also reinforces the assumption of the latent being of nothingness in understandings of the world and its history which are already amenable to this universalization.

Considering this assumption of the latent being, the circle that Nishida conceived in which beings are born from absolute nothingness and return to it reveals itself to be close to the circle in which absolute spirit moves, departing from and returning to itself. Despite the ideal that nothingness would envelop all beings as they are meaning this circle would neither unify nor totalize them, this circle that moves from the latent-being to its realization justifies the state that claims to embody absolute nothingness par excellence and realize its latent-being, subordinating others and integrating them under its rule. What would result is the empire organized around a being of nothingness through the agency of the state in which that being dwells, under a banner of the promulgation of the morality of absolute nothingness. This is not so different from Western imperialism subjugating non-Western countries and peoples in order to "civilize" or "enlighten" them. The commonality of the aforementioned operation of projecting the diachronic order into the synchronic and transcribing the former onto the latter in Hegel and Nishida's philosophies illustrates this isomorphism.

Nishida's project of overcoming Western modernity collapsed by his failure to be thoroughly faithful to the very principle he himself professed to adhere to. The replacement of one system of domination for another, along with the change of thrones, does not indicate any success in this project. Likewise, the use of a trick similar to that used in order to give the appearance of legitimacy to such a system, even if that logic is professed to be rooted in another culture, does not help break the spell of the existing power structure. I am not claiming "first come, first served," in the sense that, given modernization originated in the West, all non-Western regions and peoples, as late comers to modernization, are doomed to be bad imitators of the West, and thus be subordinated to its hegemony. I am simply pointing to the fact that if one reproduces the same evil as one's enemy, one will end up following the same path. Here, one becomes a poor imitator of the enemy. To avoid falling into this trap, we need to make efforts to search for another path, even if it is difficult to realize, or to even conceive.

Chapter 12

Reconsidering the Issues of *Kokutai* and Overcoming Modernity

In the previous chapter, I argued that Nishida's idea of the Imperial Family as a being of nothingness at the center of the structure of the Japanese state enabled him to claim this state's status as the norm of the realization of the latent being of this nothingness, allowing him to universalize this particular nation-state. It was Nishida's gesture of doing this, echoing Hegel's gesture of universalizing another particular (such as Europe or Germany) and contradicting Nishida's criticism of Hegel that made the collapse of his project of overcoming modernity decisive.

In this final chapter in part 2, I will first turn again to Nishida's idea of *kokutai* as the epitome of his universalization of the particular. I will reconsider the problems entailed in this idea with regard to its inadvertent complicity with imperialism. The idea of an exclusive national identity, infused with a sense of national superiority and implicit in the idea of this state structure, is in no way peculiar to Nishida's philosophy. Similar ideas not only permeated the "Overcoming Modernity" symposium and "The Philosophy of World History" symposia. They still survive in other similar arguments to the present. Second, I will return to the problematic of "overcoming modernity" and address its relationship with this kind of national identity from contemporary perspectives.

Section 1: *Kokutai* as the Epitome of the Universalized Particular

Considering Nishida's arguments about the structure of the Japanese state as above, the question of whether or not Nishida really did support Imperial ideology or whether he used it to express his own ideal does not make a great difference in his attitude of universalizing the particularity of Japan and Japaneseness. The same would be true even if what was really precious to him was not the Imperial Family itself but the continuity represented by it as, for example, a sign of a long-lasting peace. What matters is his gesture defining this continuity (or whatever attribute) as unique to a particular nation-state and then asserting this attribute's universal applicability to all countries and peoples. The Imperial Family is merely one element, although apparently the central one, which constitutes this discourse that universalizes the particular.

Leaving aside the motif of the Imperial Family, there are multiple lines of thought that lead to the universalization of Japan's apparent particularities in Nishida's writings. I have referred to a few such lines: the idea of environmental determinism, drawing upon Japan's geopolitical condition of being surrounded by the sea and isolated from other countries; the idea of linear progress from ethnic society to state; and the idea of the state that preserves continuity with the original ethnic society, and can therefore realize within itself morality as the self-expression of absolute nothingness that originally created this society. These ideas cooperate to qualify a particular state—that of Japan, allegedly composed of a single ethnic group and maintaining the original conditions of the foundation of its society—as the universal norm.

Still, the importance of *kokutai* to this universalization of the particular, and to Nishida himself, is undeniable. As discussed previously, he regarded the Japanese particularities-as-universalities defined by the above lines of thought as something exemplarily fostered and sustained by the structure of the Japanese state as he conceived of it. Plus, Nishida insisted on the significance of this state structure in his private letter. This letter was meant to be read by his dear disciples, including the aforementioned four thinkers, who received it as his "will":

> No matter what happens, we Japanese should never lose *spiritual confidence* at this juncture. Even if we are defeated with force, in terms of morality and culture, we must by no means lose our confidence in the historical worldliness of the structure of our state and the standpoint of the world-historical world formation. We must firmly stick to this standpoint and make our people build confidence in their future development. (NKZ XXI 398; Letter No. 2143, March 11, 1945)[1]

This letter was written several months before the end of the World War II when it became clear that Japan was losing the battle. Considering this, these words from Nishida, including the phrase "spiritual confidence," would be understood as an expression of his wish (in anticipation of the defeat) to encourage his compatriots in a disastrous and hopeless situation. Still, Nishida's "confidence in the historical worldliness of the structure of our state" is not just a spiritual matter but has obvious political implications. The emphasis upon "the world-historical world formation" in juxtaposition with the "worldliness of the structure of our state" in this private letter suggests clearly that his aforementioned published statement that this structure should be the principle for the formation of the world was a strong reflection of his real intentions. Even if he might not believe that this world-formation should be achieved by military force, it should not be forgotten that the invocation of a certain people's "spiritual confidence" (which could be sustained or recovered through the universalization of the particular attributes or political system of their own nation or state) inherently implies a sense of that group's superiority to other apparently "subordinate" peoples who do not share such particulars. As discussed before, the claim of a certain people's spiritual, cultural, or moral superiority so as to universalize their particularity can easily amount to the justification of their violence against others, or can lend itself to this justification regardless of any supposed gap between the spiritual, cultural, or moral ideals and mundane, physical, or military violence. This is not just a matter of possibility but what actually happened. The problem is that this kind of risk, when inherent in seemingly genuinely spiritual, cultural, or moral messages, is not taken so seriously, therefore such messages largely pass as pacifist and potentially "universally" valid, leaving the universalization of the particular operative there unquestioned.

Heisig understands Nishida's meaning in his wartime discourse as an intent to clarify Japan's mission of providing spiritual guidance through Japanese spirit to other Asian countries, as distinguished from expansionist and military invasion into them:

> Despite rejection of the idea of the *Japanese nation* extending its own center to absorb other nations, he does hold that the *Japanese spirit* has a special mission to lead the other countries of Asia, through political and economic initiatives, to take new shape in conjunction with one another. (*Philosophers of Nothingness* 98)

However, even if Nishida aimed at providing genuine spiritual guidance to other Asian countries (although what this means can be still be questioned), his discourse on the Japanese spirit as the banner of this guidance points toward a thought process that bridges the gap between such spiritual guidance and the expansion of the Japanese state's territories, or at least its sphere of influence. As discussed previously, Nishida defined national spirit as the formative force for the structure of the state, and the structure of the state as the form that is formed by this force (NKZ XII 420). Given this, Japanese spirit and the structure of the state of Japan are indissociable. Besides, once this structure is formed, it continues to form itself, in turn determining the spirit that has worked as its formative force. Nishida argued that the structure of the Japanese state, formed around the center of the Imperial Family, determined the particularity of Japanese culture and the quintessence of Japanese spirit. Insofar as Japanese spirit, thus determined by this structure, resides in the attitude of sustaining one's self-identity around this center, then upholding Japanese spirit entails upholding this structure and modeling oneself upon the Imperial Family as the state center. To guide other countries with Japanese spirit is to also unite them around this center. The extension of the centrality of the Imperial Family and the Japanese hereditary monarchy, from a specific political system in a specific state to outside Japan, means that other countries must come to share this system as their centers as well. Since each and every country has its own political system, this state of affairs would be impossible without expanding the Japanese state's sphere of influence, even though it might be possible to just talk about the spiritual guidance through Japanese spirit, without invoking this expansion. Even when speaking of spiritual guidance alone, the assertion that a certain people exceptionally embody absolute nothingness and practice its morality so well that others should follow their lead and tread in their footsteps is undeniably ethnocentric, regardless of how anti-egocentric this morality is depicted to be.

Certainly, Nishida's philosophy, including his arguments about *kokutai*, may have a universal dimension and may convey moral or spiritual messages that can be deduced from the insights into this dimension. However, as insisted repeatedly, given that he closely associated this universality with the particularity of the nation-state to which he belonged, the existence of a universal dimension in his philosophy alone is not enough to offset the problematic political implications in this universalization of the particular. Instead, this very universality, due to its special tie with a specific particular, legitimizes the subjugation of other particulars and lends itself to attempts to enact such implications in reality.

On this point, Ariska's remarks on the entanglement between the claim of universality in Nishida's philosophy and the imperialist regime ("Beyond 'East' and 'West' " 560) are revelatory. Against largely accepted positive images of universalism, Arisaka draws attention to the duality that "the very universalism which is presented as the vehicle of liberation became a tool of oppression" ("Beyond 'East' and 'West' " 558). Considering that the universal at issue is that which a specific particular has become, Arisaka's remark is more convincing. In a situation in which the particularity of a certain region or people has been universalized as the standard, participation in this universality can sometimes be a means for other peoples living in other regions to get rid of their subordinate status and decolonize themselves. However, insofar as participating in this universality (or even calling for others to do so for their own liberation) entails standardizing it and subjugating the particularities of other peoples or regions to the specific particularity that became this universality, doing so amounts to reproducing the same kind of exclusion and oppression of these newly participating others. That is why, as Arisaka argues, even though "[Nishida] himself did not endorse colonialism . . . his theory nevertheless *functioned* formally in a similar way to the way European universalism was used to convince colonized subjects to submit to imperialism," despite, or rather precisely because of his optimistic belief that "Japanese philosophy could help liberate Asian nations by raising them to universality" ("Beyond 'East' and 'West'" 558). What is to be noted is that even if the particularity of a certain non-Western region or people has been universalized as the standard, this does not prevent against the production of similar exclusion or oppression on the part of the particular others for such a region or people.

As Arisaka suggests ("Beyond 'East' and 'West'" 556), these power relations that result from the universalization of the particular and that characterize colonialism are not necessarily "inherently European." Rather, it is simply that such relations found their typical configuration in Europe in such a way that other regions or peoples outside it could produce similar relations after that model. To this extent, it is not just to blame Westerners for being essentially colonizers, nor is it just to blame non-Westerners for being imitators of Western colonization. What is at issue is a common power structure, produced and reproduced by both, or any kind of people. Arisaka criticizes not only Nishida's philosophy for articulating and supporting this power structure but also the universalist discourse of "liberation" or "enlightenment" used to legitimize British colonial rule in India ("Beyond 'East' and 'West'" 556–57) and US war in Vietnam ("Beyond 'East' and 'West'" 560), with an eye to the aforementioned dual aspect of universalism that was operative in these three cases.

Exploring the problems in Nishida and the Kyoto School's philosophies (or in Japanese philosophy in general) from such perspectives has nothing to do with disparaging Japanese culture or people, or advocating Western-centrism. Rather, when critics lump these things together what is to be questioned is their presumption that challenges to Western-centrism and respect for non-Western culture or people are sufficient reasons to exempt non-Western philosophers' discourses from critical investigations. If this presumption is taken for granted, we end up disregarding the fact that the cultural particularities that apparently merit respect are sometimes conceived of in ways that disparage other cultures and peoples, relabeling ethnocentrism as an assertion of "cultural uniqueness."

Section 2: The Problematic of "Overcoming Modernity" and National Identity in the Present Context

Curiously enough, some of Nishida and his disciples' assertions on Japanese particularities professed to be universalized are largely accepted as decent formulations of "Japanese uniqueness," even today. The same applies to the problematic concerning "overcoming modernity": similar arguments still reappear in different guises.

In his commentary on Hiromatsu's *Theories on "Overcoming Modernity,"* Karatani Kōjin notes the similarity between Japan's situation in which Hiromatsu's book was published, and that in which the Kyoto School philosophers were active. In the 1980s and 1990s, in the context of the declining rivalry between the Soviet Union and the United States, Japan achieved rapid economic growth. So-called postmodernism, although it had already lost its critical impact, became popular in Japan. A movement developed that involved reevaluating theories on Japan and Oriental philosophies, and intellectuals again started to propagate the notion of overcoming modernity and the West, although differently from prewar and wartime discourses. Karatani warns that these phenomena do not necessarily indicate modernity has really been overcome (269–71). In his closing remark, Karatani emphasizes this point:

> Therefore, the topic "overcoming modernity" is important to us in a double sense, that on the one hand, we still live in the very "modernity" that we should overcome, and on the other hand, we have not essentially gone beyond the problem of "overcoming modernity" posed before the war. (272)

That one of the opposite social systems collapses, and the other moves onto the next stage so as to wield greater influence on a global scale, does not mean the aporias raised between them have been completely resolved, either theoretically or practically, nor that the problems inherent in both have disappeared. Hiromatsu precisely criticized the Kyoto School philosophers for taking advantage of the situation and presenting the aporia as resolved. In the same vein, Karatani criticizes intellectuals who are excited by the Japanese economic miracle and optimistically celebrate Japan's "overcoming modernity."

Several decades have passed since the publication of *Theories on "Overcoming Modernity."* Yet the question remains as to whether we can go beyond Hiromatsu and Karatani's critical insights and find a response to the aporia they raised—or at least tackle it squarely. As if the problematic brought up by these two thinkers had already become obsolete, in the epilogue of his 2011 *Philosophia Japonica* (*Firosofia yaponika*), Nakazawa Shin'ichi writes:

> [Nishida and Tanabe's] creation neither fits into the scheme of the modern, nor can be confined within the pre-modern, nor is even the postmodern. Rather, I dare say, non-modern, which means the outside of such a scheme itself, this is the term to express the position of "Japanese philosophy" exactly. (375)

Certainly, given that any problematic is relative and far from all-encompassing, it is always possible to pursue a productive line of thought outside a certain problematic. But what matters is how to do so. Nakazawa insists Nishida and Tanabe "did not attempt at transvaluation, advocating the value of the pre-modern against the modern or the uniqueness of 'Oriental culture' against Western Europe." Nakazawa concludes that these philosophers "tried to stand outside the system of the modern deliberately" (373). However, considering the fact Nishida actually advocated the value and uniqueness of Oriental culture's tradition, it is a dubious claim to suggest that he stood outside the problematic of modernity. By ignoring the problematic he himself assumes, and by presenting this thought as if it were outside of this problematic, Nakazawa's approach is not so different from the attitude of presenting an aporia as resolved when it is not. This is precisely what Hiromatsu and Karatani criticize. Whether positing the postmodern outside the modern, or the non-modern outside the modern and the postmodern, the aporia is evaded and left unresolved.

In light of Hiromatsu and Karatani's critical remarks, Williams's nonchalant optimism manifests itself more conspicuously. He expresses this in his declaration that "the aspirations embodied in the wartime slogans of 'Overcoming Modernity' and 'The Standpoint of World History and Japan' were fulfilled after 1945" thanks to "the Japanese economic miracle" (Williams, *Defending Japan's Pacific War* 55). It is easy to assume the economic success of non-Western countries would be enough to realize an alternative modernity, or that such an alternative modernity would be free from the power structures characteristic of Western modernity. Or, even if it were not, the existence of such structures could be justified in the cause of the fight against Western-centrism. However, when one assumes this, one inadvertently makes a gesture similar to that of prewar and wartime Japanese intellectuals, who assisted in the colonial invasion of other Asian countries by appealing to the cause of anti-Western imperialism, or by asserting that Japan's colonial rule over these countries was not actually colonial rule because Japan belongs to Asia. Then, the aporia of the problematic of "overcoming modernity" reproduces itself under a different guise.

Koyasu Nobukuni reflects upon why the slogan "overcoming modernity" impressed intellectuals back then, in spite of its deceptiveness: "It was because this [slogan] was uttered in the geopolitical scheme of Asia against Europe, as the scheme of the modern world, and because Japan thus disguised itself as the representative of Asia" (248). Nishida and his four disciples' claim that Japan, as the epitome of Oriental tradition, can surpass Western modernity surely takes part in this guise, even though such a claim was not originally created by them but configured in response to the collective desire of a certain nation in a specific situation.

Isomae Jun'ichi, in the afterword to the 2010 anthology, *"Overcoming Modernity" and the Kyoto School* (*"Kindai no chōkoku" to kyōto gakuha*), further reflects on the problems involved in this guise, fabricated in the scheme of Asia vs. the West:

> Certainly, to represent one's own culture under the logic of non-Western particularity can be an effective means to criticize the West. But doing so amounts to making this culture prone to exclusionist essentialism and consequently solidifying the representation of binary opposition "the West vs. Japan or Asia." The discourses of "overcoming modernity" were but those which established such dichotomous ways of thinking. Such narratives made people forget that Japan itself was within the space of Western modernization, a space having no exit, and they produced an illusion as if the cultural region of Japan or Asia, marked by its unique and particular culture, had existed outside this space. After all, the logic of Japanese empire did not lead to the universality supposing the transformation of the self by others but ended up with the universalism imposing the homogenized particularity of the self upon others. This was the case, because the desire to unitarily subsume that wide area under homogenous particularity won, in spite of Japan's situating itself in the cultural region of Asia to counter the West. (355)

Japan's aspiration to make Asia a culturally homogeneous political unit to counter the West became a pretext to justify Japan's colonial rule in Asia.

Rationalized in terms of Asian self-determination, it prevented Japanese people from acknowledging their own colonial ambitions—ambitions which they criticized the West for having. At the same time, the idea that Asia is one, with Japan as its representative, smacked of arrogance in presupposing Japan's desire is Asia's desire. This idea averted the attention of the Japanese people away from the brutality of imposing their particularity upon others within Asia, while giving them the illusion that Japanese particularity was the only kind with which they should mark themselves. Isomae draws our attention to the irony that the insistence on the particularity of one group of people to counter another group's particularity, which is professed to be universal, results in the suppression of many other different particularities within the former group in the same way as the latter subjugates them. The project of bringing together areas and peoples that are multiple and diverse into a homogenous unit cannot be separated from the hegemony that would be necessary to carry out such a forceful unification. Such hegemony, which seeks to assimilate many different particularities within the unit into one particularity, has a tendency to expand in order to subjugate other particularities outside by professing itself to be the true universal.

Wrongly assuming that all East Asians are Confucians—an assumption that is far from the truth—Williams envisions "a future in which Confucian East Asia may be very well able to resist the homogenization of the world into a 'liberal flatland'" (*Japanese Wartime Resistance* xxv). He even asserts that "there is finally only one best way to which all Confucians will subscribe because it is the most practical" (Williams, *Japanese Wartime Resistance* 87). Williams goes on to claim that "in Confucian societies . . . there is in practice never more than one episteme that legitimates the power and morality of a system of rule (*toku*) at any one time because one and only episteme is supremely practical. However, should the episteme be legitimate in this way, if it succeeds, then everyone will willingly submit to its authority" (Williams, *Japanese Wartime Resistance* 87). In addition to his advocacy for Japan's Pacific War as a fight against the liberalist West, Williams here posits one Asia, unified under one ruling system, and dichotomously opposed to the global hegemony of the West. In doing so, he encourages the reproduction of the aporia raised in discourses of "overcoming modernity" without questioning it. The only issue for Williams is what country he believes should have hegemony in Asia now. It is unlikely that all East Asians would agree on his pejorative and delusional representation of them. His one-sided perception of all East Asians as Confucians, including those who do not identify themselves as such, and his declaration that they must be happy to submit to the authority of one ruling system, exemplifies in a typical fashion one of the Orientalist biases identified by Said. Specifically, this is the bias that "Only an Occidental could speak of Orientals, for example, just as it was the White Man who could designate and name the coloreds, or nonwhites" (Said 228).

Needless to say, Said does not mean that only Orientals can speak of Orientals, of their truth, as if there were only one infallible truth. This is made clear by his statement, "I certainly do not believe the limited proposition that only a black can write about blacks, a Muslim about Muslims, and so forth" (Said 322). In fact, Orientalism is not lacking among Orientals. For example, in the attitude of establishing the East as a substantial entity to counter Western-centrism, as discerned in the discourses of "overcoming modernity," Isomae identifies a trend of self-Orientalism (355), that is, Orientalism that Orientals apply to other Orientals.

Self-Orientalism can take many different forms. "Self," here, can refer to either the Orientals who adopt this attitude, or other Orientals. Stefan Tanaka, in his 1993 book, *Japan's Orient*, offers an example of the self-Orientalism at issue here through an analysis of Japan's Orientalism toward other regions of Asia during the Fifteen Years War, especially China. Tanaka expounds how Japan produced the discourses on Asia, as well as a specialized field of research, in order to dominate and control Asia in the same way the Occident produced the discourses on the Orient (21–23). Japan's Orientalism toward Asia thus aimed at establishing an equivalence between modern Japan and Europe, and differentiating Japan from the Orient in spite of the former's location in Asia (Tanaka 12–18). Even if this Orientalism can be qualified as self-Orientalism—meaning the Orientalism of Orientals toward other Orientals—the prefix "self" in this case is there simply to emphasize the dominators' status as siblings of the dominated, in order to legitimize Japanese domination in relation to that of Europeans. This sibling status is one that Europeans do not have. Thus, self-Orientalism does not necessarily exclude power relations of domination and subjugation among Orientals. Sometimes, it even implies the claim of dominance of Orientals over Occidentals. The Kyoto School philosophers' argument that Oriental tradition can surpass Western modernity, and that Japan represents the epitome of this tradition, was formed in a context in which self-Orientalist discourses were predominant and cooperated to justify Japan's invasion of Asia in the fight against Western imperialism and colonialism.

Even if a certain group of people proclaims they stand on the side of oppressed people, this proclamation does not guarantee the former are completely free from the desire to wield power over the latter under the pretext of protecting them against oppressors. By saying this, I do not mean to naturalize or justify the oppression of the weak by the strong. My intention is to draw attention to the risk involved in the hasty application of simplistic and sweeping dichotomous schemes, and to the necessity of scrutinizing power relations, forces, and mechanisms that cooperate to support such relations.

Going back to the theme of overcoming modernity, proclaiming to surmount it does not necessarily enable us to go beyond or outside it, especially given that we ineluctably live in the space of modernity. As such, we are always vulnerable to being caught by problems inherent in modernity. If we do not keep this vulnerability in mind, we cannot really explore the ways of thinking or modes of existence that can resist these problems. Also, we would not notice when we get caught by them. In this respect, Isomae's following admonition is telling:

> To continue our thinking while putting ourselves within such aporias of modernity, without easily sympathizing with the discourses of "overcoming modernity" or "the universality of world history"—it would mean searching for the ways of resistance to make dysfunctional the borderlines between dichotomous categories from within the space of Western modernity, without falling into the illusion that we can stand outside this space or "overcome" modernity. (356–57)

Searching for such ways of resisting dichotomous categorizations is inseparable from reconsidering and reconstructing our own identities. In his 1996 essay, "In Range of the Critique of Orientalism" (*Datsu orientarizumu no shikō*), Kang Sangjung argues a prevailing idea that people have pure and single identities is an outcome of Orientalism and imperialism:

> The belief that a person can have a single pure identity is, if anything, the product of a brilliant fusion between imperialism and culture, a product of the mode of cultural hegemony I have been calling Orientalism. It results from the way identity and culture were combined and fixed as imperialism attained a global scale, allowing individuals to think that they were exclusively white or black, western or eastern. Of course, just as people create their own histories, so too they create their own identities. We cannot deny the longevity and continuity of traditions and customs, languages and cultural geography. But this is markedly and crucially different from requiring a stubborn attachment to notions of separateness or conspicuous difference. The problem is how best to go about establishing relationships among and between these indices of difference. (128)

The belief in a person's "single pure identity," defined by belongingness to a unitary group of humans separated from others—as if being of mixed-race was aberrant—presupposes a sense of discrimination between this group and others, and involves power relations of superiority/inferiority and domination/subjugation. Based on these implications, Kang perceives in this belief the effects of Orientalism intended for domination and control over groups of people marked "others," and the effects of imperialism that aim to incorporate them into one empire.

Regarding Japanese people's allegedly "single pure identity," Sakano Tōru, in his 2005 *Japanese Empire and Anthropologists* (*Teikoku nihon to jinruigakusha*), points out the commonly held idea of the Japanese as a single and pure race was formed at the time of the Asia-Pacific War, concurrently with the formation of Japan's imperialism and the beginning of its colonial rule. According to Sakano, before the war various theories on Japanese people held currency in the field of anthropology in Japan. Some of these included theories that tribes other than the Japanese had inhabited ancient Japan, that the ancestors of the Japanese had come from the continent, and that the Japanese were a mixed race of multiple lineages. However, once the war began, theories insisting the racial unity and purity of Japanese people, or claims that the Japanese had lived in Japan since time immemorial, became predominant. Sakano observes how these new theories were in conformity with Japan's wartime policies, which consisted of endorsing Japanese rule over other ethnic groups, and making the unity of the Japanese the basis for the integration of these groups (496).

What is to be questioned, considering the outcome of such research, is not the fact that a group of people calling themselves Japanese existed in an area called Japan for a certain length of time. Rather, we should question what kind of view toward others the self-recognition of the Japanese as a single and pure race presupposes, and what kind of relation between the Japanese and other groups this self-recognition intends to establish. Needless to say, such problems are not specific to the Japanese, but can occur within any group of people.

Reconsidering or reconstructing our identities does not necessarily mean completely negating or abandoning them. While retaining our identities, we can still challenge notions of their fixedness and separateness, and the senses of superiority/inferiority and domination/subjugation that infiltrate through the received ideas of our identities. If we can reconceive our identities in the mutual exchange and transformation with others, all these identities cannot but undergo change so that the differences between us no longer entail exclusion or hierarchy, but become genuine differences. Perhaps connecting our identities through such differences while making our identities multiplicities is close to what Kang describes as, "establishing relationships among and between [the] indices of difference" (128). There is also a possibility of solidarities traversing these identities *qua* multiplicities, without the rule of one hegemonic power.

The idea of a unified and homogenized Asia is the antithesis of an Asia based on multiplicities and solidarities. When Koyasu remarks that the act of posing Asia as a substantial entity concealed the aporia in the discourses of overcoming modernity, he refers to Takeuchi's idea of "Asia as method" in contrast to "Asia as a substantial entity" (Koyasu 249–50). At the end of his 1960 lecture, "Asia as Method" (*Hōhō toshiteno ajia*), Takeuchi states:

> When [the] rollback [of culture or values from the Orient] takes place, we must have our own cultural values. And yet perhaps these values do not already exist, in substantive form. Rather I suspect that they are possible as method, that is to say, as the process of the subject's self-formation. (165)

Koyasu argues that when Takeuchi describes Asia as a subject, he does not regard it as a substantial entity. Rather, what matters here is that he describes it as a subject of resistance, that is, a subject that forms and transforms itself in each act of resistance. Koyasu writes, "Asia exists where there is resistance" (250). Given his criticism of the attitude of concealing the existence of what is to be overcome by those who attempt this overcoming, resistance here does not only mean a resistance to Western-centrism or various mechanisms that support it. Resistance also implies a pushback to similar hegemonies and mechanisms operative within the people who attempt the rollback of culture or value from the non-West.

The Asia thus conceived, which forms itself in each act of resistance, incessantly transforms itself, while creating new connections and disconnections among various regions and peoples without uniting them. Gayatri Chakravorty Spivak presents a similar vision of Asia (or more precisely "Asias") in her essay, "Our Asias," which is included in her 2008 book *Other Asias*. She proposes, "We must therefore attempt to think [of Asia] as one continent in its plurality, rather than reduce it only to our own regional identity" (Spivak 214). Spivak claims that her use of the term "Asias" in the titles of her essay and book is a sensible expression of the plurality of Asia. But, for this plurality, she has in mind more than that of diverse regions and peoples within the Asian continent. She writes, "I propose to deal with 'Asia' as the instrument of an altered citation: an iteration" (Spivak 217). According to Spivak, "Asia" is a point of reference to which people repeatedly refer, and which alters itself with every reference, while retaining its oneness only in the repetition of such alteration. Thus, the plurality she expresses with the term "Asias" also entails the plurality of "Asia" itself as a whole, differently composed and recomposed of various regions and peoples. This vision of plural Asias is in line with the vision of Asia forming and transforming itself in each act of resistance, while creating connections and disconnections among different regions and peoples.

Just as the subject of such resistance cannot be the subject of the state, various regions and peoples connected in this resistance do not have to agree with states or nations, nor do such connections have to be confined within them or thwarted by the dichotomous division between East and West. Diverse things appear and disappear in perpetual change; they affirm themselves as they are in their mutual relation. This is also a vista whose possibility Nishida hinted at when he conceived of beings in the relation of absolutely contradictory identity with absolute nothingness. This vista was also present when he conceived many particular worlds coexisting without unification, and enveloping individuals as absolute nothingness envelops these worlds. Nevertheless, he limited the effectuation of such worlds to states, and put individuals under the inescapable compulsion by them in the name of a specific form of morality alleged as the self-expression of absolute nothingness. He saw the complete form of the state and the exceptional embodiment of absolute nothingness exclusively in Japan. He reintroduced the hierarchical relation between many worlds—the very relation he criticized. Thus, he ruined the vista in which the plurality of beings and worlds are fully affirmed, tainting it with ethnocentrism and the morality permeated by it.

It may be easy to ignore such disgraceful obstacles to Nishida's thought, and to those of his four disciples, on account of their insistence on morality and their intellectual battle against Western-centrism. Doing so may even make things easier, and might please some people. But, if we do this, we risk returning to the point before Takeuchi's criticism of the "Overcoming Modernity" symposium, and invalidate the accumulated reflections on the aporias implied in a wider range of discourses concerning overcoming modernity since that time. In order to not repeat this aporia, what is needed now is for us to face these obstacles squarely, save the thought interrupted by them, and connect the multiple lines of flight discerned in this thinking with those that resist what these philosophers could not.

Conclusion

What I have meant to elucidate so far was that the Kyoto School's wartime project of overcoming modernity ended up reproducing certain power relations characteristic of the very modernity they sought to overcome. Here, the universal or moral aspects of the school's philosophy or metaphysics provided a façade to hide this state of affairs. Thus creating the false appearance that modernity had indeed been overcome prevents us from actually facing the question of how to tackle modernity.

Moreover, when the philosophy or metaphysics that camouflages the deception of this overcoming also works to buttress the assertion that only a certain group of people are qualified to become the privileged agents of this overcoming, it fosters the illusion that they are, as exclusive bearers of universal truth or morality, superior to others. Then, the ideal upheld by this philosophy, however profound it may seem, helps infuse these people with dogmatic self-conviction, rather than urging them to reflect on their actions. Even though the dividing line between "us" and "them" for these people had not been historically clear-cut, once their exclusive identity is established, the questions as to how it has become what it is, and whether it has been eternally categorical, are forgotten.

The discourses that reduce universal or moral ideals to a matter of a certain group's privilege and use of these ideals to endorse the reproduction of problematic power structures that should undergird this privilege cannot but amount to justifying, or even aggravating, the terrible *fait accompli*— whether that is a war, oppression, or discrimination. Thus, ideals lose their critical potential and ability to transform reality. Interpreting such discourses as pacifist agendas or resistances to the regime on the pretext of the morality or universality invoked lends itself, even if inadvertently, to resuscitating the ideologies that promoted the war to which such discourses were supposed to present a challenge.

When political criticisms of the Kyoto School's philosophy are accused of being disrespectful, or even discriminatory to the Japanese people and culture, how such people and culture are represented and what is at issue in these representations tend not to be questioned. It is as if critical insights contributed by a number of Japanese intellectuals—including those who are not so-called "ethnic Japanese"—since the postwar era until the present into the relation between the school's philosophy and the war have not existed (or, strangely, it is as if these people did not count as "Japanese" proper). It is undeniable that these philosophers themselves suffered from the war and were drawn into tragic situations. However, when this point is emphasized, it is often disregarded that tragedy occurred not only to these philosophers, but also to the people manipulated by their words, and to other peoples those influenced by the Kyoto School invaded. If one takes seriously the casualties of the war—which included many different kinds peoples who lived in different regions not limited to Japan—and if one wishes to avoid the repetition of similar tragedies, the words one utters now should never be, "the ideal of the war was right."

Certainly, these philosophers' discourses did not bring about such grave consequences on their own; they were just one of many factors that concertedly did so. But to completely ignore their involvement and to tolerate their discourses by saying they were just forced to utter them does not help prevent similar wars or disasters from happening in future. By exploring what was wrong with the ideal of the war in question, this book was a modest attempt to call for increased efforts to learn from past mistakes and prevent them from being repeated.

Notes

Introduction

1. I omitted the phrase "and it must not be directed against those unwilling to embrace the rule of the victors," because this phrase has no relevance to Shaku's statements quoted above.

2. For Shaku's enthusiastic support for Japan's war efforts in the Russo-Japanese War, for instance, see Brian Victoria, "Zen as a Cult of Death in the Wartime Writings of D. T. Suzuki," 4–5. See also Shaku's statement, which explains his wish when he went to a battlefield as a military chaplain: "I also wished to inspire, if I could, our valiant soldiers with the ennobling thoughts of the Buddha, so as to enable them to die on the battlefield with the confidence that the task in which they are engaged is great and noble" (Victoria 5; quoted from Shaku, "Sermons of a Buddhist Abbot," 203, at http://www.sacred-texts.com/bud/zfa/index.htm). In this statement, it is a given that "the task" in which the soldiers were engaged, namely, Japan's war efforts, are "great and noble." Shaku's aim was to convince soldiers, who were going to die in the battlefield, of this task's greatness and nobleness. For this purpose, he inspired soldiers with "the ennobling thoughts of the Buddha." Here, the accord between the moral ideal of Buddha's law and Japan's war efforts, regardless of whatever they were, is presupposed as unquestionable. What is also to be noted in passing is another citation by Victoria from the works of Suzuki Daisetsu, who was mentored by Shaku. In this citation, Suzuki dismisses the Korean people's wish for independence and one-sidedly judges that they were fortunate to be governed by Japan after the war (Victoria 5). Goto-Jones's thesis on the conditional that, even when Buddhists justify war "in the name of the Buddha," for them, "[war] must not be directed against those unwilling to embrace the rule of the victors" (*Political Philosophy in Japan* 36) at least does not apply to Suzuki's statement here.

3. Some people may find it problematic to use the categories of "Westerners," "non-Westerners," and "Orientals" etc. My use of such terms is not intended to endorse or solidify the status quo in which their referents are substantialized and dichotomized, but rather to criticize and challenge it. To elucidate and describe the state of affairs in which such identities have been substantialized and unequal power dynamics have

been established between them, in view of challenging such a status quo I think it is sometimes inevitable to use such generalized and dichotomous terms.

4. I de-italicized these two citations, which are italicized in Heisig's book.

Chapter 1

1. My translation. Translations of Japanese texts are mine except direct quotations from those written in English.

2. Takeuchi Yoshimi has a similar view on the basic strand of the arguments made during the symposium. In his "Overcoming Modernity," Takeuchi points out that although Nakamura Mitsuo questioned the simple equation between modernity and the West in his contribution submitted after the symposium, he did not develop this topic when he participated in roundtable discussions (115). See also Nakamura's statement on this point in OM 136. When Takeuchi discerns in Nakamura's essay "a critique of the symposium *in toto*" ("Overcoming Modernity" 115), Takeuchi implies the tendency of equating modernity and the West swayed the entire symposium.

3. Harootunian, in *Overcome by Modernity*, also discusses that, in this symposium, not only Kobayashi and Nishitani but also Suzuki Shigetaka, another Kyoto School philosopher among the participants, shared the belief in what is thus eternal and permanent in history (85–88).

4. I replaced "the human's" for "man's" and "one's" for "his." In rendering Nishitani's phrase 「主体としての人間の主体性は、「生命」よりも一層深く、たゞ自発的な自由を以て働くといふ自己内面の事実からのみ捉へられる」, the translator understands that it is the human's "self-interiority" that "operates through spontaneous freedom" and, based on this understanding, puts "his" before "spontaneous freedom." I interpret this phrase as meaning that the human's true subjectivity, what Nishitani calls subjective nothingness, which is deeper than life and beyond personal consciousness, "operates through spontaneous freedom." The freedom through which this subjective nothingness operates, even when it does so within the human's self-interiority, cannot be one's mere personal freedom. As such, I deleted "his" before "spontaneous freedom." The idea that spontaneous freedom resides primarily in the human's personal self-interiority, and therefore that this freedom is personal, is characteristic of Western modern philosophy, which is usually formulated as centering on human subjectivity. This idea is alien to the philosophers of the Kyoto School, including Nishitani, who claimed to challenge the premises of Western modern philosophy.

5. Although the terms "*muga*" and "*mushin*" in the context of Zen Buddhism are usually translated as "no-self" and "no-mind," these terms here do not simply mean the absence of the self and mind, but designate ethical states of mind disinterested in and freed from egoism, which is why they are regarded as moral virtues. In order to make such connotations explicit, I chose "selflessness" and "no-mindedness" as the translation of "*muga*" and "*mushin*."

6. As the translation of "*kami no mikokoro*," I replaced "gods' minds" for "gods' intentions." When Nishitani refers to "*kami no mikokoro*," he does not mean the supposed specific intentions of gods, nor does the way of the gods as he describes it here

consist in following such intentions. Quoting the passage "The mirror transparently and selflessly illuminates all things in the world. . . . This is the source of honesty," from *Jinnō shōtōki* (*Chronicle of Gods and Sovereigns*), he likens gods' minds to the mirror (OM 58). What he means is that gods' minds are in themselves nothingness, like the mirror reflecting and illuminating everything as they are without casting its figure upon them. The moral virtue of honesty results from emptying one's mind of selfish thoughts after the manner of gods' minds, which are in fact the origin of everything, including human minds. Nishitani's association of Oriental religiosity, whose core is subjective nothingness, and Japanese Shintoism is possible based on this understanding of the way of the gods. Certainly, Nishitani and other philosophers in the Kyoto School loaded nothingness with many religious, moral, and political implications, just as myths and legends have so often been arbitrarily interpreted or even fabricated. But this is a matter to be discussed on another occasion. I replaced "one's" for "their" and "mind" for "minds" simply to suit the citation to the current argument.

7. I replaced "toward" for "behind," so as to be true to Nishitani's phrase 「世界倫理への原動力」. I also replaced "country" for "nation," to maintain consistency in translation.

8. I changed the order between "become grounded in subjective nothingness" and "attain the source of their minds," according to Nishitani's Japanese phrase 「自己の心源に達することが出来、主体的無に立脚することが出来るならば」. The source of mind mentioned here is subjective nothingness, and people can become grounded in it only after they attain it. I also replaced "clean and bright" for "pure and clear" as the translation of *seimeishin* or *kiyoki akaki kokoro* (清明心).

9. I replaced "clean and bright" for "pure and clear" as above. I added "while" between "that" and "these individuals." I also deleted "will not only" between "these individuals" and "acquire" and replaced "can" for "will also" between "they" and "merge." Nishitani's Japanese phrase is 「個人はその職域に於ける練達と滅私とに努める行に於て清明の心を自得するにつれて、国家の歴史を貫く国家生命の本源に合し、同時に世界歴史の底に潜む世界倫理（古人の所謂天の道）に触れることが出来る。」. Precisely speaking, the purport of this phrase is not simply that individuals will "acquire clean and bright minds . . ." as well as "merge with the fountainhead of state life . . . ," but that they can do the latter as they do the former.

10. I added "can" between "state" and "first," to be true to Nishitani' s Japanese phrase 「国家は．．．倫理的であり得る」.

Chapter 2

1. Although Williams's *The Philosophy of Japanese Wartime Resistance* includes, as its subtitle shows, "a reading with commentary" of the three roundtable discussions, I do not cite from this "reading" (part 2 of the book) in this book. In fact, in reference to the Japanese original, the text of Williams's book includes, many interpolations, in addition to those within [ ], and transformations, and therefore does not seem to be especially true to the Japanese original. At the beginning of his book, Williams states that it "is not a translation" but his "interpretative rendering or close paraphrase of the

whole of the Japanese original" (*The Philosophy of Japanese Wartime Resistance* xxi). He asserts that he had to adopt this path because translating the Japanese texts of these roundtable discussions before or during the Second World War into modern English, which remains tainted by Wilsonian or anti-war liberalism, would end up ruining what the participants of these discussions really meant. This, he claims, could also cloak fact under moral judgment. However, under the pretext of rendering the true meanings of the Japanese original texts in a way freed from a certain bias, Williams quite often inserts his own ideas as "facts" or "truths" into his "reading," and thus biases the meanings of the texts in another way. At least from my viewpoint, many of these ideas seem to lack textual evidences and distort the factuality of the original Japanese texts. As such, I do not consult this Williams's "reading" here, although I have no intention of denying a possibility that this "reading" might be useful to someone else for other purposes.

One example of a twist Williams gave to the Japanese original is that he translated the title of the third roundtable discussion, "*Sōryokusen no tetsugaku*," as "The Philosophy of World-historical War" (*The Philosophy of Japanese Wartime Resistance* xxxiv), instead of the literal translation, "The Philosophy of Total War." The term "*sōryokusen*" corresponds to the literal Japanese translation of Erich Ludendorff's *Der totale Krieg* (usually translated as "The Total War"), the book to which the Kyoto School philosophers refer in the third symposium as *Sōryokusen ron*. Williams explains that he does not render "*sōryokusen*" as "total war" because he believes the contributors of the three symposia do not see "*sōryokusen*" as a form of "total mobilization" or "absolute war," as conceived by Ernst Jünger and Carl von Clausewitz, under whose influence Ludendorff formed his idea of total war. Williams points out that the four Kyoto philosophers share neither Ludendorff's stress on morale nor Wilson's notion of just war. What matters for them, he says, is the struggle to create a new, non-Western centered world in which the plurality of historical worlds is respected (*The Philosophy of Japanese Wartime Resistance* xxxii–xxxiv). However, this view turns out to be one-sided when we read Kimoto Takeshi's "Antinomies of Total War," published five years prior to *The Philosophy of Japanese Wartime Resistance*. Throughout this essay, Kimoto argues that while the four contributors understood "*sōryokusen*" as a struggle to overcome Western modernity and construct a new world order from the world-historical standpoint, they also regarded total mobilization and absolute war—which they reconceived differently from Jünger, Clausewitz, or Ludendorff and pushed to the extreme so as to entail the thorough totalization of all aspects of citizens' life beyond the distinction between wartime and peacetime—as the indispensable constituents of this "*sōryokusen*." Rendering "*sōryokusen*" as "world-historical war" and using the term "world-historical" is confusing, as it has as its literal Japanese translation another term, "*sekaishiteki*." This also amounts to emphasizing only one of the two aspects of the concept, while ignoring or concealing the other. This is just one of the many instances in which the factuality of the Japanese original texts seems to be distorted in Williams's "reading." Moreover, strangely enough, while Williams condemns Ludendorff's stress on morale and Wilson's notion of just war, he does not blame the four thinkers of the Kyoto School for justifying the war their state waged through recourse to a certain kind of ethicality or morality, which they allude to here and there in the roundtable discussions held after the war was launched. This is a point I will discuss later in this book.

In passing, I could not find any unusual or meaningful " 'tear' or 'burn hole' in the fabric of the text of the third symposium," as Williams claims to have found in *The Philosophy of Japanese Wartime Resistance* (xxxiii). Whether or not a person uses the Japanese language does not seem to affect the perception of such a thing. Even if this existed, such a thing would not seem to be enough textual evidence to support his "reading" that "*sō* is not an adjective, but a noun" (*The Philosophy of Japanese Wartime Resistance* xxxiii), which is simply a grammatically inappropriate understanding. Aside from the dubiousness of this "reading," the term "*sōryokusen*" can be used and understood among contemporary Japanese people in the sense of effort or struggle with "all of our powers, strengths, capabilities and capacities," as Williams understands it (*The Philosophy of Japanese Wartime Resistance* xxxiii), independently from Ludendorff's theory of total war. This effort or struggle can be, but does not necessarily have to be, war. But even this meaning of the term does not sufficiently support his reading that "*sō ryoku sen*" should be taken solely as "world-historical war," given that the term "*sōryokusen*" used in the symposium still retained the meaning of "total war," and referenced the people's effort or struggle with "all of [their] powers, strengths, capabilities and capacities" in all the aspects of their lives.

2. The "practical" subject I have discussed so far based on the four thinkers' statements in the three symposia has nothing to do with "the *practice* of Confucian revolutions," as Williams claims to find in the texts of the transcripts in *The Philosophy of Japanese Wartime Resistance* (39). Williams asserts that "Confucianism not only revealed the authentic structure of Kyoto School political thought but illuminated in an unrivalled way the nature of the political struggle these Japanese thinkers waged with the Tōjō faction in the unfolding drama of what I call the 'Post-Meiji Confucian Revolution' " (*The Philosophy of Japanese Wartime Resistance* xxii). Certainly, the relation between the Kyoto School and Confucianism is an interesting research theme, if explored properly. But what should be questioned is Williams's assertion that Confucianism exerts such a strong effect on the four thinkers in these roundtable discussions that "there was no escaping the influence of the *practice* of Confucian revolutions" (*The Philosophy of Japanese Wartime Resistance* 39). The reason he brings forth to allege that "the participants in the *Chūō Kōron* discussions never broke free of the Confucian moral framework" (*The Philosophy of Japanese Wartime Resistance* 39), in spite of these thinkers' apparent rejection of the Chinese philosophy in the roundtable discussions, is Kōyama's statement on the Meiji Restoration referring to the decisive rejection of the Edo Shogunate. Williams regards "[t]his phase of radical and unsparing criticism of a now *passé* regime" (*The Philosophy of Japanese Wartime Resistance* 39) by Kōyama, and presumably shared by his three colleagues, as unmistakably Confucian. He invokes it as evidence of the inescapable influence of Confucianism upon the four thinkers. Aside from the question of whether the understanding of Confucianism presented here is appropriate or not, a reading of the Japanese original text disproves Williams's opinion. In the subsequent part of this very statement, Kōyama specifies that the view of the radical break before and after Meiji Restoration he has just presented needs to be reconsidered more scrupulously from a contemporary standpoint. He then says that Japan, even before this event, had a modern spirit. Therefore, Kōyama ends his statement by saying there were two kinds of modernity in Japan that have discontinuous

continuity (SN 158). Reading his statement as a whole, Kōyama's emphasis is on the continuity between two kinds of modernity before and after Meiji Restoration, and not the radical break between them. Even if these two modernities are of different types and described as "discontinuous," insofar as Kōyama's intention is to connect them by calling them commonly "modernity" (*kindai*) against the ordinary Japanese usage of this word designating the period after Meiji Restoration, it is impossible to see the "radical and unsparing criticism of a now *passé* regime" in Kōyama's statement here. He himself denies the existence of such a radical break, just after he has referred to it.

3. Christian Uhl in "What was the 'Japanese Philosophy of History'?" provides an extensive look at the four Kyoto philosophers' intention of overcoming Hegel by means of Ranke, who himself tried to overcome Hegel. As Uhl observes, the four thinkers also worked to overcome Ranke in their conception of the philosophy of world history.

Still, whether this philosophy of world history could successfully overcome Hegelianism is a question that needs further exploration. For example, Sakai calls our attention to the aspects in which these philosophers, in spite of their ostensible criticism of Hegel, continue to build upon Hegelian frameworks ("Modernity and its Critique" 109–10).

4. In spite of the ideal of the truly worldly world, in which many historical worlds coexist and all countries are neutrally included as its members, it is undeniable that the actual worldview of the philosophers of the Kyoto School is partial. When they talk about the East or the Orient (*tōyō*) in contrast to the West (*seiyō*), in many cases they have in mind only the region spreading roughly from China to India, including Japan, and disregard the Arab or Islamic world, which occupies a large part of the area usually called "the Orient." By the term "the West," these philosophers mostly refer to Europe, and sometimes include America, but not Australia. They discuss the *seiyō* and *tōyō* as if they were the two halves of the world, and neglect Africa and South America. Besides, in their frequent use of the terms "the West" and "the East," or "the Orient," these philosophers tend to represent the regions designated by each term as homogeneous and to ignore internal differences within them. Although such a terminology and worldview are problematic in themselves, I limit myself to noting this point here and will discuss the thought of these philosophers based on their terminology and worldview.

5. Aside from Kōyama's "The Ideal of World History," the four thinkers' essays cited above were originally compiled in the anthology titled, *Sekaishi no riron* and published by Kōbundō in 1944. The anthology I consulted, with the same title, *Sekaishi no riron*, published in 2000 by Tōeisha, is a volume in a series of selected works of the Kyoto School. It only compiles the first half of the former anthology, which includes the essays of the Kyoto School thinkers, and leaves out most of the second half that includes essays by other writers. See Mori Tetsurō's "*kaisetsu*" of the latter *Sekaishi no riron* (396).

Chapter 3

1. I changed the places of "annihilate their selves in their work" and "serve the state" in order to arrange these phrases as per Nishitani's structure in the Japa-

nese text. According to his thought, it seems that if moral energy realizes popular or national ethics, it is primarily through the people's self-annihilation in their work, even though doing so is after all reduced to their service for the state. For it is the former aspect, rather than the latter, that enables people to live ethically by making them face absolute nothingness.

I also changed the order of "furnishing a high degree of concentrated energy to the state" and "which [the state] qua community of the people is itself made ethical" to reflect Nishitani's original organization in the Japanese text. I adjusted the latter part so as to be true to his entire phrase 「その国民の共同体としての国家自身をして倫理的たらしめ、且つ集中された強度のエネルギーを之に与へしめる」. In rendering this phrase, the translator changed the order of the first and second halves of the phrase. However, since the "high degree of concentrated energy" at issue comes from moral energy, "making the state . . . ethical," as the first effect, it should precede "furnishing a high degree of concentrated energy to the state." Otherwise, Nishitani's emphasis on "moral" energy, not mere labor force, would be omitted. The same applies to the case in which the people's service to the state is taken to be prior to their self-annihilation in their work, as I have noted above.

2. Nishitani is not the only thinker who developed a theory of subject and substratum. Tanabe Hajime, who was a representative figure of the Kyoto School alongside his mentor Nishida Kitarō, also thematized the relation between subject and substratum. See Sakai, "Subject and Substratum: On Japanese Imperial Nationalism." While Nishitani underlines the intimate unity between the subject and the substratum of the state, according to Sakai, Tanabe introduces negativity into their relation, in that individuals, in order to become subjects, must negate their substratum, which is their species. However, by insisting that individuals who have thus become such subjects can transform their species by choosing to belong to it out of their own free will, Tanabe consequently recommends the subject's return to the substratum. Moreover, claiming that the negation of species as substratum is possible through the mediation of the state, as the genus subsuming multiple species, Tanabe provides a theory that encouraged the colonized people to identify with the state of the colonizers within the Empire of Japan, while always bringing the colonized back to their own species. Thus, Tanabe's thoughts on subject and substratum, in spite of their differences from Nishitani's, theorized a means to lead people to serve the state voluntarily, and was complementary to Nishitani's, in view of the broader scope of Japan's empire outside its state.

Chapter 4

1. The logic of "putting each in the right place" (*onoono sono tokoro wo eshimeru*), to which the philosophers of world history attached so much importance, was the officially announced principle of the Greater East Asia Co-Prosperity Sphere. Although this logic has been often invoked to radically distinguish between Japanese and European colonial rule, Sakano Tōru expounds the contradiction in this logic and rejects such a distinction. From the standpoint of the rule of different ethnic

groups in the Co-Prosperity Sphere, it was necessary to emphasize the affinity of the Japanese with other ethnic groups in order to solidify the unity of the Sphere, and simultaneously negate the equality of all ethnic groups in order to secure Japan's ruling position. The ideal of "cooperative division of labor" comparable to the "family relationship" was held up for the purpose of responding to this dual need. But the reality under the veneer of this ideal was the hierarchical discrimination of different ethnic groups with Japan on top (Sakano 420–22). Sakano insists, "If [Japanese] people promote a policy to rule different ethnic groups on the basis of 'the relation of domination-subjugation,' such a policy would be no different from the European imperialism and colonialism Japan criticizes, even though [Japanese] people try to embellish this policy with flowery words like 'cooperative division of labor' or 'family relationship'" (422). This criticism also applies to the four thinkers' arguments invoking the ideal of "putting each in the right place."

Chapter 5

1. Here, Nishitani uses the Japanese term *kotogara*, while giving the kana *zahhe*, designating the German term *Sache*. Subsequently, in the same statement, he uses only the katakana *zahhe*. Although *Sache* can be translated as *kotogara* in Japanese, and as "thing" in English, when he describes *zahhe* as "objective" (*mokuhyō*) and "motive" (*dōki*), he draws upon other meanings of *Sache*, including "ideal," "purpose," "reason," etc. Considering the context in which a good or holy war is at issue, "cause" in the sense of *taigi* in Japanese seems close to what Nishitani means by *zahhe* here.

Chapter 6

1. This seems to be the case with Ōhashi Ryōsuke's 2001 book, *The Kyoto School and the Japanese Navy: On the Newly Discovered "Ōshima Memoranda* (*Kyōto gakuha to Nihon kaigun: Shin shiryō "Ōshima memo" wo megutte*). Drawing upon a recently discovered document called Ōshima Memoranda, Ōhashi claims that the Kyoto School during wartime aimed to stop the war and overthrow the cabinet. Kimoto Takeshi, in his "Antinomies of Total War," succinctly summarizes the problems with Ōhashi's claim (99–102). Kimoto spots discrepancies between the documents Ōhashi draws upon and finds aspects that contradict Ōhashi's claims. Kimoto also argues that Ōhashi seeks to revive the ideology that the Kyoto School philosophers shared with the wartime regime, under the pretext that the philosophers were actually against such ideologies (101). When done properly, deciphering the true intentions of the Kyoto philosophers through consulting materials beyond their texts, such as diaries and memoranda, can bring about fruitful results. However, to distort what is written in these philosophers' texts by invoking external materials, as Ōhashi does, is another matter. If it were assumed that the Kyoto School philosophers' thoughts were completely free of the common wartime ideology, it becomes easy to assign

opposite meanings to their public discourses. Such an assumption, coupled with the excuses made retrospectively or the materials whose credibility is questioned, allows people to arbitrarily stretch the meaning of these philosophers' texts, even against what is written in them. This can result in interpretations where the philosophers' statements endorsing the war or imperial nationalism strangely become perceived as resisting the war and promoting pacific cosmopolitanism. Even if we can understand that these philosophers' true intentions may be different from their actual statements, their discourses, once published and widely accepted, will never change. As Kimoto comments: "[I]t is through the exoteric rather than esoteric thought war that these scholars could influence the public" (102). That is to say, it is the upfront content of such discourses, and not the arcane secrets hidden in them, that influenced people and caused disaster. From this standpoint, Kimoto insists that "with the disclosure of [the] secret meetings [of the Kyoto School and the navy], it becomes all the more important to examine the public discussions" (102). Additionally, now that some scholars are distorting the meanings of the Kyoto School philosophers' discourses, it becomes all the more important to clarify what is actually stated in such discourses, and to elucidate the problems involved in them.

2. The passage cited in the English translation of Tsurumi's work is slightly different from the original passage in Ba Maw's *Breakthrough in Burma: Memories of a Revolution, 1939–1946*. Here I cited the latter passage.

3. In this passage, Koyasu quotes Shimomura Toratarō's statement, "Modernity is us, and the overcoming of modernity is the overcoming of ourselves" (OM 111), from his essay contribution to the "Overcoming Modernity" symposium (Koyasu 248). The point Shimomura thus made, even though in a de-politicized context, was however not pursued appropriately. Calichman's overview of the discussions in this symposium illustrates that, although some other participants commented on this point, in the subsequent discussions, "overcoming ourselves" was largely taken as overcoming the influence of Western culture that infiltrated the Japanese. This was ultimately reduced to a matter of restoring the purity of Japanese culture. See OM 17–18.

4. For example, in looking at the wartime discourses of Nishitani, John C. Maraldo finds similarities between Nishitani's rhetoric and that of US President George Bush soon after the outbreak of the Gulf War (354–55). Through examining the past nationalism of the Kyoto School philosophers, Maraldo casts a critical eye over the present nationalism in America and notes that "the past is a problem of the present. Critique of nationalism is ultimately also self-critique" (362).

5. For example, Takahashi Tetsuya, in his 2005 *The State and Sacrifice* (*Kokka to gisei*), delineates how the seemingly innocuous act of mourning the war's dead as precious sacrifices for peace contributes to reproducing the unit of a nation distinguished from, and opposed to, other nations. This makes it possible to restart another war against them, while promoting people's self-sacrifice for the state. Exemplifying the force of "the national" strongly binding our thought and behavior, Takahashi observes, in which country we live, or whether the agent of this act is the state, mass, bereaved families of victims, or affiliates of resistant soldiers, does not change the way in which this act functions to thus reinforce national identity.

Chapter 7

1. Although the essay refers to this passage as being quoted from NKZ XII 344, the correct page number is 341.

Chapter 8

1. For the summary of the courses in which these texts were written and published/mimeographed, see the afterword (*atogaki*) by Shimomura Toratarō, one of the editors of the old version of NKZ and a member of the Kyoto School (NKZ XII 470–73). Shimomura also participated in the *Bungakukai* symposium. As also stated in the above afterword, "The Principle of the New World Order," the best-known of the three appendixes was specifically written at the request of the Tōjō government, and aimed to formulate a philosophical principle for the Greater East Asia Co-Prosperity Sphere. For a summary of the process through which this essay was first written, edited, and finally revised to become the official essay compiled in the first edition of NKZ, and the circumstances in which Nishida thus became involved in politics, see Arisaka's "The Nishida Enigma," 84–87. There are dissident testimonies concerning this political engagement. In comparing the two opposite testimonies, Kobayashi situates this engagement between voluntary cooperation and forced surrender, and undermines their dichotomy. See Kobayashi, *The Melancholy of Nishida Kitarō* 257–63.

2. The term "species [*shu*]," which Nishida uses here, originally comes from his disciple Tanabe Hajime, who famously elaborated the "logic of species." Tanabe articulated this logic through his criticism of Nishida's idea of the place of nothingness. In response to this criticism from Tanabe, as well as those from Marxists (including Nishida's students Tosaka Jun and Miki Kiyoshi), Nishida developed his later philosophy, which focused upon the themes concerning history, society, state, or politics. As his later philosophy developed, Nishida adopted the term "species" with his own particular understanding. For more on Nishida and Tanabe's intellectual exchanges, including harsh criticism and the commonalities between Nishida's philosophy and that of Tanabe, see Sugimoto Kōichi, "Tanabe Hajime's Logic of Species and the Philosophy of Nishida Kitarō: A Critical Dialogue within the Kyoto School."

3. I replaced "objective" with "object," to be true to Nishida's original term, "*kyakkan*." I also deleted the adjective, "intentional," which qualifies "action" in the English translation. In Nishida's original text, there is no word corresponding to this adjective. From this discussion, it is obvious the "action" at issue here is "[t]he fact that the subject determines the object and the object determines the subject." This interaction is not necessarily intentional, at least on the part of the object when it is not a living thing. To qualify the action of active intuition as "internal" does not seem to fit with Nishida's idea.

4. I replaced "objective" with "object," to be true to Nishida's original term, "*kyakkan*." I also deleted "to speak of" or "to say," and added "that" where necessary. The Japanese phrase "*to iukoto*" can mean either "to speak of"/"to say," or "that"

(followed by a clause). The translator understands this phrase in the citation in the former sense, and puts "to speak of" and "to say." However, this phrase in this context should be understood in the latter sense.

5. In Nishida's argument here, which based on the assumption that the environment determines the characteristics of the people living in it and their culture, one may hear the echoes of a theory from one of his students, Watsuji Tetsurō. Watsuji's masterpiece *Climate and Culture* (*Fūdo*) discusses various types of the cultures and how they may be environmentally determined. For critical analyses of the problems entailed in Watsuji's cultural typology, in which a special emphasis is placed upon Japanese particularity and the presuppositions within the discipline of Asian Studies that tend to tolerate such problems, see Sakai Naoki, "Subject and/or *Shutai* and the Inscription of Cultural Difference."

6. Similar logic is still used today to disguise ethnocentrism. For example, Arai Masao maintains Nishida's philosophy epitomized the logic inherent in Japanese culture, the logic that consists of " 'transform[ing]' ('translating' in Japanese manners) foreign cultures once accepted, so that they fit the mentality of Japanese people without bringing about a complete change in traditional culture, and let[ting] all stuffs spontaneously make up Japanese civilization" (30). Then, Arai insists that this logic "neither leads up to the doctrine centering upon the single state, nor completely assimilates itself into foreign civilization" (30). This kind of claim, allegedly free from ethnocentrism, is in fact a claim of disguised ethnocentrism, privileging the Japanese as the only people who can accept everything from the outside and preserve their tradition so that everything forms one national culture, a common cliché of *Nihonjinron*. In order to unmask this disguise, or at least to notice the absurdity of its underlying assumptions, it would be enough to raise the question: "Cannot any other people accept and transform foreign cultures suitable for their mentality and also preserve their tradition so that all stuffs make up their own culture?"

Chapter 9

1. For the details of the course, background, and aftermath of the Minobe incident, see Frank O. Miller, "The Minobe Affair." The incident was not merely a matter of the academic debate about constitutional interpretation. This debate was inextricably intertwined with conflicts between opposing factions within the military and bureaucracy. A major driving force of such conflicts was dissatisfaction with the existing government and its policies of liberal constitutionalism, which manifested in different, sometimes conflicting, actions. As such, the outcome of the incident (that is, the defeat of Minobe as a representative liberal intellectual) decisively determined the subsequent direction of Japanese history toward the establishment of a fascist regime.

2. For Miki's life, his participation in the Shōwa Research Group, his theory of cooperativism, and the role it played in relation to the Japanese empire, see Lewis E. Harrington, "Miki Kiyoshi and the Shōwa Kenkyūkai: The Failure of World History." Miki conceived of cooperativism as a principle to unify not only Japan but also East

Asia. Harrington articulates how Miki's appeal to the universality beyond Japanese particularity aided the Japanese empire rather than resisting it, by facilitating the accomplishment of the empire's objectives. As I will discuss later, the same is true of Nishida's pursuit of universality.

Chapter 10

1. As I will mention later in another note, Hegel's famous phrase, "*Was vernünftig ist, das ist wirklich; und was wirklich ist, das ist vernünftig,*" is commonly translated into English as, "what is rational is real, and what is real is rational." To keep consistency in the translation of technical terms as much as possible, I replaced "actual" with "real" as the translation of "*wirklich,*" according to this common translation.

2. For consistency in the translation of technical terms, I replaced "concept" in the translation of "*Begriff*" with "notion." As for the translation of "*Geist,*" I replaced "mind" with "spirit." I also replaced "actualization" with "realization" for the translation of "*Verwirklichung.*"

3. I replaced "Concept" with "Notion" as the translation of "*Begriff.*"

4. With recourse to his idea of communicative rationality, Habermas criticizes the solipsism and dogmatism of the traditionally conceived rational subject, including that found in Hegelianism. Given this, one may expect the modernity he reformulates would be free from Eurocentrism. However, this is not necessarily the case. By contradicting Habermas from the perspective of Michel Foucault, James Tully draws our attention to the problem inherent in the common argument about Western modernity, which Habermas also shares. See Tully, "To Think and Act Differently: Foucault's Four Reciprocal Objections to Habermas' Theory."

5. As aforementioned, I replaced "actual" with "real" for the translation of "*wirklich.*"

6. I added the word "World" to the phrase, "'National Spirits' of History," which is lacking in the translation of "*die welthistorischen Volksgeister.*" I also replaced "moral" with "ethical" as the translation of "*sittlich.*"

7. I deleted "the goal of" before "its irresistible urging," for this phrase has no corresponding part in Hegel's German text. I also replaced "Idea" with "Notion" as the translation of "*Begriff.*"

8. I replaced "Idea" with "Notion" as the translation of "*Begriff.*" I also replaced "assumes successive forms" with "posits in itself determinations" as the translation of "*Bestimmungen in sich setzt.*" I replaced "concrete shape" with "concrete determination" as the translation of "*konkretere Bestimmung.*" As the translation of the verb "*aufheben,*" I replaced "transcend" with "sublate," given that what is at issue in this passage is "the *dialectical* nature" of the Notion. "*Aufheben,*" when it is used to describe the dialectical movement, is usually translated as "sublate."

9. Hegel not only presented a worldview in which Asia and Africa, along with their cultures, are undervalued. He also played a decisive role in excluding these regions from the discipline of philosophy, which (despite its apparent neutrality) is undeniably Eurocentric. For more on the course of this exclusion, see Peter K. Parks,

"Absolute Idealism Reverts to Kantian Position: Hegel's Exclusion of Africa and Asia." On Hegel's ideas of racial hierarchy of different peoples in the world, as seen more broadly, and the importance of his philosophy of religion to this hierarchy, see Michael H. Hoffheimer, "Race and Law in Hegel's Philosophy of Religion."

10. For the translation of "*wirklich*," I replaced "actual" with "real," according to the common English translation of Hegel's famous phrase. I also de-italicized the sentence, since it is not italicized in Hegel's German original text.

11. I replaced "moral" with "ethical" as the translation of "*sittlich*."

12. I replaced "mind objectified" with "objective spirit" as the translation of "*objektiver Geist*." I also replaced "himself" with "oneself."

13. Although the German term "*allgemein*" can be translated into either "general" or "universal," the German phrase "*der allgemeine Wille*" is commonly translated as "general will" considering Hegel's reference to Rousseau's "*volonté générale*." However, Hegel's view of the general will presented here is directly relevant to his discussion of the state as the concrete universal and, as I will discuss later, his discussion of logic, concerning the relation among the universal, the particular, and the individual. To make both connotations explicit, I put both "general" and "universal" here. Considering the relevance of Hegel's view of the general will to his discussions of logic and the state as the concrete universal, I use only "universal" unless there is the obvious reference to Rousseau's general will in the discussion hereafter.

I replaced "individual" with "subjective" as the translation of "*subjektiv*." I also replaced "Morality" with "Ethicality" as the translation of "*Sittlichkeit*," and "moral" with "ethical" as the translation of "*sittlich*."

14. Hegel explains the relation between these three elements in his discussion of the judgment of reflection, in which the predicate transcends its primal immediacy through reflection. For his brief account of the judgment of reflection, see *The Encyclopedia Logic* 251–52.

15. I changed "single" with "individual" as the translation of "*einzeln*."

16. I changed "of the single instance" with "of the individual" as the translation of "*des Einzelnen*."

17. I changed "over and above" with "alongside" as the translation of "*außer und neben*."

18. I replaced "Concept" with "Notion" as the translation of "*Begriff*." I put both "general" and "universal" as the translation of "*allgemein*" for the reason aforementioned in the note 13.

19. I replaced "Concept" with "Notion" as the translation of "*gainen*," a Japanese word corresponding to the German word, "*Begriff*." This was done to keep the consistency in the translation of technical terms and to show the relevance of Nishida's statement here to Hegel's argument about "*Begriff*." I also replaced "a singular entity" with "a singular individual," as the translation of "*yuiitsu no kobutsu*." "*Kobutsu*" is a key term in Nishida's philosophy and is usually translated as "individual." The term "entity" obscures Nishida's reference to the arguments in logic, including those of Hegel, concerning the relation among the universal, the particular, and the individual.

20. I replaced "infinitely" with "infinite" to be true to Nishida's phrase 「無限なる動的統一」.「無限なる」 is an adjective qualifying the noun 「統一」.

21. Hegel's German phrase is "*So ist der Staat die vernünftige und sich objektiv wissende und für sich seiende Freiheit.*" To be true to his original phrase, I deleted "the embodiment of" and "realizing," and added "being-for-itself." Although there is no space to discuss further, *Für-sich-Sein*, paired with *An-sich-Sein*, is an important term in Hegel's philosophy, and its significance is irreducible to simple embodiment or realization. I chose to use the term to express the relevance of *Für-sich-Sein*, even at the cost of being clumsy.

22. I changed "general" to "universal" for the translation of "*allgemein*," and "particular" to "individual" for the translation of "*einzeln*."

23. I deleted the quotation marks added to the term "place" by the translator. I replaced "a mere individual" with "merely an individual" to be true to Nishida's Japanese phrase 「単に一つの個物といふものでもない」. I added "solely a place where individuals face each other" to translate his phrase, 「唯個物が個物に対し...の場所」, and "must" to translate 「なければならぬ」or「なければならない」, which were all omitted in the English translation. I also adjusted some parts to the additions.

24. I replaced "include" with "envelop" as the translation of 「包む」, which is a key term in Nishida's philosophy. I added "must" to supplement the meanings of his words 「なければならない」. I also changed "the concept of the dialectical universal" to "what I call the dialectical universal" as the translation of his phrase 「私が...弁証法的一般者といふのは」. This was done as it is the dialectical universal, not its concept, that envelops and determines individuals.

25. I deleted the quotation marks added to the term "place" by the translator.

26. I changed "of individual-qua-universal" to "that the determination of the individual is immediately the determination of the universal" to be true to Nishida's original phrase 「個物的限定即一般的限定」.

27. Nishida's Japanese phrase is 「個物的限定と一般的限定とが弁証法的に対立し而もそれが一である世界」. I added "determination" to translate 「限定」, omitted in the English translation, and changed the past tense of the verb to the present tense to be true to the original phrase.

28. I inserted "presumably" to translate Nishida's phrase 「と考へられる」. I replaced "the unity of the race" with "the ethnic unity" as the translation of "*minzokuteki tōitsu*," because "*minzoku*" for him does not necessarily correspond to race as aforementioned.

29. I changed the translation in order to true to Nishida's Japanese phrase 「ジットリッヒカイトといふものはゲマインシャフト的なるものの合理化せられたものでなければならない」. What is to be rationalized is not *Sittlichkeit* as misunderstood in the English translation, but "the *gemeinschaftlich*."

Chapter 11

1. This essay was published several months after "Prolegomena to Practical Philosophy" and was included in *Philosophical Essays*, vol. 4, along with the "Prolegomena" and "The Problem of the Reason of the State."

2. I replaced "state" for "nation" as the translation of "*kokka*" to maintain consistency in translation. I replaced "an ethnic society" for "a racial society" as the translation of "*minzokuteki shakai*" for aforementioned reasons. I also replaced "Only such is the state" for, "This is the prerequisite of nationhood," to be true to Nishida's phrase 「此の如きもののみが国家である」.

3. This phrase is omitted in the English translation.

4. I discussed the totalizing and unifying tendency in Nishida's philosophy of absolute nothingness from another angle, in comparison with William James and Alfred North Whitehead's philosophies, in my "Pure Experience in Question: William James in the Philosophies of Kitarō Nishida and Alfred North Whitehead."

Chapter 12

1. Nishida's original Japanese phrase for "the historical worldliness" is "*rekishiteki sekaisei*." Although Yusa's translation of this phrase as "the historical universality" (*Zen and Philosophy* 329) exactly indicates Nishida's gesture of universalizing the particular (which is in this case the Japanese *kokutai*), I translated "*sekaisei*" as "worldliness" for consistency in the translation of technical terms, and to distinguish it from "*fuhensei*," which I translated as "universality."

Bibliography

Arai Masao. *Nishida tetsugaku dokkai: Hēgeru kaishaku to kokkaron* (A Reading of Nishida's Philosophy: An Interpretation of Hegel and a Theory of the State). Kōyōshobō, 2001.

Arisaka Yoko. "Beyond 'East and West': Nishida's Universalism and Postcolonial Critique." *The Review of Politics*, vol. 59, no. 3, "Non-Western Political Thought," Summer 1997, pp. 541–60. www.jstor.org/stable/1408551. Accessed on Aug. 13, 2017.

———. "The Nishida Enigma: 'The Principle of the New World Order.'" *Monumenta Nipponica*, vol. 51, no. 1, Spring 1996, pp. 81–105. www.jstor.org/stable/2385317. Accessed on Aug. 10, 2017.

Ba Maw. *Breakthrough in Burma: Memories of a Revolution, 1939–1946*. Yale University Press, 1968.

Butler, Judith. *Subjects of Desire: Hegelian Reflections in Twentieth-Century France*. 1987. Columbia University Press, 1999.

Calichman, Richard F., editor and translator. *Overcoming Modernity: Cultural Identity in Wartime Japan*. Columbia University Press, 2008.

———. "Preface" and "Introduction: 'Overcoming Modernity' The Dissolution of Cultural Identity." *Overcoming Modernity: Cultural Identity in Wartime Japan*, edited and translated by Calichman, Columbia University Press, 2008, pp. VII–XVI, pp. 1–41.

Davis, Bret W. "Turns to and from Political Philosophy: The Case of Nishitani Keiji." *Re-Politicising the Kyoto School as Philosophy*, edited by Christopher Goto-Jones, Routledge, 2008, pp. 26–45.

Davis, Bret W., Brian Schroeder, and Jason M. Wirth, editors. *Japanese and Continental Philosophy: Conversation with the Kyoto School*. Indiana University Press, 2011.

Deleuze, Gilles, and Félix Guattari. *What Is Philosophy?* Translated by Graham Burchell and Hugh Tomlinson, Verso, 1994.

Doak, Kevin M. "Nationalism as Dialectics: Ethnicity, Moralism, and the State in Early Twentieth-Century Japan." *Rude Awakenings: Zen, the Kyoto School, & the Question of Nationalism*, edited by James W. Heisig and John C. Maraldo, University of Hawai'i Press, 1995, pp. 174–96.

———. "Romanticism, Conservatism and the Kyoto School of Philosophy." *Re-politicising the Kyoto School as Philosophy*, edited by Christopher Goto-Jones, Routledge, 2008, pp. 137–60.
Sun Ge. "In Search of the Modern: Tracing Japan's Thought on 'Overcoming Modernity.'" Translated by Peter Button. *Impact of Modernity*, edited by Thomas Lamarre and Kang Nae-hui, *Traces* vol. 3, 2004, pp. 53–75.
Goto-Jones, Christopher S. *Political Philosophy in Japan: Nishida, the Kyoto School, and Co-Prosperity*. Routledge, 2005.
———, editor. *Re-Politicising the Kyoto School as Philosophy*. London: Routledge, 2008.
Habermas, Jürgen. *The Philosophical Discourse of Modernity: Twelve Lectures*. Translated by Frederick Lawrence, The MIT Press, 1987.
Harrington, Lewis E. "Miki Kiyoshi and the Shōwa Kenkyūkai: The Failure of World History." *Positions: East Asia Cultures Critique*, vol. 17, no. 1, Spring 2009, pp. 43–72.
Harootunian, Harry. *Overcome by Modernity: History, Culture, and Community in Interwar Japan*. Princeton University Press, 2000.
Hegel, Georg W. F. *Enzyklopädie der philosophischen Wissenschaften im Grundrisse: Erster Teil Die Wissenschaft der Logik mit den mündlichen Zusätzen. Werke VIII*. Edited by Eva Moldenhauer and Karl M. Michel, Suhrkamp, 1970.
———. *Grundlinien der Philosophie des Rechts oder Naturrecht und Staatswissenschaft im Grundrisse. Werke VII*. Edited by Eva Moldenhauer and Karl M. Michel, Suhrkamp, 1970.
———. *Hegel's Phenomenology of Spirit*. Translated by A. V. Miller, Oxford University Press, 1977.
———. *Hegel's Philosophy of Right*. Translated by T. M. Knox, At the Clarendon Press, 1952.
———. *Hegel's Science of Logic*. Translated by A. V. Miller, Humanity Books, 1969.
———. *Phänomenologie des Geistes. Werke III*. Edited by Eva Moldenhauer and Karl M. Michel, Suhrkamp, 1969.
———. *The Encyclopaedia Logic* with the Zusätze: Part I of the *Encyclopaedia of Philosophical Sciences* with the Zusätze. Translated by T. F. Geraets, W. A. Suchting, and H. S. Harris, Hackett, 1991.
———. *The Philosophy of History*. Translated by J Sibree. 1899. Dover, 1956.
———. *Vorlesungen über die Philosophie der Geschichte. Werke XII*. Edited by Eva Moldenhauer and Karl M. Michel, Suhrkamp, 1970.
Heisig, James W. *Philosophers of Nothingness: An Essay on the Kyoto School*. University of Hawai'i Press, 2001.
Heisig, James W., and John C. Maraldo. "Editor's Introduction." *Rude Awakenings: Zen, the Kyoto School, & the Question of Nationalism*, edited by James W. Heisig and John C. Maraldo, University of Hawai'i Press, 1995. pp. vii–x.
———, editors. *Rude Awakenings: Zen, the Kyoto School, & the Question of Nationalism*. University of Hawai'i Press, 1995.
Hiromatsu Wataru. *Kindai no chōkoku ron: Shōwa shisōshi eno ichi shikaku* (Theories on "Overcoming Modernity": A Perspective on Shōwa Intellectual History). 1980. Kōdansha, 1989.

Hobsbawm, Eric J. "Introduction: Inventing Traditions." *The Invention of Tradition*, edited by Eric J Hobsbawm and Terence O. Ranger, Cambridge University Press, 2012, pp. 1–14.
Hoffheimer, Michael H. "Race and Law in Hegel's Philosophy of Religion." *Race and Racism in Modern Philosophy*, edited by Andrew Valls, Cornell University Press, 2005, pp. 194–216.
Isomae Jun'ichi. "*Atogaki*" (Afterword). "*Kindai no chōkoku*" *to kyōto gakuha: Kindaisei, teikoku, huhensei*, edited by Sakai Naoki and Isomae Jun'ichi, Ibunsha, 2010, pp. 350–57.
Kado Kazumasa. *Nishida Kitarō to kokka e no toi* (Nishida Kitarō and the Question of the State). Ibunsha, 2007.
Kang Sangjung. "In Range of the Critique of Orientalism." Translated by Margherita Long. *Deconstructing Nationality*, edited by Naoki Sakai, Brett de Bary, and Iyotani Toshio, East Asia Program, Cornell University, 2005, pp. 113–29.
Karatani Kōjin. "*Kaisetsu: Kindai no chōkoku ni tsuite*" (Commentary: On "Overcoming Modernity"). *Kindai no chōkoku ron: Shōwa shisōshi eno ichi shikaku*, by Hiromatsu Wataru. 1980. Kōdansha, 1989, pp. 263–72.
Kawakami Tetsutarō. "Concluding Remarks to 'Overcoming Modernity.'" *Overcoming Modernity: Cultural Identity in Wartime Japan*, edited and translated by Richard F. Calichman, Columbia University Press, 2008, pp. 149–50.
Kawakami Tetsutarō et al. *Kindai no chōkoku* (Overcoming Modernity). Fuzanbō, 1979.
Kawamura Satofumi. "The National Polity and the Formation of the Modern National Subject in Japan." *Japan Forum*, vol. 26, no. 1, 2014, pp. 25–45. http://www.tandfonline.com/doi/abs/10.1080/09555803.2013.802367. Accessed on June 1, 2017.
Kimoto Takeshi. "Antinomies of Total War." *Positions: East Asia Cultures Critique*, vol. 17, no. 1, Spring 2009, pp. 97–125.
Kobayashi Toshiaki. "*Nishida Kitarō 'Nihonbunka no mondai'*" (Nishida Kitarō "The Problem of Japanese Culture"). *Nashonarizumu no meicho 50* (50 Masterpieces of Nationalism), edited by Ōsawa Masachi. Heibonsha, 2002, pp. 56–64.
———. *Nishida Kitarō no yūutsu* (The Melancholy of Nishida Kitarō). Iwamani Shoten, 2003.
———. *Nishida Kitarō tasei no buntai* (Nishida Kitarō: The Writing of Otherness). Ohta Shuppan, 1997.
Kōsaka Masaaki. "*Sekaishikan no ruikei*" (Types of the View of World History). *Sekaishi no riron. Kyoto tetsugaku sensho XX*, edited by Mori Tetsurō. Tōeisha, 2000, pp. 59–97.
Kōsaka Masaaki et al. "*Sekaishiteki tachiba to nihon*" (The World-Historical Position and Japan). *Chūōkōron*, vol. 57, no. 1, Jan. 1942, pp. 150–92.
———. "*Sōryokusen no tetsugaku*" (The Philosophy of Total War). *Chūōkōron*, vol. 58, no. 1, Jan. 1943, pp. 54–112.
———. "*Tōa kyōeiken no rinrisei to rekishisei*" (The Ethicality and Historicity of the East Asia Co-Prosperity Sphere). *Chūōkōron*, vol. 57, no. 4, Apr. 1942, pp. 120–61.
Kōyama Iwao. "*Sekaishi no dōgaku*" (The Dynamics of World History). *Sekaishi no riron. Kyoto tetsugaku sensho XX*, edited by Mori Tetsurō. Tōeisha, 2000, pp. 207–50.

———. "Sekaishi no rinen" (The Ideal of World History) (1) I–III. *Shisō*, vol. 215, Apr. 1940, pp. 329–48.
———. "Sekaishi no rinen" (The Ideal of World History) (2) IV–VIII. *Shisō*, vol. 216, May 1940, pp. 531–82.
Koyasu Nobukuni. "*Kindai no chōkoku*" *towa nani ka* (What Is "Overcoming Modernity"?). Seidosha, 2008.
Maraldo, John C. "Questioning Nationalism Now and Then: A Critical Approach to Zen and the Kyoto School." *Rude Awakenings: Zen, the Kyoto School, & the Question of Nationalism*, edited by James W. Heisig and John C. Maraldo, University of Hawai'i Press, 1995, pp. 333–62.
Matsumoto Ken'ichi. "*Kaidai*" (Annotation). *Kindai no chōkoku*, by Kawakami Tetsutarō et al., Fuzanbō, 1979, pp. i–ix.
Miller, Frank O. "The Minobe Affair." *Minobe Tatsukichi: Interpreter of Constitutionalism in Japan*, by Miller, University of California Press, 1965, pp. 196–253.
Minamoto Ryōen. "The Symposium on 'Overcoming Modernity.'" *Rude Awakenings: Zen, the Kyoto School, & the Question of Nationalism*, edited by James W. Heisig and John C. Maraldo, University of Hawai'i Press, 1995, pp. 197–229.
Mori Tetsurō. "*Kaisetsu*" (Commentary). *Sekaishi no riron. Kyoto tetsugaku sensho XX*, edited by Mori. Tōeisha, 2000, pp. 395–443.
———, editor. *Sekaishi no riron* (Theories of World History). *Kyoto tetsugaku sensho XX*. Tōeisha, 2000.
Nakazawa Shin'ichi. *Firosofia yaponika* (Philosophia Japonica). Kōdansha, 2011.
Nishida Kitarō. "*Bashoteki ronri to shūkyōteki sekaikan*" (The Logic of Place and a Religious Worldview) *Nishida Kitarō zenshū* XI. 1949. Iwanami Shoten, 1979, pp. 371–464.
———. "*Benshōhōteki ippansha toshiteno sekai*" (The World as Dialectical Universal). *Nishida Kitarō zenshū* VII. 1949. Iwanami Shoten, 1979. pp. 305–428.
———. "*Dentōshugi ni tsuite*" (On Traditionalism). *Nishida Kitarō zenshū* XIV. 1951. Iwanami Shoten, 1979. pp. 371–85.
———. *Fundamental Problems of Philosophy: The World of Action and the Dialectical World*. Translated by David A. Dilworth, Sophia University, 1970.
———. "*Jissen tetsugaku joron*" (Prolegomena to Practical Philosophy). *Nishida Kitarō zenshū* X. 1950. Iwanami Shoten, 1979, pp. 7–123.
———. "*Kōiteki chokkan no tachiba*" (The Standpoint of Active Intuition). *Nishida Kitarō zenshū* VIII. 1948. Iwanami Shoten, 1979, pp. 107–218.
———. "*Kokka riyū no mondai*" (The Problem of the Reason of the State). *Nishida Kitarō zenshū* X. 1950. Iwanami Shoten, 1979, pp. 265–337.
———. *Last Writings: Nothingness and the Religious Worldview*. Translated by David A. Dilworth, University of Hawai'i Press, 1987.
———. "*Nihon bunka no mondai*" (The Problem of Japanese Culture). *Nishida Kitarō zenshū* XII. 1950. Iwanami Shoten, 1979, pp. 277–394.
———. "*Nihon bunka no mondai*" (The Problem of Japanese Culture: Lectures). *Nishida Kitarō zenshū* XIV. 1951. Iwanami Shoten, 1979, pp. 387–417.
———. *Ontology of Production: Three Essays*. Translated by William Haver, Duke University Press, 2012.

———. "*Poiēshisu to purakushisu: Jissen tetsugaku joron hosetsu*" (Poiesis and Praxis: The Addendum to Prolegomena to Practical Philosophy). *Nishida Kitarō zenshū* X. 1950. Iwanami Shoten, 1979, pp. 124–76.

———. "*Shokanshū* II" (Collection of Letters II). *Nishida Kitarō zenshū* XIX. 1953. Iwanami Shoten, 1980.

———. "*Tetsugaku ronbunshū daiyon hoi*" (Supplement to *Philosophical Essays* vol. 4). *Nishida Kitarō zenshū* XII. 1950. Iwanami Shoten, 1979, pp. 397–434.

———. "The Logic of the Place of Nothingness and the Religious Worldview." *Last Writings: Nothingness and the Religious Worldview*. Translated by David A. Dilworth, University of Hawai'i Press, 1987, pp. 47–123.

———. "The Standpoint of Active Intuition." *Ontology of Production: Three Essays*. Edited and translated by William Haver, Duke University Press, 2012, pp. 64–143.

———. "The World as Dialectical Universal." *Fundamental Problems of Philosophy: The World of Action and the Dialectical World*. Translated by David A. Dilworth, Sophia University, 1970, pp. 163–235.

———. "*Watakushi no tachiba kara mita hēgeru no benshōhō*" (Hegelian Dialectic Seen from My Standpoint). *Nishida Kitarō zenshū* XII. 1950. Iwanami Shoten, 1979, pp. 64–84.

Nishitani Keiji. "'*Kindai no chōkoku' shiron*" (My Views on "Overcoming Modernity"). *Kindai no chōkoku*, by Kawakami Tetsutarō et al., Fuzanbō, 1979, pp. 18–37.

———. "My Views on 'Overcoming Modernity.'" *Overcoming Modernity: Cultural Identity in Wartime Japan*, edited and translated by Richard F. Calichman, Columbia University Press, 2008, pp. 51–63.

———. "*Sekaikan to kokkakan*" (Worldview and Stateview). *Nishitani Keiji chosakushū* IV. Sōbunsha, 1987, pp. 261–384.

———. "*Sekaishi no tetsugaku*" (The Philosophy of World History). *Nishitani Keiji chosakushū* IV. Sōbunsha, 1987, pp. 221–57.

Ōhashi Ryōsuke. *Kyōto gakuha to nihon kaigun: Shin shiryō "Ōshima memo" wo megutte* (The Kyoto School and the Japanese Navy: On the Newly Discovered Ōshima Memoranda). Tokyo: PHP Kenkyūsho, 2001.

Osaki Harumi. "Dialectic of Hegel and Nishida: How to Deal with Modernity." *European Journal of Japanese Philosophy*, vol. 2, Oct. 2017, pp. 85–112.

———. "Pure Experience in Question: William James in the Philosophies of Kitarō Nishida and Alfred North Whitehead." *Philosophy East and West*, vol. 65, no. 4, Oct. 2015, pp. 1234–52.

Osborne, Peter. *The Politics of Time: Modernity and Avant-Garde*. Verso, 1995.

Parkes, Graham. "The Definite Internationalism of the Kyoto School: Changing Attitudes in the Contemporary Academy." *Re-Politicising the Kyoto School as Philosophy*, edited by Christopher Goto-Jones, Routledge, 2008, pp. 161–82.

Parks, Peter K. "Absolute Idealism Reverts to Kantian Position: Hegel's Exclusion of Africa and Asia." *Asia, Africa, and the History of Philosophy*, by Parks, State University of New York Press, 2013, pp. 113–31.

Said, Edward W. *Orientalism*. Vintage Books, 1979.

Sakai Naoki. "Modernity and its Critique: The Problem of Universalism and Particularism." *Postmodernism and Japan*, edited by Miyoshi Masao and Harry D. Harootunian, Duke University Press, 1989, pp. 93–122.

———. "Resistance to Conclusion: The Kyoto School Philosophy under the *Pax Americana*." *Re-Politicising the Kyoto School as Philosophy*, edited by Christopher Goto-Jones, Routledge, 2008, pp. 183–98.

———. "Subject and/or *Shutai* and the Inscription of Cultural Difference." *Translation and Subjectivity: On Japan and Cultural Nationalism*, translated by Meaghan Morris, The University of Minnesota Press, 2008, pp. 117–52.

———. "Subject and Substratum: On Japanese Imperial Nationalism." *Cultural Studies*, vol. 14, no. 3–4, Jul. 2000, pp. 462–530.

Sakai Naoki, and Isomae Jun'ichi, editors. *"Kindai no Chōkoku" to kyoto gakuha: Kindaisei, teikoku, huhensei* ("Overcoming Modernity" and the Kyoto School: Modernity, Empire, and Universality). Ibunsha, 2010.

Sakano Tōru. *Teikoku nihon to jinruigakusha 1884–1952* (Japanese Empire and Anthropologists 1884–1952). Keisō Shobō, 2005.

Spivak, Gayatri Chakravorty. "Our Asias—2001: How to Be a Continentalist." *Other Asias*, by Spivak, Blackwell, 2008, pp. 209–38.

Stevens, Bernard. "Overcoming Modernity: A Critical Response to the Kyoto School." *Japanese and Continental Philosophy: Conversation with the Kyoto School*, edited by Bret W. Davis, Brian Schroeder, and Jason M. Wirth, Indiana University Press, 2011, pp. 229–46.

Suares, Peter. *The Kyoto School's Takeover of Hegel: Nishida, Nishitani, and Tanabe Remake the Philosophy of Spirit*. Lexington Books, 2011.

Sugimoto Kōichi. "Tanabe Hajime's Logic of Species and the Philosophy of Nishida Kitarō: A Critical Dialogue within the Kyoto School." *Japanese and Continental Philosophy: Conversation with the Kyoto School*, edited by Bret W. Davis, Brian Schroeder, and Jason M. Wirth, Indiana University Press, 2011, pp. 52–67.

Suzuki Shigetaka. "*Sekaishikan no rekishi*" (The History of the View of World History). *Sekaishi no riron. Kyoto tetsugaku sensho XX*, edited by Mori Tetsurō. Tōeisha, 2000, pp. 98–170.

Takahashi Tetsuya. *Kokka to gisei* (The State and Sacrifice). Nippon Hōsō Shuppan Kyōkai, 2005.

Tanaka, Stefan. *Japan's Orient: Rendering Pasts into History*. University of California Press, 1993.

Takeuchi Yoshimi. "Asia as Method." *What Is Modernity?: Writings of Takeuchi Yoshimi*, edited and translated by Richard F. Calichman, Columbia University Press, 2005, pp. 149–65.

———. "Overcoming Modernity." *What Is Modernity?: Writings of Takeuchi Yoshimi*, edited and translated by Richard F. Calichman, Columbia University Press, 2005, pp. 103–47.

Tsurumi Shunsuke. *An Intellectual History of Wartime Japan 1931–1945*. KPI, 1986.

Tully, James. "To Think and Act Differently: Foucault's Four Reciprocal Objections to Habermas' Theory." *Foucault contra Habermas: Recasting the Dialogue between Genealogy and Critical Theory*, edited by Samantha Ashenden and David Owen,

SAGE Publications, 1999, pp. 90–142.

Ueda Shizuteru. "Nishida, Nationalism, and the War in Question," translated by Jan Van Bragt. *Rude Awakenings: Zen, the Kyoto School, & the Question of Nationalism*, edited by James W. Heisig and John C. Maraldo, University of Hawai'i Press, 1995, pp. 77–106.

Uhl, Christian. "What was the 'Japanese Philosophy of History'?: An Inquiry into the Dynamics of the 'World-Historical Standpoint' of the Kyoto School." *Re-Politicising the Kyoto School as Philosophy*, edited by Christopher Goto-Jones, Routledge, 2008, pp. 113–33.

Victoria, Brian. "Zen as a Cult of Death in the Wartime Writings of D. T. Suzuki." *The Asia Pacific Journal: Japan Focus*, vol. 11, issue. 30, no. 4, Aug. 2013. http://apjjf.org/-Brian-Victoria/3973/article.pdf.

Wilkinson, Robert. *Nishida and Western Philosophy*. Ashgate, 2009.

Williams, David. *Defending Japan's Pacific War: The Kyoto School Philosophers and Post-White Power*. RourtledgeCurzon, 2004.

———. *The Philosophy of Japanese Wartime Resistance: A Reading, with Commentary, of the Complete Texts of the Kyoto School Discussions of "The Standpoint of World History and Japan."* Routledge Studies in the Modern History of Asia XCIX, Routledge, 2014.

Yonetani Masafumi. "'*Sekaishi no tetsugaku*' *no kiketsu: Senchū kara sengo e*" (The Consequences of the "Philosophy of World History": From Wartime to the Postwar Era). *Gendai shisō*, vol. 23, no. 1, Jan. 1995.

Yusa Michiko. "Nishida and Totalitarianism: A Philosopher's Resistance." *Rude Awakenings: Zen, the Kyoto School, & the Question of Nationalism*, edited by James W. Heisig and John C. Maraldo, University of Hawai'i Press, 1995, pp. 107–31.

———. *Zen & Philosophy: An Intellectual Biography of Nishida Kitarō*. University of Hawai'i Press, 2002.

Index

Absolute present, 136–138, 141, 144–145, 224, 231–233
Active intuition / active-intuitive, 128, 136–138, 231–232, 268n3
Africa / African, 192–194, 264n4, 270n9
Alternative modernity, 249
Altruism / altruistic, 32 107
Appiah, Kwame Anthony, 158
Arisaka Yoko, 122–123, 125, 246–247, 268n1 of chapter 8
Asia / Asian, 9–11, 13–14, 24, 35, 37, 44, 82, 106, 107, 193–194, 245, 247, 250–252, 255, 270–271n9
  See also East Asia / East Asian, Greater East Asia
  Asia as a homogenous unit, 250–251
  "Asia as Method," 255
  Asian self-determination, 251
  Asian Studies, 269n5
  Asias, or Asia as multiplicity, 255
  Southeast Asia, 106
Asia-Pacific War / Pacific War, 10, 13, 16, 25, 28, 34, 97–99, 104, 106, 109–110, 251, 254
  See also Greater East Asia War, Second World War / World War II
Atomistic view, 76–78, 153
Awareness / aware, 31–32, 43, 47, 53–54, 71, 80, 90, 133, 135, 144, 150–151

Ba Maw, 106

Being (capitalized), 208, 215, 218, 234–235, 237
Being-for-itself, 204, 272n21
Buddhism / Buddhist, 5–6, 259n2
Bungakukai [Literary World], 23–25, 29, 38–39, 41, 48, 51–52, 83, 101, 104, 112, 268n1 of chapter 8
Burma / Burmese, 106–107
Bushidō, 54. See also Samurai
Butler, Judith, 219

Calichman, Richard F., 25, 33, 39, 48, 112, 267n3
Censorship, 15, 104, 123
China / Chinese, 6, 10, 45, 97, 154, 252, 263n2, 264n4
Christianity, 30, 146
Chūōkōron [Central Review], 23–24, 39, 41–42, 48, 52, 61, 63, 85, 88, 90, 101, 104, 110–112, 117, 128–129, 159–160, 263n2
Civilizational transference, 9
Clean and bright mind [*seimeishin / kiyoki akaki kokoro*], 36, 91, 261n9. See also Clean and right spiritual power
Clean and right spiritual power [*kiyoku tadashii seishinryoku*], 90–91. See also Clean and bright mind
Coercion / coercive, 57–59, 62. See also Command, Compulsion / compulsive

283

Coeval modernity, 17
Colonialism / colonial / colonialist. *See also* Imperialism
  Advocacies of Japanese colonialism and their problems, 13–14, 108–109, 122, 250–252
  British colonialism, 247
  Ideal and reality of Japanese colonialism, 106–107, 265–266n1 of chapter 4
  Parallels between Japanese and Western colonialisms, 18, 108
  Kyoto School and colonialism, 33–37, 51, 152, 161, 247
  Universalist philosophy and colonialism, 10–14
  Western colonialism and modernity, 182
Command, 131–133, 148, 226–231, 235. *See also* Coercion / coercive, Compulsion / compulsive
Compulsion / compulsive, 132–133, 228–230, 256. *See also* Coercion / coercive, Command
Concrete universal, 197–198, 204, 206–209, 210–213, 215, 224, 234, 271n13
Confucianism / Confucian, 7, 251, 263n2
Consciousness / conscious, 30–31, 53, 156, 191, 194, 205, 260n4 of chapter 1
  Ancient Japanese consciousness, 90–92
  Consciousness of West or Western modernity, 180–184, 238–239
Contradictory self-identity / contradictorily self-identical, 119–120, 147–148, 161, 167, 212, 224
  Absolutely contradictory self-identity, 212, 224–229, 232–234, 240
Cooperativism, 170–171, 269n2
Cosmopolitanism / cosmopolitan, 10, 104–105, 107, 157–158, 267n1

Davis, Bret W., 2, 15, 35
Deleuze, Gilles, and Félix Guattari, 220–221
Descartes, René, 220–221
Dialectic / dialectical, 179, 180–181, 184–193, 195–196, 202–204, 206–208, 210–212, 214–215, 217–218, 221–222, 236, 238, 270n8
Doak, Kevin M., 26–29, 37, 130, 173

East / Eastern, xi–xii, 2, 7, 77, 79–80, 121, 154–155, 182. *See also* Orient / Oriental, Asia / Asian, East Asia / East Asian
  East-West divide / contrast, 3–4, 8–9, 23, 68–69, 83, 103, 153, 252–253, 256, 264n4
  Eastern culture, 4, 23
  Eastern philosophy (or system of thought), 4, 7
  Eastern religions, 2, 7
  Eastern tradition, 4, 7–8, 23
East Asia / East Asian, 1, 107, 109, 251, 269–270n2. *See also* Greater East Asia
Edo period, 53
Ego / egoism / egoistic / egoistical, 6, 31, 159, 260n5
  Anti-egocentric, 246
  Ethnic egoism, 152–154, 156–158, 160
  National egoism, 102
  Non-ego, 35
Eliot, T.S., 135, 138, 140–141
Emperor, 120–121, 144, 163–165, 168–175. *See also* Imperial Family, Imperial Way
Emperor organ theory [*tennō kikan setsu*], 165–166, 168–173
Emperor system, 120
Emperor-worship, 164–165
Empire, 241, 254
  Asiatic Empires, 193
  Japanese empire / Empire of Japan,

6–7, 101, 104, 250, 265n2, 269–270n2
Roman Empire, 146
Empty (verb)
  Empty one's mind, 91, 261n6
  Empty one's subjectivity, 148, 156
  Empty oneself / one's own self, 148, 154, 237
Enlightenment / enlighten, 6–7, 15, 78, 182–183, 241, 247
Envelop, 144, 147, 154–159, 163–164, 187, 195, 210, 212, 215, 217, 224, 226, 232–235, 237–241, 256, 272n24
Environmental determinism, 155, 244
Essentialism / essentialist, 38, 113, 159, 250
Eternal / eternalize, 28–29, 92–95, 99–100, 108, 175, 260n3 of chapter 1
  Eternal present (or now), 137–138, 141, 145
  Eternal warfare, 111
  Living tradition as eternal and temporal, 135, 138, 140–141
Ethicality, 11, 33, 35–38, 41, 51, 57, 69, 98, 102–103, 132–133, 159–160, 262n. *See also* Morality
  Ethicality in Hegel, 197, 199, 206, 213–214, 222
  Nishida's criticism of Hegel's idea of ethicality, 213–214
  World-historical necessity qua ethicality, 43–46, 49, 67–69, 72–73, 88, 92, 95–99
Ethical substance, 199, 206, 214
Ethical vitality, 71–72. *See also* Moral energy, Moral power, Moral vitality
Ethnocentrism / ethnocentric
  Ethnocentrism in Hegel and Nishida, 237
  Ethnocentrism in the assertion of cultural uniqueness, 247–248, 269n6

Kyoto School and ethnocentrism, 14, 26–27, 38, 67–68, 74, 104–105, 121–122, 157, 160, 246, 256
Eurocentrism / Eurocentric, 13, 193, 270n4, n9
Eurocentric world (or world order), 44–45, 72–73
Europe / European, 1, 17, 44–45, 60, 65, 72–73, 89, 93–94, 108, 146, 155, 182, 192–196, 243, 247, 249, 250, 252, 264n4, 265–266n1 of chapter 4. *See also* West / Western
Existenz, 53

Family system [*ie*], 77–80, 158
Feenberg, Andrew, 125
Fifteen Years War, 252
Foucault, Michel, 169–170, 270n4
Freedom, 30, 32, 54–55, 58–65, 75–76, 78, 105, 108, 141, 153, 165–166, 181–182, 193, 199–200, 202, 204, 237, 260n4 of chapter 1

Gemeinschaft / *gemeinschaftlich*, 213, 225, 272n29
Germany / German, 193, 237, 243
Goto-Jones, Christopher S., 2–3, 5–7, 160, 259n2
Greater East Asia [*Daitōa*], 35, 106
  Greater East Asia War [*Daitōa sensō*], 23, 25, 160 (*see also* Asia-Pacific War / Pacific War, Second World War / World War II)
  Greater East Asia Co-Prosperity Sphere [*Daitōa kyōeiken*], 24, 33, 35, 37, 51, 79, 81, 265n1 of chapter 4, 268n1 of chapter 8

Habermas, Jürgen, 179–183, 270n4
Harootunian, Harry, 17–18, 28–29, 39, 260n3 of chapter 1
Hayashi Fusao, 39, 48
Hegel, Georg W. F., 179–210, 212–215, 217–219, 221–223, 227–228,

Hegel, Georg W. F. *(continued)*
234–241, 243, 264n3, 270n1, n4, n7, 270–271n9, 271n10, n13, n14, n19, 272n21
Hegemony / hegemonic, 10, 13–14, 24, 29, 33, 74–75, 83, 85–86, 89–90, 97, 103–105, 108, 111, 120, 122, 152–153, 158–159, 183, 214, 239–240, 242, 251, 253–255
Heidegger / Heideggerian, 2, 174–175
Heisig, James W., 2–3, 11–12, 245, 260n4 of Introduction
Hierarchy / hierarchical / hierarchize / hierarchization, 9, 54, 77, 79–80, 111, 159, 183, 191–193, 196–197, 206–207, 211, 213–215, 222, 236, 238–241, 254, 256, 266n1 of chapter 4, 271n9
Hiromatsu Wataru, 109–110, 160, 248–249
Historicity / historicize, 93–94, 108
Hobsbawm, Eric J., 140
Homo poieticus, 129

Idea (Hegelian; capitalized), 205–206, 214, 228
Immanence / immanent, 30–31, 35, 38, 144
  Plane of immanence, 220–221
Imperial Family, 120–121, 125, 144–149, 156–157, 163–164, 167–169, 171–175, 241, 243–244, 246
  See also Emperor
Imperialism / imperial / imperialist / imperialistic, xi, 5–7, 12–13, 111, 182, 253–254, 267n1
  See also Colonialism
  Cause of anti-imperialism to justify Japanese imperialism, 35, 109, 111, 122, 159, 250, 252
  Hegelianism and European imperialism, 194–195, 291
  Internationalist philosophy and imperialism, 104

Nishida and imperialism, 118–120, 122, 152–154, 156–160, 243
Parallels between Japanese and Western imperialisms, 18, 241, 266n1 of chapter 4
Universalist philosophy and imperialism, 125, 246–247
Western imperialism and modernity, 182–183
Imperial Rule Assistance Association [*Taisei yokusan kai*], 171
Imperial Way, 120–122, 125, 163. *See also* Emperor
India / Indian, 154, 247, 264n4
Individualism, 123, 129, 165, 168
International communality (or community), 34–37, 51, 121, 159
Isomae Jun'ichi, 250–253

Japan Romantic School [*Nihon rōmanha*], 25–27, 29, 38
Japanize / half-Japanize, 79–80

Kado Kazumasa, 166–169, 171, 173–176
Kamakura period, 5
Kang Sangjung, 253–254
Kant, Immanuel, 220–221, 271n9
Karatani Kōjin, 248–249
Kawakami Tetsutarō, 25
Kawamura Satofumi, 169–171
Kimoto Takeshi, 97, 111–112, 262n, 266n1 of chapter 6, 267n1
Kobayashi Hideo, 38, 39
Kobayashi Toshiaki, 105, 124, 126, 161, 174–175, 268n1 of chapter 8
Kojiki, 144
Konoe government, 171
Korea / Korean, 6, 10, 107, 259n2
Kōsaka Masaaki, 18, 41, 43–47, 68–69, 71–72, 74–76, 81–82, 89–91, 96–98, 105, 127, 160
Kōyama Iwao, 18, 41, 43–44, 46, 52–57, 59–61, 64, 67–72, 75–80, 82–83, 89–94, 97–98, 263–264n2, 264n5

Koyasu Nobukuni, 110-111, 250, 255, 267n3

Latent being, 189-190, 196, 203, 207, 214, 217, 221-223, 225, 228, 234, 236-237, 240-241, 243
Law, 5-6, 64, 130-132, 144-145, 166-168, 172-174, 198-201, 226-230, 233, 259n2
Lese-majeste, 165
Liberal constitutionalism, 165, 269n1
Liberalism, 123-124, 126, 165, 169, 262n

Malaya, 69
Man'yōshū, 90
Manchukuo, 107
Maraldo, John C., 2, 267n4
Matsumoto Ken'ichi, 25
Mediation, 53, 74, 80-82, 97-98, 130, 133, 136-137, 176, 180, 185-186, 231-233, 265n2
　Dialectical mediation, 185
　Mediation of non-mediation, 133, 137, 231
Medieval Japan, 53
Meiji Constitution / Constitution of the Empire of Japan, 165
Meiji period, 16, 25, 28
Meinecke, Friedrich, 204
Metaphysics / metaphysical, xi, 9, 15, 125, 133, 175, 257
Middle Ages, 60
Miki Kiyoshi, 164, 170-172, 268n2, 269-270n2 of chapter 9
Minamoto, Ryōen, 23, 26, 35-36
Minobe incident (or affair), 164-166
Minobe Tatsukichi, 164-166, 168-172, 269n1 of chapter 9
Moral energy (or *Moralische Energie*), 27, 33-34, 36-37, 43, 46, 51, 57-60, 62, 69, 71, 73, 81-82, 88, 96, 265n1 of chapter 3. *See also* Ethical vitality, Moral power, moral vitality

Morality, 1-2, 24, 27, 35, 37-38, 43, 51, 88-89, 96, 98-99, 132-133, 144-146, 148-149, 159-160, 167, 194, 197, 199, 206, 213-214, 228-30, 237, 240-241, 244, 246, 251, 256-257, 262n, 271n13. *See also* Ethicality
Morality and state, 29, 128-130, 132, 138, 144-146, 148-149, 197-199, 204, 213-214, 240, 244
Morality in Japanese tradition, 24, 29, 33, 53, 145, 148-149, 163
Morality of nothingness, 133, 138, 145-146, 148-149, 163, 199, 237, 241, 244, 246, 256
Moral power, 43-46, 71-72, 76. *See also* Ethical vitality, Moral energy, Moral vitality
Moral vitality, 43, 46-47, 56, 90. *See also* Ethical vitality, Moral energy, Moral power
Mori Tetsurō, 119, 264n5

Nakazawa Shin'ichi, 249
Nara period, 90, 92
Nationalim / nationalist / nationalistic, xi, 267n1, 267n4
　Ethnic nationalism of Japan Romantic School, 26
　Internationalism and nationalism in Kyoto School, 68, 70, 104, 158
　Kyoto School and nationalism, 2, 5, 10, 24-29, 32-33, 38, 104, 67-68, 121-123, 125-126, 160, 168-169, 171, 173
　Minobe and ultranationalism, 170
National spirit / spirituality. *See also* Spirit / spirituality / spiritual
　Hegel on national spirit, 191, 193, 197, 213, 237, 270n6
　Kyoto School on national spirit / spirituality, 34, 92, 143, 146-148, 245-246
Negation, 30-32, 34, 63, 65, 80, 118-122, 152-159, 180-181, 186,

Negation *(continued)*
189–190, 195–196, 198, 202, 204, 207, 210, 213–215, 219, 229, 234–237, 265n2, 266n1 of chapter 4. *See also* Self-negation

Absolute negation, 30, 190, 195, 202

Negation of negation, 185–186. *See also* Dialectic / dialectical

New Japanese, 46–47, 52, 56–57, 60–61, 69

New world order, 45, 56, 71, 73–74, 79–80, 108, 150–152, 157, 159, 164, 236, 238–239, 262n

Nietzsche, Friedrich, 98

Nihon Shoki, 144

Nishida Kitarō, 1, 3–7, 16, 19, 81, 117–161, 163–164, 166–177, 179–180, 184–191, 193–199, 202–204, 206–215, 217–219, 221–241, 243–250, 256, 265n2, 268n1 of chapter 8, 268n2–3, 268–269n4, 269n5–6, 270n2 of chapter 9, 271n19–20, 272n23–24, 272n26–29, 273n2, n4 of chapter 11, 273n1 of chapter 12

Nishitani Keiji, 3, 18, 24, 27, 29–39, 41–43, 45–49, 51–53, 56–65, 67, 69–70, 73–75, 79, 83, 86–87, 90–91, 98–99, 101, 104, 108, 129, 132–134, 158–159, 260n3–n4 of chapter 1, 260–261n6, 261n7–10, 264–265n1, 265n2, 266n1 of chapter 5, 267n4

Noema / noematic, 184, 186–189, 196

Noesis / noetic, 187–188

Non-West / non-Western / non-Westerner, 13, 17, 18, 29, 44, 76, 89, 97, 182–184, 214, 241–242, 247, 249–250, 255, 259n3, 262n1

Non-Western modernity, 17

Non-Western philosophy, xi, 5, 9, 247

Nothingness, 30–31, 54–55, 64–65, 81–82, 86–87, 103–105, 117–119, 132–134, 137, 149, 156–159, 161, 166–167, 174–176, 185–190, 202, 207–210, 228, 237, 240–241, 261n6

Absolute nothingness, 54–55, 68–69, 73–74, 82, 93, 103, 117, 133–134, 136–138, 144–149, 156, 166, 173–176, 186, 199, 207–213, 215, 217–218, 222–228, 230–241, 244, 246, 256, 265n1 of chapter 3, 273n4

Being of nothingness [*mu no yū*], 147–149, 157, 163–164, 166–167, 173, 175, 237–238, 241, 243

Being-qua-nothingness [*yū soku mu*], 209

Japanese nothingness, 124

Oriental nothingness, 68, 83, 103

Nothingness qua place, xii, 81–82, 133, 158–159, 167, 208, 211, 268n2

Self-awareness of nothingness, 185–187

Subjective nothingness, 30–34, 36, 260n4 of chapter 1, 261n6, n8

Substantialization of nothingness, 174–176, 237, 241

Notion (Hegelian; capitalized), 181, 184, 191–192, 196, 200–203, 205–206, 208, 270n3, n7, n8, 271n18–19

Occident / Occidental, 9, 251–252. *See also* West / Western

Orient / Oriental, xi, 8–9, 44, 154, 252, 255, 259n3, 264n4
See also East / Eastern, Orientalism / Orientalist

Oriental culture, 2, 69, 74, 153–155, 158–159, 193, 195, 249

Oriental ethics, 77

Oriental nothingness, 68, 83, 103

Oriental philosophy (or system of thought), 4, 248

Oriental religiosity, 24, 29–35, 37, 83, 261n6

Oriental tradition, 77, 83, 158–159, 238, 249–250, 252

Index   289

Orientalism / Orientailst, 8–9, 251–254
  Self-Orientalism / self-Orientalist, 252
Osborne, Peter, 182–183, 191

Parkes, Graham, 158
Particularism / particularist /
    particularistic
  Eastern (or Oriental) particularism,
    xi, 8
  Japanese particularism, 8–11, 14, 126
  Kyoto School's particularist stance, xi,
    10, 11, 12, 13, 14, 158
Particularization of the universal, 10–14,
    18, 250. See also Universalization
    of the particular
Pastral power, 169, 171–172
Peace Preservation Law [chian iji hō],
    165
Pearl Harbor, 69
Place, xii, 76–77, 81–82, 133, 158–159,
    167, 208–209, 210–213, 215, 224,
    234, 272n23
  Absolute being-qua-place [zettai no
    bashoteki yū], 224
  Awareness of place, 133
  Ethics of place, 81
  Logic of place, 81
  Place qua nothingness, xii, 81–82,
    133, 158–159, 167, 208, 211, 268n2
  Putting or being put in the right
    place [tokoro wo eru / eshimeru],
    76–81, 152, 158, 265–266n1 of
    chapter 4
Platonic Form (or Idea), 92–94
Pluralistic world order, 73–75, 77–81,
    85, 158
Polis, 129
Postmodernism / postmodern, 248–249
Practical subject of world history, 43,
    45–46, 49, 51, 67, 71–73, 88–90,
    92, 94–96, 99, 102

Ranke, Leopold von, 43, 264n3

Responsibility, 45, 53–56, 64, 71, 79,
    103, 124, 173, 132, 235
  Ethics of responsibility, 53–54, 56, 83
  Subject / subjectivity of responsibility,
    51, 53–56, 60, 64, 67–69, 82, 86,
    104, 117, 132, 134, 149, 156, 158,
    235
  World-historical responsibility, 49, 51,
    56, 67–69, 71, 73, 89, 94, 103
Rousseau, Jean-Jacques, 198, 212,
    271n13
Russia, 45
Russo-Japanese War, 6, 259n2

Said, Edward W., 8, 251–252
Sakai Naoki, vii, 8–11, 13–14, 17, 80,
    83, 183, 264n3, 265n2
Sakano Tōru, 254, 265–266n1 of chapter
    4
Samurai, 53–56, 59–61, 64, 67–70, 83,
    94. See also Bushidō
Schroeder, Brian, 2
Second Chino-Japanese War [Shina
    jihen], 97
Second World War / World War II, 1,
    16, 106, 244, 262n. See also Asia-
    Pacific War / Pacific War, Greater
    East Asia War
Seizing an opportunity [toki wo eru],
    93–94
Self-abandonment, 92, 95. See also
    Self-annihilation, Self-negation,
    Self-sacrifice
Self-annihilation, 36, 38, 55, 57–58,
    60, 64, 74, 82, 91, 93, 103, 105,
    132–134, 138, 148–150, 158, 163,
    264n1, 265n1 of chapter 3. See also
    Self-abandonment, Self-negation,
    Self-sacrifice
Self-annihilation and devotion to
    public service [messhi hōkō],
    33, 37–38, 47, 53, 56–58, 61–62,
    87

Self-awareness, 11, 31, 34, 53, 56, 60, 74–75, 79, 136, 185, 186–187, 231–233, 235
Selfless / selflessness [*muga*], 54–56, 82, 90–91, 160, 260n5, 261n6
Selflessness and no-mindedness [*mushin*], 31, 34–35, 37–38, 51, 159, 260n5
Self-negation / self-negativity / self-negating, 30, 32, 34, 105, 148, 153–156, 158–159, 185–187, 202 237. *See also* Self-abandonment, Self-negation, Self-sacrifice
Self-negation of nothingness, 133, 145–146, 185–187, 190, 207–209, 211, 224–226, 234, 238
Self-sacrifice, 38, 53, 70, 105, 148, 267n5
See also Self-abandonment, Self-annihilation, Self-negation
Shintoism, 7, 32, 261n6
Shōwa period, 110, 170
Shōwa Research Group [*Shōwa kenkyūkai*], 171, 269n2
Sittlichkeit, 213, 271n13, 272n29
South America, 264
Sovereignty / sovereign, 34, 143, 169, 233
Sovereignty interpreted as the absoluteness of law, 166–168, 172–176
Soviet Union, 248
Species, 129–130, 135, 143, 161, 225, 234, 265n2, 268n2
Spirit / spirituality / spiritual, 34–35, 37, 47, 56, 70, 78, 90–93, 98–99, 145, 154, 182, 191, 203–205, 244–246, 263n2, 270n2 of chapter 10
Absolute spirit, 180–182, 184–186, 189–199, 202–207, 211, 213–215, 217, 221–222, 228, 234, 237–238, 241
Ethnic spirit, 212–213
German spirit, 193

Japanese spirit / spirituality, 31–32, 53–54, 61, 70, 78, 83, 90–92, 95, 147–149, 168, 237, 245–246
National spirit / spirituality, 34, 92, 143, 146–148, 191, 193, 197, 213, 237, 245–246, 270n6
Objective spirit, 197, 271n12
Universal spirit, 181
World Spirit, 121
Spivak, Gayatri Chakravorty, 255
State control, 7, 59–62, 64–65
State power, 57, 60–61, 169–172, 175
Stereotype / stereotyping, xi, 4, 7–9
Stevens, Bernard, 182
Suares, Peter, 218–219
Sublate / sublation, 58, 60–61, 65, 108, 188, 190, 192, 202, 270n8. *See also* Dialectic / dialectical
Substratum = subject, 59–65, 86–87, 91–92, 102–103, 108, 119, 127–129, 132, 134, 265n2
Sun Ge, 28–29
Suzuki Shigetaka, 18, 41–44, 73, 75, 89, 96, 128, 260n3 of chapter 1

Taishō Democracy, 169
Taishō period, 169–170
Taiwan, 10
Takeuchi Yoshimi, 23–24, 38, 109, 111, 255–256, 260n2
Tanabe Hajime, 3, 249, 265n2, 268n2
Tanaka, Stefan, 252
Tōjō government, 52, 171, 263n2, 268n1 of chapter 8
Tosaka Jun, 171, 268n2
Totalitarian, 160, 166, 168, 198, 204, 235
Total mobilization, 112, 170–171, 262n
Total war, 41, 111–113, 262–263n
Tradition / traditional, 33, 48, 113, 127, 135–136, 138–145, 231–232, 239–240, 253, 269n6
Continental tradition, 2

Index   291

East Asian tradition, 1
Eastern tradition, 4, 7–8, 23
Invented tradition, 140
Japanese tradition, 5, 8, 23–28,
  32–33, 37–39, 46–47, 49, 53, 56,
  61, 67–69, 71, 74, 82–83, 87–88,
  102–103, 108, 112–113, 139,
  141–142, 144, 149, 158, 239,
  269n6
Living tradition, 135, 141, 231–233,
  235, 239
Non-Western tradition, xi
Oriental tradition, 77, 83, 158–159,
  238, 249–250, 252
Tradition as active-intuitive, 136–138,
  231–232
Western tradition, 186
Transcendent / transcendental, 11, 13,
  30–31, 92, 144, 233
Tsurumi Shunsuke, 106, 267n2
Ueda Shizuteru, 119–120, 123, 125,
  152
United States, 17, 248
Universalism / universalist /
  universalistic
Japanese universalism, 11
Kyoto School's universalist
  philosophy, 10–14, 18, 125–126
Philosophical universalism, 10
Western (or European) universalism,
  8–11, 14, 246–247
Universalization of the particular, 16,
  18, 121, 125–126, 164, 175–176,
  180, 183–184, 215, 217–218, 236–
  237, 241, 243–248, 273n1. *See also*
  Particularization of the universal

Verfallen, 174–175

Way of the gods [*kannagara no michi*],
  32, 260–261n6
West / Western, xi–xii, 2–5, 8–11,
  13–14, 16–18, 23, 25, 28–29,
  32–33, 36, 41, 44–45, 68–71,
  74–76, 78, 83, 89–91, 93, 103, 106,
  122, 106–109, 146, 152–153, 180,
  182–184, 191, 193, 214–215, 222,
  241–242, 247–253, 256, 259n3,
  260n2, 264n4. *See also* Europe /
  European, Occident / Occidental
West-East divide / contrast, 3–4, 8–9,
  23, 68–69, 83, 103, 153, 252–253,
  256, 264n4
Western-centrism /-centric /
  -centered, 5, 17–18, 45, 69, 79, 152,
  247, 249, 252, 255–256
Western culture, 4, 25, 29–30, 32, 47,
  153–155, 158, 194–195, 267n3
Western modernity, 17–18, 24–25,
  28–29, 31–33, 52, 60–62, 65, 83,
  108, 117, 158, 179–180, 182–184,
  191, 196, 207, 215, 217–218, 222,
  236, 238–241, 249–250, 252–253,
  262n, 270n4
Western moral ideals, 75
Western philosophy (or thought),
  1–5, 7–9, 11, 14, 16, 165, 168, 186,
  214, 260n4
Western religiosity, 30
Wilkinson, Robert, 3–4, 8, 223
Will, 30, 59–60, 63–65, 131–132, 165,
  199–202
Absolute will, 226, 228
Ethnic will, 131, 144, 146
Free will, 58, 62, 70, 198, 200, 214,
  235, 265n2
General / universal will, 198–202,
  204, 206, 212, 214, 271n13
Individual will, 65, 198, 199, 200,
  201, 202, 204, 206, 212, 214
Objective will, 230
Particular will, 198
Will of collectivity / community, 60,
  63–65, 131
Will of the state, 59–60, 63, 65,
  198–199, 200–201, 204, 214

Williams, David, 26, 52, 249, 251,
  261–263n1, 263n2
Wirth, Jason M., 2
Worldly world, 151–152, 154, 156, 264n4

Yasuda Yojūrō, 26

Yonetani Masafumi, 12, 161
Yusa Michiko, 119–121, 123, 125, 147,
  152, 273n1

Zen, 1, 2, 4, 30, 260n5. *See also*
  Buddhism / Buddhist

www.ingramcontent.com/pod-product-compliance
Lightning Source LLC
Chambersburg PA
CBHW021214240426
43672CB00026B/82